An Introduction to

Student-Involved
Assessment FOR Learning

An Introduction to

Student-Involved Assessment FOR Learning

Sixth Edition

RICK STIGGINS

Pearson Assessment Training Institute

JAN CHAPPUIS

Pearson Assessment Training Institute

PEARSON ASSESSMENT TRAINING INSTITUTE

Boston   Columbus   Indianapolis   New York   San Francisco   Upper Saddle River
Amsterdam   Cape Town   Dubai   London   Madrid   Milan   Munich   Paris   Montreal   Toronto
Delhi   Mexico City   Sao Paulo   Sydney   Hong Kong   Seoul   Singapore   Taipei   Tokyo

Vice President/Editor-in-Chief: Paul A. Smith
Editorial Assistant: Matthew Buchholz
Marketing Manager: Joanna Sabella
Production Supervisor: Karen Mason
Copy Editor: Robert L. Marcum
Full-Service Vendor: Element LLC
Manufacturing Buyer: Megan Cochran
Cover Design: Elena Sidorova

Between the time website information is gathered and then published, it is not unusual for some sites to have closed. Also, the transcription of URLs can result in typographical errors. The publisher would appreciate notification where these errors occur so that they may be corrected in subsequent editions.

Library of Congress Cataloging-in-Publication Data

Stiggins, Richard J.
   An introduction to student-involved assessment for learning/Rick Stiggins. — 6th ed.
        p. cm.
   Includes bibliographical references and index.
   ISBN-13: 978-0-13-256383-3
   ISBN-10: 0-13-256383-5
1. Educational tests and measurements—United States. 2. Examinations—United States. I. Title.
   LB3051.S8536 2011
   371.26—dc22

                                                                          2010044249

10 9 8 7 6 5 EBM 15 14 13

www.pearsonhighered.com

ISBN-10:   0-13-256383-5
ISBN-13: 978-0-13-256383-3

This book is dedicated to all of those students who struggled to learn but, with the help of their teachers, found academic success and gained confidence in themselves as learners.

BRIEF CONTENTS

CONTENTS

Chapter 6   Written Response (Essay) Assessment   121

Chapter 7   Performance Assessment   138

Chapter 8   Personal Communication as Assessment   173

PREFACE

We have written this sixth edition of *An Introduction to Student-Involved Assessment FOR Learning* for those who have little or no classroom experience as a teacher. So it provides the reader's first conceptual introduction to a teacher's day-to-day classroom assessment responsibilities.

We also have prepared parallel versions for practicing teachers who have classroom experience, entitled *Classroom Assessment FOR Student Learning: Doing It Right—Using It Well* and *Seven Strategies of Assessment FOR Learning.* These are published by Pearson too and are distributed through the Pearson Assessment Training Institute, Portland, Oregon, and by Pearson Education. They are intended for graduate-level courses and inservice professional development programs being completed by practicing teachers who can work with these ideas in their own classrooms with their own students.

In addition, we have prepared yet another version of keys to productive assessment for school leaders, entitled *Assessment Balance and Quality: An Action Guide for School Leaders*, published by Pearson. It helps local district and building administrators understand how to establish learning environments in their schools in which teachers and principals can carry out sound assessment practices.

The vision of excellence in assessment presented in these three complementary programs of study arises from decades of research and extensive interaction with practicing teachers whose instincts have taught them how to use assessment both to support and to verify student learning. They have helped us see that students are assessment users too, interpreting the evidence of their learning we provide to them through classroom assessment and making crucial instructional decisions based on those data. Students themselves decide whether learning success is within reach, whether to try for that success, and how much to invest in achieving it. Our challenge as teachers is to make sure they come down on the right side—the productive side—of these decisions.

What's New to This Edition

This sixth edition of *An Introduction to Student-Involved Assessment FOR Learning* includes several new features designed to help readers understand and learn to apply commonsense standards of assessment quality. They reflect the evolution of our society, corresponding changes in the mission of its schools, and keys to productive assessment in those schools. For example, the first new feature is labeled "Exploring the Cultural Context of Assessment." In this case, periodic probes encourage readers to reflect on and discuss challenging community issues and concerns that have troubled or continue to trouble society in its use of assessment in schools. These connect classroom assessment to life and student well-being in the neighborhood that surrounds school.

Second, in this same spirit, this edition centers completely on the use of assessment to promote student well-being in standards-driven schools. This means we take the position that the most productive assessments are those that tell the user how each student did in mastering each standard or learning target. So every teacher's mission is to use assessment to maximize student confidence and success.

Third, again consistent with the tenor of our social and educational times, we provide a more sharply focused and complete portrait of a balanced assessment system than did previous editions—that is, a system that meets the information needs of all key instructional decision makers. We explore the role of classroom assessment in the larger context of assessment in schools.

The most prominent addition to this edition is a new chapter on the specifics of classroom assessment record keeping. Here, readers learn why and how to differentiate achievement records by assessment purpose and learning target. This change, then, lays the foundation for corresponding revisions in which we teach readers why and how to differentiate between feedback intended to support student learning and that which is intended to certify or report learning, such as report card grades.

Finally, with respect to the matter of what teachers need to assess—that is, learning targets—this edition includes an enhanced treatment of reasoning and problem-solving proficiencies. For each pattern of reasoning, to assist with the evaluation of student work we include a rubric defining levels of proficiency, from emerging to developing to competent.

Supplementary Material

The power of classroom practice

In *Preparing Teachers for a Changing World*, Linda Darling-Hammond and her colleagues point out that grounding teacher education in real classrooms—among real teachers and students and among actual examples of students' and teachers' work—is an important, and perhaps even an essential, part of training teachers for the complexities of teaching in today's classrooms. MyEducationLab is an online learning solution that provides contextualized interactive exercises, simulations, and other resources designed to help develop the knowledge and skills teachers need. All of the activities and exercises in MyEducationLab are built around essential learning outcomes for teachers and are mapped to professional teaching standards. Utilizing classroom video, authentic student and teacher artifacts, case studies, and other resources and assessments, the scaffolded learning experiences in MyEducationLab offer pre-service teachers and those who teach them a unique and valuable education tool.

For each topic covered in the course you will find most or all of the following features and resources:

Connection to National Standards

Now it is easier than ever to see how coursework is connected to national standards. Each topic on MyEducationLab lists intended learning outcomes connected to the appropriate national standards. And all of the activities and exercises in MyEducationLab are mapped to the appropriate national standards and learning outcomes as well.

Assignments and Activities

Designed to enhance student understanding of concepts covered in class and save instructors preparation and grading time, these assignable exercises show concepts in action (through video, cases, and/or student and teacher artifacts). They help students deepen content knowledge and synthesize and apply concepts and strategies they read about in the book. (Correct answers for these assignments are available to the instructor only under the Instructor Resource tab.)

Building Teaching Skills and Dispositions

These learning units help students practice and strengthen skills that are essential to quality teaching. After presenting the steps involved in a core teaching process, students are given an opportunity to practice applying this skill via videos, student and teacher artifacts, and/or case studies of authentic classrooms. Providing multiple opportunities to practice a single teaching concept, each activity encourages a deeper understanding and a more complete mastery of important concepts and principles.

Study Plan Specific to Your Text

A MyEducationLab Study Plan is a multiple choice assessment tied to chapter objectives, supported by study material. A well-designed Study Plan offers multiple opportunities to fully master required course content as identified by the objectives in each chapter:

- *Chapter Objectives* identify the learning outcomes for the chapter and give students targets to shoot for as you read and study.
- *Multiple Choice Assessment*s assess mastery of the content. These assessments are mapped to chapter objectives, and students can take the multiple choice quiz as many times as they want. Not only do these quizzes provide overall scores for each objective, but they also explain why responses to particular items are correct or incorrect.
- *Study Material: Review, Practice and Enrichment* give students a deeper understanding of what they do and do not know related to chapter content. This material includes text excerpts, activities that include hints and feedback, and interactive multi-media exercises built around videos, simulations, cases, or classroom artifacts.
- *Flashcards* help students study the definitions of the key terms within each chapter.

Certification and Licensure

The Certification and Licensure section is designed to help students pass their licensure exam by giving them access to state test requirements, overviews of what tests cover, and sample test items.
The Certification and Licensure tab includes the following:

- **State Certification Test Requirements:** Here students can click on a state and will then be taken to a list of state certification tests.
- Students can click on the **Licensure Exams** they need to take to find:
  - Basic information about each test
  - Descriptions of what is covered on each test
  - Sample test questions with explanations of correct answers
- **National Evaluation Series™ by Pearson:** Here students can see the tests in the NES, learn what is covered on each exam, and access sample test items with descriptions and rationales of correct answers. They can also purchase interactive online tutorials developed by Pearson Evaluation Systems and the Pearson Teacher Education and Development group.

- **ETS Online Praxis Tutorials:** Here students can purchase interactive online tutorials developed by ETS and by the Pearson Teacher Education and Development group. Tutorials are available for the Praxis I exams and for select Praxis II exams.

Visit www.myeducationlab.com for a demonstration of this exciting new online teaching resource.

Online Instructor's Manual

Available for instructors to download from Pearson's Instructor's Resource Center (http://www.pearson.com), this supplement includes teaching and learning activities for the effective presentation of chapter material.

Acknowledgments

We would like to thank Judy Arter and Steve Chappuis, our colleagues at the Pearson Assessment Training Institute, for their contributions to our collective understanding of the principles of sound assessment OF and FOR learning. Also, special thanks to Sarah Gandolfo for providing a practical teacher's point of view in revising this edition.

In addition, we appreciate those who use this text in their teaching and were generous enough to suggest how to improve the sixth edition to better meet the needs of their students: Debra J. Anderson, Minnesota State University, Mankato; Christine DiStefano, University of South Carolina; Sharon A. Feaster-Lewis, Southern Wesleyan University; Jean Ann Foley, Northern Arizona University; Jean Shepherd Hamm, Radford University Lynn Keyne-Michaels, Concordia University; and Jack Robinson, Old Dominion University.

Each edition has been improved immeasurably in the hands of our copyeditor partner for nearly two decades, Robert L. Marcum. Robert has known from the very beginning of our work together how critically important it is to speak to our readers in a manner and a voice that keeps them believing in themselves as learners. From the beginning, he has sensed and shared our passion for student well-being. The text he has helped us create shows this.

Thanks too to colleagues Kevin Davis and Paul Smith, publishers at Pearson Education, who have understood and embraced our vision from the outset and over the years. Without their confidence, we would not have been able to influence life in the classroom as we have. Thanks also to Karen Mason, production supervisor at Pearson, and Heidi Allgair of Element LLC, for transforming this edition from manuscript to final form.

We all must remember that we know far more together than any of us does alone. Let us all continue to both teach and learn from each other.

Rick Stiggins and Jan Chappuis
Portland, Oregon

Rick Stiggins, B.S., M.A., Ph.D., founded the Assessment Training Institute in Portland, Oregon, in 1991 to provide professional development for educators facing the challenges of day-to-day classroom assessment. In 2009, the Institute joined the Pearson Education team to extend its professional development services around the world.

Dr. Stiggins received his bachelor's degree in psychology from the State University of New York at Plattsburgh, master's degree in industrial psychology from Springfield (MA) College, and doctoral degree in education measurement from Michigan State University. Dr. Stiggins began his assessment work on the faculty of Michigan State before becoming director of research and evaluation for the Edina, Minnesota, Public Schools and a member of the faculty of educational foundations at the University of Minnesota, Minneapolis. In addition, he has served as director of test development for the ACT, Iowa City, Iowa; as a visiting scholar at Stanford University; as a Libra Scholar, University of Southern Maine; as director of the Centers for Classroom Assessment and Performance Assessment at the Northwest Regional Educational Laboratory, Portland, Oregon; and as a member of the faculty of Lewis and Clark College, Portland.

Jan Chappuis, educator and author, has been an elementary and secondary teacher as well as a curriculum developer in English/Language Arts, Mathematics, Social Studies, and World Languages. For the past twenty years she has written books and developed workshops focused on classroom assessment literacy, presenting both nationally and internationally. She is recognized as a national thought leader in the area of formative assessment for her work in translating research into practical classroom applications. She currently works with Rick Stiggins at Pearson Assessment Training Institute in Portland, Oregon.

Chappuis is author of *Seven Strategies of Assessment* FOR *Learning* (2009), *Learning Team Facilitator Handbook* (2007), and co-author of *Creating and Recognizing Quality Rubrics* (2006), *Classroom Assessment for Student Learning: Doing It Right—Using It Well* (2004), and *Understanding School Assessment—A Parent and Community Guide to Helping Students Learn* (2002).

INTRODUCTION TO STUDENT-INVOLVED ASSESSMENT FOR LEARNING

In this book, we form a team with you and your professor to lay the foundation of professional competence you need to manage the assessment process in your classroom. That process can command a quarter to a third of your available professional time, sometimes more. Your success and satisfaction as a teacher can turn on your ability to manage this facet of your professional practice effectively.

As we move forward, you will see two very strong themes emerge. First, assessment is, in part, the process of gathering information to inform instructional decisions. Those decisions, when made well, drive student learning success. Effective instructional decision requires accurate assessment.

Second, we can use classroom assessment as far more than merely a source of evidence for grading. We also can use it to build student confidence, motivation, and engagement in their learning. In other words, assessment isn't merely an index of the amount learned—it can also be the cause of that learning. We can promote such learning success with deep student involvement in the classroom assessment, record keeping, and communication process. Used in this way, classroom assessment can become a very strong contributor to student success.

It has not been our tradition to involve students in self-assessment. Rather, we have used assessment merely to hold students accountable for learning—to grade them. However, recent research has instructed us that we also can use classroom assessment to advance learning. We achieve excellence in classroom assessment when we balance a continuous array of assessments used to help students learn (we will call these *assessment FOR learning*) with periodic assessments used to verify that they did, in fact, meet prescribed academic achievement standards (*assessment OF learning*).

The presentation unfolds in three parts. In Part I we set the stage for sound assessment practice by articulating commonsense keys to quality classroom assessment. Those keys link assessment directly to productive instructional decision making by (1) identifying the users and uses of assessment results, (2) describing the various kinds of achievement to be assessed, and (3) connecting these learning targets to appropriate assessment methods.

Part II is about how to use of the different assessment methods well. The presentation takes you inside each of the four families of assessment methods one at a time: selected response (e.g., multiple-choice, true/false) assessments, essay assessments, performance assessments, and assessments based on direct personal communication with students. We will explore how to apply each method in appropriate contexts, detailing how to develop good ones, how to avoid biased results, and when and how to involve students in their use in ways that promote increased achievement.

In Part III we delve deeply into the alternative ways of managing assessment results and communicating them to their many users, such as students, parents, other teachers, administrators, and so on, in timely and understandable terms. The communication vehicles we will explore are report cards and grades, portfolios, conferences, and annual large-scale standardized test scores. We will explore the strengths and limitations each offers when it comes to using assessment to improve student learning.

Become a Reflective Learner

Our mission is to help you begin to develop the know-how and practical skills you need to be confident in and comfortable with your assessment practices. Ultimately, we want you to know that your practices are sound and that they will support, not stifle, your students' learning. We will support your learning with a variety of interactive learning strategies in this text. Our hope is that you will continue to refine your assessment proficiencies throughout your career.

But before we describe those learning aids, we need to be sure you are clear about something very important: *Your study of the material presented herein is JOB TRAINING. As specified previously, you are going to spend a great deal of your professional time directly involved in assessment-related activities. Do it well and you and your students will prosper. Do it badly and both you and your students will suffer. If you merely study this book with the purpose of committing to short-term memory for course exams, or a course grade, you will finish neither confident with nor competent in your assessment practices. We urge you to think of this text as a long-term resource guide and take this learning task very seriously, striving to master the lessons that follow for the sake of the well-being of your students.*

Now to the learning aids built into this presentation to help you succeed: As we go, we will ask you for your personal reflection during learning and practice exercises in order to help you connect new ideas to your personal experiences as a learner. These "Times for Reflection" will serve to integrate your new learning about assessment into the structures of knowledge and understanding you have derived from your personal experiences. Further and in this same spirit, periodically we will be "Exploring the Social Context of Assessment," an exercise connected to the current topic for you to think about and perhaps discuss with your classmates. These explorations will help you explore your own values and fit classroom assessment into the social world around you—both within and outside of your classroom.

In addition, you will be able to practice applying the concepts and procedures as you learn about them. These practice activities include the following:

- Case studies that ask you to confront real-world classroom assessment dilemmas and use what you are learning to find solutions
- Examples of unsound assessments that you can practice fixing
- Examples of high-quality assessments for you to study and learn from
- Projects that you can complete to meld these ideas directly into your classroom

Only with practice can you develop the level of personal understanding needed to make these concepts and procedures part of your teaching routine. We offer here several methods for you to develop this understanding. First, we plan to model in our relationship the very partnership that must exist between you and your students. We want the work you do in conjunction with this book to keep you in touch with, and therefore feeling in control of, your own ongoing professional competence in assessment. Specifically, this presentation models in your adult learning environment the very student-involved assessment, record-keeping, and communication tactics that have been demonstrated to yield profound achievement gains when used with your students in classrooms.

Next, extensive experience in helping teachers learn about classroom assessment leads us to suggest that you maintain a learning log, journal, or diary as you proceed. From time to time we will suggest entries that may be useful particularly in helping you watch yourself grow. This will be a confidence builder.

Finally, it has been our experience that we learn more, faster, and with deeper understanding when we collaborate with others who are seeking the same learning. The research literature on adult learning and professional development supports this contention. In fact, we rely exclusively on learning teams in our in-service professional development at the Pearson Assessment Training Institute to provide experiences to practicing educators around the world. Teamwork works! For this reason, consider forming a small team of classmates to help you learn about classroom assessment. Meet between class meetings, taking time to talk about the big ideas, help each other through difficult parts, compare your responses to Times for Reflection and to the practice exercises, or discuss the social/cultural issues raised. This "talking time" is very important to solidifying your understanding.

An Introduction to

Student-Involved
Assessment FOR Learning

PART 1

Keys to Classroom Assessment Quality

Part I provides your introductory orientation to sound classroom assessment practice. Chapter 1 introduces a brief series of universal keys to quality assessment, centering on the critical roles of accurate assessment and emphasizing the power and thus the importance of student involvement in the process. Chapter 2 centers on instructional decision making by identifying the users and uses of assessment information (that is, the decision makers) from the classroom to the school building to the district and beyond. Chapter 3 describes the various kinds of achievement, contending that we can dependably assess only those learning targets that we have clearly and appropriately defined. We will map the route to student success in mastering state or local achievement standards by breaking each standard down into the classroom-level achievement targets that underpin mastery and by transforming those targets into student-friendly versions to be shared with our students from the very beginning of their learning. Chapter 4 frames commonsense standards of classroom assessment quality, explaining how to select proper assessment methods given particular users and achievement targets. This chapter connects these various assessment methods to the various kinds of achievement discussed in Chapter 3.

CHAPTER 1

Classroom Assessment for Student Success

CHAPTER FOCUS

This chapter answers the following guiding question:

> What are my classroom assessment responsibilities as a teacher and how can I fulfill them?

From your study of this chapter, you will understand the following:

1. How classroom assessment fits into the big picture of your job as a teacher and as part of the team in your school and district.
2. What it means to develop and use assessments that dependably reflect important learning targets.
3. The relationships among assessment, student confidence, and student success at learning.
4. Guiding principles or keys to quality that underpin sound classroom assessment practice.

A Teacher's Classroom Assessment Responsibilities

Assessment is, in part, the process of gathering evidence of student learning to inform instructional decisions. This process can be done well or poorly. To promote student success we all must be able to do it well. That means we must do both of the following:

- Gather *accurate evidence* of the achievement of our students—the quality and impact of our instructional decisions depend on it.
- Weave the classroom assessment process and its results into instruction in ways that *benefit students;* that is, that enhance both their desire to learn and their achievement.

Gather dependable information and use it well and we can get our students on winning streaks and keep them there. In short, we succeed as teachers by promoting their success. Gather inaccurate information or use it poorly and we can do severe and perhaps long-lasting damage to some (perhaps many) of our students. Let me introduce you to Ms. Weathersby, a teacher who has mastered her classroom assessment responsibilities and who carries them out very effectively. She and her student, Emily, can teach us valuable lessons.

A STORY OF ASSESSMENT FOR STUDENT SUCCESS

At a local school board meeting, the English department faculty from the high school presents the results of their evaluation of the new writing instruction program that they had implemented over the past year. The audience includes a young woman named Emily, a junior at the local high school, sitting in the back of the room with her parents. She knows she will be a big part of the presentation. It has been a good year for her. It was unlike any she has ever experienced in school before. She also knows her parents and teacher are as proud of her as she is of herself.

In preparation for their new program, the faculty attended a summer institute on integrating their writing assessments into their teaching and their students' learning. The teachers were confident that this professional development and their subsequent program revisions would produce much higher levels of writing proficiency.

As the first step in presenting program evaluation results, the English department chair, Ms. Weathersby, who also happens to be Emily's English teacher, distributes a sample of student writing to the board members (with the student's name removed), asking them to read and evaluate this writing. Here is that work:

BEGINNING OF THE YEAR Writing Sample

Computers are a thing of the future. They help us in thousands of ways. Computers are a help to our lives. They make things easier. They help us to keep track of information.

Computers are simple to use. Anyone can learn how. You do not have to be a computer expert to operate a computer. You just need to know a few basic things.

Computers can be robots that will change our lives. Robots are really computers! Robots do a lot of the work that humans used to do. This makes our lives much easier. Robots build cars and do many other tasks that humans used to do. When robots learn to do more, they will take over most of our work. This will free humans to do other kinds of things. You can also communicate on computers. It is much faster than mail! You can look up information, too. You can find information on anything at all on a computer.

Computers are changing the work and changing the way we work and communicate. In many ways, computers are changing our lives and making our lives better and easier.[*]

---

[*] *Source:* Personal writing by Nikki Spandel. Reprinted with permission.

They are critical in their commentary. One board member reports that, if these represent the best results of that new writing program, then clearly it is not having the impact they had hoped for. The board member is right. This is, in fact, a pretty weak piece of work. Emily's mom puts her arm around her daughter's shoulder and hugs her.

But Ms. Weathersby urges patience and asks the board members to be very specific in stating what they don't like about this work. As the board registers its opinion, a faculty member records the criticisms on chart paper for all to see. The list includes repetitiveness, no organization, short, choppy sentences, and disconnected ideas.

Next, Ms. Weathersby distributes another sample of student writing, asking the board to read and evaluate it.

END OF THE YEAR Writing Sample

So there I was, my face aglow with the reflection on my computer screen, trying to come up with the next line for my essay. Writing it was akin to Chinese water torture, as I could never seem to end it. It dragged on and on, a never-ending babble of stuff.

Suddenly, unexpectedly—I felt an ending coming on. I could wrap this thing up in four or five sentences, and this dreadful assignment would be over. I'd be free.

I had not saved yet, and decided I would do so now. I clasped the slick, white mouse in my hand, slid it over the mouse pad, and watched as the black arrow progressed toward the "File" menu. By accident, I clicked the mouse button just to the left of paragraph 66. I saw a flash and the next thing I knew, I was back to square one. I stared at the blank screen for a moment in disbelief. Where was my essay? My ten-billion-page masterpiece? Gone?! No—that couldn't be! Not after all the work I had done! Would a computer be that unforgiving? That unfeeling? Didn't it care about me at all?

I decided not to give up hope just yet. The secret was to remain calm. After all, my file had to be somewhere—right? That's what all the manuals say—"It's in there *somewhere*." I went back to the "File" menu, much more carefully this time. First, I tried a friendly sounding category called "Find File." No luck there; I hadn't given the file a name.

Ah, then I had a brainstorm. I could simply go up to "Undo." Yes, that would be my savior! A simple click of a button and my problem would be solved! I went to Undo, but it looked a bit fuzzy. Not a good sign. That means there is nothing to undo. Don't panic … don't panic …

I decided to try to exit the program, not really knowing what I would accomplish by this but feeling more than a little desperate. Next, I clicked on the icon that would allow me back in to word processing. A small sign appeared, telling me that my program was being used by another user. Another user? What's it talking about? *I'm* the only user, you idiot! Or at least I'm trying to be a user! Give me my paper back! Right now!

I clicked on the icon again and again—to no avail. Click … click … clickclickclickCLICKCLICKCLICK!!!! Without warning, a thin cloud of smoke began to rise from the back of the computer. I didn't know whether to laugh or cry. Sighing, I opened my desk drawer, and pulled out a tablet and pen. It was going to be a long day.[*]

---

[*] *Source:* Personal writing by Nikki Spandel. Reprinted with permission.

Ah, now this, they report, is more like it! But be specific, she demands. What do you like about this work? They list positive aspects: good choice of words, sound sentence structure, clever ideas, and so on. Emily is ready to burst! She squeezes her mom's hand.

The reason she's so full of pride at this moment is that this has been a special year for her and her classmates. For the first time ever, they became partners with their English teachers in managing their own improvement as writers. Early in the year, Ms. Weathersby made it crystal clear to Emily that she was, in fact, not a very good writer and that just trying hard to get better was not going to be enough. She expected Emily to improve—nothing else would suffice.

Ms. W. started the year by working with students to implement new state writing standards, including understanding quality performance in word choice, sentence structure, organization, and voice, and by sharing some new "analytical scoring guides" written just for students. Each scoring guide explained the differences between good and poor-quality writing in understandable terms. When Emily and her teacher evaluated her first two pieces of writing using these standards, she received very low ratings. Not very good. . . .

But Ms. W. also provided samples of writing that Emily could see were very good. Slowly, Emily began to understand why they were very good. The differences between these and her work started to become clear. Ms. W. began to share examples and strategies that would help her writing improve one step at a time. As she practiced and time passed, Emily and her classmates kept samples of their old writing to compare to their new writing, and they began to build their "growth" portfolios. Thus, she literally began to watch her own writing skills improve before her very eyes. At midyear, her parents were invited in for a conference at which Emily, not Ms. Weathersby, shared the contents of her growing writing portfolio and described her emerging writing skills. Emily remembers sharing thoughts about some aspects of her writing that had become very strong and some examples of things she still needed to work on. Now, the year was at an end and here she sat waiting for her turn to speak to the school board about all of this.

Now, having set up board members by having them analyze, evaluate, and compare these two samples of student work, Ms. W. springs a surprise. The two pieces of writing they had just evaluated, one of relatively poor quality and one of outstanding quality, were produced by the same writer at the beginning and at the end of the school year! This, she reports, is evidence of the kind of impact the new writing program is having on student writing proficiency.

Needless to say, all are impressed. However, one board member wonders aloud, "Have all your students improved in this way?" Having anticipated the question, the rest of the English faculty joins the presentation and produces carefully prepared charts depicting dramatic changes in typical student performance over time on rating scales for each of six clearly articulated dimensions of good writing. They accompany their description of student performance on each scale with actual samples of student work illustrating various levels of proficiency.

Further, Ms. W. informs the board that the student whose improvement has been so dramatically illustrated with the work they have just analyzed is present at this meeting, along with her parents. This student is ready to talk with the board about the nature of her learning experience. Emily, you're on! Interest among the board members runs high. Emily talks about how she has come to understand the truly important differences between good and bad writing. She refers to differences she had not understood before, how she has learned to assess her own writing and to fix it when it doesn't "work well," and how she and her classmates have learned to talk with her teacher and one another about what it means to write well. Ms. W. talks about the improved focus of writing instruction, increase in student motivation, and important positive changes in the very nature of the student–teacher relationship.

This board member turns to Emily's parents and asks their impression of all of this. They report with pride that they had never before seen so much evidence of Emily's achievement and that most of it came from Emily herself. Emily had never been called on to lead the parent-teacher conference before. They had no idea she was so articulate. They loved it. Their daughter's pride in and accountability for her achievement had skyrocketed in the past year.

As the meeting ends, it is clear to all in attendance this evening that this application of student-involved classroom assessment has contributed to important learning. The English faculty accepted responsibility for student learning, shared that responsibility with their students, and everybody won. There are good feelings all around. One of the accountability demands of the community was satisfied with the presentation of credible evidence of student success, and the new writing program was the reason for improved student achievement. Obviously, this story has a happy ending.

Success from the Student's Point of View

The day after the board meeting, an interview with Emily about the evening's events revealed even more about what really works for Emily.

"You did a nice job at the school board meeting last night, Emily," I started.

"Thanks," she replied. "What's most exciting for me is that, last year, I could never have done it."

"What's changed from last year?"

"I guess I'm more confident. I knew what had happened for me in English class and I wanted to tell them my story."

"You became a confident writer."

"Yeah, but that's not what I mean. Last night at the board meeting I was more than a good writer. I felt confident talking about my writing and how I'd improved."

"Let's talk about Emily the confident writer. What were you thinking last night when the board members were reacting to your initial writing sample—you know, the one that wasn't very good? Still confident?"

"Mom helped. She squeezed my hand and I remember she whispered in my ear, 'You'll show 'em!' That helped me handle it. It's funny, I was listening to the board members' comments to see if they knew anything about good writing. I wondered if they understood as much about it as I do—like, maybe they needed to take Ms. Weathersby's class."

"How did they do?" I asked, laughing.

"Pretty well, actually," Em replied. "They found some problems in my early work and described them pretty well. When I first started last fall, I wouldn't have been able to do that. I was a terrible writer."

"How do you know that, Em?"

"I understand where I was then, how little I could do. No organization. I didn't even know my own voice. No one had ever taken the time to show me the secrets. I'd never learned to analyze my writing. I wouldn't have known what to look for or how to describe it or how to change it. That's part of what Ms. W. taught us."

"How did she do that?"

"To begin with, she taught us to do what the board members did last night: analyze other people's writing. We looked at newspaper editorials, passages from books we were reading, letters friends had sent us. She wanted us to see what made those pieces work or not work. She would read a piece to us and then we'd brainstorm what made it good or bad. Pretty soon, we began to see patterns—things that worked or didn't work. She wanted us to begin to see and hear stuff as she read out loud."

"Like what?" I asked.

"Well, look, here's my early piece from the meeting last night. See, just read it!"

(Refer back to the "Beginning of the Year Sample" above, if you wish.)

"See, there are no grammar or usage mistakes. So it's 'correct' in that sense. But these short, choppy sentences just don't work. And it doesn't say anything or go anywhere. It's just a bunch of disconnected thoughts. It doesn't grab you and hold your attention. Then it stops. It just ends. Now look at my second piece to see the difference."

(Refer back to "End of the Year Sample," if you wish.)

"In this one, I tried to tell about the feelings of frustration that happen when humans use machines. See, I think the voice in this piece comes from the feeling that 'We've all been there.' Everyone who works with computers has had this experience. A writer's tiny problem (not being able to find a good ending) turns into a major problem (losing the whole document). This idea makes the piece clear and organized. I think the reader can picture this poor, frustrated writer at her computer, wanting, trying to communicate in a human way—but finding that the computer is just as frustrated with her!"

"You sound just like you did last night at the board meeting."

"I'm always like this about my writing now. I know what works. Sentences are important. So is voice. So are organization and word choice—all that stuff. If you do it right, it works and you know it," she replied with a smile.

"What kinds of things did Ms. W. do in class that worked for you?"

"Well, like, when we were first getting started, Ms. Weathersby gave us a big stack of student papers she'd collected over the years—some good, some bad, and everything in between. Our assignment was to sort them into four stacks based on quality, from real good to real bad. When we were done, we compared who put what papers in which piles and then we talked about why. Sometimes, the discussions got pretty heated! Ms. W. wanted us to describe what we thought were the differences among the piles. Over time, we formed those differences into a set of rating scales that we used to analyze, evaluate, and improve our writing."

"Did you evaluate your own work or each other's?"

"Only our own stuff to begin with. Ms. W. said she didn't want anyone being embarrassed. We all had a lot to learn. It was supposed to be private until we began to trust our own judgments. She kept saying, 'Trust me. You'll get better at this and then you can share.'"

"Did you ever move on to evaluating one another's work?"

"Yeah. After a while, we began to trust ourselves and each other. Then we were free to ask classmates for opinions. But Ms. W. said, no blanket judgments—no saying just this is good or bad. And we were always supposed to be honest. If we couldn't see how to help someone improve a piece, we were supposed to say so."

"Were you able to see improvement in your writing along the way?"

"Yeah, see, Ms. W. said that was the whole idea. I've still got my writing portfolio full of practice, see? It starts out pretty bad back in the fall and slowly gets pretty good toward spring. This is where the two pieces came from that the board read last night. I picked them. I talk about the changes in my writing in the self-reflections in here. My portfolio tells the whole story. Want to look through it?"

"I sure do. What do you think Ms. Weathersby did that was right, Emily?"

"Nobody had ever been so clear with me before about what it took to be really good at school stuff. It's like, there's no mystery—no need to psych her out. She said, 'I won't ever surprise you, trust me. I'll show you what I want and I don't want any excuses. But you've got to deliver good writing in this class. You don't deliver, you don't succeed.'"

"Every so often, she would give us something she had written, so we could rate and provide her with feedback on her work. She listened to our comments and said it really helped her improve her writing. All of a sudden, *we* became *her* teachers! That was so cool!

"You know, she was the first teacher ever to tell me that it was okay not to be very good at something at first, like, when you're trying to do something new. But we couldn't stay there. We had to get a little better each time. If we didn't, it was our own fault. She didn't want us to give up on ourselves. If we kept improving, over time, we could learn to write well. I wish every teacher would do that. She would say, 'There's no shortage of success around here. You learn to write well, you get an A. My goal is to have everyone learn to write well and deserve an A.'"

"Thanks for filling in the details, Em."

"Thank you for asking!"

The Keys to Success

Let's consider the conditions that needed to be in place in Ms. W.'s classroom for Emily and her classmates to have experienced such success. To begin with, Ms. W. was intent on using the classroom assessment process and its results to help her students become better writers. Therefore, assessment was a student-involved activity *during the learning;* that is, Emily and her classmates assessed their own achievement repeatedly over time, so they could watch their own improvement. Ms. W. shared with her students the wisdom and power that come from being able to assess the quality of ones own writing and fix it when it isn't working. She showed her students the secrets to their own success. So, in this sense, her assessment *purpose* during the learning was crystal clear.

Second, Ms. Weathersby started with a highly refined vision of the *learning target.* She conveyed this to her students by engaging them in the study with her of samples of writing that varied greatly in quality. From this, she drew them into creating written descriptions of the levels of writing quality, each reflecting one key attribute of the learning target. With these learning progressions in place, she was able to help her students remain in touch with their current level place on the learning continuum. She wanted her students to continually see the distance closing between their present position and their goal. She used ongoing student-involved assessment, not for entries in the grade book, but as a confidence-building motivator and teaching tool. The grading part came later—after the learning. This turned out to be incredibly empowering for her students.

Third, Ms. W. and her colleagues knew that their *assessments* of student achievement had to be very accurate. Writing exercises had to elicit the right kinds of writing. Scoring criteria and procedures needed to focus on the facets of writing that make it effective. As faculty members, they needed to train themselves to apply those scoring standards dependably—to avoid making biased judgments about the quality of student work.

But just as importantly from a classroom assessment point of view, Ms. W. understood that she also had to train her students to make dependable judgments about the quality of their own work. *This represents the heart of competence. She understood that any student who cannot evaluate the quality of her own writing and fix it when it isn't working cannot become an independent, lifelong writer.* Her job is to bring her students to a place where they didn't need her any longer to tell them they had produced good writing—to a place where they could determine that on their own and act on their own self-assessment results if their writing was there yet.

Finally, Ms. W. needed to take great care throughout to *communicate effectively* about student achievement. Whether describing for Emily improvements needed or achieved in her work or sharing with the school board summary information about typical student gains in writing proficiency, she took pains to speak simply, using shared vocabulary and relying on examples to ensure that her meaning was clear.

Some Students Aren't So Lucky

Sadly, for every such positive story in which sound assessment feeds into productive instruction and important learning, there may be another story with a far less constructive, perhaps even painful, ending. For example, consider the story of Rick's daughter Kristen Ann, when she was just beginning to learn to write:

Krissy arrived home from third grade one afternoon full of gloom. She said she knew we were going to be angry with her. She presented us with a sheet of paper—the third-grade size with the wide lines. On it, she had written a story. Her assignment was to write about someone or something she cares about deeply. She wrote of Kelly, an adorable tiny kitten who had come to be part of our family, but who had to return to the farm after two weeks because of allergies. Kelly's departure had been a painful loss of a very real family member.

On the sheet of paper was an emergent writer's version of this story—not sophisticated, but poignant. Krissy's recounting of events was accurate and her story captured her very strong sadness and disappointment at losing her new little friend. Actually, she did a pretty darn good job of writing, for a beginner. At the bottom of the page, which filled about three quarters of the page, was a big red circled "F". We asked her why, and she told us that the teacher said she had better learn to follow directions or she would continue to fail. Questioning further, we found that her teacher had said that students were to fill the page with writing. Krissy had not done that, so she hadn't followed directions and deserved an F.

When she had finished telling us this story, Kris put the sheet of paper down on the kitchen table and, with a very discouraged look, said in an intimidated voice, "I'll never be a good writer anyway," and left the room. My recollection of that moment remains vivid after 30 years.

In fact, she had *succeeded* at hitting the learning target at some level. She produced some pretty good writing. But her confidence in herself as a writer was deeply shaken because her teacher failed to disentangle her expectation that students comply with directions with her expectation that they demonstrate the ability to write well. Let's analyze this in a bit more detail.

In this case, the purpose of the assessment turned out to be one of controlling student behavior, not advancing academic achievement. Kris didn't know that. The learning target the teacher was assessing was length of writing, not quality. Kris didn't know that. The evaluation criterion was "fill the page," not attributes of effective writing. As a result, both the assessment and the feedback had a destructive impact on this naïve student. Without question, it's quite easy to see if the page is full. But is that the point? It's somewhat more challenging to assess accurately and to formulate and deliver understandable and timely feedback that permits a student to write better the next time and to remain confident about her ability to continue to grow as a writer.

In sum, the purpose was not clear, the learning target was not clear, and the assessment was of inferior quality because the target and its performance criteria had no educational value; as a result, the feedback delivered confused and disappointed the learner. So the bottom line impact of the assessment experience from the learner's point of view was destructive.

Do not *ever* underestimate the power of your evaluations of student performance and the impact of your feedback on your students' (1) learning success and (2) sense of control over their own academic well-being in school. For us as adults, the result of assessing may merely be a grade that goes in a gradebook or a score we average with other scores. But for students, it's always far more personal than that. Their interpretation of the feedback we provide helps them decide how (or if!) they fit into the world of people who do these things called "writing," or "reading" or "math problem solving." And depending on how they "come down" on this, we may or may not be able to influence their learning lives. Never lose sight of this very personal dimension of your classroom assessment processes.

Time for Reflection

Analyze and compare the assessments experienced by Emily and Kristen. Considering the keys to success discussed here, what were the essential differences? Where were assessment purposes and learning targets clear? Unclear? Appropriate? Inappropriate?

Other Potential Problems

Some unfortunate students may be mired in classrooms in which they are left on their own to guess the meaning of academic success. Their teachers may lack a vision of success, focus on an incorrect one, or intentionally choose to keep the secrets of success a mystery to retain power and control in the classroom. When their students guess at the valued target and guess wrong, they fail. Under these circumstances, they fail not from lack of motivation, but from lack of insight as to what they are supposed to achieve. This can be very discouraging. It destroys confidence. Besides, it can be very unfair. These students may well have succeeded had they been given the opportunity to strive for a clear objective.

Consider the plight of those students who prepare well, master the required material, but fail anyway because the teacher prepares a poor-quality test, thus inaccurately measuring their achievement. Or how about students whose achievement is mismeasured because a teacher places blind faith in the quality of the tests that accompanied the textbook, when in fact that confidence is misplaced. Indeed, some students fail, not because of low achievement, but because their teacher's subjective judgments are riddled with the effects of bias.

When these and other such problems arise, an environment of assessment illiteracy dominates, assessments are of poor quality, and students are placed directly in harm's way.

ANTICIPATING AND AVOIDING ASSESSMENT PROBLEMS

Your job is to avoid problems like these by applying the basic principles of sound assessment. As you will see, assessments can serve many masters, take many different forms, reflect many different kinds of achievement, and fall prey to any of a variety of problems that may lead to inaccurate results. When our journey together through the chapters of this book is complete you will have developed your own framework for understanding all of the options and for selecting from among them for each classroom assessment context. You need to understand what can go wrong and how to prevent assessment problems. In short, you will be prepared to assemble the parts of the classroom assessment puzzle as artfully as Ms. Weathersby does.

We Need "Valid" Assessments

One way to think about the quality of an assessment is in terms of the fidelity of the results it produces. Just as we want our recorded music or high-definition TV to provide a high-quality representation of the real thing, so too do we want assessments to provide a high-fidelity representation of the desired learning. In the assessment realm, this is referred to as the *validity* of the test. All assessment results (scores, for example) provide outward indications of inner mental states of the learner. We must always seek assessment results that accurately represent student learning. If they are to master content knowledge, then assessments must sample the content to be mastered. Whether assessing reasoning proficiency, performance skills, or ability to create products that meet certain standards of quality, our assessment exercises and scoring schemes must accurately reflect the learning. Such assessments are said to yield valid inferences about student mastery. We will discuss this in many ways as we study together.

Another way to think about the validity of an assessment is in terms of the usefulness of its results. A valid assessment is said to serve the purpose for which it is intended. For instance, a diagnostic test helps the user see and understand specific student needs. A college admission test leads to appropriate selection decisions among candidates. We always seek to develop and use assessments that fit the context at hand—that are valid for a specific purpose or set of purposes. Again, as we go, we will fill in details about this important concept of validity.

We Need "Reliable" Assessments

Still another way to think about assessment quality is in terms of its ability to give us consistent results. Assume that, in the truth of the world, a student possesses a specific and stable level of proficiency in reading comprehension. So we know that achievement in this case is not changing. A dependable or *reliable* assessment will reflect that stable level of achievement (a consistent score) no matter how many times we administer it.

Additionally, as that proficiency improves, a reliable assessment will track those changes in proficiency with changing results. We need to be able to count on our assessments to deliver dependable information about that student's evolving proficiency.

As we progress, you will come to see that factors other than students' actual level of achievement can influence test scores—bad test items, test anxiety, distractions during testing, and the like. When this happens the score is muddled by these extraneous factors and is said to have given us *unreliable* results. This is a bad thing and we will discuss how to anticipate and avoid these kinds of problems.

Assessment FOR Learning: GPS for Student Success

Here's a very practical way to think about quality assessment: think of it is as an orienting and tracking system for student learning success. These days, global positioning systems (GPS) are wired into our cars, boats, airplanes, and so on. The satellites help us keep ourselves located so we don't get lost on the streets, on the water, or in the air—so we can track our progress and arrive safely. Think about how they work. We enter our current location and a destination. Then the information wired into the GPS system of maps determines our best route. We travel that path with the GPS screen and its friendly voice (or, in planes, air traffic controllers) keeping us posted on our progress. If we deviate, the system knows it and redirects us. We arrive safe and sound.

Assessment FOR learning is a GPS for student learning. The teacher is the satellite, in effect, loading the system with the student's current location, destination, and route in the form of points along the way. In an assessment FOR learning classroom, all of this is given to the student traveler who then relies on classroom assessments to know where they are at the start, track themselves as they travel toward academic success, and understand when they have arrived. If the student gets off course, the teacher (air traffic controller) knows it and redirects the learner. But in addition, students get to self-assess and see the preset way points pass by as they go, becoming partners in redirecting their own efforts if necessary. Clearly, this represents preparation for lifelong learning.

THE CHANGING MISSION OF SCHOOLS AND ROLE OF ASSESSMENT

For a variety of good and important reasons, recently, our society has expanded the social mission of its schools. This new assignment necessitates rethinking the role of assessment.

For decades, the mission of schools has been to weed out the unable and unwilling learners (we call them our "dropouts") and to rank those who remain at the end of high school from the highest to lowest achiever. Thus, our schools served the social mission of beginning to sort us into the various segments of our social and economic system.

Recently, however, society has come to realize the insufficiency of this mission for schools in today's increasingly complex and rapidly changing world. Because of the accelerating technical evolution, rapid expansion of our ethnic diversity, and ever-increasing international interconnectedness, society has realized that all students must master lifelong learner proficiencies. These include the reading, writing, and mathematics problem-solving capabilities needed to survive in and contribute to our collective prosperity. So society has decided that schools that merely sort no longer meet our needs. Rather, in addition to sorting, schools need to assure universal lifelong learner competence. The problem with the traditional sorting mission is that those who finish low in the rank order (along with those who give up in hopelessness and drop out before they are ever ranked) fail to master the fundamental reading, writing, math problem-solving, and other proficiencies needed to survive in and contribute to an increasingly demanding and technical society.

This new vision of effective schools has continued to evolve over the decades, leading to today's dominant view that truly effective schools help all students meet the more rigorous academic achievement standards that prepare them for success in college and the workplace.

In response, virtually every state has developed its own standards defining the important academic learning that students are expected to master. Beyond this, at the time of this writing, new common core achievement standards are being developed for national dissemination. Once articulated by experts in each academic field, these standards are to be adopted by states, translated into state assessments, and used as a measure of the effectiveness of schools. Thus, policy makers have decreed that schools will be judged effective not merely in terms of their ability to rank students, but also on their ability to produce competent students in these terms.

Given this shift in mission assessments are going to have to do far more than merely serve as the basis for grading and ranking students. Failure to master essential achievement standards can no longer be dismissed as the student's problem—now it becomes the faculty's problem too. Our assessments have to help us accurately diagnose student needs, track and enhance student growth toward standards, motivate students to strive for academic excellence, and verify student mastery of required standards. This book will help you understand how classroom assessment can help us accomplish these things at whatever level and in whatever subject(s) you teach.

To be more specific, as a teacher, your job is to gather solid information about student achievement and feed it into instructional decision making. You can do this only when you are able to do the following:

- *Anticipate the information needs* of those instructional decision makers who will use your assessment results. Your assessments must be designed specifically to meet those needs.
- *Identify the achievement targets* (goals, objectives, expectations, standards) that you expect your students to hit. These must be the focus of your assessment exercises and scoring procedures.
- *Select proper assessment methods* that accurately reflect your achievement expectations.
- *Design and build high-quality assessments* that can lead you to confident conclusions about student achievement.
- *Communicate assessment results* in a timely and understandable manner into the hands of their intended user(s).

Exploring the Cultural Context of Assessment

Do you believe that everyone is supportive of this shift in the social mission of schools from one of sorting students to one of ensuring some level of universal competence for all? Who is likely to be supportive? Opposed? What would be the implications of each position for the future of assessment practice?

Important Benefits to You

There are three specific reasons why it is in your best interest to understand the principles of sound classroom assessment. First, remember that you will spend a great deal of your available professional time involved in assessment-related activities. This includes designing and building them, selecting them from other sources, administering them, scoring them, and managing and reporting results. It is hard work and can be tedious. The procedures described herein can *make that job MUCH easier.* The time savings detailed in the chapters that follow are legion.

Second, the routine application of the principles of sound classroom assessment offered herein, under the proper circumstances can *yield remarkable gains in student achievement* versus environments where they are missing (Black & Wiliam, 1998; Hattie & Timperley, 2007). These gains accrue for all students, but especially for low achievers. In other words, the consistent application of these ideas can help you reduce achievement gaps between those who do and do not meet standards.

Third, understanding the elements of sound classroom assessment will allow you to build a strong defense for their use in your classroom. The ideas presented herein run counter to decades of assessment traditions in schools. As a result, you will work with colleagues of long experience who will challenge you on them and try to draw you back into "conventional" practice. If you master the principles of sound practice, you will be able to carry them out and help others understand why they should do the same.

A FUNDAMENTAL ASSESSMENT BELIEF

Our assessment traditions are built on the belief that assessment results inform the instructional decisions made by the adults who manage schools and classrooms (teachers, principals, curriculum directors, superintendents, etc.). If the adults have the right data, we have assumed, they will make the right instructional decisions and schools will work effectively. However, in this book we manifest a fundamentally different belief. While we too believe the adults in the system play crucial roles and certainly must rely on good evidence to make instructional decisions that contribute to student success, in fact, other players make even more important instructional decisions based on assessment results. Those other assessment users, as we're sure you have inferred by now, are students themselves. We will consider the various assessment users—adults and students—and the decisions they make in great detail in Chapter 2.

But for now, we simply ask that you put your students on your radar screen as players in the assessment process, and not merely as recipients of the scores and grades you assign. Based on their interpretation of their own academic record, students decide whether (1) they are even capable of learning what you ask them to learn, (2) trying to learn is worth the reward of public success or risk of possible public failure, and (3) the learning to be gained is worth the effort needed to acquire it. If they come down on the wrong side of these decisions in your classroom, then it doesn't matter what you decide to try to impact their learning. The learning stops.

Therefore, whatever else we do, we must help them believe that success in learning is within reach. Student-involved classroom assessment, as described herein, is entirely about building and maintaining that confidence.

To make their decisions well, students need continuous access to accurate and understandable descriptions of their work and how to improve it. They need to know their achievement status and see their academic improvement. When they are partners in this process and have continuous access to descriptive (not judgmental) feedback during their learning, teachers tell us, it's almost shocking how fast they can grow. The purpose of this book is to enable you to join the ranks of these very strong teachers.

This book details the different ways you can use day-to-day classroom assessment, record keeping, and communication to help learners feel in control of control their own success. It's about avoiding circumstances in which assessments have the effect of destroying student confidence. This book aspires to assessment without victims.

We are not opposed to holding students accountable for their learning. Indeed, they need to know that, at some point in the future their work will be evaluated and will be judged sufficient or insufficient—that grades may be assigned. But in between those graded events there needs to be time for practice, time for learning. Next, we consider why.

THE EMOTIONAL DYNAMICS OF ASSESSMENT

So our aspiration is to keep students feeling in control of their own learning success. We want them confident that they probably will succeed if they try and that trying will enhance that probability. We want to promote hope and help our students see the relevance of practice—we don't want them giving up in hopelessness or seeing assignments as just a meaningless assignment. We want (indeed need) to promote student buy-in to the learning.

The label psychologists have coined for this emotional state is *self-efficacy.* As with other psychological characteristics, we each fall somewhere on a continuum from, in this case, strong to weak self-efficacy. Bandura (1994) maps the anchor points of this particular continuum as follows. While he refers to a generalized personality trait here, as educators, we can think about and refer more specifically to academic self-efficacy—a student's sense of control of her or his chances of academic success:

> Self-efficacy is defined as peoples' beliefs in their own capabilities. . . . People with high assurance in their capabilities approach difficult tasks as challenges to be mastered rather than as threats to be avoided. Such an efficacious outlook fosters intrinsic interest and deep engrossment in activities. They set themselves challenging goals and maintain strong commitment to them. They heighten and sustain their efforts in the face of failure. They quickly recover their sense of efficacy after setbacks. They attribute failure to insufficient effort or deficient knowledge and skills which [they believe] are acquirable. . . .
>
> In contrast, people who doubt their capabilities shy away from difficult tasks which they view as personal threats. They have low aspirations and weak commitment to the goals they choose to pursue. When faced with difficult tasks, they dwell on their personal deficiencies, on the obstacles they will encounter, and all kinds of adverse outcomes rather than concentrate on how to perform successfully. They slacken their efforts and give up quickly in the face of difficulties. They are slow to recover their sense of efficacy following failure or setbacks. Because they view insufficient performance as deficient aptitude, it does not require much failure for them to lose faith in their capabilities. (p. 71)[*]

When our students are partners with us in assessment during learning (that is, traveling the GPS route) we help them link their efforts directly to success early and often. In effect, this encourages them to take the risk of trying and invest the energy needed to move boldly toward the strong end of this continuum. We can help them get on winning streaks and stay there as they gain confidence in themselves as learners. This emotional dynamic can feed on itself, leading students into learning trajectories where optimism overpowers pessimism, effort replaces fatigue, and success leaves failure in its wake. We will return to this concept of self-efficacy often in subsequent chapters, as it represents the emotional foundation and reason for the power of assessment FOR learning.

As you will learn in the next chapter, there are many important assessment users at all levels of the educational system. However, students, who use the results to set expectations of themselves, are among the most important. Students decide how high to aim based on their sense of the probability that they will succeed. They estimate the probability of future success based on their record of past success as reflected in their classroom assessment experience. *No single decision or combination of decisions made by any other party exerts such influence on student success.* For this reason, to be considered valid for this context, your classroom assessments must help both you and your students clearly understand the results of each individual assessment and track increments in their achievement over time.

---

[*]Bandura, A. (1994). Self-efficacy. In V. S. Ramachaudran (Ed.), *Encyclopedia of human behavior* (Vol. 4, pp. 71-81). New York: Academic Press. Reprinted with permission by Elsevier.

A Special Note about Struggling Learners

When students are academically challenged, we and they face the constant danger that they will sense their learning difficulties and develop a sense of futility in that regard. As we proceed, we will discuss specific ways to deal with this. But for now, suffice it to say that you must be aware of this danger and its origins. The achievement targets we set for those who struggle to learn will be framed in their Individual Educational Plans (IEPs). We must be sure those are based on their real level of learning to date—that is, their current place in the learning progression you have planned for them. There is no place for "ought to be" or "should have learned" or "grade-level expectation" in this context if they fail to represent a student's actual starting point for learning. It is only with dependable diagnostic evidence that we can answer the driving question that must be the focus of classroom assessment and instruction: What comes next in the learning? It is neither ethical nor pedagogically sound to hold students accountable for achievement targets they have no hope of hitting. This dooms them to inevitable failure and that is unacceptable. The effect of doing so will be a loss of confidence for the student and the rapid development of that sense of futility that leads to hopelessness.

FIGURE 1.1
Keys to Assessment Quality

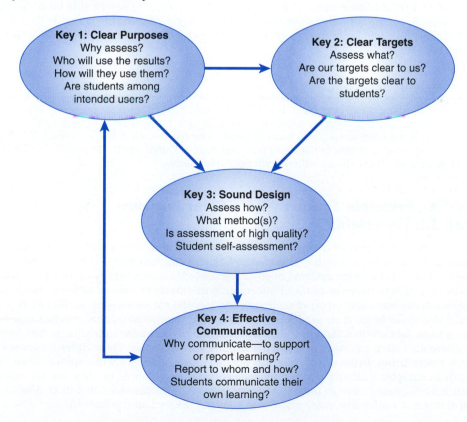

On the other hand, if we manage their learning in a continuous-progress manner and at a rate appropriate for them, keeping them in touch with their own improvement through their involvement in assessment, we can keep them believing that success (as defined for them in terms of their special needs) is within reach.

GUIDES TO VALID AND RELIABLE ASSESSMENT EFFECTIVELY USED

Starting now, our job herein is to teach ourselves out of jobs. In other words, our job is to help you reach a place where you no longer need us or your professor to tell you whether your assessment practices are sound—a place where you know when you have done well because you can *apply the criteria that define sound assessment to your own work.*

Your job in your classroom is exactly the same as ours here: to take your students to a place where they no longer need you to tell them whether they have done well, but rather where they know this in their own minds because they understand the criteria that define high achievement—just as Ms. W. helped Emily and her classmates learn.

As we proceed toward this end, you will see (indeed, already have seen) repeated reference to a set of guiding principles. They are represented graphically in Figure 1.1. We highlight them with you here at the outset as interrelated themes that map the path to valid and reliable assessment. The order in which they are presented is immaterial; each principle is profoundly important. Together, they represent the concrete foundation on which we will build the structure of your understanding of how to assess well in your classroom.

Time for Reflection

As you read about these principles, keep Ms. W. and Emily in mind and you will see why we started our journey together with their story. In fact, it might be helpful to take a few minutes to reread the story if you wish to be in close touch with it (not essential). In any event, make note of where in the story you find evidence that Ms W. attended to each of these principles. Then, discuss them with your teammates.

Guiding Principle 1: Start with a Clear Purpose: Why Am I Assessing?

Classroom level is part of a larger assessment system that exists within schools and districts to meet the information needs of a variety of different users. In other words, as specified previously, such systems need to acknowledge that a variety of decision makers need access to different kinds of information in different forms at different times to help students learn and report of their success. Beyond the classroom, we find instructional decisions focused on program evaluation and improvement that reaches across classrooms and schools. And beyond these, annual district accountability, policy, and resource allocation assessment users make more key decisions. These different assessment users bring different information needs to the table. We will explore these in depth in Chapter 2. If any users' information needs are ignored or they are provided with misinformation due to inept assessments, ineffective decisions will filter down to harm student confidence, motivation, and learning, as well as teacher efficacy.

For this reason, the starting place for the creation of a quality assessment for use in any particular context must be a clear sense of the information needs of the assessment user/decision maker to be served. Without a sense of what kind of information will help them and, therefore, what kind of assessment must be conducted, the assessor cannot proceed with productive assessment development or use. If they do proceed in the absence of a clear purpose, the results will be (and often is) the inept assessment and ineffective communication and use of results.

Guiding Principle 2: Start with Clear and Appropriate Achievement Targets: Assess What?

The quality of any assessment depends on how clearly and appropriately you define the achievement target you are assessing. In our opening vignette, a breakthrough in student writing achievement occurred in part because the English department faculty returned from that summer institute with a shared vision of writing proficiency. They built their program, and thus the competence of their students, around that vision.

You cannot validly (accurately) assess academic achievement targets that you have not precisely and completely defined. There are many different kinds of valued achievement expectations within our educational system, from mastering content knowledge to complex problem solving, from performing a flute recital to speaking Spanish to writing a strong term paper. All are important. But to assess them well, you must ask yourself, "Do I know what it means to do it well? Precisely what does it mean to succeed academically?" You are ready to assess only when you can answer these questions with clarity and confidence.

If your assignment is to promote math problem-solving proficiency, you must become a confident, competent master of that performance domain yourself. Without a sense of final destination reflected in your standards, and signposts along the way against which to check students' progress, you will have difficulty being an effective classroom assessor or teacher.

Guiding Principle 3: Create High-Quality Assessments That Yield Dependable Information

To be of high quality (that is, to consistently produce accurate results), assessments need to satisfy four specific quality standards. They must do all of the following:

1. Rely on a proper assessment method (a method capable of reflecting the target).
2. Sample student achievement appropriately (provide enough evidence).
3. Be built with high-quality ingredients (good test items and scoring schemes, for example, not bad).
4. Minimize distortion of results due to bias (more about this later).

Assessments that meet these standards can support *valid* and *reliable* inferences about student learning. All assessments must meet these standards. No exceptions can be tolerated, because to violate any of them is to risk inaccuracy, placing student academic well-being in jeopardy. This is the first of many discussions and illustrations of these quality standards that permeate this book. On this first pass, we intend only to give you a general sense of the meaning of *quality.*

Guiding Principle 4: Communicate Results Effectively

Mention the idea of communicating assessment results and the first thoughts that come to mind are of test scores and grades attached to very briefly labeled domains of achievement such as *reading, writing, science, math,* and the like. When the purpose of the communication is to report the sufficiency of student learning for accountability purposes, this level of detail can work. Remember in our opening vignette the English faculty started with a clear vision of the meaning of academic success in writing in their classrooms and communicated that meaning effectively to students, parents, and school board members. They accomplished this with summary performance ratings depicting typical gains in achievement.

However, when the purpose of the communication is to support learning—not merely report it—then mere summaries (grades, scores or ratings) will not do the job. In those cases, students need access to descriptive feedback focused on specific attributes of their work revealing how they can do better the next time. In other words, numbers and grades are not the only—or in certain contexts even the best—way to communicate about achievement. We can use words, pictures, illustrations, examples, and many other means to convey this information.

So effective communication of assessment results turns on the purpose for the communication. Teachers must understand how to balance their use of feedback to support learning with communication about the sufficiency of student learning at accountability time. Using our GPS metaphor, we must communicate in ways that keep student on track as they learn and that report their arrival at the achievement destination when that is appropriate.

AN OVERARCHING PRINCIPLE: STUDENT INVOLVEMENT

Within each of these four guiding principles—clear purpose, clear target, quality assessment, and effective communication—we can form a solid link to student involvement in classroom assessment during their learning. The strongest belief or value underpinning this book is that the greatest potential value of classroom assessment is realized when we open the process up *during the learning* and welcome students in as full partners. By now you understand that we refer here to far more than merely suggesting that students trade test papers or homework assignments and grade each other's work. That's strictly clerical stuff. We are suggesting something that goes far deeper.

Students who participate in the thoughtful analysis of quality work to identify its critical elements or to internalize valued achievement targets become better performers. When students learn to apply these standards so thoroughly that they can confidently and competently evaluate their own and each other's work, they are well on the road to becoming better performers in their own right. Consider Emily's case in our opening vignette. Ms. W. helped her to internalize key elements of good writing so she could understand the shortcomings of her own writing, take responsibility for improving them, and watch herself improve. Her confidence and competence as a partner in her classroom assessment came through loud and clear, both in the parent-teacher conference she led at midyear and in her commentary to the school board at the end of the year. Throughout this text, we offer many specific suggestions for melding assessment, instruction, and students in this way.

Time for Reflection

During your K–12 schooling years, did your teachers engage you in this kind of self-assessment? If they did, when they did involve you, how did they do so? What was that experience like for you—what impact did it have? If they did not, why do you think that was the case? Discuss this with your teammates.

Summary: The Importance of Sound Assessment

The guiding principles discussed in this chapter (and illustrated with Emily's experience) form the foundation of the assessment wisdom all educators must master in order to manage classroom assessment environments effectively.

Teachers who are prepared to meet the challenges of classroom assessment understand that they need to do their assessment homework and be ready to think clearly and to communicate effectively at assessment time. They understand why it is critical to be able to share their expectations with students and their families and why it is essential that they conduct high-quality assessments that accurately reflect achievement expectations.

Well-prepared teachers realize that they themselves lie at the heart of the assessment process in schools and they take that responsibility very seriously. Competent teachers understand the complexities of aligning a range of valued achievement targets with appropriate assessment methods so as to produce information on student achievement that both they and their students can count on to be accurate. They understand the meaning of *valid assessment* and they know how to use all of the assessment tools at their disposal to produce valid information to serve intended purposes.

Effective classroom assessors/teachers understand the interpersonal dynamics of classroom assessment and know how to set students up for success, in part through using the appropriate assessment as a teaching tool. They know how to make students full partners in defining the valued targets of instruction and in transforming those definitions into quality assessments. They understand how to use them as satellite signals in a GPS-style classroom assessment environment.

As teachers involve students in assessment, thus demystifying the meaning of success in the classroom, they acknowledge that students use assessment results to make the decisions that ultimately will determine if school does or does not work for them. Our collective classroom assessment responsibility is to be sure students have access to and understand the information they need to see themselves growing over time.

Final Chapter Reflection

Each chapter in this text will conclude with a brief and consistent set of questions for you to reflect on to solidify your understanding and ease your transition to subsequent chapters. Please take time to record your answers in your journal. They will help you make key connections as we continue our journey through the realm of classroom assessment.

1. *What are the three most important new insights to come to you as a result of your study of this chapter?*
2. *What questions come to mind now about classroom assessment that you hope to have answered in subsequent chapters?*

Practice with Chapter 1 Ideas

The following activities provide opportunities for your personal reflection on ideas presented in Chapter 1 and may serve as an excellent basis for discussion of those ideas among classmates:

1. Read the following classroom assessment scenarios. Is each likely to increase or decrease student confidence and motivation to learn? Why?

   - Alan is having his students score each other's quizzes and then call out the scores so he can enter them in his gradebook.
   - Students in Eileen's class are discussing some samples of anonymous science lab notes to decide which are great examples, which have some good points, and which don't tell the story of the lab at all well. They're gradually developing criteria for improving their own lab "learning logs."
   - Catherine has just received back a grade on a report she wrote for social studies. She got a D+. There were no other comments.
   - Students in Henry's basic writing class are there because they have failed to meet the state's writing competency requirements. Henry tells students that the year will be a time of learning to write. Competence at the end will be all that matters.
   - Jeremy's teacher tells him that his test scores have been so dismal so far that no matter what he does from then on he will fail the class.
   - Pat is reading her latest story aloud for the class to critique. Like each of her classmates, she's been asked to take notes during this "peer assessment" so that she can revise her work later.

2. Think of an assessment experience from your personal educational past that was a GOOD experience for you. What made it a productive experience? What emotional and learning impact did if have for you? Now think of one that was a BAD experience for you. What made it a counterproductive experience? What was its emotional and learning impact? What were the procedural differences between the two experiences? How do those differences relate to the Guiding Principles described at the end of this chapter?

Now go to www.myeducationlab.com to take a Pretest to assess your initial comprehension of chapter content, study chapter content with your individualized Study Plan, take a Posttest to assess your understanding of chapter content, practice your teaching skills with Building Teaching Skills exercises, and build a deeper, more applied understanding of chapter content with Homework and Exercises.

CHAPTER 2

Understanding Why We Assess

CHAPTER FOCUS

This chapter answers the following guiding question:

Who are the various users of the assessment process and its results within and outside the classroom and how do (can, should) they use them?

From your study of this chapter, you will understand the following:

1. How your classroom assessments fit into the big picture of assessment in schools.
2. How classroom assessments can affect the quality of instruction.
3. How interim and annual assessments can support and certify learning.

OUR BALANCED ASSESSMENT MISSION

In Chapter 1, we established that we assess for two reasons: (1) to gather information about student achievement to help us make instructional decisions that will enhance learning, and (2) to motivate students by keeping them in touch with their learning success. Although our natural tendency is to see teachers as the instructional decision makers (and we certainly need to be), it turns out many others make critically important decisions, too. Our traditions and societal values have us thinking we assess to hold students accountable; that is, to assign report card grades; in fact, grading decisions represent only one entry on the long list of assessment uses. This chapter explores the other uses of assessment, placing you, the classroom teacher, right in the center of this assessment universe.

Figure 2.1 highlights the facet of assessment quality we will be addressing: clear purposes. One must always start the assessment process with a clear answer to the question, *Why am I assessing?*

The various tables in this chapter analyze the range of potential answers; that is, the array of potential assessment users and uses. We begin by describing the assessment demands of the *classroom level* of use, where students and teachers make the key instructional decisions. Next, we progress to *interim/benchmark assessments* where periodic assessments are used across classrooms every few weeks to identify weaknesses in instructional programs and to focus immediate program and faculty improvements. Finally, we move to *annual standardized tests* whose results influence resource allocation and large-scale programmatic, policy, and other decisions made by school, district, and community leaders.

FIGURE 2.1
Keys to Assessment Quality: Clear Purpose

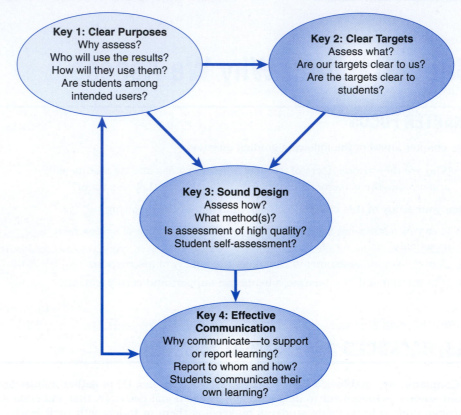

To see how your assessment role as a classroom teacher fits into the big picture, you must understand that assessments at each of these levels can serve either of two purposes: they can support student learning (*formative* applications) or verify that learning has been attained (*summative* applications). When we cross the three levels of assessment use (classroom, interim, and annual) with formative and summative applications, as shown in Table 2.1, we frame the big assessment picture in schools. To bring this picture into focus, in each cell of the table we need to provide specific answers to four essential questions:

- What key decisions are to be informed by assessment results?
- Who are the decision makers?
- What information do they need to make sound decisions?
- What essential assessment conditions must be satisfied to ensure a productive decision?

In a truly productive balanced assessment system those essential conditions are always satisfied, permitting quality evidence to flow into the hands of the proper decision maker, who is ready to make the right instructional decisions.

TABLE 2.1
Elements of a Balanced Assessment System

Level of Assessment/Key Issues	Formative Applications	Summative Applications
Classroom assessment		
• *Key decision(s) to be informed?*	What comes next in the student's learning?	What standards has each student mastered? What grade does each student receive?
• *Who is the decision maker?*	Students and teachers	Teacher
• *What information do they need?*	Evidence of where the student is now on learning continuum leading to each achievement standard	Evidence of each student's mastery of each relevant standard
• *What are the essential assessment conditions?*	• Clear curriculum maps leading to each standard • Accurate assessment results showing how each student did in mastering each standard • Descriptive feedback pointing student and teacher clearly to next steps in the learning	• Clear and appropriate standards • Accurate evidence for each standard • Focus on achievement only • Evidence well summarized • Grading symbols have clear and consistent meaning for all
Interim/benchmark assessment		
• *Key decision(s) to be informed?*	Which standards students consistently struggling to master? Which students are struggling? Where/how can we improve instruction for them right now?	Did the program of instruction deliver as promised? Should we continue to use it or terminate its use?
• *Who is the decision maker?*	Instructional leaders; faculty departments or teams of teachers	Curriculum and instruction leaders
• *What information do they need?*	Evidence of achievement standards students are struggling to master	Evidence of mastery of particular standards
• *What are the essential assessment conditions?*	• Clear and appropriate standards • Accurate assessment results by standard • Results reveal how *each* student did in mastering *each* standard	Accurate assessments of mastery of program standards aggregated over students
Annual testing		
• *Key decision(s) to be informed?*	What standards are our students not mastering? Where and how can we improve instruction next year?	Are enough students meeting standards?
• *Who is the decision maker?*	Curriculum and instructional leaders	School and community leaders
• *What information do they need?*	Standards students are struggling to master	Percent of students meeting *each* standard
• *What are the essential assessment conditions?*	Accurate evidence of how *each* student did in mastering *each* standard aggregated over students	Accurate evidence of how *each* student did in mastering *each* standard aggregated over students

School districts must implement a productive, multilevel assessment system to ensure that all users make the most effective instructional decisions. If we fail to meet the information needs of anyone on this list or fail to implement quality assessments at any level, we place students directly in harm's way. Because your responsibility is to deliver sound assessment practices in your classroom, the classroom level of Table 2.1 will be the focus of most of our attention in the chapters that follow. However, you also may be invited to participate in the development of local interim/benchmark assessments. The lessons that follow also will prepare you to do that job well.

As you read on, bear in mind that an assessment is *valid* when it serves its intended purpose well.

Time for Reflection

Before continuing, please study Table 2.1 carefully. Based on the information provided, write down whatever insights or generalizations you can draw about assessment's role in promoting student success.

Classroom Users and Uses

Let's begin at the classroom level to define your assessment role more completely. In this context, students and teachers gather and use the results of student assessments to inform a variety of decisions that influence both students' motivation and their level of success. Some of these decisions are *formative*, supporting learning: How can we help students understand the target? Self-assess? Improve over time? Others are *summative*, for accountability purposes: Did the student learn enough? What standards did the student master and fail to master? What grade should go on the report card?

After reflecting on the classroom-level questions listed in Table 2.1, can you imagine the dire consequences for student success if students, teachers, and parents were to try to answer them based on misinformation about student achievement due to inaccurate classroom assessment? What if students were, in fact, not hitting the target, but the assessments said they were? What if they were succeeding, but the assessments said they were not?

Clearly, inaccurate assessments would lead to teacher misdiagnosis of student needs, failure to understand which instructional strategies work and which do not, and communication of misinformation to parents, among other problems.

The point is that accurate information derived from quality classroom assessments is essential for instruction to work effectively and for students to learn. In addition, analyzing the questions in Table 2.1 leads to the following critically important generalizations:

- Although we most often think of students as the examinees and not as examiners, they clearly are assessors of their own academic progress, and they use those results in compelling ways.
- Given the manner in which assessment results fit into day-to-day classroom decision making, assessment must occur regularly. These are recurring decisions, and are precisely why classroom assessment events are so much more frequent in a student's life than are annual, formal standardized tests.

- At this level, on the summative side, assessment virtually always focuses on each individual student's mastery of specified material. You, the teacher, must set standards of acceptable achievement if your assessments are to show whether students have succeeded. This is either reported on a standards-based report card, or the report card grade assigned is a function of the extent of each student's mastery of a preset list of standards.

Interim/Benchmark Assessment Users

It has become popular across the land to administer interim assessments quarterly or every few weeks to track student progress in mastering established achievement standards. Users at this level take advantage of assessment results to answer questions such as these: Are there particular standards that our students typically struggle to master? How can we improve our instruction on those standards right now? Can we identify students who are consistently struggling? What can we do right away to help these students?

We see the following patterns emerge from this level of Table 2.1:

- The decisions to be made often focus on the instructional program or the classroom; that is, the effect on groups of students.
- Decisions are made periodically and thus assessment need only be periodic (typically every few weeks or months).
- At this level, heavy reliance is placed on using assessment results from instruments or procedures held constant across classrooms (often termed *common* assessments). In other words, some standardization is required if sound information and good decisions are to result.
- The evidence generated must reveal how each student is doing in mastering each standard. Assessments that cross many standards and blend results into a single overall score will not help, due to their lack of sufficient detail.
- Summative applications take the form of program evaluations in which the purpose of data gathering is to test the efficacy of the program on trial. Once and for all, is this program of instruction worth continuing or should it be abandoned (replaced)? Students become the data source for research but are not held accountable (graded).

These periodic assessments can carry any of a number of labels, including *interim, benchmark, short-cycle,* or *common* assessments, depending on the school district. Under any heading, they will be standardized across classrooms and will be administered every few weeks.

Comparing Classroom and Interim Formative Applications

It should be self-evident that both classroom and interim/benchmark assessments are important, because they can inform decisions that, if made well, can enhance student learning right away. But it is critical that you understand that they are different, and that they accomplish different things. Table 2.2 highlights the differences.

Users and Uses of Annual Tests

The final level of assessment users includes curriculum directors, school leaders, policy makers, and citizens of the community. They establish achievement standards to guide instruction in classrooms, provide instructional personnel and resources, and

TABLE 2.2
Comparing Classroom and Interim Levels of Formative Assessment Use

	Classroom Level	Interim Level
Achievement focus	Student progress toward each standard	Student mastery of each standard
Student focus	Results provide achievement info for each individual student separately	Results are aggregated across students to summarize group results
Frequency of assessment	Continuous	Periodic (every few weeks)
Results inform	Student and teacher	Teachers and school leaders
Key instructional decision	What comes next in the learning?	How can instruction be improved?
Consistency of assessment	Can be unique to an individual student	Typically standardized across students (same test for all)

then demand evidence of achievement to verify that students are meeting the standards. Based on the evidence they receive, they allocate district resources to overcome weaknesses, set personnel policies to regulate who gets to teach, and set procedural policies that guide teaching practices. Once again, we find both formative and summative applications.

We can make the following generalizations on the basis of the information in Table 2.1:

- Their focus is on mastery of standards, not student progress toward each standard; in short, on the summative side, they ask: Who attained mastery of each standard? Did enough students achievement mastery?
- On the formative side, the key question is the same as with interim assessments: Which standards do students consistently struggle to master? Where do we need to improve our programs long term?
- As with the interim/benchmark level, assessments are summarized across students to fulfill program improvement and accountability need.
- As with the interim level, periodic assessment will suffice—typically once a year.
- At this level too, assessment procedures must be standardized across contexts and over time—the decisions to be made require it.

These points having been made, we feel the need to sound a note of caution regarding this level of assessment. Because of the very large numbers of students tested in annual district or statewide testing programs, the costs of test development, administration, scoring, and reporting are high. For this reason, it has been our tradition to rely on the most economical of testing formats, multiple-choice tests. We will discuss this point further in later chapters on test development and standardized testing. But for now, you need to understand that when we choose to stick only with that format we severely restrict the array of achievement targets we can assess. Thus, the danger exists that more complex and very important twenty-first century learning proficiencies will be left out. This reliance on one testing format, along with the infrequency of annual testing, has rendered scores on these tests of little value for classroom-level instructional decision making. For this reason, from here on as we address the challenges of classroom assessment, we will refer infrequently to these tests.

Generalizations across Levels of Users and Uses

Having reflected on classroom, interim, and annual formative and summative uses of assessment, do any general conclusions come to your mind regarding the role of assessment in determining and enhancing the effectiveness of schools? See if you agree:

- Obviously, assessment is intricately woven into the effectiveness of school functioning. Often the depth and complexity of the contributions of the various assessment levels are surprising to many educators. As teachers and instructional leaders, we must all face this complexity and become organized to meet the full range of users' information needs.
- Students count on many people at all levels and in many decision-making contexts to use sound assessment results in productive ways. Every question listed in the tables is critical to student well-being. This is why we must continually strive for the most valid assessments—those that fit the purpose and reflect the target most closely. It is a moral, ethical, and professional imperative of the highest order.
- Considering Tables 2.1 and 2.2 together, it is clear that information both gathered continuously on individual student mastery of specified material and gathered periodically for the purpose of comparing students serve important roles. Different users need different information at different times in different forms to do their jobs.

Given this summary of all of the decision-oriented users and uses of assessment, it becomes clear that we need to maintain a balanced perspective about assessment's valuable role at all levels. High-quality classroom assessment serving its important users must be balanced with high-quality interim and annual standardized assessments serving their important users. Appendix A offers more in-depth analyses of assessment uses organized by user at each of these levels.

Exploring the Cultural Context of Assessment

Historically, assessment priorities in the United States have centered almost exclusively on large-scale annual testing for accountability purposes. This began with districtwide assessment in the 1960s and evolved to statewide testing in the 1970s, national assessment in the 1980s, international assessment in the 1990s, and every-pupil annual testing most recently. Why do you think assessment priorities have evolved in this manner? What have been the driving social and educational forces? Has this been a healthy state of assessment affairs? Why or why not?

Therefore, the Keys to Assessment FOR Learning

This book is about how to use classroom assessment in the service of student success. We speak here not merely of dependable assessment OF learning but also of dependable assessment FOR learning. We seek to use the process and its results, not merely to keep track of learning, but to help students learn more. The tools and strategies offered herein will permit you to help your students go on internal control and take responsibility for their own learning.

Both assessments OF and FOR learning are important. In the case of the former, we use assessment to verify that students have met standards in an accountability sense. For instance, statewide standardized tests ask students to demonstrate that they have met required achievement standards. Or in the classroom, teachers administer final examinations to determine a student's report card grade. These are periodic events that happen after learning is supposed to have occurred, to let others know if students have learned.

But assessment FOR learning is different. In this case, we rely on the process not merely to check for learning, but to increase it. As stated, we refer to these as formative applications. These are the assessments that we use early in learning to diagnose student needs. *These have no place in the determination of report card grades.* They are the continuous assessments that we conduct while learning is happening to help students see and feel in control of their own ongoing growth; in short, to inform students about themselves during learning. In between periodic assessments OF learning we rely on a steady flow of assessments FOR learning. This is what Ms. W. did for Emily and her classmates while they were learning to write—before assigning grades.

In this sense, teachers who help students understand the learning targets, engage in self-assessment, watch themselves grow, talk about that growth, or anticipate next steps in learning are applying the principles of assessment FOR learning.

Following this line of reasoning, we at the Pearson Assessment Training Institute have developed a set of strategies of assessment FOR learning (Figure 2.2). They help students understand where they are headed in their learning (that is, what success will look like when they get there), where they are now in relation to that expectation, and how to close the gap between the two (Sadler, 1989, as interpreted by Chappuis, 2009).

We put students in touch with our vision for their academic success by starting instruction with a student-friendly version of the target and by accompanying that with samples of student work that illustrate the performance continuum they will travel to get there. We help them locate themselves on that continuum by providing descriptive feedback on strengths and areas in need of improvement. And then we teach them how

---

Where am I going?

Strategy 1: Provide students with a clear and understandable vision of the learning target.
Strategy 2: Share with them examples and models of strong and weak work.

Where am I now?

Strategy 3: Provide regular descriptive feedback.
Strategy 4: Teach students to self-assess and set goals.

How can I close the gap?

Strategy 5: Design lessons to focus on one learning target or aspect of quality at a time.
Strategy 6: Teach students to revise their work one key attribute at a time.
Strategy 7: Engage students in self-reflection so they can track and share their learning.

FIGURE 2.2
Seven Strategies of Assessment FOR Learning
Source: Adapted from *Seven Strategies of Assessment* for *Learning* (p. 12), by Jan Chappuis, 2009, Portland OR: Pearson Assessment Training Institute. Adapted by permission.

to self-assess so they can generate their own descriptive feedback. This permits them to begin to set goals for their own learning. From here, we help them learn to improve their work one key facet at a time, tracking and describing the changes in the quality of their work as they go.

When teachers carry out these steps as a matter of routine, they are using assessment FOR learning—assessment in support of student success. In the chapters that follow, we will show you the specifics of how to make these keys come alive in your classroom. But for now, remember that we have been addressing the crucial matter of assessment *purpose* in this section. A quality assessment arises from and serves its intended purpose. We must fit the assessment into its context, and often that context needs to be one of supporting student learning, before we grade it.

Summary: Assessment for Many Purposes

Assessment is, in part, the process of gathering information about student learning to inform instructional decisions. For any assessment to work effectively, it must be developed with an intended purpose in mind: What decision(s) is it to help inform, who will be making the decision(s), and what kind of information is likely to be helpful? Therefore, your starting place for the effective creation and use of any assessment is this driving question: *Why am I assessing?*

One level of assessment use is the classroom, where students and teachers must decide what comes next in the learning and who has mastered which achievement standards. They need continuous access to information about how each individual student is doing on her or his journey to each standard.

Another level of assessment use focuses at the interim/benchmark level across classrooms. Teacher teams, principals, and curriculum personnel must decide which standards are and are not being mastered by students, and which programs are working and which need adjustment. They need periodic evidence (perhaps quarterly during the school year) of student mastery of each standard aggregated across students, classrooms, and sometimes even buildings to focus their program improvement efforts.

Finally, there is the annual district or policy level of assessment use where school, district, and community leaders must determine if enough students are meeting standards. This is the purview of the annual standardized achievement tests typically administered districtwide or statewide.

All levels of use are important because they provide valuable information to important decision makers. However, our journey together through the realm of assessment in this book will center mostly on the classroom, where you, the classroom teacher, will be in charge. You will be responsible for ensuring the accuracy of the evidence gathered with your assessments, and you will need to be sure your assessments and their results are used well to benefit student learning. Included in this latter responsibility is the need to use classroom assessment to keep students believing they are capable learners. The chapters that follow will show you how to fulfill all of these responsibilities.

Always remember, assessment is not merely something adults to do students. Students interpret their assessment results to decide whether success is (1) within reach for them, (2) worth the effort, and (3) worth the risk of public failure. If they come down on the wrong side of these, it doesn't matter what you decide. The learning stops. This book is about using assessment to keep them believing in themselves just as you believe in them.

Table 2.3 presents the first entry in a set of rating scales, or *rubrics,* for evaluating assessment quality that we will build through the rest of the book. (These rubrics appear in their entirety in Appendix B.) This entry asks, Does the assessment arise from and serve clearly articulated purposes?

TABLE 2.3
Guide for Evaluating Assessments for Clear Purpose

Still Needs Work	Well on Its Way	Ready to Use
It is not clear why the assessment is being conducted. No reason for assessment is inferred from the context.	Users and uses can be inferred but are not made explicit. There is some question about whether the assessment can fulfill its intended purpose.	Intended users and uses are explicitly stated. It is clear that the assessment will help them.
The assessment couldn't possibly serve all intended purposes.	If an assessment FOR learning context, the assessment may be encouraging to some learners.	If an assessment FOR learning, the assessment will assist students to strive for excellence.
The specified purpose is inappropriate—the information gathered will not serve the needs of the intended users.		
If an assessment FOR learning context, the assessment probably will not serve students well.		

Final Chapter Reflection

1. *What are the three most important new insights to come to you as a result of your study of this chapter?*
2. *Which of your Chapter 1 questions about assessment can you now answer based on your study of this chapter?*
3. *What new questions have come to mind as a result of your study of this chapter that you hope to have answered as your study continues?*

Practice with Chapter 2 Ideas

1. Consider the strategies of assessment FOR learning in Figure 2.2. Reflect on and write briefly about the extent to which the assessments you are experiencing in your college life meet these requirements and therefore could be considered assessments FOR learning.

2. Traditional school improvement plans and strategies have operated on the belief that the most important instructional decisions—the ones that contribute the most to student learning—are made by teachers and other adults in the system. Little attention has been given to students as assessment users

and instructional decision makers. Why do you think that has been the case?

3. Reflect on, list, and discuss with your class-mates classroom assessment activities with which you are familiar that you believe manifest the principles of assessment FOR learning, noting why or how they manifest those principles.

Now go to www.myeducationlab.com to take a Pretest to assess your initial com-prehension of chapter content, study chapter content with your individualized Study Plan, take a Posttest to assess your understanding of chapter content, practice your teaching skills with Building Teaching Skills exercises, and build a deeper, more applied understanding of chapter content with Homework and Exercises.

CHAPTER 3

Clear Achievement Expectations: The Foundation of Sound Assessment

CHAPTER FOCUS

This chapter answers the following guiding question:

> What kinds of achievement must teachers be ready and able to assess in their classrooms?

From your study of this chapter, you will understand the following:

1. Clear and appropriate achievement standards and corresponding classroom learning targets represent essential foundations of sound assessment and student success.
2. Sound achievement standards and learning targets satisfy certain quality criteria.
3. Teachers must be prepared to assess four different kinds of achievement targets, plus dispositions, if their students are to succeed.

VALIDITY IN TERMS OF LEARNING TARGETS

In Chapter 2, we established that valid classroom assessments arise from and serve clear purposes. So in every context, we must know why we are assessing—that is, who will use the assessment and how. Different users need different information in different forms at different times to do their jobs. Every assessment must be valid for its intended purpose.

In this chapter, we move on to the next key to excellence in classroom assessment: quality assessments arise from and accurately reflect clear and appropriate achievement targets (Figure 3.1). So in preparation for assessing, one must ask, What do I expect my students to learn? Teachers who cannot articulate their achievement expectations will not be able to develop assessment exercises and scoring procedures that reflect them. Further, they will find it impossible either to share a clear vision of success with their students or to select instructional strategies and assignments that promise and deliver student success.

Only when the target is clear can the assessor pick an appropriate assessment method and develop and implement it properly so as to produce a high-fidelity representation of student learning. Assessments that appropriately cover the material to be learned are said to have *content validity*.

FIGURE 3.1
Key to Assessment Quality: Clear Targets

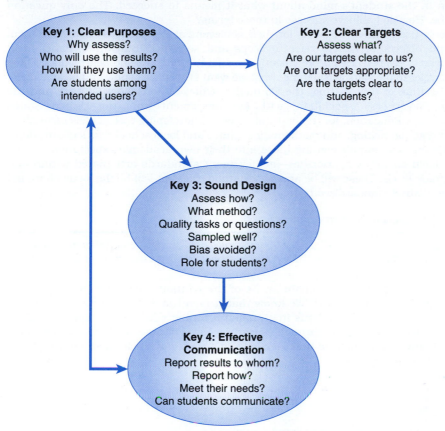

Defining Achievement Targets

Achievement or learning targets define academic success—what we want students to know and be able to do. Visualize a target with its concentric circles and a bull's-eye in the middle. The center circle defines the highest level of performance students can achieve; a very high-quality piece of writing, the most fluent oral reading, the highest possible score on a math problem-solving test. Each concentric ring on the target defines a level of performance further from the highest level. As students improve, they need to understand that they are progressing toward the bull's-eye.

Our mission as teachers in standards-driven schools is to help the largest possible percentage of our students get there. To reach that goal, we must take charge of defining where "there" is. What are the attributes of a good piece of writing, such as Emily's end-of-year sample from Chapter 1? How does this level of performance differ from performance of lesser quality—that is, from the outer rings of the target? Ms. Weathersby knew, and gave Emily the insights she needed to understand as well.

We have adopted the target metaphor to permit us to point out now and repeatedly throughout this book that *students can hit any target that they see and that holds still for them.* But if they are guessing at what success looks like, in effect trying to learn while blindfolded, success will be a random event for them. There should never be a question in the student's mind about what it means to succeed. The only question should be, How do I achieve success in those terms?

Schools use a variety of labels for their achievement expectations. Some call them *goals* and *objectives.* Others refer to *scope* and *sequence.* Still others label them *proficiencies* or *competencies.* More recently, we refer to *standards* and *benchmarks.* These terms all refer to the same basic thing: what we want students to know and be able to do.

At the time of this writing, the Council of Chief State School Officers and the National Governors Association, with encouragement from the United States Department of Education, for the first time ever are developing core achievement standards in reading, writing, and mathematics. States and local school districts are adopting, adapting, and supplementing these into their own academic expectations in the form of local curriculum priorities—achievement standards articulated within and across grade levels. These will be among the standards that will be the focus of annual state and district standardized tests.

Exploring the Social Context of Assessment

Why do you think this team took on the task of developing our first ever national standards? What political forces were at work? Do you think this is a good idea? Why or why not?

As teachers, we need to remain aware of the relation of these standards to our teaching and student learning. We know that it is virtually never the case that students attain mastery of standards in an instant. Rather what really happens is that, over time, students progress through ascending levels of proficiency to a place where they are ready to demonstrate that they have met each state or local standard. This is illustrated in Figure 3.2.

FIGURE 3.2
Relationship of Standards to Enabling Classroom Targets

The scaffolding on which they climb during the process of becoming competent can be thought of as enabling *classroom-level learning targets.* They must be the focus of classroom instruction and day-to-day classroom assessment if students ultimately are to arrive at success. Figure 3.3 provides two examples of state standards that have been unpacked into their enabling classroom-level achievement targets.

Our standards and learning targets form a solid foundation for effective teaching and learning (and therefore classroom assessment) when they meet the following universal and nonnegotiable criteria:

1. *Center on Important Learnings*—Academic achievement expectations cannot merely be a matter of local opinion. Rather, they must be steeped in the best, most current thinking of leading experts in the field. We don't get to vote on what

---

Sample State Standard

History: Students will evaluate different interpretations of historical events.

The teacher must translate this into relevant classroom targets:

Knowledge and Understanding: Students must know and understand each historical event, and must understand each of the alternative interpretations to be evaluated. The teacher must determine if students are to know those things outright or if they can use reference materials to retrieve the required knowledge.

Reasoning: Evaluative reasoning requires judgment about the quality of each interpretation. Thus students must demonstrate both an understanding of the criteria by which one judges the quality of an interpretation and the ability to apply these criteria.

Performance Skills: None required

Products: None required

Sample State Standard

Writing: Students will use styles appropriate for their audience and purpose, including proper use of voice, word choice, and sentence fluency.

The teacher must translate this into relevant classroom targets:

Knowledge and Understanding: Writers must possess appropriate understanding of the concept of style as evidenced in voice, word choice, and sentence structure. In addition, students must possess knowledge of the topic they are to write about.

Reasoning: Writers must be able to figure out how to make sound voice, word choice, and sentence construction decisions while composing original text. The assessment must provide evidence of this ability.

Performance Skills: One of two kinds of performance will be required. Either respondents will write longhand or will compose text on a keyboard. Each requires its own kind of skill competence.

Products: The final evidence of competence will be written products that present evidence of the ability to write effectively to different audiences.

FIGURE 3.3
Converting State Standards to Classroom Achievement Targets

our local faculty means by "good writer." Those traits have been clearly defined in our professional literature. Nor is it merely a matter of individual teacher opinion of what it means to do good science or solve math problems appropriately. As teachers, it is our personal and collective responsibility to remain in touch with our professional literature.

2. *Are Unambiguously Stated and Public*—Our achievement expectations must be written in clear language. When achievement targets are clearly stated, all who read and paraphrase them interpret them to mean essentially the same thing. Similarly, one criterion by which we should judge the appropriateness of our achievement expectations is our ability to provide actual samples of student work that clearly illustrate different levels of proficiency. Our definitions and illustrations must be made available to all within the community to see and understand.

3. *Are Organized to Unfold in Proper Order over Time within and across Grades*— Achievement expectations held as important at any grade level must fit into a continuously progressing curriculum that guides instruction across grade levels in that school and district. The overall curriculum should define ascending levels of competence that spiral through grade levels, mapping a journey to academic excellence. Each teacher's goals and objectives, therefore, must arise directly from what has come before and lead in a commonsense manner to what will follow. Because of differences in academic capabilities, students will ascend such con-tinuously progressing curricula at vastly different rates. Some will zoom through, while others will crawl very slowly. Please realize that the path to academic suc-cess doesn't change as a function of how fast students travel it. Prerequisites will remain foundations for what follows, and must be mapped to guide progressive learning—for students with learning disabilities, for midrange students, and for those who are gifted and talented.

   Typically, these roadmaps to academic success are created by teams of expe-rienced teachers for use across the school district by all teachers. But when that has not been done, you must map the journey for your own students. This requires that you become a competent master of the standards your students are expected to meet. More about this in item 7.

4. *Have Been Unpacked and Backed Down into the Curriculum to Create the Scaffolding Students Will Climb to Reach Them*—Not only must standards unfold in proper order over time, but each standard must be analyzed to determine the foundations of knowledge, reasoning, performance skills, and/or product development capabilities that, if mastered, will take the student through ascending levels of competence to learning success as represented in that standard.

5. *Have Been Transformed into Student- and Family-friendly Versions*—Once articulated in these terms, as specified, our expectations should be made public for all—school and community—to see and understand. First and foremost, this includes our students. This requires transforming classroom achievement targets into student-friendly versions that we are prepared to share with them from the very beginning of their learning. This is one of several specific strategies that we will discuss later as foundational to creating an "assessment FOR learning" classroom.

6. *Are Manageable in Number and Scope*—It is always the case that time and resources available to promote student learning are limited. Besides, students vary in the rate at which they are capable of learning. Still further, achievement expectations vary in the complexity of the demands they place on teacher and learner. It is essential that these variables be considered in defining the scope of each teacher's assigned teaching responsibilities. In the productive classroom

assessment environment, the amount to be learned fits within those limited resources. Too much overwhelms, too little leads to boring frustration. Both excesses discourage both teacher and learner.

For this reason, at the beginning of any unit of study, one must articulate the learning targets in manageable terms. This includes setting priorities. One must know from the outset which standards are absolutely essential and which can slip if necessary. It is best if this is a faculty decision based on the big picture. But if those priorities have not been established in any particular context, it falls to you, the teacher, to make those decisions.

7. *Fall within the Teacher's Repertoire*—As a classroom teacher, it will fall to you to deliver instruction and to conduct both formative and summative classroom assessments that focus on an assigned set of achievement expectations. To fulfill this responsibility, you must become a confident, competent master of the learning targets that you expect your students to hit. This doesn't mean, for example, that elementary teachers must become masters of high school physics. But it does mean these teachers must understand those physics (or math or social studies) concepts that their students must master on their journey toward high-level study. If they do not, then important prerequisites will be missing, dooming some students to later failure.

An Example of Learning Targets Carefully Defined

Figure 3.4 presents sample learning requirements for the state of Wisconsin as transformed by the Milwaukee Public Schools. This example centers on one Language Arts standard in writing that Wisconsin school leaders feel is important for their students. The standard, written at a general statewide level of specificity at the top, is clearly stated and specific. Most importantly, the Milwaukee team made sure the learning requirements are vertically articulated within and across grade levels (Col. 1). A sample of that progression appears in the figure. Further, achievement expectations at each level are transformed into student- and community-friendly vocabulary (Cols. 2 & 3). In this form, they provide a foundation for assessments that both support and verify learning—assessments OF and FOR learning.

ARGUMENTS IN FAVOR OF CLEAR AND APPROPRIATE TARGETS

The energy you invest in becoming clear about your classroom targets will pay big dividends.

Benefit 1: Control of Your Professional Success

One major benefit of defining specific learning targets is that you set clear limits on your own professional responsibility. These limits provide you with a standard by which to gauge your own success as a teacher. In short, defining targets helps you control your own professional destiny. The better you become at bringing your students to mastery of your delimited learning outcomes, the more successful you become as a teacher. The thoughtful use of classroom assessment can help.

Wisconsin Content Standard: Students in Wisconsin will write clearly and effectively to share information and knowledge, to influence and persuade, to create and entertain.

MPS learning target	MPS student-friendly language	MPS public language
Grade 2 B.2.1–Communicate ideas in writing using complete sentences sequentially organized around a specific topic for a variety of audiences and purposes. B.2.2–Independently create multiple drafts of writing in a variety of situations. B.2.3–Correctly compose complete sentences.	B.2.1–I can organize my ideas into a paragraph with a main idea and details by using a web. B.2.2–I can write a first draft and then make it better. B.2.3–I can write a sentence that begins with a capital letter, ends with an end mark, and has a subject and a verb.	Students will: B.2.1–write in complete sentences organized around a topic. Write for different purposes; for example, to entertain or to provide information. B.2.2–create and improve a piece of writing through multiple drafts. B.2.3–write complete sentences that contain subjects and predicates.
Grade 3 B.3.1–Organize sentences into paragraphs to create meaningful communication for a variety of audiences and purposes. B.3.2–Independently apply revision and editing strategies to create clear writing in a variety of situations. B.3.3–Employ standard American English including correct grammar to effectively communicate ideas in writing.	B.3.1–I can write paragraphs with main ideas and details to share my ideas with others. B.3.2–I can change my writing to make it easier to read and understand. B.3.3–I can use correct nouns and verbs when I write; for example, The boys were playing outside. Instead of: The boys was playing outside.	Students will: B.3.1–write a variety of well organized paragraphs that contain main ideas and details. B.3.2–improve writing by revising and editing, for example, choosing specific words and applying proper grammar, spelling, and punctuation. B.3.3–use standard American English to communicate ideas in writing.
Grade 4 B.4.1–Prepare multi-paragraph writing, adapting style and structure to suit a variety or audiences and purposes. B.4.2–Independently employ purposeful revision and editing strategies to improve multiple drafts of writing in a variety of situations. B.4.3–Identify various sentence forms and structures while applying the rules of standard American English to written communications.	B.4.1–I can write more than one paragraph on or different reasons. B.4.2–I can use the writing process to check my writing for mistakes and make my writing better. B.4.3–I can choose different kinds of sentences to make my writing more interesting.	Students will: B.4.1–write reports and stories several paragraphs in length. Change the style and structure according to the type of writing and the reader. B.4.2–plan, draft, revise, edit, and publish their writing. B.4.3–apply standard American English to written communication. Know different types of sentence forms, such as declarative, exclamatory, imperative, and interrogative.

		Students will:
Grade 8 B.8.1–Compose clear and effective writing including literary commentaries, critiques and interpretations that analyze a reading or viewing experience. B.8.2–Independently identify questions and strategies for improving drafts in writing conferences. B.8.3–Apply the rules of standard American English to written communications.	B.8.1–I can write my personal thoughts about something I read or saw. B.8.2–I can think of questions and make a plan to improve my writing. B.8.3–I can check writing and make the right changes in grammar, capitalization, and punctuation.	B.8.1–write for a variety of purposes, to include clear commentaries and critiques about something that was read or viewed. B.8.2–identify and apply strategies to improve their own and others' writing. B.8.3–apply the rules of standard American English to their writing.
Grade 11 & 12 B.11/12.1–Create substantial pieces of proficient writing to effectively communicate with different audiences for a variety of purposes, including literary analyses. B.11/12.2–Apply the writing process to create and critique writing composed in a variety of situations. B.11/12.3–Edit and critique writing for clarity and effectiveness.	B.11/12.1–write longer compositions of different types. Analyze literature and communicate their analyses using written reports. B.11/12.2–apply the writing process to any writing they undertake. B.11/12.3–edit and critique writing for clarity and effectiveness.	B.11/12.1–write longer compositions of different types. Analyze literature and communicate their analyses using written reports. B.11/12.2–apply the writing process to any writing they undertake. B.11/12.3–edit and critique writing for clarity and effectiveness.

FIGURE 3.4

Sample of Milwaukee Public Schools (MPS) Map of Achievement Expectations

Source: Milwaukee Public Schools, Milwaukee, Wisconsin. Reprinted by permission.

As a community of professionals, all of us must be ready to take responsibility for our own success. If we succeed as teachers and our students hit the target, we want acknowledgement of that success. If our students fail to hit the target we want to know it, and we want to know why they failed.

We can think of at least five possible reasons why our students might not have mastered our standards:

1. They lacked the prerequisites needed to achieve what we expected of them.
2. We didn't understand the learning target to begin with, and so could not convey it appropriately.
3. Our instructional approach, strategies, and materials were inappropriate or inadequate.
4. Our students lacked the confidence to risk trying—the motivation to strive for success wasn't there.
5. Some force(s) outside of school and beyond our control (family issues or other emotional upset, for example) interfered with learning.

As a professional educators whose students failed to hit the target, we need to know which of these problems inhibited learning if we expect to remedy the situation. Only when we know what went wrong can we make the kinds of decisions and take the kinds of action that will promote success for us and our students next time.

For example, if our students lacked prerequisites (reason 1), we need to work with our colleagues in the lower grades to be sure our respective curricula mesh. If we lack mastery of the valued targets ourselves or fail to implement solid instruction (reasons 2 & 3), we have to take responsibility to complete some pretty important professional development. Similarly, if our students lacked the confidence or motivation needed to try learning (reason 4), we may need to investigate ways to help them experience enough learning success to regain their sense of academic self efficacy. And finally, if reason 5 applies, then we need to reach out into their community beyond school to seek solutions.

In any event, as teachers employed in a school setting committed to helping all students meet state or local academic standards, our success hinges on our understanding the reasons for any lack of success.

Note that we can choose the proper corrective action if and only if we take the risks of (1) gathering dependable evidence about student success or failure using our own high-quality classroom assessments, and (2) becoming enough of a classroom researcher to uncover the causes of student failure. If we as teachers simply bury our heads in the sand and blame our students for not caring or not trying, we may doom them to long-term failure for reasons beyond their control. Thus, when they fail, we must risk finding out why. If it is our fault or if we can contribute to fixing the problem in any way, we must act accordingly.

We believe that the risk is greatly reduced when we start out with clear and specific targets. If we can share the vision with our students, they can hit it! If we have no target, how can they hit it?

Exploring the Cultural Context of Assessment

In many urban schools, the dropout rate can exceed 50 percent. Thinking about the possible reasons for failure discussed here, why might this be happening and what actions might such schools consider taking to address this serious educational problem? Please discuss this with your learning team. Also, please keep this question in mind as you continue your study of this text.

Benefit 2: Enhanced Student Academic Self-Efficacy

If teachers can help students understand their achievement expectations from the outset, they set their students up to take responsibility for their own success. The motivational implications of this for students can be immense.

Personalize this! Say you are a student facing a big test. A great deal of material has been covered. You have no idea what will be emphasized on the test. You study your heart out but, alas, you concentrate on the wrong material. Nice try, but you fail. How do you feel when this happens? How are you likely to behave the next time a test comes up under these same circumstances?

Now, say you are facing another test. A great deal of material has been covered. But your teacher, who has a complete understanding of the field, points out the parts that are critical for you to know. The rest will always be there in the text for you to look up when you need it. Further, the teacher provides lots of practice applying the knowledge to solving real-world problems and emphasizes that this is a second key target of the course. You study in a very focused manner, concentrating on the important material and its application. Your result is a high score on the test. Good effort—you succeed. Again, how do you feel? How are you likely to behave the next time a test comes up under these circumstances?

Given clear requirements for success, students can approach learning from a more efficacious perspective; that is, they are better able to gauge the appropriateness of their own preparation and thus gain control over their own academic well-being. Students who feel in control of their own chances for success are more likely to care and to strive for excellence.

Benefit 3: Greater Assessment Efficiency

Clear achievement targets can make assessment quicker and easier. Here's why: Any assessment is a sample of all the questions we could have asked if the test were infinitely long. But because time is always limited, we can never probe all important dimensions of a particular achievement standard. So we sample, asking as many questions as we can within the allotted time. A sound assessment asks a representative set of questions, allowing us to infer a student's mastery of the standard based on that student's performance on the shorter sample. If we have set clear limits on our valued target, then we have set a clear sampling frame. This allows us to sample with maximum efficiency and confidence; that is, to gather just enough information to lead us to a confident conclusion about student achievement without wasting time over testing. When we have a clear sense of the desired ends, we can use the assessment methods that are most efficient for that particular situation. When we get to specific assessment methods in Part II, we will explore matters of sampling efficiency in greater detail by method. Also in Part II, we will argue that some methods work well with certain kinds of achievement targets but not with others. In that context, it also will become clear that some methods produce achievement information more efficiently than do others.

Benefit 4: Accurate Classroom Assessments

Because, as just stated, assessment methods work differentially well with different kinds of achievement targets, one cannot make a smart choices about which method to use in any particular situation without knowing the learning target(s) to be assessed.

Thus, the quality of any assessment turns, first, on the choice of a *proper* assessment method given the target. As you will learn later, we have a variety of assessment methods at our disposal. They are not interchangeable. Skillful classroom assessors understand what methods to use when. Your skill as an assessor in this sense increases with the clarity of your vision of your learning targets.

SOURCES OF INFORMATION ABOUT ACHIEVEMENT EXPECTATIONS

You can search out, identify, come to understand, and even place limits around the achievement targets and thus your teaching responsibilities in three ways: analyzing state, and local standards; studying your local written curriculum; and interacting with professional colleagues. Let's explore each.

Common Core Achievement Standards

At the time of this writing, for the first time in our history, states are collaborating with the federal government in developing mathematics and literacy curricula in the form of core standards for student learning. This represents an attempt to unify an American vision of the meaning of academic success across states. Not all states will adopt these as their state standards, but if your state does these will be a very important part of your professional practice.

State and Local Standards

Virtually every state has written its own standards of academic excellence, possibly including federal core standards but extending beyond those to cover additional grade levels and school subjects. States disseminate their standards for local use and administer statewide assessments reflective of their standards. Local schools adopt or adapt those standards and are held accountable for demonstrating student mastery of state standards by scoring high on these tests. Contact your district office or state department of education for information about these standards.

Local Written Curriculum

Every school district will transform its state standards into its own local written curriculum. This statement of learning expectations presents learning targets in much greater detail, typically identifying how the standards that define success within subjects will unfold over time within and across grade levels. Specific topics to be covered will be described, revealing how they are woven together into progressions that engage students in learning over time. This guiding curriculum document also will state if teachers are to emphasize integration across subjects or grades, such as writing across the curriculum. For all of these reasons, you can turn to your local curriculum description for insights regarding your assigned achievement expectations.

Professional Development and Networking

Besides state standards and your local curriculum, the next most important source of insight into key achievement targets is your team of professional colleagues. This includes your principal, other teachers whose instructional responsibilities are similar to yours, and others with experience in teaching in your context. This list all includes the appropriate local and national professional associations of teachers, most of whom have assembled commissions of members to articulate their version of relevant achievement standards. Work with the resource personnel in your professional library if you have one. Often they can route special articles and information to you when they arrive. In short, keep learning.

Exploring the Cultural Context of Assessment

Historically, the locus of control for defining what is to be learned in schools has migrated steadily from individual teachers to the local community or school district to the state with the development of state standards; the new core standards have added a level of federal responsibility. This has been accompanied by the progressive addition of district, then state, then national, and finally international assessments of student learning. Why do you think this shift away from local and toward more centralized control of the curriculum and assessment has taken place?

LEARNING TARGETS FOR THE TWENTY-FIRST CENTURY

As you explore the resources mentioned previously and begin to understand the achievement expectations that are your assigned responsibility, you will see that your students need to master a number of different kinds of achievement as they work toward ultimate academic success in college and the workplace. Our challenge as teachers is to understand which of these kinds of academic achievement is relevant for our particular students at any particular point in their academic development.

As we analyzed the task demands of classroom assessment along with our colleagues, we tried to discern the various kinds of learning targets teachers need to address (Stiggins & Conklin, 1992). We collected, studied, categorized, and tried to understand the various kinds of expectations reflected in teachers' classroom activities and assessments. The following categories or types of achievement targets consistently emerge as important; that is, we ask our students to master the following:

- *Knowledge*—subject matter content to be mastered, where mastery includes both knowing and understanding; examples include science knowledge, knowledge of vocabulary and syntactic structure of language, and knowledge of numbers and numeration systems

- *Reasoning*—the ability to use that knowledge and understanding to figure things out and to solve problems, as in scientific inquiry, algorithmic math problem solving, reading comprehension, and composing original text
- *Performance Skills*—the development of behavioral or process skills, such as playing a musical instrument, reading aloud fluently, speaking in a second language fluently, or using psychomotor skills
- *Products*—the ability to create tangible products, such as term papers, science fair models, and art products, that meet certain standards of quality
- *Dispositions*—the development of the attitudes, interests, and motivational intentions that support learning success in school

As you will see, these categories are very useful in thinking about classroom assessment because they subsume all possible learning targets, are easy to understand and relate to one another in very helpful ways. But most importantly in the context of this text they form the rungs on the scaffolding leading up to standards and they tell us what assessment methods to use in any particular classroom assessment situation. But before we discuss assessment, let's understand these categories of learning targets.

Time for Reflection

As we proceed through the various kinds of learning targets, make a written outline. Label each kind of achievement and define it very briefly in your own words. This will help you internalize this framework. It really is the case that your success in the classroom will hinge, in part, on your understanding of this facet of assessment and teaching.

Knowing and Understanding Targets

When we were growing up, we were asked to learn important content. What happened in 1066? Who signed the Declaration of Independence? Name the Presidents of the United States in order. What does the symbol "Au" refer to on the periodic table of elements? Learn the vocabulary for a quiz on Friday. Here is your spelling list for this week. Learn your multiplication tables.

"Learn the content" typically meant memorize it by test time. And, in fact, at least some of what we learned in this way was important. For example, we can communicate our ideas to others using written or spoken language because we mastered and retain a sufficient vocabulary to do so. We may have attained proficiency in speaking a second language because we learned its vocabulary and syntax. We would not have been able to read our science text if we had not mastered some amount of science knowledge.

Because mastery of knowledge is prerequisite to all other forms of achievement, part of our jobs as teachers is to be sure our students gain control of important content. This is precisely why we have structured this book in part to help you know and understand the foundations of sound assessment practice. You cannot do the classroom assessment part of the teaching job well unless you *know* certain things. In that sense this knowledge represents a foundation of your teaching competence.

But remember three important things about mastery of content knowledge—all of which have direct implications for classroom assessment: (1) to know and to understand are not the same; (2) there are two ways of "knowing"; and (3) there are many ways of coming to know.

1. To Know and to Understand Are Not the Same

The world around us is full of things we know but don't understand. For instance, suspension bridges span rivers and bays. We know this, but we don't understand how their structures keep them from falling into the water. We know that our computers will save the text that we compose, but we don't understand how it does this. We know that $E = MC^2$, so if someone asked us what E equals, we can say, "MC^2." But we don't understand what it means and can't use it to help us solve physics problems. Thus, for us this simply represents useless knowledge.

On the other hand, there are lots of things that we know and understand. Airplanes fly, we understand, because of the vacuum formed when air accelerates over the top of the curved wing. We can say and spell the science word *watershed* and we understand what it means. We even understand what not to do in a watershed environment. We can read and understand guidebooks on fly fishing, because we know and understand its vocabulary. These represent elements of knowledge that are useful to us because we know and understand them.

So it is with our students. They must come to know and understand if they are to be able to use their knowledge productively.

2. Two Ways of "Knowing"

When we were high school and college students, consequences were dire if anyone was caught with a crib sheet in a test. We were expected to know the required material outright. We were expected to have burned the content into the neural connections of our brains. We remember all the tricks we used to promote learning in this sense: Color-coded flash cards. Repetition—over and over. Cramming. All nighters. Playing recordings repeatedly while sleeping. If we didn't memorize it, we failed. There can be no question, some of that stuff stuck and that's a good thing. Regardless of how one gets there, knowing something outright can be a powerful way of knowing. But this is not the only way of knowing.

The reason is that, these days, we are every bit as much masters of content if one knows where to find it as if one is know it outright. In other words, the world does not operate solely on information retrieved from memory. This is a crucial twenty-first century learning perspective. To understand how crucial knowledge retrieval is, just try to fill out your income tax return, operate a new computer, or use an unfamiliar transit system without referring to the appropriate (hopefully well-written!) user's guide. When we confront such challenges in real adult life, we rely on what we know to help us find what we don't know.

In short, this "knowledge" category of achievement targets includes both those targets that students must learn outright to function within an academic discipline (core facts, principles, concepts, relationships within structures of knowledge, and accepted procedures) and other learning targets they can access as needed through their use of reference resources. Each presents its own unique classroom assessment challenges. And remember, each way of "knowing" must be accompanied by "understanding."

To help our students know and understand content, we ourselves must be masters of the disciplines we expect them to master. Thus, we must be prepared to share the topics, concepts, generalizations, and theories that hold facts together. We also must be ready to share with them our skills and methods of researching information. Further, as classroom teachers, part of our job is to devise assessment exercises that require students to demonstrate their understanding of those connections.

3. Many Ways of Coming to Know

These are at least five ways one can come to "know" something.

- If I don't know it already I can go look it up.
- If it is startling, important, or useful to me—that is, triggers an emotional reaction for some reason, I probably will remember it.
- Or, give me a list to memorize and in the end I will know it.
- Or, put me in a situation where I must use the same body of knowledge repeatedly, and habits of use eventually will entitle me not to have to look it up every time.
- Or, present me with a novel problem whose solution forces me to combine two pieces of knowledge previously mastered, and once I figure it out, that solution will probably become part of the knowledge to which I will return to the next time that problem or one like it comes up.

Think about the assessments Ms. W. had Emily involved in as she was learning to write. What were the foundations of knowledge that Emily needed to master to become a proficient writer? Vocabulary for word choice, alternative sentence structures, various ways to organize ideas, and so on. How did Ms. W. help Emily master these things? Did she give her definitions of the attributes of good writing and corresponding performance rating scales to memorize? We think not. She helped Em and her classmates figure out what it was they needed to know and then she provided lots of guided practice in applying that knowledge of good writing. Emily came to know and understand them.

Time for Reflection

Apply this set of ideas to the content domains relevant to your teaching context. Identify at least five knowledge achievement targets that you would expect students to learn outright at the grade level(s) and in the subject(s) you teach or plan to teach. Also identify at least three knowledge targets you expect them to know where to find if and when they need them.

Relationship to Other Targets

Content knowledge forms the foundation of all other forms of academic competence. This seems to run counter to current twenty-first century thinking about valued learning targets. We are supposed to be developing "higher-order thinking" capabilities to solve complex problems. We agree that this is very important. But understand that one cannot speak a foreign language unless we *know* the vocabulary—it's never sufficient, but is always essential. We cannot solve science problems unless we bring science *knowledge* to the table, or find algebra solutions without procedural *knowledge* in that domain. We can't read with comprehension something we don't already *know* something about. So it is with every academic subject. Without foundational knowledge, little else can be achieved.

The point is that we must exercise caution in our haste to embrace "higher-order thinking." Our enthusiasm in this case can cause us to deemphasize what we have traditionally called "lower-order thinking." But what have we traditionally defined as "lower order"? The mastery of content knowledge. So by deemphasizing content mastery, in effect, we deny our students access to the very content knowledge they need to solve the problems that we want them to solve. Does that make sense to you? We hope not! Without a foundation of relevant knowledge in any context, problem solutions will remain beyond reach. For this reason, you will find no further reference to higher- or lower-order thinking in this book. Rather, we will honor both the ability to retrieve useful knowledge and the ability to use it to reason and solve problems as important school outcomes. Think of them as a team.

Time for Reflection

Identify the academic discipline you regard as your greatest strength. How strong is your underlying knowledge of facts, concepts, and generalizations in this area? Think about your weakest area of academic performance. How strong is your knowledge and understanding base here? From this two-part analysis, what inference would you draw about how much a part of academic success is a strong, basic understanding of facts, concepts, and generalizations?

Reasoning Targets

Asking students to master content merely for the sake of knowing it and for no other reason is a waste of everyone's time—theirs and ours. Rather, we want students to learn to access their knowledge and understanding in order to use it to reason, to figure out how things interrelate, to solve certain kinds of problems. Every academic discipline defines itself, at least in part, in terms of certain consistent ways of reasoning. For example, we want them to

- *Analyze* story problems in math because those problems mimic life after school, *deduce* what math operations to apply, and practice using *problem solving algorithms* in order to become confident in this domain.
- *Compare and contrast* current or past political events or leaders because they need to be able to reason in this manner to be productive, active citizens; elections are entirely about this kind of reasoning.
- Draw *inductive and deductive inferences* in science to find solutions to classroom problems so they can use science to find solutions to everyday problems; every profession presents complex problems to solve.
- *Evaluate* opposing positions on political and scientific issues because life constantly requires this kind of *critical thinking.*

If we hold such twenty-first century learning targets as valuable for students, we must define precisely what they mean. It is incumbent on us to define *reasoning and problem-solving proficiency* in each relevant learning context. What does it mean to reason "analytically"? It means that we can take things apart to understand what's inside them and how the parts come together to form a whole. But what is the difference between doing this well and doing it poorly? That's the key question. What does it mean to reason "comparatively"? We do this when we think about similarities and differences. But why is that relevant? That is another key question. What does it mean to classify, synthesize, to reason inductively or deductively? What is evaluative reasoning or critical thinking, anyway? Not only must we be clear about the underlying structures of these patterns of reasoning, but we must help students understand and take possession of them, too. And, of course, we must be ready to translate important reasoning patterns into high-quality classroom assessment exercises and scoring procedures.

If we are to help our students learn to use their knowledge productively to reason and solve problems, we must understand that any form of reasoning can be done either well or poorly. Our assessment challenge lies in knowing the difference. Our success in helping students learn to monitor the quality of their own reasoning—a critical part of lifelong learning—hinges on helping them learn the differences between strong and weak performance. Remember, our mission is to bring our students to a place where they no longer need us to tell them if they have reasoned well—to a place where they can confidently judge the quality of their own reasoning.

To accomplish this, as with the other kinds of learning targets, we who presume to help students master effective reasoning must first ourselves become confident, competent masters of these patterns. In other words, we must strive to meet standards of intellectual understanding and rigor in our own reasoning if we are to make this vision come alive in our students' minds. This requires analysis of a few key points. Let's consider these next.

All Reasoning Arises from a Foundation of Knowledge

It is important that we understand that there is no such thing as "content-free" thinking. An auto mechanic can diagnose the reason for a car problem in large part because he knows and understands the systems that make a car run. An attorney can help with legal problems because she knows or can look up relevant law and judicial precedent. CPAs prepare taxes correctly because they know proper procedures. A physician can help someone get well because she knows the human body and understands medical remedies. If the knowledge isn't there, there will be no problem solving.

Students Are Natural "Thinkers"

With a few notable exceptions, our students arrive at school from day one with natural cognitive capabilities either in place or developing. You don't have to teach them to "think." Rather, you must help them learn to focus and organize their thinking into reasoning. The vast majority of students possess those cognitive abilities they need to survive and even prosper in school and beyond. Hidden within them is the capacity to interact purposefully with their world, confronting problems, reflecting on solutions, solving problems, and deriving or constructing personal meaning from experience.

But there's a problem. According to scholars of the topic, the unschooled human mind is a mixed bag of good and bad thinking, of sharp focus and fuzzy thinking, of ignorance and sound knowledge, of accurate conceptions and misconceptions, of misunderstanding and important insight, of open-mindedness and prejudice (see for example Paul, 1995). Our challenge as teachers is to help students learn to clean out and organize their mental houses as needed, to clear out the waste and let sound reasoning prevail. But how should we do this?

There Are Consistent Patterns of Reasoning

The answer lies in understanding how the ways we tend to organize our thinking come together to solve problems. Let's start by exploring a few of the commonly referenced forms of reasoning. Then we'll explore their dynamic interrelationships.

In the real world, we frequently find ourselves needing to figure out relationships among things by reasoning analytically, comparatively, or in an evaluative manner. Real-life thinkers need to be able to synthesize, classify, and reason inductively or deductively. But what do these mean? As you will see each has its own definition. Each can be illustrated in understandable terms within the context of any academic discipline. Nevertheless, realize that in real-world problem solving, sometimes we use these reasoning patterns independently and other times in combination. For now, as you read about each pattern, take a few seconds to see if you can identify ways they fit together. We'll discuss the interconnections among patterns later.

To ensure you see your own learning path ahead, we intend to argue that both you and your students must understand these or similar patterns if they are to learn to use them productively to reason and solve problems. We need to be ready to teach and assess student mastery of each. But more important, *we must prepare our students to be lifelong assessors of the quality of their own reasoning.*

Analytical Reasoning. Consider, for example, the performance arena of writing and the assessment of writing proficiency. Here we draw the distinction between "holistic" and "analytical" evaluation (i.e., scoring) of student writing. In *holistic* scoring we consider all aspects of the written piece at once and base our judgment of quality on this overall impression, assigning one overall score. In *analytical* scoring, we break performance down into its component parts (word choice, organization, voice, and the like), evaluating and rating each part. It is this meaning of *analytical* that we are addressing here.

When we reason analytically, we draw inferences about the component parts of something: its ingredients, how they fit together, and how they function as a whole. When good reporters do "news analysis" they go into a story in greater depth to study its parts. When we try to figure out how a machine works (to go inside and see how the pieces fit and work together) we are reasoning analytically. When we think about what typically goes into making something good, such as food, a movie, or a teacher, we are involved in analytical reasoning. Figure 3.5 presents a graphic representation of this pattern of reasoning, analyzing key classroom assessment concepts, in the form of an expanding concept map.

It may be helpful for you to "see" an illustration of this kind of reasoning as it plays out in your own mind's eye. We are about to ask you a focused question. When we do, you need to stop reading this text and think about your answer before reading the second paragraph. As you generate that answer in your mind, try to notice what you are doing mentally. Ready? Here goes: How do the parts of an automobile engine work to move the car forward? Think about this for a minute. Then read on.

First, if you lacked any knowledge of automobile engines, you were dead in the water from the start. You have no answer. That was the point we made earlier about knowledge as the foundation of reasoning—there is no such thing as content-free reasoning.

If you know engines, you automatically began to create a mental picture of an engine including drive shaft, crank shaft, pistons, spark plugs, etc. Notice that you were not merely regurgitating a previously memorized list of engine parts or their relationship. Rather, you were dipping into your foundations of knowledge and thinking about how things come together to make the whole—how the parts relate and function. That is the analytical reasoning process in action.

In the case of analytical reasoning, our instructional challenges are to be sure that students have the opportunity to master whatever knowledge and understanding they need to be able analyze the things we want them to understand, and that they receive guided practice in exercising their analytical (component part) thought processes. We must help them understand that, if they wish to conduct a proper

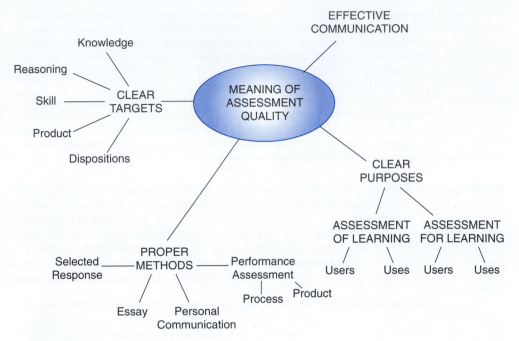

FIGURE 3.5
Illustration of Analytical Reasoning

analysis and don't possess the required knowledge, they must go and get it from a dependable source.

At assessment time, we ask them to tap into their own knowledge base and apply their practiced reasoning skills to a *novel* analytical task. For example, in literature, we might provide practice in character analysis by having students read a story (gathering knowledge of those particular characters) and asking them to practice analyzing some character they have just "met." Then, at assessment time, we present a new story and character(s), asking them to demonstrate their ability to analyze in this context.

As a teacher, you want your students to know exactly what is called for whenever you ask them to "analyze" something. You might even put a chart on the wall detailing the process and highlighting examples of analytical inferences. These might include character analyses from literature, storyline or plot analyses, breakdown diagrams of machines, or depictions of the subparts of a scientific process such as the water cycle. We want students to recognize when analysis is needed and to understand how to apply that pattern of reasoning in novel problem situations.

Figure 3.6 provides a portrait of the continuum of quality (we will call such scales *rubrics*) along which one's analytical reason might vary, from strong to weak.

Synthesizing. Let's say you have just finished helping students analyze the structure of two short stories. Then, you have them pool or synthesize these into a set

Definition: *Analysis* is the examination of the components or structure of something to determine how the parts relate to each other or how they come together to form a whole.

Strong	Developing	Weak
The response reveals a thorough and accurate understanding of the component parts and how they come together to form a whole, identifies the important information in a problem statement, or has a clear sense of the order of steps in a process, if that is the nature of the target, and why that order is important. This is indicated by	The student understands some component parts but gaps or inaccuracies are apparent. Thus, the student has a general sense of key parts of a whole, the important information in a problem statement, or steps in a process but lacks key insights as to the contribution of each. This is indicated by	The student has a superficial or inaccurate understanding of the component parts, has little sense of how parts work together to form a whole, incorrectly identifies the information needed to solve a problem, or has an inaccurate sense of steps in a process and why the order is important. This is indicated by
• Specific and appropriate references to elements, components, or steps	• Accurate identification and discussion of only part of the relevant elements, components, or steps	• The object, issue, or event treated as a vague whole, there are few references to elements, components, or steps
• Correct and relevant description of most elements, components, or steps	• Accurate description of only some elements, components, or steps	• Inaccurate or irrelevant description of most elements, components, or steps
• Correct relationships among or interconnectedness of parts or steps	• Some of the relationships of parts is appropriate, some not	• Incorrect use of most vocabulary
• Correct use of vocabulary	• Some incorrect use of vocabulary	

FIGURE 3.6
Rubric for Analysis

of generalizations about the typical structure of a short story. Thus, two different sources of knowledge and understanding about short stories are integrated. This is *synthesizing.* You then ask them to draw the following inference: How does the story you just read align with what you know about the typical structure that you just developed? Figure 3.7 presents a description of the flow of ideas leading to a synthesis, and Figure 3.8 describes the quality continuum.

We find a great deal of interest being expressed these days in the development of "integrated" or "thematic" instruction or curricula. This often is described as being different from discipline-based instruction, in which students study separately math, science, writing skills, and so on. Thematic instruction encourages students to bring knowledge and productive patterns of reasoning together from several disciplines, as they explore their particular theme, whether it be the study of a particular culture, scientific problem, or social issue. Such curricula place a premium on synthesizing insights from divergent sources and present wonderfully rich opportunities to develop and assess student mastery of this pattern of reasoning.

Comparative Reasoning. *Comparative reasoning* refers to the process of figuring out or inferring how things are either alike or different—a specialized kind of synthesis. Sometimes we compare in terms of similarities, other times we contrast in terms of differences, still other times we do both. To understand this kind of reasoning, we must

Questions that help students *synthesize*:
1. What is the problem to be solved by combining ideas?
2. Why is synthesis relevant in this context?
3. What are the various understandings that can be combined to help?
4. How do those parts fit together to help us find a solution?

Key concepts:
- Convergence
- Generalization
- Whole is more than the sum of its parts

Example:
Understanding 1: My personal experience has shown me that students who are involved in the ongoing assessment of their own achievement are much more highly motivated to learn than are those who are not involved.

Understanding 2: The professional literature in both reading and writing instruction tells us that students must learn to monitor their own comprehension and the quality of their own writing to become independently literate adults.

Understanding 3: Research from around the world provides irrefutable evidence that students who are deeply involved in high-quality classroom assessment environments learn more.

Synthesis: It would be a very good idea for me, the teacher, to involve my students in assessment, record keeping, and communication to increase motivation.

FIGURE 3.7
Illustration of Synthesis as a Pattern of Reasoning

Definition: *Synthesis* is the process of combining relevant discrete elements or ingredients to create something new. It involves identifying the relevant ingredients to combine and then combining them to create a pleasing or complete new inference, generalization, or insight.

Strong	Developing	Weak
The student tapped the most relevant, accurate information or elements to bring together into the synthesis.	Some of the ideas brought to the synthesis are relevant and accurate, but inaccuracies or irrelevancies cloud the synthesis.	Directly relevant ideas or information are overlooked or misrepresented.
The resulting synthesis of ideas yields an inference or generalization that is clearly defensible.	The inference or generalization resulting from the blending of ideas is defensible but is not particularly insightful or original.	The synthesis drawn from the blending of the background is naïve or indefensible.
Ideas or elements are organized in a new way as the student makes new connections and demonstrates original thinking.	The student's way of describing the background and blending into new thinking works sometimes but is confusing, interrupts the flow, or impedes the blending of ideas.	There is no evidence of original thought or new connections.
The student's way of describing the synthesis brings out the main points and enhances the blend of ideas into the new insight.		The student's representation of the thinking is confusing, hides rather than reveals main points, interrupts the flow, or impedes the blending of ideas.

FIGURE 3.8
Rubric for Synthesis

FIGURE 3.9
Understanding Comparative Reasoning

Questions that help students *compare and contrast:*

1. What is to be compared?
2. Why is it relevant to draw the comparison?
3. Upon what basis will we compare them?
4. How are they alike?
5. How are they different?
6. What important lessons can we learn from this *comparison?*

Key concepts:

- Similar
- Different

Example:
Compare classroom and standardized assessment

Criterion	Classroom Assessment	Standardized Test
Focus	Narrow Targets	Broad Targets
Developer	Teacher	Test Publisher
Frequency	Continuous	Once a year
Users	Teacher	Principal
	Student	Curriculum Director
	Parent	Superintendent
		School Board
		Legislator

see that those who are proficient begin with a clear understanding of the things they are to compare. They then identify the dimensions of each that they will examine for similarities or differences. And finally, they detail the comparison, highlighting why those particular points are important. Here are simple examples: In what way are these two poems alike and different? Given this early and this late work by this particular author, how are they different in style? How are these insects alike and different? Figure 3.9 illustrates the structure and Figure 3.10 provides a simple rubric or performance continuum.

Classifying. Sometimes, life presents us with reasoning challenges that ask us to categorize, or *classify,* things. When we budget, we classify expenses. When we budget how we use our time, we organize events into different categories. In science, we classify plants and animals. In politics, we categorize issues and candidates. To reason productively in this manner, we must first know the defining characteristics of each category and the attributes of each thing to be classified. Then we classify. Figure 3.11 depicts a quality continuum.

Definition: *Comparison* involves describing the similarities or differences between or among items. In its more complex form, items are compared or contrasted based on several salient features, while simple comparisons differentiate on a single criterion.

Strong	Developing	Weak
The student understands and has articulated why a comparison would be relevant or useful.	The reason for the relevance comparison can be inferred but is not explicitly stated.	The student has not established the relevance of the comparison.
The things to be compared are clearly defined.	The things to be compared are clear.	It is not clear what is being compared.
The criteria to be used in comparing are appropriate and clearly define the specific features to guide thinking about similarity or difference.	The criteria to be applied are appropriate but some key features are overlooked or vaguely articulated.	Criteria are not specified, inappropriate or unclear criteria are used, or some key criteria are missing.
The similarities or differences articulated in the comparison are correct or defended with sound rationale.	Similarities or differences are mostly correct and defensible but some are not drawn as clearly as they could be.	The similarities or differences articulated are incorrect or vaguely drawn; or important ingredients are missing from the comparison.
If or when relevant, appropriate generalizations are drawn with rationale at the conclusion of the comparison.	Sound generalizations are drawn from the comparison but some possible inferences are overlooked or not as strong as they might be.	If drawn, generalizations about the comparison are incorrect, inappropriate, or confusing.

FIGURE 3.10
Rubric for Comparison

Definition: *Classification* is the process of sorting items into categories based on specified characteristics.

Strong	Developing	Weak
The items to be classified are clear.	When sorting items into predetermined categories, the student is correct sometimes and incorrect sometimes.	The student is mostly inaccurate when sorting items into predetermined categories.
The characteristics of the categories into which they are to be sorted are clear.	When explaining why items were sorted as they were, the student sometimes is correct and sometimes incorrect on reasons, or sometimes cites unimportant distinctions.	The student frequently is incorrect when providing the reasons for sorting.
The student accurately sorts items into predetermined categories.		
The student can explain the most important features that resulted in the classification made.		

FIGURE 3.11
Rubric for Classification

Inductive and Deductive Inference. In the case of *inductive* reasoning, we reason productively when we can infer principles, draw conclusions, or glean generalizations from accumulated evidence. Induction results from synthesis. Reasoning travels from particular facts to a general rule or principle. Here are two examples:

- Now that you have read this story, what do you think is its general theme or message?
- Given the evidence provided in this article about the stock market [note that this is an example of using knowledge gained through reference], what is the relationship between interest rates and stock values?

We help students gain control over their inductive reasoning proficiency when we make sure they have the opportunity to access the proper knowledge from which important rules or principles arise and when we provide guided practice in drawing inferences, conclusions, or generalizations.

We also reason when we apply a general rule or principle to find the solution to a problem. This is *deductive* reasoning. Here, reasoning travels from the general to the specific:

- Given your theory about criminal behavior, who did the killing?
- Given what you know about the role of a tragic hero in classic literature, if this character is a tragic hero, what do you think will happen next in the story?
- If the chemical test yields this result, what element is it?

Obviously, the key instructional challenge is to be sure students have the opportunity to learn and understand the rules, generalizations, or principles we want them to apply. Then and only then can we assess their reasoning proficiency by presenting them with novel contexts within which to apply those rules. Figure 3.12 introduces a rubric for this pattern.

Evaluative Reasoning. We reason in an evaluative manner when we apply certain criteria to judge the value or appropriateness of something. The quality of the reasoning depends on our ability to logically or dependably apply proper judgmental criteria. Synonyms for this pattern of reasoning include *critical thinking* and *judgmental reasoning.*

Definition: An *inductive or deductive inference* is a conclusion from evidence and reasoning.

Strong	Developing	Weak
The conclusion is based on sufficient high-quality, relevant evidence.	The conclusion drawn is based on evidence only part of which is defensible.	The conclusion is either a wild guess based on no evidence or based on unverified, questionable, or irrelevant evidence.
The student explains convincingly why the evidence is relevant and should be accepted.	The student provides justification for the inference only part of which is convincing or correct.	The student provides little justification for the inference or is unable to connect it to relevant evidence.
The student describes any relevant limitations of the inference or evidence cited in its defense.	The student notes limitations in the inference or evidence but important limitations are overlooked.	The student does not acknowledge important limitations or is incorrect about those limitations.

FIGURE 3.12
Rubrics for Inductive/Deductive Inference

Within the context of our journey together, the very process of evaluating the quality of student work in terms of some predetermined achievement standards, such as writing assessment, is a classic example of evaluative reasoning. When we express and defend a point of view or opinion, we reason in an evaluative manner. When we judge the quality of an assessment using our five keys to quality (see Figure 3.1), we reason in an evaluative manner.

Our instructional task is to help students understand the criteria they should be applying when they defend their point of view on an issue. Who is the best candidate for mayor? That's a matter of opinion. What are the important characteristics of a good mayor? As we discuss these criteria in class, we must address how to apply these standards logically.

Our assessment challenge is to determine if students are able to apply those criteria appropriately, given a novel evaluative challenge. Students who are able to appropriately evaluate a piece of writing they have never seen before using a learned set of analytical rating scales are demonstrating proficiency in evaluative reasoning. It is in this sense that we say this entire book is about developing critical thinkers. See Figure 3.13 for a for a quality rubric.

Why These Patterns?

Three reasons. First, a careful analysis of the various frameworks of reasoning processes found in the professional literature tends to bring consistent attention to these. Further, that literature holds that these patterns generalize across academic disciplines. Obviously, the content being brought to bear differs across subjects, but these patterns tend to be universally applicable.

Definition: *Evaluation* is expressing and defending an opinion, point of view, judgment, or decision. It can be thought of as having three facets: an assertion, criteria the assertion is based on, and evidence that supports the assertion.

Strong	Developing	Weak
The student states her or his position or judgment clearly and explains it in understandable terms; key issues are identified and explained.	The student's position or judgment can be inferred from what is said, but it is not explicitly stated.	The student's position or judgment is vaguely stated or the student changes positions upon being questioned.
The student defends his or her judgment clearly by applying clear and appropriate criteria with supporting evidence in a logical manner.	The criteria used to support the judgment are mostly appropriate but some are marginally relevant or correct.	The student offers no justification in defense of her or is positions, the criteria applied are inappropriate, or the evidence cited is weak.
The student acknowledges other positions or judgments and addresses them by identifying and evaluating assumptions, citing limitations of evidence, or pointing out faulty reasoning.	Key issues are summarized but with some errors or confusion.

Alternative judgments, criteria, or evidence is suggested but not thoroughly or clearly explained. | Other positions or judgments are not addressed or, if it is, points made are irrelevant or inaccurate. |

FIGURE 3.13
Rubric for Evaluation

Second, they include what we normally think of as reasoning processes in the real world. These patterns are simple, understandable, and practical—they describe what happens in the adult world beyond school.

Third, they describe and illustrate in terms that students (your students!) can easily understand and master. The fact that we can diagram or illustrate each pattern and easily find examples makes them approachable by our students. That's a good thing.

About the Bloom Taxonomy

Finally, we want to distinguish between reasoning generally conceptualized in current professional literature and another conceptualization about which you may tend to hear a great deal: the Bloom Taxonomy (Bloom, Englehard, Furst, Hill, & Krathwohl, 1956). Because this has been the dominant conceptualization of reasoning proficiency for decades, it is important that you become aware of it. That original framework includes the following patterns: knowledge, comprehension, application, analysis, synthesis, and evaluation. As you can see, they are somewhat consistent with those described previously. But there are important differences.

First, Bloom defined these as representing ascending levels of cognitive complexity from knowledge through evaluation with each carrying greater mental challenge. In fact, however, each pattern described can vary profoundly in cognitive demand from simple to very challenging. Thus, it is possible to conceive of an advanced analytical problem that far outreaches a simple evaluation in cognitive demand. So the idea of differential cognitive complexity doesn't hold up.

Second, Bloom separates knowledge and comprehension. This differentiation is impractical. Knowledge without comprehension cannot feed productively into reasoning in any academic context.

Third, Bloom includes *application* as a unique level of reasoning. Every reasoning context requires that the user apply their knowledge to that cognitive challenge and apply the appropriate reasoning proficiencies to arrive at a defensible solution. Thus, there is no reasoning that is not an application.

But that having been said, after studying and reflecting on the reasoning targets that you are assigned in your local curriculum or that you want your students to master, if you find other classifications or definitions, including Bloom's, work better for you, use them. Just be clear enough about your vision of excellence in reasoning that your definitions are practical, based on the best current understanding, and student friendly. Table 3.1 presents sample reasoning targets for Language Arts and Science.

Links among Patterns

As we wrote about these patterns of reasoning and their classroom applications, we tried to use consistent vocabulary so you could begin to see key connections. We hope that your study of and reflection on the six patterns or organizing structures permitted you to notice the important connections among them on your own. We list some here to establish the dynamic nature of reasoning. You may see more.

- All reasoning arises from a foundation of knowledge.
- Reasoning is seeing relationships among things.
- Synthesis requires inductive inference; that is, we do it well when we can infer or see a new insight arising from divergent parts.
- Complex comparisons involve a prior step of analyzing the things to be compared to identify points of potential similarity and difference.

TABLE 3.1
Reasoning Learning Targets in Language Arts and Science

Pattern of Reasoning	Language Arts	Science
Analysis	Describe the process you used in writing your term paper.	Conduct an investigation to determine the active ingredient in an herbal medicine.
Synthesis	Write a fictional narrative.	Write a lab report.
Comparison	Identify similarities and differences between an Egyptian version of *Cinderella* and a Chinese version.	Make a chart showing ways in which the natural environment and the constructed environment differ.
Classification	Given a selection of words, sort them into categories representing parts of speech.	Sort and order objects by hardness.
Inductive and Deductive Inference	Inference: What does this story suggest about _____? Inductive inference: Now that you have read this story, what do you think is its general theme or message? Deductive inference: Given what you know about the role of a tragic hero in classic literature, if this character is a tragic hero, what do you think will happen next?	Inference:Draw a conclusion based on inquiry. Inductive inference: Plot the locations of volcanoes and earthquakes to make a generalization about plate motions. Deductive inference: Use characteristic properties of liquids to distinguish one substance from another.
Evaluation	Evaluate accuracy of information from a variety of sources.	Evaluate conclusions drawn from an experiment for legitimacy.

Source: From *Classroom Assessment for Student Learning: Doing It Right—Using It Well* (p. 70), by R. J. Stiggins, J. A. Arter, J. Chappuis, and S. Chappuis, 2004, Portland, OR: Pearson Assessment Training Institute. Copyright 2006, 2004 by Pearson Education. Reprinted by permission.

- Classification involves comparison of each item to be classified to the attributes of each category to infer which goes where.
- Inductive inference requires that we compare the pieces of evidence at hand to see what they have in common.
- Evaluation often requires analysis and comparison of different points of view before coming to a defensible judgment.
- Evaluative judgments about the quality of any reasoning can be made only if we have standards for what it means to do it well.

So it is that different ways of reasoning form a puzzle whose pieces can fit together in various ways to permit you and your students to figure things out. It is appropriate to help students see and understand the different organizing structures.

Reason in School Subjects and Beyond

Students who encounter a new math problem, debate a volatile social issue, or confront an unknown substance in a science lab bring these ways of reasoning into play. Depending on the context, they will use them in a rapid-fire manner, analyzing the problem to infer what knowledge bases they must bring to bear. When confronted with a math problem, learners must analyze it to discover its component parts, infer what math operations are needed to arrive at a solution, and understand the steps to carry out to solve it properly. The keys to success are knowledge teamed with productive reasoning. Your job is to take them to a place where they don't need you any longer to tell them if they have done well. Build lifelong learners.

In writing, one must bring to bear a sufficiently well-developed vocabulary and syntactic awareness to communicate ideas, infer what words, sentences, and organization of ideas will best bring those ideas to the page, evaluate the effectiveness of the writing as it unfolds, and fix it when it isn't working. Create independent writers.

To read with comprehension in order to learn something new, readers must possess sufficient prior knowledge of the author's topic to be able to draw it off the written page and understand it, be able to compare their own current structure of knowledge to the author's message, and to evaluate where and how their prior understanding needs to be changed. Any student who leaves school unable to do this cannot become an independently functioning lifelong learner.

So it is with each school subject: our students need the opportunity to master important knowledge within that subject and to practice applying whatever patterns of reasoning comprise the routines of that academic discipline, whether literature, science, social studies, music, and so on. Key parts of your teaching challenge are to be ready to assess student reasoning proficiencies and to help students learn to assess their own.

Beyond school, when students are confronted with a drug pusher, must make career choices, or need to deal with the demands of peer pressure, they must think clearly and select a proper course of action. Those who are masters of their own reasoning and who know how to use their minds effectively have a strong chance of generating productive responses to such circumstances.

Time for Reflection

Identify at least five reasoning or problem-solving achievement targets that might be relevant for students to master at the grade levels and in the subjects you teach or plan to teach.

Relationship to Other Targets

As previously mentioned, we can use our reasoning powers to generate new knowledge and understanding. When one combines two ideas that one understood previously to derive new insight, that insight can remain with us for future use. Further, our reasoning powers will come into play as we strive for skillful performance or product development—the next two kinds of targets. You'll see how as you read on.

Performance Skills Targets

In most classrooms, there are things teachers want their students to *be able to do,* instances for which the measure of attainment is students' ability to demonstrate certain observable behaviors—to perform well, if you will. For example, at the primary-grade level, a teacher might look for certain fundamental social interaction behaviors or oral reading fluency skills. At the elementary level, a teacher might observe student performance in cooperative group activities. In middle school or junior high, manipulation of a science lab apparatus might be important. And at the high school level, public speaking or the ability to converse in a second language might be a valued outcome.

In all of these cases, success lies in "actually *doing* it well." One assessment challenge lies in being able to define in clear terms, using words, examples, or both, what it *means* to do it well—to read or speak fluently, work productively as a team member, or carry out the steps in a lab experiment. A second, equally important, assessment challenge is to map the continuum of performance learners will travel from the beginning to the end of their journey. This will allow students to know where they are on that continuum at any point in time in relation to where they were and where they ultimately want to be.

Then, obviously, to assess effectively on an ongoing basis, we must provide opportunities for students to show their skills, so we can observe and evaluate while they are performing.

Time for Reflection

Identify at least three achievement targets that take the form of performance skills that might be relevant for students to master at the grade levels and in the subjects you teach or plan to teach.

Relationship to Other Targets

To perform skillfully, one must possess the fundamental procedural knowledge and reasoning proficiency needed to figure out what skills are required. Further, skillful performance must combine with this knowledge and reasoning proficiency to create quality products (discussed in the next section). In this way, performance skills represent an end in and of themselves as well as a building block for other competencies. For example, one cannot produce a quality piece of writing (a product) unless one has handwriting or computer keyboarding proficiency (performance skills) *and* the ability to think about the topic in ways that permit us to write fluently and coherently. We cannot deliver an effective spontaneous speech (a skill) unless we know something about the subject and can figure out what needs to be said about that topic at this moment. It is critical that we understand that, in this category, the student's performance objective is to integrate knowledge and reasoning proficiencies and to be skillful. This is precisely why achievement-related skills often represent complex targets requiring sophisticated assessments. Success in creating products—the next kind of target—virtually always hinges on the ability to perform some kinds of skills. Performance skills underpin product development.

Product Development Targets

Yet another way for students to succeed academically in some contexts is by developing the capacity to create products that meet certain standards of quality. These represent tangible entities created by the performer, and that present evidence in their quality that the student has mastered basic knowledge and requisite reasoning and problem-solving proficiencies needed to create a quality product.

For example, a high school social studies teacher might have students prepare a term paper to gather evidence of proficiency applied in that particular context. A technology teacher might ask students to repair a computer to judge job-related preparedness. An elementary or primary-grade teacher might collect samples of student art or craft work and judge their evolving quality as students learn.

In all cases, student success lies in creating products that possess certain key attributes when completed. The learning target and thus the focus of instruction is the attributes of quality products. The assessment challenge is to be able to define clearly and understandably, in writing and/or through example, what those attributes are. We must be able to specify exactly how high- and low-quality products differ and we must be prepared to express those differences in student-friendly language.

Time for Reflection

Identify at least two product development achievement targets that might be relevant for students to master at the grade levels and in the subjects you teach or plan to teach.

Relationship to Other Targets

Note once again that successful product creation arises from student mastery of prerequisite knowledge and through the application of appropriate reasoning and skill strategies. In addition, students will probably need to perform certain predefined steps to create the desired product. Prerequisite achievement thus underpins the creation of quality products, but evidence of ultimate success resides in the product itself. Does it meet standards of product quality?

Disposition Targets—the Affective Domain

This final category of aspirations that we have for our students includes those characteristics that go beyond academic achievement into the realms of affective and personal feeling states, such as attitudes, sense of academic self-confidence, or interest in something that motivationally predisposes a person to act or not act.

Many teachers set as goals, for example, that students will develop positive academic self-concepts or positive attitudes toward school subjects predisposing them to strive for excellence. Without question, we want our students to develop strong interests, as well as a strong sense of internal control over their own academic well-being. We can define each disposition in terms of these essential elements: It has a focus: we have attitudes about things, interests in things, or are motivated to do certain things. Further, those dispositions always vary along a continuum from strong to weak feelings.

Examples of things about which we might have attitudes (feelings) include ourselves as learners, school in general, specific subjects, classmates, and teachers. Those feelings about things can be positive, neutral, or negative. For instance, our academic self-concepts are positive or negative. We might hold positive or negative attitudes about math or English. Sometimes those feelings are very strong, other times very weak—we range from passionate to disinterested. In school, we seek to impart strong positive dispositions toward learning new things, among other attitudes.

Relationship to Other Targets

Teachers can take advantage of a potentially very powerful relationship between achievement and student dispositions. In fact, the concept of assessment FOR learning is build around tapping this relationship. It takes the form of an interactive loop. Let us illustrate with the case of the struggling learner. Let's say a student has experienced considerable failure over time and has begun to believe that success is beyond reach in school. To the extent that a teacher can (1) assess well and find out where that student is now on a relevant achievement progression, (2) thus identify what comes next in the learning for this struggling learner, (3) plan an instructional intervention that works, and thus (4) help this student self assess and watch him or herself succeeding in some important way (that is, making it to the next target), that student might become just slightly more confident about learning (a key disposition). To the extent that the teacher can then repeat that experience and get that student on a winning streak and experiencing successes, that student's sense of academic self-efficacy (control over ones own well being in school—a disposition) might begin to turn around. This might empower this student to be willing to take the risk of continuing to strive for even more success. Note the key sequence here: success triggers confidence which leads to motivation to try which leads to productive action which leads to success, and so on. A productive achievement/disposition loop.

Because these affective and social dimensions are quite complex, thoughtful assessment is essential. We define success in assessing them exactly as we do success in assessing achievement: Sound assessment requires a crystal-clear vision or understanding of the characteristic(s) to be assessed. Only then can we select a proper assessment method, devise a sampling procedure, and control sources of bias and distortion so as to accurately assess direction and intensity of feelings about specified objects. We will address this matter in great depth in Chapter 9, Assessing Dispositions.

Time for Reflection

Identify at least three dispositional targets that might be relevant for students to master at the grade levels and in the subjects you teach or plan to teach.

Summary of Targets

We have discussed four different but interrelated visions of achievement plus the affective component of student learning. Knowledge and understanding are important. Reasoning and problem solving require applying that knowledge. Knowledge and reasoning are required for successful skill performance and/or product development. And dispositions very often result from success or lack of success in academic performance. But once again, remember that these can all grow and change in dynamic, interrelated ways within students. Figure 3.14 summarizes the kinds of targets we have discussed, and Table 3.2 presents sample achievement targets from various academic disciplines. Read down each column.

Time for Reflection

Let's say we wanted to extend Table 3.2 to include more columns. Identify examples of knowledge, reasoning, skill, product, and dispositional targets that would be relevant for Foreign Language (spoken and written, separately), Social Studies, Physical Education, and Visual Arts. Or, pick another subject important to you.

FIGURE 3.14
An Overview of Kinds of Achievement

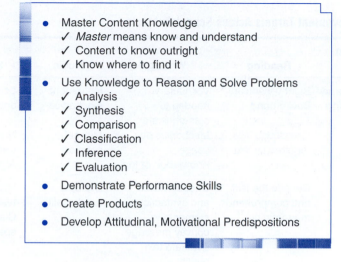

- Master Content Knowledge
  - ✓ *Master* means know and understand
  - ✓ Content to know outright
  - ✓ Know where to find it
- Use Knowledge to Reason and Solve Problems
  - ✓ Analysis
  - ✓ Synthesis
  - ✓ Comparison
  - ✓ Classification
  - ✓ Inference
  - ✓ Evaluation
- Demonstrate Performance Skills
- Create Products
- Develop Attitudinal, Motivational Predispositions

THE CRITICAL CONNECTION: STANDARDS TO CLASSROOM LEARNING TARGETS

As noted earlier, our emergence into the era of standards-driven schools has spurred a great deal of high-powered reexamination of important achievement expectations. This is a boon to teachers because in virtually every field, we have at our disposal today definitions of academic competence that hold the promise of allowing us to produce better achievers faster than ever before. This applies to reading, writing, science, math, reasoning and problem solving, foreign languages, and many other subjects. Virtually every state and lots of local districts have standards of academic excellence, typically developed by teams of experienced teachers. Success in reaching these standards turns, at least in part, on two actions we teachers can take on behalf of student learning: scaffolding each standard, or mapping how students will climb to success; and transforming the resulting classroom learning targets into student-friendly versions.

Scaffolding Standards

On investigation, you will find that standards developed in these contexts typically are articulated in the form of relative broad or global learning outcomes. Examples appeared earlier in Figure 3.3, one in history and the other in writing. A critically important step in laying the foundation for quality classroom assessments is the transformation of state or district standards into the classroom-level achievement targets that students can acquire over time as they climb the scaffolding to a place where they are ready to demonstrate the required proficiency. To accomplish this, we must ask the following questions about each standard:

- What do students need to come to *know and understand* in order to be ready to demonstrate that they can meet this standard when the time comes to do so?

TABLE 3.2
Sample Achievement Targets Across School Subjects

Achievement Target	Reading	Writing	Music	Science	Math
Knowledge and Understanding	Sight vocabulary Background Knowledge required by text	Vocabulary needed to communicate Mechanics of usage Knowledge of topic	Instrument mechanics Musical notation	Science facts and concepts Numeration systems Algorithms	Number meaning Math facts
Reasoning	Decode the text and comprehend the meaning	Choose words and syntactic elements to convey message Evaluate text quality	Evaluate tonal quality	Hypotheses testing Classifying species	Formulate math problem from situation
Performance Skills	Oral reading fluency	Letter formation Keyboarding skills	Instrument fingering Breath control	Manipulate lab apparatus correctly	Use manipulatives while solving problem
Products	Diagram revealing comprehension	Samples of original text	Original composition written in musical	Written lab report Science fair model notation	Well-reasoned problem solution
Dispositions	"I like to read."	"I can write well."	"Music is important to me."	"Science is worth understanding."	"Math is useful in real life."

- What patterns of *reasoning*, if any, must they gain mastery of on their journey to this standard?
- What *performance skills*, if any, are called for as building blocks beneath this standard?
- What *products* must students become proficient at creating, if any, according to this standard?

The answers map the route to student success. We believe this scaffolding of our valued standards into the foundations of student success is best done at the school or district level to gain consistency in the faculty's vision of how to get students to competence. If that has not happened, then it becomes your responsibility to do it for your classroom.

Be advised, as mentioned previously, that all academic competence (and therefore each standard) rests on a foundation of knowledge. As the faculty, you and your colleagues must divide up responsibility for providing students with the opportunity to master it. Further, many standards expect mastery of specific reasoning proficiencies, while others also imply performance skill and product development capabilities. These must be identified and your collective curriculum and instruction, as well as your assessment system, must be built around them.

As a teacher, you may or may not practice in a district that has engaged in this kind of integrated planning. You may or may not practice in a school in which staff collaborate in articulating achievement targets across grade levels or subjects. In short, you may or may not receive the kind of school and community support needed to do a thorough job of generating a continuous progress portrait of student success.

Nevertheless, each of us has a responsibility to our particular students to be clear, specific, and correct about our achievement expectations. The point is, regardless of what is going on around you, tomorrow or as soon as you enter a classroom, a bunch of students will show up wanting and needing to master content knowledge, learn to solve problems, master important performance skills, learn to create important products, and/or develop certain dispositions. They count on you to know what these things mean and to know how to teach and assess them. When it comes to being clear about what it means to be successful in your classroom, the responsibility stops with you! Embrace this responsibility.

Student-Friendly Targets

You will recall that the Milwaukee, Wisconsin, team took the step of transforming their state standards into student- and community-friendly versions (see Figure 3.4), to be ready to show students from the very beginning of their work where the learning will take them. This team believes that students can hit any target they can see and that holds still for them.

This transformation to a student-friendly version is quite straightforward:

1. Identify the learning target: Let's say we want students to understand what it means to *summarize.*
2. Define the key term(s) in the simplest language: Start with the dictionary definition: "to give a brief statement of the main points, events, or ideas."
3. Rewrite that definition as an "I can" statement that the intended learner can understand: "I can summarize text. This means I can make a short statement of the main ideas."
4. Try it out on some students and adjust as needed to ensure understanding.

This can be a very productive way to introduce reasoning targets. For example:

1. *compare*
2. to cite similarities and differences
3. "I can compare things. This means I can tell how they are alike or different."

Or

1. *infer*
2. to draw conclusions from evidence
3. "I can make good inferences. This means I can use the information I have to make a good guess about something."

In fact, your students can be excellent partners, working with you to create student-friendly versions of the targets you and they care about.

Summary: Clear Targets Are Essential for Sound Assessment

In this part of our journey into the realm of classroom assessment, we have argued that the quality of any assessment rests on the clarity of the assessor's understanding of the achievement target(s) to be assessed. We strive for content-valid assessments, and they start with clear and appropriate targets. Therefore, your second starting place for the effective use of any particular assessment is your answer to this driving question: *What achievement do I need to assess?*

We have identified four kinds of interrelated types of achievement expectations plus affect as useful in thinking about and planning for assessment and for integrating it into your instruction:

- Mastering content knowledge (including understanding)
- Using that knowledge to reason and solve problems
- Demonstrating certain kinds of performance skills
- Creating certain kinds of products
- Developing certain dispositions

Each teacher faces the challenge of specifying desired targets in the classroom, relying on a commitment to lifelong learning and having strong professional preparation, community input, and collegial teamwork within the school to support this effort.

When we are clear, benefits accrue for all involved. Limits of teacher accountability are established, setting teachers up for time savings and greater success. Limits of student accountability are established, setting students up for success. And, the huge assessment workload faced by teachers becomes more manageable.

We will make this clarity the second criterion by which to judge classroom assessment quality. High-quality assessments arise from easily identified and clearly articulated learning targets. They reflect the best current thinking in the field and are obviously important—that is, they deserve instructional and assessment time and effort. Poor-quality achievement targets, on the other hand, either (1) are missing, (2) are too broad or vague to guide assessment development, (3) fail to link to important academic standards, or (4) fail to reflect the wisdom of the field of study.

Thus, clarity and appropriateness will be the second entry in our set of comprehensive rubrics for judging classroom assessment quality (see Appendix B). You will have opportunities throughout your study to practice applying these standards of good practice.

We urge that you specify clear expectations in your classroom. Do so in writing and publish them for all to see. Eliminate the mystery surrounding the meaning of success in your classroom by letting your students see your vision. If they can see it, they can hit it. But if they cannot see it, their challenge turns into pin the tail on the donkey—blindfolded, of course. You will see in the next chapter how the target triggers key decisions about how to assess the achievement of your students.

Figure 3.15 presents the second entry in our set of rating scales for evaluating assessment quality (the complete set of rubrics appears in Appendix B). This entry asks, Does the assessment arise from and promise to accurately reflect clearly articulated achievement targets?

Final Chapter Reflection

1. *What are the three most important new insights to come to you as a result of your study of this chapter?*
2. *Which of your previous questions about assessment can you now answer based on your study of this chapter?*
3. *What new questions have come to mind as a result of your study of this chapter that you hope to have answered as your study continues?*

FIGURE 3.15
Guide for Evaluating Assessments for Clear Targets

Still Needs Work	Well on Its Way	Ready to Use
The learning targets the assessment is to reflect are not stated and are not clear.	Learning targets are stated but they leave lots of room for interpretation; as a result there may be some disagreement or confusion among teachers as to their meaning.	Targets are stated and clear; all will interpret them to mean the same thing.
There is no link established to relevant state or district standards.	Some learning targets link to relevent standards, while others do not.	They are clearly linked to relevant and important standards.
Targets do not reflect the best current thinking of the field.	Scaffolding is incomplete or vague in certain instances.	They reflect the best current thinking of the field of study.
Standards have been improperly deconstructed into the scaffolding students will climb to achieve them.	Some accommodation to student understanding has been attempted.	Scaffolding is clear and complete.
Targets have not been transformed into student-friendly language.		Student-friendly versions have been prepared.

Practice with Chapter 3 Ideas

1. Engage your professor in a discussion of the intended standards and achievement targets of the course in which you are using this text. How do those expectations relate to the attributes and types of targets discussed in this chapter?

2. Here are several state standards. Deconstruct each into the enabling classroom-level knowledge, reasoning, performance skill, or product achievement targets (as appropriate) that underpin it.

   Reading—The student understands the meaning of what is read. Specifically, the student comprehends important ideas and details.

   Writing—The student writes effectively. Specifically, the student uses style appropriate to the audience and purpose; uses voice, word choice, and sentence fluency for intended style and audience.

   Mathematics—The student uses mathematical reasoning. Specifically, the student analyzes information from a variety of resources; uses models, known facts, patterns, and relationships to validate thinking.

   Science—The student understands and uses scientific concepts and principles. Specifically, the student recognizes the components, structures, and organization of systems and the interaction within and among them.

   Geography—The student understands the complex physical and human characteristics of places and regions. Specifically, the student identifies the characteristics that define the regions within which she or he lives.

   Civics—The student analyzes the purposes and organization of governments and laws. Specifically, the student compares and contrasts democracies with other forms of government.

3. Select three state achievement standards from a state in which you may teach—any grade level or content area—and analyze them in terms of the foundations of classroom targets that students must master on their journey up to each of those standards.

4. Transform each of the following classroom learning targets into student-friendly versions:

- The student will be able to reason analytically.
- The student will be able to synthesize information.
- The student will be able to classify things.
- The student will be able to carry out evaluative reasoning.
- The student will be able to reason inductively.
- The student will be able to reason deductively.

Now go to www.myeducationlab.com to take a Pretest to assess your initial comprehension of chapter content, study chapter content with your individualized Study Plan, take a Posttest to assess your understanding of chapter content, practice your teaching skills with Building Teaching Skills exercises, and build a deeper, more applied understanding of chapter content with Homework and Exercises.

CHAPTER 4

Designing Quality Classroom Assessments

CHAPTER FOCUS

This chapter answers the following guiding question:

> As a classroom teacher, how should I assess the achievement of my students?

From your study of this chapter, you will understand the following:

1. Quality assessments display four key design features: (1) the assessment method selected is capable of reflecting the intended target(s); (2) they sample achievement sufficiently to lead to appropriate conclusions about student mastery; (3) they are built of quality items, tasks, exercises, and scoring schemes; and (4) they are constructed and used in ways that minimize bias that can distort results.

2. We have four categories of assessment methods from which to choose for any particular classroom assessment situation: selected response, essay, performance assessment, and personal communication.

3. The method of choice in any particular classroom assessment context is a function of the learning target to be assessed.

THE ASSESSMENT OPTIONS

Having introduced the ideas that any particular assessment must (1) serve its intended purpose(s) (users and uses) and (2) accurately reflect its intended learning target(s), we now turn to our third key to assessment quality: creating or selecting an assessment capable of fitting well into its intended purpose and target context. In this chapter, we begin to explore the available methods by addressing when to use each and how to use each effectively (Figure 4.1).

We're going to study four categories of assessment methods, each of which is familiar to you: selected response assessments, essay (written) assessments, performance assessments, and assessments that rely on direct personal interaction or communication with students. Each presents unique development challenges and provides its own special form of evidence of student learning. We introduce all four in this chapter, and then in Part II devote an entire chapter to the effective use of each method.

Our two-part mission as teachers and assessors is to gather valid and reliable evidence of student mastery and to use that evidence to promote maximum student learning success or accurately report achievement status, depending on the context. As

FIGURE 4.1
Proper Method: One Key to Effective Classroom Assessment

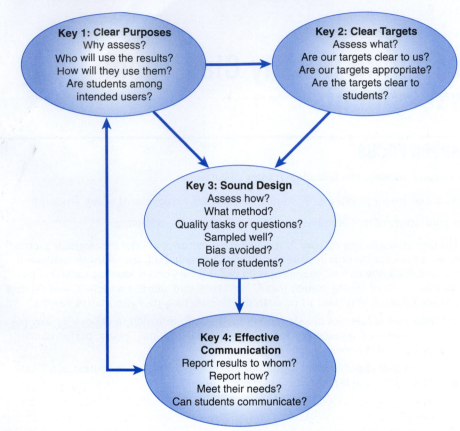

mentioned previously, quality classroom assessments rely on appropriate assessment methods, sample achievement appropriately, are built of high-quality test items, tasks, and scoring schemes, and minimize bias. We address the first feature—selecting the right method—in depth in this chapter, and then just introduce the other three. In the chapters of Part II, we explore how each of these remaining three design features applies to each assessment method.

To understand how to select a proper assessment method for each classroom assessment context, you need to know which methods work well with which of the kinds of targets described in the previous chapter. We will do this by filling in the cells of Figure 4.2 with commentary on the viability of the match represented in each cell. When you understand these alignments, you will be well down the road to understanding quality assessment.

The point is that, say, an assessment of instrumental music proficiency is likely to look very different from a spelling test in language arts. The former relies on the assessor to listen to and subjectively judge proficiency. The latter can be accomplished by evaluating a set of fill-in responses as correct or incorrect yielding a score reflecting proficiency. Different targets, different assessment methods.

FIGURE 4.2
A Plan for Matching Assessment Methods with Achievement Targets

	Selected Response	Essay	Performance Assessment	Personal Communication
Knowledge				
Reasoning				
Performance Skills				
Products				
Dispositions				

Further, it should be self-evident that, in the primary grades, before students have become confident readers and writers, selected response or essay methods cannot be used, as they require competence in those modes of communication. In that case, teachers are compelled to rely completely on performance assessment (observing them) and personal communication (talking to them). On the other hand, when assessing middle school science, for example, selected response and essay methods may make perfect sense. Different settings require different methods.

Also as a quick reminder, note that an assessment of instrumental music proficiency for the purpose of planning a student's next lesson demands a different kind of assessment from one designed to determine who receives a scholarship to the conservatory. The former requires a narrowly focused, brief assessment; the latter a much larger, more diverse sampling of proficiency. As purpose varies, so do the attributes of a sound assessment.

In this chapter, we're going to study how to pick a method that is capable of reflecting the target you wish to assess. We also will continue to fill in details about the idea of student involvement with each assessment method.

Selected Response Assessment

This category includes all of the "objectively" scored paper and pencil test formats. Respondents are asked a series of questions, each of which is accompanied by a range of alternative responses. Their task is to select either the correct or the best answer from among the options. The index of achievement in this instance is the number or proportion of questions answered correctly. Format options within this category include the following:

- multiple-choice items
- true/false items
- matching exercises
- short answer fill-in items

Fill-in-the-blank items are included here because they require a very brief response selected from within a respondent's knowledge base or reasoning that is judged right or wrong.

Essay Assessment

In this case, respondents are provided with exercises that call for them to prepare original extended written answers. Respondents might answer questions by relying on their content knowledge or provide a problem solution arising from their reasoning. For example, they might be asked to compare historical events, interpret scientific information, or solve open-ended math problems, where they must show and explain all their work. The examiner reads this original written response and evaluates it by applying specified scoring criteria.

Evidence of achievement is seen in the conceptual substance of the response (i.e., ideas expressed and the manner in which they are tied together). The student's score is determined by the number of points attained out of a total number of points available.

Performance Assessment

In this case, respondents actually carry out a specified activity under the watchful eye of an evaluator, who observes their performance or its results and judges the level of achievement demonstrated. Performance assessments can center on observations of respondents as they are demonstrating certain behaviors (skills), or on evaluation of the products they create as a result of performing. In this sense, as with essay assessments, performance assessments consist of two parts: a performance task or assignment and a set of evaluation or scoring criteria that underpins judgments of quality.

Respondents may evidence achievement by carrying out a proper sequence of activities or by doing something in the appropriate manner. Examples include musical performance, reading aloud, communicating conversationally in a second language, or carrying out some motor activity, as in the case of physical education or dance. In this case, it is the doing that counts. The index of achievement typically is a performance rating or profile of ratings reflecting levels of quality in the performance.

Alternatively, respondents may demonstrate proficiency by creating complex achievement-related products intended to meet certain standards of quality. The product resulting from performance must exist as an entity separate from the performer, as in the case of term papers, science fair exhibits, or art and craft creations. The assessor examines the tangible product to see if those attributes of quality are indeed present. In this instance, it is not so much the process of creating that counts (although that may be evaluated, too) but rather the characteristics of the creation itself. Again in this case, the index of achievement is the rating(s) of product quality.

Personal Communication as Assessment

One of the most common ways teachers gather information about student achievement to inform instructional decisions *during learning* is to talk with them. While this does not seem to be assessment in the same sense as a multiple-choice test or a performance assessment, clearly a well-placed question eliciting an immediate response from students can provide clues as to student needs.

This form of classroom assessment includes questions posed and answered during instruction, interviews, conferences, conversations, listening during class discussions, and oral examinations. For instance, a math teacher might have a student "think out loud" as they talk through their approach to solving a math problem. In such a case, the assessor listens to responses and either (1) judges them right or wrong if correctness is the criterion, or (2) makes subjective judgments according to some continuum of quality. Depending on the context, that teacher might respond with feedback to support learning (correctives) or a judgment about the sufficiency of learning. Personal communication is a very flexible means of assessment that we can bring into play literally at a moment's notice and can be used strategically to advance learning.

Time for Reflection

Think about the assessments you have experienced in the classroom, either as a student or as a teacher, and identify an example from your personal experience of each of the four assessment methods described.

Keep All Options in Play

As you assess in your classroom, strive to maintain a balanced perspective regarding the viability of these assessment options. As you are about to see, each has a contribution to make. At various times in the United States one method or another has become dominant. For decades it was the multiple-choice (selected response) test. But, because this method can tap only a narrow range of our valued learning, in recent years, we have embraced the more expansive range of performance and essay assessment. This is a good development because none of these methods is inherently superior to the others. Each can provide rich and useful information about student learning when in the hands of a competent user. Unfortunately, each also can be a formula for disaster in the hands of an incompetent user.

PRIOR TO BEGINNING DESIGN: KNOW YOUR LEARNING TARGET(S)

We realize that we just spent a chapter on this, but it is so central to sound assessment design that we simply want to reiterate:

- Knowledge targets: What content is to be sampled within the assessment? Outline it.
- Reasoning targets: What are the specific patterns of reasoning to be assessed? Define them.
- Performance skills: What skills and what are the attributes of sound performance?
- Product development: What is the product and what are the attributes of a good one?

Remember that assessments only provide us with external indicators (i.e., their achievements) of learner's internal mental states. These indicators take the form of visible manifestations that we can see and count or evaluate, such as correct or incorrect responses to test items or ratings of a performance skill. In other words, because we can't just lift the tops off students' heads and look inside to see if math problem-solving proficiency is in there, we administer an assessment in the form of several math problems from which we infer mastery of the desired achievement. Your job is to choose the method for any particular form of achievement that permits you to draw the most valid (defensible) inference about student learning. For this reason, we reiterate yet again, **you** *must be a master of the targets your students are expected to hit if you are to select, develop, and use sound assessments of those targets*. This mastery may take some time. As you launch your career in the classroom, don't hesitate to seek the advice of the most highly regarded veteran teachers around you to help you refine your sense of the key learning targets. Invest the time and effort.

Also remember that any assessment will represent a sample of all the exercises we could have posed if the assessment were infinitely long. A sound assessment relies on a sample that is sufficient in its size and systematically representative of the possibilities, from which we infer how much of the target students have mastered.

Our goal in assessment design is to use the most powerful assessment option we can. Power derives from the accuracy and efficiency with which a method can represent our valued standard. We always want the highest-resolution picture of that valued target we can get using the smallest possible sample of student performance; maximum information for minimum cost. You will study the specifics of this by method in the chapters of Part II.

Finally, anticipate that the plan for aligning achievement targets and assessment methods outlined here is going to sound somewhat complex to you the first time through it. The remainder of the book is about how to make these matches work to your benefit and to the benefit of your students. All we intend here is that the alignments described next make sense to you.

DESIGN FEATURE 1: MATCHING METHODS WITH LEARNING TARGETS

Note that three of the four assessment methods described herein call for students to develop original responses. Some require written responses, others demonstration of complex performance skills, or still others the creation of multidimensional products. These take more time to administer and certainly more time to score than, say, a true/false test. Thus, if the amount of assessment time is held constant and if it aligns well with the target in question, selected response assessments can provide a much larger sample of achievement per unit of assessment time.

So given this fact, you might ask, why not just use this most efficient option— selected response—all the time? The reason is that selected response assessment formats cannot validly represent (sample) all of the kinds of achievement we expect of our students. Different kinds of assessment methods align well with different kinds of achievement targets. Your challenge, given a choice of methods, is first to pick the viable candidates (those methods capable of reflecting the target) and then select the most efficient method for your context—the one providing the most valid evidence per unit of time). As it turns out, the recipes for creating these matches are not complicated.

As you saw in Figure 4.2, we visualize this challenge by crossing the five kinds of outcomes with the four methods to create a table depicting the various matches of targets to methods. We may then explore the nature and practicality of the match within each cell of this table. The result, though not a simple picture, is both understandable and practical. Table 4.1 presents brief descriptions of the various matches.

Time for Reflection

Please take a few minutes now to study Table 4.1 in the following way: Starting with the knowledge line at the top, think about the following question and then read across the first line of the table: If you wanted to assess your students' mastery of content knowledge, what methods do you think you might be able to use? Carry out this reflect-then-read sequence for each line of the table. When you have completed your study of the table, please read on.

Assessing Content Knowledge and Understanding

Selected Response/Knowledge Match

We can use selected response, objective paper and pencil tests to measure student mastery of facts, concepts, and even generalizations. Typically, each item tests mastery of its own isolated elements of knowledge, such as knowledge of United States history, spelling, vocabulary, earth science, and the like.

These tests are efficient in that we can administer large numbers of multiple-choice or true/false test items per unit of testing time. Thus, they permit us to sample widely and draw relatively confident generalizations from the content sampled. For this reason, when the target is knowledge mastery, selected response formats fit nicely into the resource realities of most classrooms. Just remember, this option only works well when students bring to the table a sufficiently well-developed reading proficiency to be able apprehend what each question is asking. So use it cautiously in primary grades and with special needs students.

In other words, always remember that even when the method aligns well with the target, we are not guaranteed a quality assessment. Things can go wrong that can bias or distort results leading us to an incorrect inference about student learning. For instance, a nonreader or a student who is still learning English might actually know the material but score low on a test because of poor reading proficiency. If we concluded that their low score means a lack of knowledge, we would be wrong. We'll explore these and other potential sources of mismeasurement in later chapters.

Essay/Knowledge Match

When the domain of knowledge is defined not as elements in isolation but rather as important relationships among elements, larger concepts, and important generalizations—in other words, where the knowledge to be mastered is organized in complex relationships—we can test student mastery by having them portray their knowledge using an extended written essay format. Examples of larger information chunks we might ask students to know are the causes of westward migration in U.S. history or differences among igneous, metamorphic, and sedimentary rocks.

In this case, we sample with fewer exercises, because each exercise requires longer response times, but each provides us with relatively more information than any single selected response item would.

Further, essay assessments present us with a more complex scoring challenge, and not just in terms of the time it takes. Because we must subjectively judge response quality, not just count it right or wrong, bias can creep in if we are not cautious. The

TABLE 4.1

Matching Achievement Targets to Assessment Methods

TARGET TO BE ASSESSED	ASSESSMENT METHOD			
	Selected Response Short Answer	Extended Written Response	Performance Assessment	Personal Communication
Knowledge Mastery	Multiple choice, true/false, matching, and fill-in can sample mastery of elements of knowledge	Exercises can tap understanding of relationships among elements of knowledge	Not a strong choice for this target—three other options preferred for knowledge targets	Can ask questions, evaluate answers, and infer mastery, but a time-consuming option
Reasoning Proficiency	Can assess application of some patterns of reasoning, but not all	Written descriptions of complex problem solutions can provide a window into reasoning proficiency	Can watch students solve some problems or examine some products and infer about reasoning proficiency	Can ask student to "think aloud" or can ask follow up questions to probe reasoning
Performance Skills	Can assess mastery of the knowledge prerequisites to skillful performance, but cannot rely on these to tap the skill itself		Can observe and evaluate skills as they are being performed	Strong match when skill is oral communication proficiency; also can assess mastery of knowledge prerequisite to skillful performance
Ability to Create Products	Can assess mastery of the knowledge prerequisite to the ability to create quality products, but cannot use these to assess the quality of products themselves		Can assess: (1) proficiency in carrying out steps in product development, and (2) attributes of the product itself	Can probe procedural knowledge and knowledge of attributes of quality products, but not the quality of products themselves
Dispositions	Selected response questionnaire items can tap student dispositions	Open-ended questionnaire items can probe dispositions	Can infer dispositions from behavior and products	Can talk with students about their feelings

only way to prevent this is reliance on carefully thought-out scoring guidelines. And remember, in this case, students also must bring writing proficiency into the assessment context. We must remain aware of the danger that students might know and understand the material but be unable to communicate it in this manner.

Performance Assessments of Knowledge Mastery

When it comes to the use of performance assessment (observation and professional judgment) to detect mastery of content knowledge, things quickly become complicated. To see why, consider a brief example.

Let's say we ask a student to complete a rather complex repair of a piece of technical equipment to determine if she understands the equipment. So this is an instance of product-based performance assessment. We will evaluate the student's success based on whether the piece of equipment works when she is done. If the student successfully completes the repair and the piece works properly, then obviously, she possesses the prerequisite knowledge of equipment assembly and operations needed to both identify and solve the problem. In this case, the match between performance assessment and assessment of mastery of knowledge works—but only when the student succeeds.

But what if the student fails at the performance assessment? Is her failure due to lack of knowledge? Or does she possess the required knowledge but cannot use it properly to identify the problem (a flaw in reasoning)? Or does the student possess the knowledge and reason productively, but fail because of inept use of repair tools (a performance skill problem)? At the time the student fails to perform successfully, we just don't know.

In fact, we cannot know the real reason for failure unless and until we follow up the performance assessment by turning to one of the other assessment methods to gather more evidence, like by asking a few questions and interpreting the student's responses (personal communication). If our initial goal was simply to determine if she has mastery of essential content knowledge, why go through all this hassle? Why not just ask to start with—that is, turn to one of the other three options from the outset?

Also understand that the purpose of the assessment represents an important consideration here. If the reason for assessing is to certify repair technicians, we don't care why the student fails. But if teachers whose job is to help students learn to perform, will have no way to help her perform better in the future unless we know why students fail.

Personal Communication/Knowledge Match

The final option for assessing mastery of knowledge is direct personal communication with students; for example, by asking questions and evaluating answers. This is a good match across all grade levels, especially with limited amounts of knowledge to be mastered, few students to be assessed, and in contexts in which we need not store records of performance for long periods of time.

The reason we impose these conditions is that this obviously is a time- and labor-intensive assessment method. So if our domain of knowledge to assess is large, we are faced with the need to ask a large number of questions to cover it well. That just doesn't fit the resource realities in most classrooms. Further, if the number of students to be assessed is large, this option may not allow enough time to sample each student's achievement representatively. And, if we must store records of performance over an extended period of time, written records will be needed for each student over a broad sample of questions. This, too, eats up a lot of time and energy.

Assessment via personal communication works best in those situations when teachers are checking student mastery of critical content during instruction in order to make quick, ongoing adjustments. Further, sometimes with some students in some contexts, it is the only method that will yield accurate information. For various reasons, some students just cannot or will not participate in the other forms of assessment, such as those who experience debilitating evaluation anxiety, have difficulty reading English, have severe learning or communication disabilities, or simply refuse to "test."

Table 4.1 is important. Please read across the knowledge line one more time. Do these entries make sense to you now? If they do, read on. If not, please consult with your professor.

Assessing Reasoning Proficiency

We constantly use our knowledge to reason and to solve problems. In the previous chapter, we described several valued patterns of reasoning. For example, one important pattern is *evaluative* or *critical thinking,* the ability to make judgments and defend them through application of standards or criteria. In newspapers, movie or restaurant critics evaluate based on their standards of quality. So, too, can students evaluate the quality of a piece of literature or the strength of a scientific argument by learning to apply certain criteria of quality or standards of excellence. This is evaluative reasoning in action.

Another commonly valued pattern is *analytical* reasoning, the ability to break things down into component parts and to see how the parts work together. Yet another pattern involves using knowledge to *compare and contrast* things, to infer similarities and differences.

How does one assess these kinds of reasoning targets in the classroom? Our four methodological choices all provide excellent options when we possess both a clear vision of what we wish to assess and sufficient craft knowledge of the assessment methods.

Selected Response/Reasoning Match

For example, we can use selected response exercises to determine if students can reason well and find the correct or best answer. We can use them to see if students who have read a story can analyze its elements, compare them, or draw conclusions. Consider the following examples of questions from a reading test:

- *Analytical reasoning*—Which of the following sequences of plot elements properly depicts the order of events in the story we read today? (Offer alternative orderings, only one of which is correct.)
- *Comparative reasoning*—What is one essential difference between the story we read today and the one we read yesterday? (Offer alternative differences, only one of which is correct.)
- *Drawing conclusions*—If you had to choose a theme from among those listed for the story we read today, which would be best? (Offer response options, one of which is best.)

Assuming that these are novel questions posed immediately after reading the story, so students have to figure out the answers, they ask students to dip into their knowledge base (about the story) and use it to reason. Students who see themselves becoming

increasingly proficient at responding to questions like these become increasingly confident and problem solvers.

We continue to be surprised by how many educators believe that selected response
exercises can test only recall of content knowledge. While multiple-choice formats certainly can do that very well, they also can tap important reasoning proficiencies.

There are limits, however. *Evaluative reasoning*—the ability to express and defend
a judgment, opinion, or point of view—cannot be tested using multiple-choice or
true/false items because this kind of reasoning requires at least a presentation of the
defense. Answers are not merely right or wrong—they vary in quality. Essay, performance assessment, or personal communication are needed to present that defense.

In a similar sense, problems that are multifaceted and complex, involving several
steps, the application of several different patterns of reasoning, and/or several problem
solvers working together, as real-world problems often do, demand more complex
assessment methods.

But, nevertheless, for some relatively simple, straightforward patterns of reasoning,
such as analysis, comparison, classification, and the like, selected response can work. Be
advised also that we can provide students with sharply focused practice in mastering valued patterns of reasoning by having them practice writing sample test items that require
them to properly reason out the answer.

Essay Assessment of Reasoning Proficiency

This represents an excellent way to assess student reasoning and problem solving.
Student writing provides an ideal window into student thinking. Teachers can devise
highly challenging exercises that ask students to analyze, compare, draw complex
inferences, evaluate, or use some combination of these proficiencies, depicting their
reasoning in written form.

Of course, the key to evaluating the quality of student responses to such exercises
is for the assessor to understand the pattern of reasoning required and be able to
detect its presence in student writing. This calls for exercises that really do ask students to reason through an issue or figure something out, not just regurgitate something that they learned earlier. And these exercises must be accompanied by clear and
appropriate scoring criteria that reflect sound reasoning, not just content mastery. The
rubrics for the reasoning patterns provided in Chapter 3 can be very helpful in formulating those scoring guides.

Very often, we can help our students become confident masters of various patterns
of reasoning by providing them with the opportunity to assess their own reasoning and
problem solving during learning. In this assessment FOR learning context, we might,
for example, engage them as partners in creating student-friendly versions of scoring
criteria for evaluating the quality of their analytical reasoning.

Performance Assessment/Reasoning Match

We can watch students in the act of problem solving in a science lab, for example,
and evaluate their proficiency. To the extent that they carry out proper procedures or
find solutions when stymied, they reveal their ability to carry out a pattern of reasoning. When we watch students work with math manipulatives to demonstrate a
problem solution or figure out how to manipulate computer software to accomplish
something that they haven't done before, we can literally see their reasoning unfold-
ing in their actions.

However, again, evaluating reasoning proficiency on the basis of the quality of student products can be risky. If performance is weak, did the student fail to perform because of a lack of basic knowledge, failure to reason productively, or lack of motivation? As previously stated, without followup assessment by other means, we just don't know. If we don't follow up with supplemental assessment and thereby infer the wrong cause of failure, at the very least our remedy is likely to be inefficient. We may waste valuable time reteaching material already mastered or teaching reasoning skills already developed.

Personal Communication/Reasoning Match

One of the strongest matches between target and assessment method in Table 4.1 is the use of personal communication to evaluate student reasoning. Teachers can do any or all of the following:

- Ask questions that probe the clarity, accuracy, relevance, depth, and breadth of reasoning.
- Have students ask each other questions and listen for evidence of sound reasoning.
- Have students reason out loud, describing their thinking as they confront a problem.
- Have students recount their reasoning processes.
- Ask students to evaluate each other's reasoning.
- Simply listen attentively during class discussions for evidence of sound, appropriate reasoning.

Just talking informally with students can reveal so much, when we know what we're looking for! However, with this method, it will always take time to carry out the assessment and to keep accurate records of results.

Once again, as with the other subjectively scored assessments discussed, quality scoring rubrics will be the key to unbiased assessment. The rubrics provided in Chapter 3 will be helpful in developing those scoring criteria.

Please return once again to Table 4.1 and read across the reasoning line. Do these entries make sense to you? If they do, read on. If not, please consult with your professor.

Assessing Mastery of Performance Skills

When our assessment goal is to find out if students can demonstrate performance skills, such as play a role in a dramatic performance, fluently speak in a second language, effectively give a formal speech, or interact with classmates in socially acceptable ways, then there is only one way to assess. We must observe them while they are exhibiting the desired behaviors and make judgments as to their quality. This calls for performance assessment. There is no other choice. Each of the other options falls short for this kind of target.

But sometimes limited resources make it impossible to assess the actual skill. At those times, we may need to go for second best and come as close to the real target as we can. We have several options when we need to trade high fidelity for greater efficiency in skills assessment. We can use selected response test items to determine whether students can recognize high-level achievement. For example, given a number of performance demonstrations (on video, perhaps), can respondents identify the best? Or, we may use a multiple-choice format to see if students know the proper sequence of activities to carry out when that is relevant to the outcome. Given several descriptions of a procedure, can respondents identify the correct one? We can also use paper and pencil methods to ask if students have mastered the vocabulary needed to communicate about desired skills.

Realize, however, that such tests assess only prerequisite knowledge underpinning effective performance—important building blocks to competence, to be sure. But they will not assess examinees' actual levels of skill in performing.

With this same limitation, we could have students write essays about the criteria they might use to evaluate performance in a vocal music competition, knowledge that might well represent an important foundation for performing well in such a competition. But, of course, this will fall short of a real test of performance. Only performance assessment will suffice.

Finally, personal communication represents an excellent means of skills assessment when the skills in question have to do with oral communication proficiency, such as speaking a foreign language. For such an outcome, this is the highest-fidelity assessment option. For other kinds of performance skills, however, personal communication falls short of providing direct data on students' abilities.

Please return once again to Table 4.1 and read across the performance skill line. Do these entries make sense to you? If they do, read on. If not, please consult with your professor.

Assessing Proficiency at Creating Products

The same limitations discussed for performance skills assessment apply here. If our assessment goal is to determine whether students can create a certain kind of achievement-related product, there is no other way to assess than to have them actually create one. In fact, performance assessment represents the *only* means of *direct* assessment. The best test of the ability to throw a ceramic pot is the quality of the finished pot. The best test of the ability to set up a scientific apparatus is the completed arrangement. The best test of the ability to format a term paper is the finished paper.

Again, we could use selected response assessment to see if students can pick out a quality product from among several choices. Or, we could test knowledge of a quality product's key attributes. But these are limited substitutes for assessment that actually asks students to create the product.

It is also possible to have students answer questions, write brief essays, or just discuss informally the key attributes of a carefully crafted object, such as a cabinet in shop class (personal communication). In this way, we can be sure they start with the key understandings they need—a necessary, but not sufficient, condition for success. Then students won't waste valuable time working on projects they are not prepared to succeed on.

But ultimately the real issue is whether students can create a carefully crafted cabinet. When that is the question, product-based performance assessment is the method of choice.

Please return once again to Table 4.1 and read across the product line. Do these entries make sense to you? If they do, read on. If not, please consult with your professor.

Assessing Dispositions

Let's review some of the student characteristics that fall under this heading. Affective dimensions that might be the object of classroom assessment include attitudes, values, interests, academic self-efficacy, and motivation. Remember, as stated earlier, the focus of assessment in this case is to determine the direction and intensity of student feelings about different school-related topics or issues. When it comes to dispositions, sometimes we strive to develop strong positive affect: positive attitudes about school, subjects, classmates, and so on; strong values about hard work; a strong positive academic self-concept; and strong positive motivation or seriousness of purpose. Other times we seek to develop negative affect—about bullying or drugs and alcohol, for example.

The key to success in assessing these things, as with achievement, is to start with a clear reason to assess, define clearly the characteristic to be assessed, and select a proper method. In this case, our methods include questionnaires, interviews, and observations. We devote all of Chapter 9 to this assessment challenge. But for now, realize we can use questionnaires made up of selected response and written response items. We also can infer a student's affect from the behavior we see them exhibiting in the classroom. And obviously, we can talk with our students about their attitudes, values, interests, and motivations.

Time for Reflection

To review, please create your own version of the matrix crossing achievement targets with assessment methods (Table 4.1). Fill in the cells that describe the matches and mismatches in your own words. These connections are critical to your success as a classroom assessor. So please, just one more pass through the matches now.

Some Final Points about Target–Method Match

Be advised of these two final and important generalizations: (1) These various assessment methods are not interchangeable. Each works well in some contexts but not in others. So you cannot adopt a favorite and use it every time if it is incapable accurately reflecting the learning target. (2) None of these methods is inherently superior to the others. Each is capable of producing sound evidence of learning when in the hands of a competent user. But each also can be a formula for disaster in the hands of an incompetent user. Competence includes knowing when to use it and how to use it well. We consider next what it means to "use it well."

THE REMAINING THREE DESIGN FEATURES OF QUALITY ASSESSMENTS

We have established that different assessment contexts (purposes and targets) afford us opportunities to use different assessment methods. Valid assessments rely on proper methods—methods capable of tapping the learning in question.

As stated earlier, quality assessments also display three design features beyond proper method: they are built of quality ingredients; they provide valid samples of level of achievement mastery; and they are constructed in ways that minimize bias and distortion that can result in mismeasuring achievement. We introduce these three features in the following subsections and will discuss them further in Part II as they relate to each assessment method.

Design Feature 2: Sample Achievement Appropriately

We must assemble enough of the right kinds of exercises (test items, for example) to sample student performance in a manner that leads us to a confident conclusion about achievement, without wasting time gathering more than we need. Any assessment represents a subset of all the exercises we could have posed if the assessment were infinitely long. A sound assessment relies on a sample that is systematically representative of all the possibilities. We use performance on the sample to infer or generalize about how much of the target sampled each student has mastered.

Our goal in assessment design is to use the most powerful assessment option we can. As noted previously, power derives from the accuracy and efficiency with which a method represents our valued achievement target. We always want the highest-resolution picture of that target we can get using the smallest possible sample of student performance; maximum information for minimum cost. We will provide specific guidelines for how to do this for each method in the chapters of Part II.

Design Feature 3: Build the Assessment of Quality Exercises, Tasks, Items, and Scoring Procedures

Once we select an assessment method and plan how to sample, we need to use our method of choice in a manner that will ensure us an accurate portrait of achievement. This means we must build it out of high-quality ingredients. If it is to be a multiple-choice test, we must build it of good multiple-choice test items, not poor-quality items. The difference is critical to assessment quality and we will consider it in depth in Chapter 5. A sound performance assessment requires good performance tasks and scoring criteria, not poor-quality ones. You have to know the difference. Each method brings with it a set of specific procedural guidelines for creating high-quality ingredients. We will explore these in the chapters of Part II.

Design Feature 4: Minimize Bias

Further, please understand that, even if we select a proper method, build it of quality items, and sample appropriately, each method still carries with it a list of things that can go wrong that can mislead us about student achievement. As it turns out, distortions in assessment results can creep in from such sources as the scoring process, the student's emotional state, and the test administration environment. Part of assessment literacy is understanding those potential sources of bias and knowing what to do by way of assessment development and implementation to prevent such problems. Again, later chapters will provide instruction on how to anticipate and avoid bias so as to maximize assessment accuracy.

Exploring the Cultural Context of Assessment

In some high-stakes statewide assessment contexts in recent years, every student is required to take the test and students who don't read, write, or speak English are required to take the test in English. No options are offered. Why do you think such a requirement might be imposed? Does this represent sound assessment practice, in your opinion? Why or why not? Please discuss this with your classmates.

ASSESSMENT FOR LEARNING

Before we turn to further treatment of these various assessment methods we would remind you that one basic premise of this book is that we can involve students actively in classroom assessment and thus derive great motivational and learning benefits for them. Here are more suggestions for how you can assess FOR learning:

- Develop a pretest version of a multiple-choice final exam, have students take it early in the unit of study, and help them analyze their results learning target by learning target to see their own strengths and weaknesses from the beginning of the learning. This begins the unit with students sharply focused on the keys to their own success.
- During a particular unit of study (that is, while students are still learning) have students work in teams to draft practice test items. Then have teams trade items and take each other's practice tests. Engage everyone in a discussion of the experience. What do the results of this practice tell us about what we still need to work on as a class?
- Provide students with a sample of your writing—a piece of work that you have not finished yet—so they can practice giving you descriptive feedback. Then revise your work based on their feedback and show them their impact on the quality of your work.
- Have your students create their own performance assessment exercises that tap performance skill and product targets that you establish as important for them to master. Have them develop scoring guides for evaluating their own performance. Have them practice scoring samples of each other's work to internalize the keys to their own success. Do these things for practice before students take the final performance assessment.

Sprinkled throughout the remaining chapters are suggestions of ways to involve students to unlock for them the secrets of their own academic success. All four assessment methods can allow productive student involvement during learning.

Summary: A Vision of Excellence in Classroom Assessment

Let's recount some crucial connections: In Chapter 2, we asked, *Why are we assessing?* In Chapter 3 we asked, *What are we assessing?* In this chapter we blend the why and what to infer, therefore, *How should we assess?* Sound classroom assessments arise from a clear sense of purpose, have clear and appropriate targets, and rely on a proper assessment method. A proper method is one that provides the most direct view of student performance, permitting the strongest inferences from the assessment results to the actual status of the achievement target. Such assessments also are built of quality ingredients, provide valid samples of level of achievement mastery, and are constructed in ways that minimize bias.

We established four categories of assessment methods: selected response tests, essay exercises,

FIGURE 4.3
Guide for Evaluating Assessments for Assessment Design

Still Needs Work	Well on Its Way	Ready to Use
The method selected is not capable of accurately reflecting the target.	(There is no half way for this one–it either matches or does not.)	A method has been selected that fits the desired achievement target.
Note: You will learn much more about the following quality criteria in the chapters of Part II:		
The test items, essay exercises, or performance tasks and scoring guides are of poor quality.	Some of the ingredients are of good quality, but others need work.	All items, exercise, tasks, and scoring procedures are of very high quality.
The sample of items or exercises included clearly do not cover (represent) the domain to be assessed.	The sample is adequate, but could be improved in size and coverage.	The sample collected will lead to confident conclusions about student mastery of the domain.
Relevant sources of bias remain and will distort results.	Some sources of bias have been eliminated, but some remain.	All relevant sources of bias have been eliminated.

performance assessments, and direct personal communication with students. We discussed how we might use them selectively to tap student achievement on a range of kinds of achievement. Given the range of our valued achievement targets, we need to apply all of the assessment tools we have at our disposal—no single method can serve all of our assessment needs at all grade levels. We must learn to use all available methods. If we do, the results will be better information about student success gathered in less time.

Therefore, selecting a proper assessment method becomes one of our criterion, and thus the next entry in our set of comprehensive rubrics for evaluating classroom assessment quality (Figure 4.3; the complete set appears in Appendix B). Assessments are ready to go when the method matches the target.

In the chapters that follow, we provide instruction and practice on how to use each method productively by sampling student achievement properly with high-quality exercises in ways that minimize bias. We also will explore using student-involved assessment as a motivational and teaching tool.

Final Chapter Reflection

1. *What are the three most important new insights to come to you as a result of your study of this chapter?*
2. *Which of your previous questions about assessment can you now answer based on your study of this chapter?*
3. *What new questions have come to mind as a result of your study of this chapter that you hope to have answered as your study continues?*

Practice with Chapter 4 Ideas

1. If your supervisor's objective is to evaluate your teaching proficiency, what assessment method(s) should be employed and why? (Be careful here! Pause to reflect on all of the active ingredients of good teaching before answering.)

2. When you took your driver's test, what achievement targets were covered and why? What assessment methods did they use and why?

3. In the vignette presented in Chapter 1, what assessment method did Ms. Weathersby use to determine Emily's writing proficiency and that of her classmates and why?

4. Draw a blank version of Figure 4.2. In each cell, insert an example of an achievement target from a subject you are familiar with that might be assessed with that method.

Now go to www.myeducationlab.com to take a Pretest to assess your initial comprehension of chapter content, study chapter content with your individualized Study Plan, take a Posttest to assess your understanding of chapter content, practice your teaching skills with Building Teaching Skills exercises, and build a deeper, more applied understanding of chapter content with Homework and Exercises.

PART II

Understanding Assessment Methods

As we explore the keys to classroom assessment quality, keep the big picture clearly in mind as represented in the following figure. In any particular assessment context, we start with a clear answer to our opening question, *why* are we assessing? We also start with a clear sense of *what* we intend to assess. Then and only then can we determine *how* to assess that achievement. Part II is about the specifics of *how*. We will add to final key, *effective communication* of assessment results, to this table when we introduce Part III.

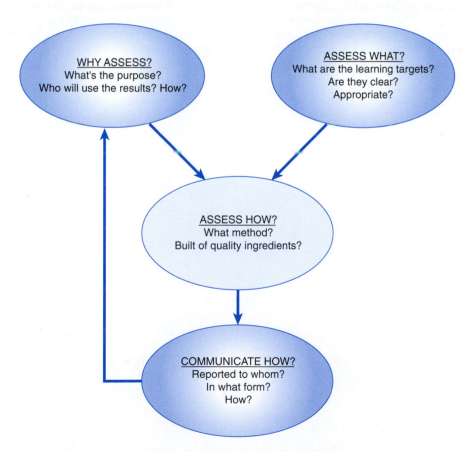

WHY ASSESS?
What's the purpose?
Who will use the results? How?

ASSESS WHAT?
What are the learning targets?
Are they clear?
Appropriate?

ASSESS HOW?
What method?
Built of quality ingredients?

COMMUNICATE HOW?
Reported to whom?
In what form?
How?

As you already know, the actual fabric of your classroom assessment environment must be woven from four basic methods: selected response, essay, performance assessment, and personal communication. Each is the focus of its own chapter in Part II. Your mission is to use these methods to create a continuously evolving portrait of each student's achievement and to keep your students in touch with and feeling in control of their own growth. Here is a quick summary of the methods addressed in each chapter:

Chapter 5: selected response assessments—multiple choice, true/false, matching, and short answer fill-in

Chapter 6: essay assessments—extended written response

Chapter 7: performance assessment methods—where you rely on observation and professional judgment

Chapter 8: personal communication—direct verbal interaction with students

Chapter 9: assessing student dispositions—attitudes, values, etc. via questionnaire, interview, or observation

As stated previously, none of these assessment methods is inherently superior to the others. Each is capable of providing vivid insights into student learning when brought into play by a competent user. At the same time, however, each also can be done poorly. An assessment-literate educator knows the difference and is committed to carrying out sound assessment practices. Each chapter reminds you when to use its particular method and then details how to create quality assessments. In addition, we will discuss how to use the method being addressed effectively to support and verify student learning. The guidelines offered in Part II chapters are intended to help you create good assessments and evaluate assessments developed by others. Never trust that someone else's test (published or otherwise) is of high quality. Always be sure to verify quality.

CHAPTER 5

Selected Response Assessment

CHAPTER FOCUS

This chapter answers the following guiding question:

When and how do I use selected response methods of assessment most effectively?

From your study of this chapter, you will understand the following:

1. Selected response assessments align well with knowledge and understanding targets, as well as with some patterns of reasoning.
2. To develop these assessments efficiently, follow three steps: (1) plan or blueprint the test; (2) find the focus for each item; (3) write the items.
3. This method can fall prey to sources of bias that can distort results if users are not careful. You will learn to avoid them.
4. By involving our students in the development and use of practice assessments while they are learning, we can set them up for confident, energetic, and successful learning.

As you study this chapter, keep our target–method matching scheme in mind. In Figure 5.1, we will be dealing in depth with the shaded areas.

	SELECTED RESPONSE	ESSAY	PERFORMANCE ASSESSMENT	PERSONAL COMMUNICATION
Knowledge				
Reasoning				
Performance Skills				
Products				
Dispositions				

FIGURE 5.1
Aligning Achievement Targets and Assessment Methods

THE "CONVENTIONAL" ASSESSMENT METHODS

According to our habits of mind and social norms, multiple-choice, true/false, matching, and fill-in tests represent what comes automatically to mind when we think of "tests." Have you ever noticed how many people contend that they were never "good test takers" in school? These usually are the kinds of tests to which they refer. There is no question that these selected response methods have been dominant in our learning and schooling lives.

These methods can serve as very powerful assessment OF and FOR learning tools when used thoughtfully by those who understand how to sample student achievement efficiently with high-quality test items, while anticipating and controlling for those bedeviling sources of bias that can creep into these assessments.

To start with, we need to think about selected response assessment quality from two points of view: how they fit into the practical realities of the classroom and the feasibility of developing an truly "objective" tests of student achievement.

When to Use Selected Response Formats

This method can come into play when your instruction is focusing on standards or classroom learning targets that center on foundations of knowledge and some reasoning proficiencies. It can help students to know where they're headed, where they are now, and how to close the gap between the two.

One obvious strength of this format can be its efficiency. When it fits the learning target, it can sample achievement efficiently (short response time per item), be administered to large numbers of students at the same time, and be scored in large numbers very quickly too using optical scanning technology. However, it has limitations, too. For example, you should consider using selected response formats only when you are absolutely certain students possess a sufficiently high level of reading proficiency in the language of the assessment to comprehend the items. With selected response formats, students' mastery of the content being assessed is always confounded with their ability to read. Therefore, this is not an appropriate format, for example, for primary-grade nonreaders or for older students who, for whatever reason, are poor readers, nonreaders, or students who are still learning the language in which the assessment is written. If your task is to evaluate their mastery of content or reasoning targets you must help them overcome their reading difficulty by reading the questions to them. This is the only way to disentangle content mastery from reading proficiency and obtain an accurate estimate of achievement of the knowledge and reasoning in question.

Obviously, however, if you are conducting an assessment of reading proficiency per se, such a remedy would be inappropriate. In this case, if students can't read, a valid and reliable assessment will, indeed must, reflect that fact.

This confounding having been noted, however, it is possible to use a selected response format in primary grades when you, the teacher, read the question to students and provide pictorial response options, one of which is the correct or best. For example, you might pose the following questions:

Which of these pictures shows what this story is about?
Which set of pictures tells the story in the right order?

The Myth of Objectivity

One common label for these formats is *objective test,* because this connotes an absence of subjectivity in development or use. Almost from the time of their first appearance on the educational scene early in the 1900s, selected response assessments have carried an air of dispassionate or scientific precision—an apparent freedom from the fallibility of human judgment to which other assessment format (say, essay tests for example) can fall prey. Our sense has been that this makes them fairer. In truth, however, subjectivity—that is, matters of teacher/assessor professional judgment—permeate all facets of selected response assessment too. First, understand that all assessments are made up of the following:

- Exercises designed to elicit some kind of response from examinees
- Scoring schemes that allow the user to judge the quality of that response

Let's be very clear about the fact that the vaunted "objectivity" in selected response assessment applies *only* to the scoring system. Well-written multiple-choice test items, for example, allow for just one best answer or a limited set of acceptable answers. This leads to the "objective" scoring of responses. No judgment required. Students' answers are either right or wrong. But this has nothing to do with the test exercise or item side of the equation.

The process of writing exercises involves a major helping of the test author's subjective professional judgment. The developer decides what learning targets to assess, how many questions to pose on a test, how to word each question, what the best or correct answers will be, and which incorrect answers to offer as choices, if needed. *All assessments, regardless of format, arise from the assessor's professional judgment.* So good assessment requires sound judgment, a matter we will address in this and each of the following Part II chapters. All assessments reflect the assessor's biases or perspectives. The key to your effective use of sound classroom assessment as a part of instruction is to make sure that your perspectives or instructional priorities are clear and public for your students from the outset. This way, they have a chance to see and understand from the very beginning of the learning what it means to be successful.

Exploring the Social Context of Assessment

One shortcoming of selected response methods of assessment is that it is more possible for students to cheat with them than with other methods. The higher the stakes, the greater is the probability of problems in this regard. What can a teacher do to try to control for this eventuality? The obvious response is to keep the test and answer key secure. But can you think of other actions that approach this problem from different directions that might help? Are there any ways to disarm this problem by rendering cheating counterproductive? Please discuss this with classmates.

MATCHING METHOD TO LEARNING TARGET

In Chapter 4, we touched on challenge of aligning various assessment methods with different kinds of achievement targets. Let's continue that discussion now by examining the kinds of targets that we can effectively translate into selected response formats. Select the best answer for the following question:

Which of the following test item formats can be used to assess both students' mastery of content knowledge and their abilities to use that knowledge to reason and solve problems?

1. Multiple choice
2. True/false
3. Matching
4. Short answer fill-in
5. All of the above

The best answer is 5, all of the above. All four formats can tap both knowledge mastery and reasoning.

Assessing Knowledge Mastery

We can use selected response test items to assess student mastery of subject matter knowledge. But remember from Chapter 4, students can know things but not understand them. If we wish to assess understanding, we need to weave it into test items. Shepard (1997) provides us with a classic illustration.* When students were presented with the following problem, 86 percent of them answered it correctly:

$$\begin{array}{r} 4 \\ \times\,3 \\ \hline \end{array}$$ A. 9
B. 12
C. 15
D. 18

But when confronted with the same problem in a manner that requires conceptual understanding the results were quite different. Here's an example:

Which choice goes with:

X   X   X   X
X   X   X   X
X   X   X   X

A. $3 \times 4 =$
B. $3 + 4 =$
C. $3 \times 12 =$

This time, only 55 percent of those same students were able to answer correctly. For many, rote learning of the answer (first problem) did not result in conceptual understanding of the mathematics involved (second problem).

If we expect students to know and understand, we must teach for and assess knowing and understanding. As this example illustrates, selected response assessment formats can help us with this but only if the tests author has mastered sufficiently deep understanding.

---

*From *Measuring Achievement: What Does It Mean to Test for Robust Understanding?* (n.p.) by L. A. Shepard, 1997, Princeton, NJ: Educational Testing Service. Copyright 1997 by ETS Policy Information Center. Reprinted by permission of Educational Testing Service.

Assessing Reasoning

When we ask students to dip into their knowledge and understanding and to use what they know in novel ways to figure something out, we ask them to *reason*. To assess this well, at testing time we must present them with new test items that they have not seen before to see if they can reason their way through the problems we present. For example, we might ask students to demonstrate proficiency in figuring out one or more of the following:

- How things are alike or different (comparative reasoning)
- How something can be subdivided into its component parts or how the parts work together (analytical reasoning)
- The main idea or theme of a story just read (inductive inference)
- The insights that can be derived from a provided data chart (deductive inference)

In such cases, our teaching challenges are to (1) make sure students have the opportunity to master the knowledge they need to solve the problems we want them to learn to solve, and (2) provide them with lots of guided practice in applying specified patterns of reasoning. But at assessment time, we must leave them alone to see if they can combine the two successfully. In other words, assessments of reasoning proficiency must ask novel questions that require new applications of available knowledge. Our intent is not to ask students merely to regurgitate solutions figured out previously and then memorized.

Skillful selected response test item writers can use multiple-choice, true/false, matching, and fill-in test items to tap the various other forms of student reasoning included in their curriculum. Examples of such questions appear in Figure 5.2. But again, to do so, these items must present students with novel problems.

Assessing Performance Skills

We cannot use selected response test formats to assess student mastery of performance skills such as speaking, drama, physical education, interacting socially, tuning an automobile engine, and the like. But we can use them to assess mastery of at least some of the procedural knowledge and understanding prerequisite to being able to demonstrate such skills.

For instance, let's say we use a performance assessment to observe two students trying to communicate effectively in a second language, and let's say they're failing to connect. If we wanted to find out why, we might follow up with by asking each of them some questions or even given them a selected response or fill in assessment to see if it was due to a lack of knowledge of vocabulary and syntactic structure. If our performance assessment reveals students failing to carry out a science lab procedure correctly, we might follow up with another kind of assessment to determine whether they understand the science knowledge to which the experiment relates or if they know and understand the steps in the lab process.

Assessing Products

Selected response exercises cannot help us determine if students can create quality products. They cannot tap proficiency in building a structurally sound model bridge, creating an authentic model of a native village, or producing an artistic creation that meets specified standards of quality. These all require performance assessments.

Reasoning	*Illustration*
Analysis	Of the four laboratory apparatus setups illustrated below, which will permit the user to carry out a distillation? (Offer four diagrams, one of which is correct.)
Synthesis	If we combine what we know about the likely impact of strong differences in barometric pressure and in temperature, what weather prediction would you make from this map? (Accompany the exercise with a map and several predictions, one of which is most likely.)
Comparison	What is one important difference between igneous and sedimentary rocks? (Offer several differences, only one of which is correct.)
Classification	Given what you know about animal life of the arid, temperate, and arctic regions, if you found an animal with the following characteristics, in which region would you expect it to live? (Describe the case and offer regions as choices.)
Inference	From the evidence provided to you in the graph, if water temperature were to go up, what would happen to the oxygen content of that water? (Provide a graph depicting the relationship between the two and offer conclusions as choices.)

FIGURE 5.2
Sample Selected Response Exercises That Require Reasoning

However, as with skills, selected response formats can test students' prerequisite knowledge of the attributes of a quality product. Students who don't understand the attributes of sound bridges, native villages, or good art—indeed, students who cannot distinguish a quality product from an inferior one—are unlikely to be able to create quality products. Selected response assessments can test these important prerequisites.

In other words, fundamental knowledge is prerequisite to performance success. It is never sufficient merely to know and understand, but it is *always* essential.

Summary of Achievement Target Matches

While we certainly can't reach all of the achievement targets we value with selected response exercises, we can tap parts of many of them. We can test student mastery of content knowledge, including what they learn outright and what they learn to retrieve through effective use of reference materials. In addition, we can tap a variety of kinds of reasoning and problem solving, including analytical, comparative, and other kinds of inferential reasoning proficiencies. And we can get at some of the underpinnings of successful performance in more complex arenas, assessing knowledge of appropriate procedures, and/or understanding of the key attributes of quality products. Table 5.1 summarizes the Selected Response column of our comprehensive targets-by-methods chart.

THE STEPS IN ASSESSMENT DEVELOPMENT

Described in its simplest form, the selected response assessment is developed in three steps, each requiring the application of special professional competence:

TABLE 5.1
Selected Response Assessment of Achievement Targets

Target to Be Assessed	Selected Response
Knowledge & Understanding	Multiple choice, true/false, matching, and fill-in can sample mastery of elements of knowledge
Reasoning Proficiency	Can assess application of some patterns of reasoning
Performance Skills	Can assess mastery of the knowledge prerequisite to skillful performance, but cannot rely on these to tap the skill itself
Ability to Create Products	Can assess mastery of the knowledge prerequisite to the ability to create quality products, but cannot assess the quality of products themselves

1. Develop an assessment plan or blueprint that identifies the material to be tested (that is, defines the achievement standards to be sampled).
2. Identify the specific elements of knowledge, understanding, and reasoning that will be the focus of each test item.
3. Transform those elements into the actual test items.

The steps of test planning and identifying elements to be assessed are the same for all four test item formats, so we will deal with those together. Then we will discuss how to write quality test items using each individual format.

Step 1: Preparing a Blueprint

Building a test without a plan is like building a house without a blueprint. Two things are going to happen and both are bad. Construction is going to take much longer than you want and the final product is not going to meet your standards. Plan well and the test will almost automatically develop itself. Fail to plan and you will struggle. In fact, the practice of test blueprinting will save you more time than any other single idea offered in this text.

Besides making test development easier and more efficient, test blueprinting offers an opportunity for teachers and students to clarify achievement expectations—to sharpen their vision of what it means to be successful. But to work well, as you will see, this kind of planning absolutely requires that the test developer understand both the underlying structure of the knowledge students are to master and the nuances of reasoning, if that is part of the focus of the assessment. Without this clarity and depth of vision, it will be impossible to develop sound assessments.

In the classroom, teachers have two types of test blueprints to choose from. The one that is currently most popular takes the form of a *list of academic achievement standards*. In any particular instructional context, achievement expectations will represent some subset of state or local standards judged important for that grade and subject. When those standards call for mastery of content knowledge or some patterns of reasoning, then items can be written to tell us how each student did in mastering each standard.

A variation on this theme that has been standard operating procedure in the professional test development field for decades is called a *table of test specifications*. When the instructional context includes several content and reasoning standards—that is, asks student to master multiple content domains and several patterns of reasoning over time such as in a high school course in U.S. History—then these can be combined into a convenient strategy for assessing them simultaneously. Let us illustrate.

Table of Specifications as a Blueprint

To explain how the table of test specifications works, we must first consider the individual assessment exercise or test question. Any test question requires respondents to do two things: (1) retrieve to a specific piece of information (either from memory or reference materials), and (2) use that knowledge to carry out a cognitive operation that will lead them to the answer (i.e., to solve some kind of problem).

For example, you might construct a test item based on knowledge of a piece of literature and ask respondents simply to demonstrate the ability to retrieve it from memory:

Who were the main characters in the story?

Or, you might ask respondents to recall two elements of content knowledge from literature and relate one to the other, as in this comparison item:

What is one similarity between two leading characters in this story?

In this case, respondents must dip into their reservoir of knowledge about the two characters (prerequisite knowledge), understand the various facets of each, and find elements that are similar (comparative reasoning). So it is in the case of all such test questions: Elements of knowledge are carried into some reasoning process.

The table of test specifications takes advantage of this combination of knowledge retrieval and its reasoning application to permit you to develop a plan that promises to sample both in a predetermined manner. Table 5.2 is a simple example of such a table. For our example, pretend that you are teaching a unit in Government. In this table, we find your plan for a unit test. The test is to include 40 questions worth one point each. You choose this number because you feel (1) you need this many questions to

TABLE 5.2
Sample Table of Test Specifications

Content	Knowledge & Understanding	Comparative Reasoning	Classification Reasoning	Total
Alternative Forms of Government	9 questions	5	1	15
Structure of U.S. Government	4	5	1	10
Rights and Responsibilities of Citizens	7	5	3	15
Total	20	15	5	40

adequately sample the knowledge and reasoning students need to master, and (2) your students can attempt all 40 in the available time.

On the left, you subdivide the content into three basic categories: Alternative Forms of Government, Structure of U.S. Government, and Rights and Responsibilities of Citizens. Each category contains many elements of knowledge within it, some of which you regard as sufficiently important to be tested—to transform into test items later. But for now, note in the last column that you have decided to include 15 questions covering knowledge of Forms, 10 on Structure, and 15 on Responsibilities. These numbers reflect your sense of the relative importance of these three categories of material.

Time for Reflection

Before reading on, please take a minute to think about how a teacher might establish the numbers of items in the row and column totals (that is, the sampling priorities). Why might some categories in a blueprint receive more questions than others? What important factors must a teacher consider in making these decisions?

The difference in the number of items assigned to each category might reflect any or all of the following:

- Amount of instructional time spent on each
- Amount of material in each category
- Relative importance of material in each category for later learning
- Important relationships among various ideas

This is an important part of the art of classroom assessment: As a teacher, your special insights about the nature and capabilities of your students and the nature and amount of material you want them to master must guide you in setting these priorities. Given this particular body of material, as a teacher/test developer, you must ask, What should be my areas of greatest emphasis now if I am to prepare students for important concepts and general principles they will confront later in their education?

Now let's continue with your table of specifications. Notice the columns in Table 5.2. Three patterns of reasoning appear, representing three different kinds of cognitive actions that were the focus of instruction: demonstrate understanding of the content, reason comparatively using elements of content, and use knowledge and reason to classify elements of content. As with the content categories, these are patterns you have emphasized during this unit of study. It might be that they are patterns that you have decided are sufficiently important to be covered across all or several units or just for this one, because they bond well with the content to be learned. In any event, your target priorities are reflected at the bottom of each column: 20 understanding items, 15 comparison items, and 5 items requiring classification.

Remember, if the test and your instruction are to align well—that is, if the test is to reflect the results of instruction accurately and fairly—then students need to have been provided with opportunities to (1) master the essential content and (2) practice with the valued patterns of reasoning. This is the kind of instruction that sets them up for success.

Once you have defined categories and specified row and column totals (which does not take long when *you* understand the material), you need only spread the numbers of questions into the cells of the table so that they add up to the row and column totals.

This will generate a plan to guide you in writing a set of test questions that will systematically sample both content and reasoning priorities as established.

How do you decide how many and what rows and columns to include in a table of test specifications? There are no rigid rules. You can include as many rows and columns as make sense for your particular unit and test. This aspect of test development is as much art as science. You should consider the following factors with respect to blueprint categories for content:

1. In Chapter 3, we discussed how to deconstruct state standards into the classroom-level achievement targets that set students up for success on state assessments. Those standards should go a long way toward identifying the knowledge and reasoning foundations of student success in your state and, therefore, in your classroom.
2. Look for natural subdivisions in the material presented in a text, such as chapters or major sections within chapters. These are likely to reflect natural subdivisions of material generally accepted by experts in the field. Each chapter or section might become a row in your table of specifications.
3. Use subdivisions of content that are likely to make sense to students as a result of their studies. Ultimately, you want them to see the vision, too.

The patterns of reasoning (columns) in your test blueprint should have the following characteristics:

1. Patterns should have clear labels and underlying meanings, both for you and your students.
2. Again, patterns taught and learned should relate to those specified in state and local achievement standards.
3. Categories should be so familiar and comfortable to you that you can almost automatically pose questions that demand student thinking in those terms.
4. Each category should represent kinds of reasoning and problem solving that occur in the real world.
5. All categories should translate into student-friendly terms, including description and examples.

Published text materials may supply the content categories for you, but you probably will have to establish the patterns of reasoning. The bottom line is this: The categories of content, kinds of reasoning tested, and proportion of items assigned to each should reflect the target priorities communicated to students from the very beginning. *Students can hit any target they can see and that holds still for them!* Do not leave them guessing.

Achievement Standards as Plans for Assessment

You also may build your assessment from a list of achievement standards or classroom learning targets that guide your instruction. When your standards or the learning targets leading up to them, like each cell in a table of specifications, specify the knowledge students must bring to bear and the action they must take (recall it, analyze it, compare it, and so on) then they can set up selected response assessments. Following are examples of such objectives:

Students will be able to compare and contrast different forms of government.
Students will understand a citizen's voting rights and responsibilities.

TABLE 5.3
Sample Test Plan for Third-Grade Mathematics Test

Learning Targets	Importance
Number Sense:	
Identifies place value to thousands	
Reads, writes, orders, and compares numbers through four digits	
Reads and writes common fractions to represent models, real-life objects, and diagrams	11 points
Number Operations:	
Subtracts whole numbers to three digits with borrowing	4 points
Measurement:	
Reads time to the nearest minute	
Identifies correct units of measurement for length, capacity, weight, and temperature	5 points

Source: From *Classroom Assessment FOR Student Learning: Doing It Right—Using It Well* (p. 130) by R.J. Stiggins, J. A. Arter, J. Chappuis, and S. Chappuis, 2004, Portland, OR: Assessment Training Institute. Copyright 2006, 2004 by Educational Testing Service. Reprinted by permission of Educational Testing Service, the copyright owner.

Like cells in a table of specifications, these objectives frame categories that contain many possible manifestations of competence—that is, many possible test items—within them. Sound standards answer the question, what knowledge must respondents use to perform what cognitive activity? Ultimately, you must prepare test items that ask students to retrieve required knowledge and use it to figure out the right answer.

Table 5.3 offers another example, in this case for early mathematics proficiencies. Three categories of learning targets center on mastery of knowledge and its use: number sense, number operations, and measurement. Note that the teacher has specified the number of items he or she thinks will be needed to lead to a confident conclusion about student mastery of each learning target.

Careful Planning Really Helps

The limits you place on content and reasoning by devising tables of specifications or lists of standards and learning targets are very important for three reasons. First and foremost, they define success for students, giving them more control over their own fate. So be sure to share your expectations with them. Turn the spotlight on your expectations so all can see them.

Second, clearly written expectations in the form of tables of test specifications and lists of objectives set limits on your accountability for your students' learning. With thoughtful plans in place, you are no longer responsible for seeing to it that every student knows every single fact about the subject. Rather, students need to know and understand specific parts and know how to reason using that information. When your students can hit such a complex target, you are a supreme success as a teacher, and there can be no question about it.

Third, once your overall plan is assembled, it becomes possible for you to develop more than one form of the same test. This can be very useful when you need to protect test security, such as when you need another form for students who were absent or who must retake the test for some reason. You can develop two tests (or more, if you like) made up of different items that you know sample the same content and reasoning patterns. This means that you provide all students with the same chance of success regardless of when they take the test.

Think Assessment FOR Learning

Remember how Ms. Weathersby involved Emily and her classmates in the process of figuring out the important attributes of good writing? Then she involved them in learning to build those attributes into their own work? She revealed her definition of success at the outset and then provided a practice environment that entitled them to master that vision before being held accountable for demonstrating proficiency.

That same kind of "assessment for practice" thinking can play out with selected response formats of assessment. For example, what if a teacher develops the table of test specifications for a unit final exam before she begins teaching the unit? And what if she provides a copy of the test plan to every student on *day one* of the unit? This establishes a contract between teacher and student saying that, our collective goal is to maximize your performance down the road on an assessment of these priorities. Let's go to work. No surprises, no excuses. When teachers do this kind of thing, achievement skyrockets for all the right reasons.

Time for Reflection

Let's say you have developed a table of test specifications and two forms of your test. You need to file one away to be brought out later as your final exam. This leaves you a "spare test" to use as you see fit to maximize student learning. How might you involve your students during instruction in productive ways with your table of specs and that "spare" assessment? Discuss this with your teammates.

Or here's another assessment FOR learning (for practice during learning) idea that is elegant in its simplicity and powerful in its impact on student success: as students take a practice quiz early in the learning, have them indicate their confidence in the correctness of their answer. If we know the learning target reflected in each item, then we can help students review their own results and zero in on those learning targets they have yet to master in future study or lack confidence in their mastery of.

Summary of Step 1

The first step in selected response assessment development is to formulate a plan or blueprint. Sound plans can be developed only when you yourself have attained complete mastery of the material (knowledge and reasoning) that you expect your students to master. Given that foundation, you can either (1) design a table of test specifications, or (2) prepare a list of achievement standards or classroom learning targets leading to those standards. Any cell of the table of specs or any objective will represent the union of two essential elements: some content knowledge students must retrieve via memory or reference and some cognitive act they must carry out using that material. These plans permit you to reveal the meaning of success to your students, giving them a visible target to shoot for.

Step 2: Selecting the Specific Material to Assess

After developing your table of specifications or list of objectives, you must select the specific and individual elements of knowledge and reasoning around which you will create test items. In Table 5.2, the cell crossing Alternative Forms of Government with Know & Understand requires the construction of nine test questions. Your next key test development question is, Can these nine questions test any facts or concepts that I wish? How do I decide which of the huge number of facts, concepts, and general principles about alternative forms of government to include in the assessment?

There are two factors to consider in answering such a question: (1) coverage of the full range of learning expectations in the unit, and (2) the relative importance of the elements within. Let me explain how these come into play.

Coverage of Material: Proper Sampling

As previously stated, any set of test questions really only represents a sample of all of the questions you could ask if the assessment were infinitely long. Clearly, if you were to test student mastery of every aspect of government, we'd be talking about an impossibly long test! The most efficient way to prevent this problem (and to create tests that fit into reasonable time limits) is to include questions that cover as much of the *important* material as time will permit. Then infer that each student's score on the sample also reflects level of mastery of the entire domain of knowledge and understanding sampled. A student who answers 80 percent of the questions on the assessment correctly probably has mastered about 80 percent of the important learnings in the domain sampled. But, you might ask, how do we decide which items to write to fill in each cell of our table of test specifications? Can we pick just any elements of content knowledge or reasoning, test them, and then generalize? The answer is No. Here is another place where classroom assessment becomes an art. We must select a sample (a subset) of *important elements* of knowledge and understanding or reasoning.

Who decides what is important, and how do they do it? If you are the teachers and are to develop the assessment, you do! If the textbook publisher developed the test and you are considering using it, you must establish your classroom achievement priorities and then evaluate the text-embedded test to see if it accurately represents them. If the instructional materials used cover more than students can master during your time with them, you must rely on your local district achievement standards to select from among the array of possibilities what to emphasize.

Other valuable sources of guidance in articulating valued knowledge and reasoning targets are the various national and state professional associations of teachers, such as science, mathematics, English, and so on. Nearly every such association has assembled a commission within the recent past to identify and publish standards of excellence for student achievement in their domain. You should be familiar with any national standards of student performance held as valuable by teachers in your field.

Please understand that the professional judgment you must exercise here is not a problem as long as you (1) are a master of the achievement targets that make up the school subject(s) you teach, (2) specify your valued achievement targets carefully, and (3) communicate them to your students. No one can do this work for you. You must possess the vision, and it must be a sound and appropriate one, given the students you teach and the latest thinking about the disciplines you teach and assess.

Identifying Important Elements

In this section, we offer a practical and efficient means of transforming your vision, whether expressed in a table of specifications or a list of targets, into quality test questions. Here is another strategy that promises to save you immense amounts of test development time while improving the quality of your tests.

Capture the elements you wish to test in the form of clearly stated sentences that reflect important elements of content and stipulate the kind of cognitive operation respondents must carry out. In the test development field, such statements are called *propositions*. As you shall see, propositions save you time in assessment development.

But before we illustrate them, we need to ask you to accept something on faith now, which we will verify for you later through example: When you have identified and listed all of the propositions that form the basis of your test, that test is 95 percent developed! While the work remaining is not trivial, we promise you that it will go so fast it will make your head spin. If you invest your time up front in identifying those things students should know and be able to do, the rest of your test development will be almost automatic.

To collect these propositions, or basic units of test items, begin by reviewing the material you will sample on the test, keeping your table of specifications or instructional objectives close at hand.

Refer to Table 5.2 once again. You need a total of 20 Knowledge & Understanding test items (bottom of column 1). Nine of these must arise from content related to Alternative Forms of Government. So as you review this material, you seek out and write down, say, 15 to 20 statements that capture important facts, concepts, or enduring understandings about Alternative Forms of Government that you think every student should know and understand. We recommend collecting about twice as many propositions as you will need to fill your final quota of test items. That way, if you need to replace some later or if you want to develop two parallel forms of the same test, you have your active ingredients (that is, additional propositions) ready to go. Remember, those collected must reflect the most important material. As you collect propositions, use clearly stated sentences like these:

> *Three common forms of government are monarchies, dictatorships, and democracies.*
> *In democracies, the power to govern is secured by vote of the people.*

And by the way, item writing is easier when you state propositions in your own words. That process forces you to understand what it is you are going for in the questions. Don't lift them verbatim from the text.

Likewise, your table of specifications calls for four questions in the Know and Understand/Structure of U.S. Government cell. Here are two sample propositions:

> *The three branches of U.S. government are legislative, judicial, and executive.*
> *Under the system of checks and balances, the executive branch balances the legislative branch through its ability to veto legislation.*

Once you have written your propositions for the cell of the first column of Table 5.2, move on to the next column, this time crossing the content categories with Comparative Reasoning. Note from the blueprint that you need 5 of these in each cell, for a total of 15. Given this expectation, try to identify and state 10 important propositions for each cell. Here's an example from the row on Structure of U.S. Government:

A difference between the U.S. Senate and House of Representatives is the term of office.

And so you proceed through all nine cells of the table, seeking out and writing down more propositions than you will need. In effect, you are creating a list of elements of the material that it is important for students to learn. Note that you have not yet attempted to write any test questions.

Remember our general sampling goal: For any given body of material, we must collect enough test propositions to confidently generalize from students' performance on the sample (score on the test) to their proportional mastery of the whole. We know we can't ask everything. But we need to be sure to ask enough. It's a matter of judgment and, as the test creator, you are the judge.

A Note on Propositions Focused on Student Reasoning

When you wish to assess your students' ability to use their knowledge to figure things out—that is, to *reason*—your challenge is to state propositions reflecting important inferences you expect them to be able to draw that you would not have explicitly covered in class. That is, they may represent the kinds of comparative inferences you want them to be able to draw using their own knowledge of government and their understanding of comparison—they apply the concepts of similarity and difference. To test their ability to reason on their feet, then, you must present cognitive challenges at assessment time that demand more than mastery of fundamental knowledge.

To reach this goal, a very special relationship must exist between the questions that appear on the test and your preceding instruction: The item must present a problem for which students (1) have had the opportunity to master appropriate prerequisite knowledge but (2) have not had the opportunity to use it to solve this particular problem. The assessment exercise challenges them to reason it out right there on the spot.

Certainly, students must dip into their reservoir of available knowledge. That is, they must retrieve the requisite information if they are to reason productively. But the aim of these propositions is to convey more than retrieval from memory, when the goal of instruction is more than just knowing. If you want students to make the leap, for example, from just knowing something to analyzing or comparing (that is, to reasoning), you must write propositions representing extrapolations you want them to be able to make. It is not acceptable for them to have solved the problem before and memorized the answer for later regurgitation. You want them to be able to use their knowledge to figure things out at assessment time. Otherwise, you have not assessed their reasoning powers.

Completing Step 2

Once you have completed your collection of propositions tapping critically important learnings to be assessed—remember, you have been writing more than you need—you must make the final cut. At this time, it is wise to step back from this list of propositions, review them one more time, and ask yourself, Do these really provide a composite picture of what I think are the important knowledge and reasoning targets of this unit? If you really know and understand the material and know how it relates to what students will confront in the future, weak propositions will jump out at you. If you find weak entries, remove them. When the list meets your highest standards of coverage, you are ready to select the specific number needed to actually fill the cells of the table. Just remember to keep those that do not make the final cut. They will come in very handy during instruction, as you will see.

Additional Thoughts on Steps 1 and 2

At this point, you may be asking, How does he expect me to find time to do all of this and teach, too? Stick with me through the third and final test development step and it will become apparent why this planning saves you a great deal of time and effort.

Trust us when we say that this kind of test development quickly becomes second nature to those who practice and master it. We promise you, if you are not confident that you have mastered all of the content or reasoning targets that you value when you start test development, by the time you finish designing some tests in this way, you will have a much stronger handle on them. In this sense, the very act of developing tests is an excellent professional growth experience.

Continue to Think Assessment for Learning

Just as it is possible to connect students to a vision of their own success by sharing your learning targets with them at the beginning of learning, so too is it possible to involve students with propositions in ways that promote their success:

- During instruction, have students jot down and share propositions they think are important.
- At the end of a day of instruction, engage students as partners in listing the important propositions of the day.
- Provide students with some sample propositions (perhaps some they developed), along with the table of test specifications, and have them practice fitting each proposition into its proper cell in the table.

All of these provide students with focused practice.

Time for Reflection

Can you think of other specific ways to involve students with the combined ideas of test blueprints and propositions in ways that set them up for success in learning content and patterns of reasoning?

Step 3: Building Test Items from Propositions

Previously, we noted that developing a high-quality test plan and specifying propositions represent 95 percent of the work in selected response test development. Complete the list of propositions and the test will almost develop itself from that point on. The reason lies in the fact that each proposition captures a complete and coherent thought. Professional test developers understand that the key to fast and effective item writing is to be sure to start with a complete and coherent thought about each fact, concept, general principle, or matter of inference that you intend to test.

Once you have a proposition in hand, you can spin any kind of selected response item out of it that you wish. Let us illustrate with the following proposition from the cell in Table 5.2 that crosses Alternative Forms of Government with Know & Understand:

In a monarchy, the right to govern is secured through birth.

To generate a true/false item out of this proposition that is true, you can simply include the proposition on the test as stated! The proposition is a true true/false test item as written. This is always the case with well-stated propositions.

If you want a false true/false item, simply make one part of the proposition false:

In a monarchy, the right to govern is secured through the approval of those governed.

To convert this proposition to a fill-in item, simply leave out the phrase dealing with the effect and ask a question:

How is the right to govern secured in a monarchy?

If you desire a multiple-choice item, add a number of response options, only one of which is correct.

How is the right to govern secured in a monarchy?

    a. With military power
    b. Through birth
    c. By popular vote
    d. Through purchase

Here's the key: Every well-conceived and clearly stated proposition, whether requiring retrieval of knowledge or its application in a reasoning context, is an automatic source of test questions.

Here's another example, this time requiring Comparative Reasoning using an understanding of Structure of U.S. Government. In its initial statement, it is a true true/false question:

The executive and legislative branches of U.S. government differ in that the latter is elected directly by the people.

As a false true/false question:

Members of executive and legislative branches are both elected directly by the people.

As a fill-in item:

Election of members of the executive and legislative branches differs in what way?

As a multiple-choice item:

Election of members of the executive and legislative branches differs in what way?

    a. Legislators are restricted by term limits; presidents are not
    b. Legislators are elected directly; presidents are not
    c. One must register to vote for legislators; not for president

Invest your time and effort up front by learning the underlying structure of the material you teach, and finding the important propositions. These are the keys to the rapid development of sound selected response assessments. Once you have identified the format(s) you plan to use, a few simple keys will aid you in developing sound test items. Some of these guidelines apply to all formats; others are unique to each particular format. They all have the effect of helping respondents understand exactly what you, the item writer, are going for in posing the exercise.

General Item Writing Guidelines

Be careful here—don't over think this process. Just follow the relatively simple guidelines we offer here and item writing will become pretty easy pretty quickly. The simplicity of these few suggestions belies their power to improve your tests.

1. *Write clearly in a sharply focused manner.* Good assessment development is first and foremost an exercise in clear communication. Follow the rules of grammar—tests are as much a public reflection of your professional standards as any other product you create. Include only material essential to framing the question. Be brief and clear. Your goal is to test mastery of the material, not students' ability to figure out what you're asking!

   Not this:

   When scientists rely on magnets in the development of electric motors they need to know about the poles, which are?

   But this:[*]
   What are the poles of a magnet called?
      a. Anode and cathode   c. Strong and weak
      b. North and south   d. Attract and repel

2. *Ask a question.* That is, when using multiple-choice and fill-in formats, minimize the use of incomplete statements as exercises. When you force yourself to ask a question, you force yourself to express a complete thought in the stem or trigger part of the question, which usually promotes respondents' clear understanding.

   Not this:

   Between 1950 and 1965
      a.   Interest rates increased.   c. Interest rates fluctuated greatly.
      b.   Interest rates decreased.   d. Interest rates did not change.

   But this:

   What was the trend in interest rates between 1950 and 1965?
      a. Increased only   c. Increased, then decreased
      b. Decreased only   d. Remained unchanged

3. *Aim for the lowest possible reading level.* This is an attempt to control for the inevitable confounding mentioned previously between reading proficiency and mastery of the content and reasoning students are to demonstrate. You do not want to let students' reading proficiency prevent them from demonstrating that they really know the material. Minimize sentence length and syntactic complexity and eliminate unnecessarily difficult or unfamiliar vocabulary. For an example, see the previous magnet questions.

---

*Item adapted from *Handbook on Formative and Summative Evaluation of Student Learning* (p. 592, item A.4-n-2.211) by B. S. Bloom, J. T. Hastings, and G. F. Madaus, 1971, New York: McGraw-Hill. Copyright 1971 by McGraw-Hill, Inc. Adapted by permission of the publisher.

4. *Eliminate clues to the correct answer either within the question or across questions within a test.* When grammatical clues within items or material presented in other items give away the correct answer, students get items right for the wrong reasons. The result is misinformation about their true achievement.

Not this:
   All of these are examples of a bird that flies, except an
   a. Ostrich   c. Cormorant
   b. Falcon   d. Robin

(The article *an* at the end of the stem requires a response beginning with a vowel. As only one is offered, it must be correct.)

Not this either:
   Which of the following are examples of birds that do not fly?
   a. Falcon   c. Cormorant
   b. Ostrich and penguin   d. Robin

(The question calls for a plural response. As only one is offered, it must be correct.)

5. *Have a qualified colleague review your items to ensure their appropriateness.* This is especially true of your relatively more important tests, such as big unit tests and final exams. No one is perfect. We all overlook simple mistakes. Having a willing colleague review your work takes just a few minutes and can save a great deal of time and assure accuracy of results.
6. *Double check the scoring key for accuracy before scoring.*

Guidelines for Multiple-Choice Items

When developing multiple-choice test items, keep these few simple, yet powerful, guidelines in mind:

1. *Ask a complete question to get the item started, if you can.* We repeat this for emphasis. This has the effect of placing the item's focus in the stem, not in the response options.
2. *Don't repeat the same words within each response option; rather, reword the item stem to move the repetitive material up there.* This will clarify the problem and make it more efficient for respondents to read. (See the previous "interest rate" example.)
3. *Be sure there is only one correct or best answer.* This is where that colleague's independent review can help. Remember, it is acceptable to ask respondents to select a best answer from among a set of answers, all of which are correct. Just be sure to word the question so as to make it clear that they are to find the "best answer."
4. *Word response options as briefly as possible and be sure they are grammatically parallel.* This has two desirable effects. First, it makes items easier to read. Second, it helps eliminate grammatical clues to the correct answer. (See the second bird example.)

Not this:
   Why did colonists come to the United States?
   a.   To escape heavy taxation by their native governments
   b.   Religion

c. They sought the adventure of living among Native Americans in the new land

d. There was the promise of great wealth in the new world

e. More than one of the above answers

But this:

Why did colonists migrate to the United States?
a. To escape taxation   c. For adventure
b. For religious freedom   d. More than one of the above

5. *Vary the number of response options presented as appropriate to pose the problem you want your students to solve.* While it is best to design multiple-choice questions around three, four, or five response options, it is permissible to vary the number of response options offered across items within the same test. Please try not to use "all of the above" or "none of the above" merely to fill up spaces just because you can't think of other incorrect answers. In fact, sound practice suggests limiting their use to those few times when they fit comfortably into the context of the question.

Some teachers find it useful to include more than one correct answer and ask the student to find them all, when appropriate. Of course, this means those questions should be worth more than one point. They need to count for as many points as there are correct answers. For example:

Which of the labels provided represents a classification category for types of rocks? (Identify all correct answers[*])
a. Geologic   c. Sandstone
b. Metamorphic*   d. Igneous*

By the way, here's a simple, yet very effective, multiple-choice test item writing tip: If you compose a multiple-choice item and find that you cannot think of enough plausible incorrect responses, include the item on a test the first time as a fill-in question. As your students respond, those who get it wrong will provide you with the full range of viable incorrect responses you need the next time you use it.

Guidelines for True/False Exercises

You have only one simple guideline to follow here: Make the item *entirely* true or false *as stated.* Complex "idea salads" including some truth and some falsehood just confuse the issue. Precisely what is the proposition you are testing? State it and move on to the next one.

Not this:

From the Continental Divide, located in the Appalachian Mountains, water flows into either the Pacific Ocean or the Mississippi River.

But this:

The Continental Divide is located in the Appalachian Mountains.

Guidelines for Matching Items

When developing matching exercises, which are really complex multiple-choice items with a number of stems offered along with a number of response options, follow all of the multiple-choice guidelines offered previously. In addition, observe the following guidelines:

1. *Provide clear and concise directions for making the match.*
2. *Keep the list of things to be matched short.* The maximum number of options is 10. Fewer is better. This minimizes the information processing and idea juggling respondents must do to be successful.
3. *Keep the list of things to be matched homogeneous.* Don't mix events with dates or with names. Again, idea salads confuse the issue. Focus the exercise.
4. *Keep the list of response options brief in their wording and parallel in construction.* Pose the matching challenge in clear, straightforward language.
5. *Include more response options than stems and permit students to use response options more than once.* This has the effect of making it impossible for students to arrive at the correct response purely through a process of elimination. If students answer correctly using elimination and you infer that they have mastered the material, you will be wrong.

Not this:

_____ 1. Texas	A. $7,200,000	
_____ 2. Hawaii	B. Chicago	
_____ 3. New York	C. Liberty Bell	
_____ 4. Illinois	D. Augusta	
_____ 5. Louisiana	E. Cornhusker	
_____ 6. Florida	F. Mardi Gras	
_____ 7. Massachusetts	G. 50th State	
_____ 8. Alaska	H. Austin	
_____ 9. Maine	I. Everglades	
_____ 10. California	J. 1066	
_____ 11. Nebraska	K. Dover	
_____ 12. Pennsylvania	L. San Andreas Fault	
	M. Salem	
	N. 1620	
	O. Statue of Liberty	

But this:

Directions: The New England states are listed in the left-hand column and capital cities in the right-hand column. Place the letter corresponding to the capital city in the space next to the state in which that city is located. Responses may be used only once.

States Capital Cities

_____ 1. Connecticut	A. Augusta
_____ 2. Maine	B. Boston
_____ 3. Massachusetts	C. Brunswick
_____ 4. New Hampshire	D. Concord
_____ 5. Rhode Island	E. Hartford
_____ 6. Vermont	F. Montpelier
	G. New Haven
	H. Providence

Guidelines for Fill-in Items

Here are three simple guidelines to follow:

1. *Ask respondents a question and provide space for an answer.* This forces you to express a complete thought. The use of incomplete statements as item stems is acceptable. But if you use them, be sure to capture the essence of the problem in that stem.

2. *Try to stick to one blank per item.* Come to the point. Ask one question, get one answer, and move on to the next question. Simple language, complete communication, clear conclusions. Does the student know the answer or not?

> *Not this:*
> In the percussion section of the orchestra are located _____, _____, _____, and _____.

> *But this:*
> In what section of the orchestra is the kettle drum found? _____

3. *Don't let the length of the line to be filled in be a clue as to the length or nature of the correct response.* This may seem elementary, but it happens. Again, this can misinform you about students' real levels of achievement.

More Assessment FOR Learning Ideas

Consider the possibility of engaging students as partners in developing practice items reflecting the important knowledge and reasoning proficiencies as given in your achievement standards, learning targets, or set of propositions. This can turn into sharply focused instruction in the form of guided practice. They must begin to tune into the important content and become so comfortable with your valued reasoning patterns that they can pose questions of their classmates that require their application. Just remember, these activities are for practice only—they are assessments *for* learning. It is not acceptable for students to develop their own assessments *of* learning—those you use to verify learning for report card grading, for example. When it comes time for accountability, the assessment must be yours, seen by your students only at the proper time.

Summary of Step 3

In this step, you transformed propositions into assessment questions. This can be very quick and easy. Regardless of the item format, however, clarity and focused simplicity must be hallmarks of your exercises. Always try to ask questions. Strive to eliminate inappropriate clues to the correct answer, seek one clearly correct answer whenever possible and appropriate, ask a colleague to review important tests, and follow just a few simple format-specific guidelines for item construction. Figure 5.3 presents a summary of these guidelines collected for your convenient use.

Further, remember to help students perform up to their potential by providing clear and complete instructions, letting students know how each exercise contributes to the total test score, starting with easy items, and making sure the test is readable.

General guidelines for all formats

_____ Items clearly written and focused

_____ Question posed

_____ Lowest possible reading level

_____ Irrelevant clues eliminated

_____ Items reviewed by colleague

_____ Scoring key double checked

Guidelines for multiple-choice items

_____ Item stem poses a direct question

_____ Repetition eliminated from response options

_____ One best or correct answer

_____ Response options are brief and parallel

_____ Number of response options offered fits item context

Guideline for true/false items

_____ Statement is entirely true or false as presented

Guidelines for matching exercises

_____ Clear directions given

_____ List of items to be matched is brief

_____ List consists of homogeneous entries

_____ Response options are brief and parallel

_____ Extra response options offered

Guidelines for fill-in items

_____ A direct question is posed

_____ One blank is needed to respond

_____ Length of blank is not a clue

FIGURE 5.3
Test Item Quality Checklist

FINE TUNING ASSESSMENT APPLICATIONS

Consider the following suggestions as you develop your selected response assessments.

Mix Formats Together

The creative assessment developer also can generate some interesting and useful assessment exercises by mixing the various formats. For example, mix true/false and multiple-choice formats to create exercises in which respondents must label a statement true or false and select the response option that gives the proper reason it is so. For example:

> _As employment increases, the danger of inflation increases._
> a. True, because consumers are willing to pay higher prices
> b. True, because the money supply increases
> c. False, because wages and inflation are statistically unrelated to one another
> d. False, because the government controls inflation

Or, mix multiple-choice or true/false questions with the fill-in format by asking students to select the correct response and fill in the reason it is correct. As a variation, ask why incorrect responses are incorrect, too.

Time for Reflection

Can you think of combinations of these formats that might be useful?

Use Interpretive Exercises

Here's another simple but effective assessment development idea: Let's say you wish to use selected response formats to assess student reasoning and problem-solving proficiency. But let's also say you are not sure all of your students have the same solid background in the content, or you want to see them apply content you don't expect them to know outright. In these contexts, you can turn to what is called an *interpretive exercise.* With this format, you provide information to respondents in the form of a brief passage, chart, table, or figure and then ask a series of questions calling for them to interpret or apply that material.

There are other very common instances when this method can be applied effectively. For instance, virtually every reading comprehension test relies on this format. We present students with passages that present the knowledge, ask them to read it, and then ask them inferential comprehension questions about that content. Such passages can deal with story comprehension or they can focus on particular content areas, such as science content. Or similarly in science, teachers often rely on table and graphs to present data and then ask students to interpret the data using analysis, comparison, or evaluation questions.

Format the Test Carefully

Finally, here are a few simple guidelines for setting up your test as a whole that will maximize the accuracy of the results:

1. Make sure your students know the point value for each assessment exercise. This helps them use their time wisely.
2. Start each test with relatively easy items. This will give students a chance to get test anxiety under control.
3. Present all questions of like format together (all multiple choice together, all fill-in, etc.)
4. Be sure all parts of a question appear on the same page of the test.
5. Make sure all copies are clear and readable.

Work Backwards to Verify Test Quality

You can reverse the three-step test development process described to evaluate previously developed (for example text-embedded) tests. To do this, begin at the test item level: Do the items themselves adhere to the quality control guidelines presented previously? If they do not, there is obvious reason for concern about test quality. If they do, proceed to the next level of evaluation.

TABLE 5.4
Reasoning Test Item Illustrations—Reading Comprehension

Reasoning Learning Targett	Item Formula
Make inferences based on the reading	Which sentence includes an idea you can get from this (selection)? a. The correct response is an idea that can reasonably be inferred from the text. b. Incorrect responses are ideas that it seems one might infer from the text but that the selection does not really support.
Make predictions based on the reading	What do you think (character) will do now that (cite circumstances at end of story)? a. The correct response is an outcome that can reasonably be predicted given the information in the text. b. Incorrect responses are not appropriate given the information in the text.
Compare and contrast elements of text	Which sentence tells how (two characters in the story) are alike? a. The correct response identifies an appropriate similarity. b. Incorrect responses do not identify similarities; they may focus on something that is true of one character or the other but not both.
Make connections within texts	Which sentence explains why (event) happened? a. The correct response is a reasonable statement of causation. b. Incorrect responses are events in the story that thoughtful reading reveals are not really the cause.
Make connections among texts	How does (story character's) feelings about (subject) compare to the poet's feeling about (subject)? a. The correct response identifies an appropriate similarity. b. Incorrect responses identify elements that exist in one passage but not in other.

Source: From *Washington Assessment of Student Learning 4th-Grade Reading Test and Item Specifications,* 1998, Olympia, WA: Office of the Superintendent of Public Instruction. Reprinted by permission.

Transform the items into the propositions that they reflect. You accomplish this by doing the following:

- Combine the multiple-choice item stem with the correct response.
- Check that true true/false items already are propositions.
- Make false true/false items true to derive the proposition.
- Match up elements in matching exercises.
- Fill in the blanks of short answer items.

Then, analyze the resulting list of propositions, asking, Do these reflect the priorities in my instruction?

Next, collect the propositions into like groups to determine the achievement standards or learning targets they represent or to create a table of specifications depicting the overall picture of the test, including the proportional representation of content and reasoning. Again, ask, Do these reflect priorities as I see them?

This kind of reverse process can both reveal the flaws in previously developed tests and help you understand the nature of the revisions needed to bring the test up to your standards of quality.

SOME FINAL REMINDERS

As you plan your development and use of selected response assessments, attend carefully to the following issues:

- Be sure time and test length permit students to attempt all test items. If a student doesn't get to try an item because time runs out, you have no way of knowing if that student has mastered the material tested. You cannot automatically assume they would get it wrong. They might not—you don't know. To avoid the problem, give everyone every chance. If that means extending test time for some, extend it.
- Remember, as mentioned previously, do not hand score unless absolutely necessary. It's a huge waste of time. Use optical scanning technology.
- Use fill-in exercises when you wish to control for guessing. And make no mistake about it, guessing can be an issue. If a student guesses an item right and you infer that the right answer means the student has mastered the material, you will be wrong. You have mismeasured that student's real achievement.

Potential Sources of Problems	*Suggested Remedies*
Lack of vision of the priority target(s)	Carefully analyze the material to be tested to find the knowledge and reasoning targets.
	Find truly important learning propositions.
Wrong method for the target	Use selected response methods to assess mastery of knowledge and appropriate kinds of reasoning only.
	Selected response can test prerequisites of effective skill and product performance, but not performance itself.
Inappropriate sampling:	
• Not representative of important propositions	Know the material and plan the test to thoroughly cover the target(s).
•Sample too small	Include enough items to cover key concepts.
•Sample too large for time available	Shorten cautiously so as to maintain enough to support confident student learning conclusions.
Sources of bias:	
•Student-centered problems	
•Cannot read well enough to respond	Lower reading level of test or offer reading support.
•Insufficient time to respond	Shorten test or allow more time.
•Poor-quality test items	Learn and follow both general and format-specific guidelines for writing quality items.
	Seek review by a colleague.
•Scoring errors	Double check answer key; use it carefully.

FIGURE 5.4
Avoiding Problems with Selected Response Tests and Quizzes

- Use multiple-choice items when you can identify one correct or best answer and a number of viable incorrect responses (also known as *distractors*). On its surface, this might sound obvious. But think about it. If you formulate your distractors carefully, you can use multiple-choice items to uncover common misunderstandings and to diagnose students' needs. That is an assessment FOR learning way of thinking.

Barriers to Sound Selected Response Assessment

Recall that we highlighted several keys to sound assessment. We must start with a clear sense of purpose (user and use) and clear targets. Then and only then can we

---

Where am I going?

1. Make targets clear.
   - _____ Write targets in student-friendly language.
   - _____ Share test plans at the outset.
   - _____ Have students match propositions with test plan cells.
   - _____ Have students develop propositions along the way.
2. Use strong and weak models.
   - _____ Students identify wrong multiple-choice and fill-in answers and say why.

Where am I now?

3. Provide descriptive feedback.
   - _____ Provide feedback target by target on a test.
   - _____ Define quality and always anchor suggested improvements to it.
4. Teach students to self-assess and set goals.
   - _____ Students use test plans as a basis for evaluation of strengths and areas for study.
   - _____ Students complete self-evaluation and goal-setting form on basis of test or quiz results.

How can I close the gap?

5. Teach focused lessons.
   - _____ Students answer question: *How do you know your answer is correct?*
   - _____ Students turn propositions into items and practice answering the items.
   - _____ Students create test items for each cell and quiz each other.
   - _____ Students use graphic organizers to practice patterns of reasoning.
6. Students practice revising.
   - _____ Students answer the question: *How do I make this answer better?*
7. Students reflect on and share what they know.
   - _____ Students engage in self-reflection: I have become better at _____.
   - I used to _____, but now I _____.

FIGURE 5.5
Ideas for Student-Involved Assessment

Source: From *Classroom Assessment FOR Student Learning: Doing It Right—Using It Well* (p. 153) by R. J. Stiggins, J. A. Arter, J. Chappuis, and S. Chappuis, 2004, Portland, OR: Assessment Training Institute. Copyright 2006, 2004 by Educational Testing Service. Reprinted by permission of Educational Testing Service, the copyright owner.

turn to test design. In this context, the four key design features we discussed in come to the fore. We must always do the following:

- Select a proper assessment method.
- Build the assessment of quality ingredients (test items in this case).
- Sample achievement appropriately.
- Control of relevant sources of bias.

These represent categories of things that can go wrong—that can keep a student's test score from being an accurate reflection of that student's real level of achievement. Listed in Figure 5.4 (see page 116) by way of summary are many of the sources of mismeasurement touched on in this chapter, together with actions you can take to prevent these problems. These remedies can help you develop sound selected response assessments.

Student Involvement in Selected Response Assessment

As you will recall from Chapter 2, as teachers, we conduct both assessments OF and FOR learning. Selected response assessments represent assessments OF learning when they look to the past to determine the amount learned for the determination of a report card grade. They become assessments FOR learning when they help students understand where they are headed, where they are now in relation to expectations, and how to close the gap between the two. Figure 5.5 (see page 117) suggests some specific ways to accomplish this with selected response assessments.

Summary: Productive Selected Response Assessment

We established at the beginning of the chapter that these options often are labeled "objective" tests because of the manner in which they are scored. When test items are carefully developed, there is only one clearly best answer. No judgment is involved. However, the teacher's professional judgment does play a major role in all other facets of this kind of assessment, from test planning to selecting material to test to writing the test items. For this reason, it is essential that all selected response test developers closely follow procedures for creating sound tests. Those procedures have been the topic of this chapter.

We discussed the match between selected response assessment methods and the four basic kinds of achievement targets plus dispositions that are serving as signposts for our journey. These selected response formats can serve to assess students' mastery of content knowledge and understanding, ability to reason in important ways, and mastery of some of the procedural knowledge that underpins both the development of performance skills and the creation of complex products.

As we examined the test development process itself, we explored several context factors that extend beyond just the consideration of match to target that must be taken into account in choosing selected response assessment. These included factors related to students' reading abilities and to the kinds of support services available to the user.

Also under the heading of test development, we explored a three-step developmental sequence: test planning, identifying propositions to test, and test item writing. In each case, we touched on specific ideas for involving students in selected response assessment to extend their learning. We reviewed a limited number of specific item and test development tactics within each step that promise to decrease test development time and increase test quality. These tactics hold the promise of saving teachers immense amounts of time in test development. Not only do they result in quick and easy test item development, but teachers can store both test blueprints and items on their personal computer for convenient reuse later.

Final Chapter Reflection

1. *What are the three most important new insights to come to you as a result of your study of this chapter?*
2. *Which of your previous questions about assessment can you now answer based on your study of this chapter?*
3. *What new questions have come to mind as a result of your study of this chapter—questions that you hope to have answered as your study continues?*

Practice with Chapter 5 Ideas

1. Make up a simple table of test specifications for a 10-item selected response assessment of the content priorities presented in this chapter.

2. Transform each of the following test items into its basic proposition:
   - True T/F: One reason for declining numbers of Pacific salmon is the destruction of salmon habitat.
   - False T/F: A tariff is a tax on real estate.
   - Fill in: If we increase the radius of a ball by 3 inches, what will be the effect on its circumference?
   - Multiple choice: Which of the following is an example of a tariff?
     a.   Income tax
     b.   Tax on Chinese imports
     c.   Real estate tax
     d.   All of the above

3. Transform the following propositions into test items:
   - Automobiles and factories are the largest sources of air pollution.
   - The water cycle depends on evaporation and condensation.
   - In the United States, we have a bicameral legislature.
   - Our free market economic system is based on the law of supply and demand.

4. Write the 10 propositions that will fill in the table of test specifications for this chapter that you designed for Practice item 1. Then write the test items. Exchange work with a classmate, if possible, and evaluate each other's work.

5. Retrieve a copy of a selected response test that you have taken in the recent past and do the following:
   - Transform its items into propositions and summarize them into a table of test specifications.
   - Rate the quality of this assessment using the rubrics for evaluating assessment quality found in the Appendix along with the more specific guidelines presented in this chapter.

Now go to www.myeducationlab.com to take a Pretest to assess your initial comprehension of chapter content, study chapter content with your individualized Study Plan, take a Posttest to assess your understanding of chapter content, practice your teaching skills with Building Teaching Skills exercises, and build a deeper, more applied understanding of chapter content with Homework and Exercises.

CHAPTER 6

Written Response (Essay) Assessment

CHAPTER FOCUS

This chapter answers the following guiding question:

> When and how do I most effectively use assessments that ask students to provide written responses?

From your study of this chapter, you will understand the following:

1. Essay assessment aligns well with knowledge and understanding targets, as well as with various patterns of reasoning.
2. This method can be efficiently developed in three steps: assessment planning, exercise development, and preparation to score student responses.
3. This method can fall prey to bias if users are not careful.
4. By involving your students in essay assessment development and use, you can set them up for energetic and successful learning.

As we start this part of our journey, keep the big picture in mind. In this chapter, we deal with the shaded areas of Figure 6.1.

ASSESSMENT BASED ON SUBJECTIVE JUDGMENT

In recent years, our increasingly complex society has asked schools to help students master increasingly complex forms of achievement. These more sophisticated reasoning and writing achievement standards have heightened interest in assessment methods that can probe student learning more deeply than can selected response assessment. One result has been a reaffirmation of essay assessment—the method, by the way, that dominated student evaluation until the appearance of the multiple-choice format early in the 1900s.

This chapter explores the potential of the essay assessment to reflect achievement targets for which selected response formats are insufficient, such as students' understanding of connections or relationships among elements of knowledge, or complex reasoning patterns. As you will see, written response assessments too can be integrated very productively into teaching and learning through student involvement, while saving teachers a great deal of scoring time.

	SELECTED RESPONSE	ESSAY	PERFORMANCE ASSESSMENT	PERSONAL COMMUNICATION
Knowledge				
Reasoning				
Performance Skills				
Products				
Dispositions				

FIGURE 6.1
Aligning Achievement Targets and Assessment Methods

As with all assessment methods, however, if we are not careful, problems can crop up. For instance, we are likely to inaccurately assess student achievement if we

- Lack sufficiently clear learning targets.
- Rely on the essay format when it doesn't fit the achievement target.
- Use this method with students who lack sufficient writing skills to convey their achievement of content or reasoning proficiencies.
- Do not sample the achievement target with enough high-quality essay exercises.
- Disregard the many sources of bias that can invade subjective assessments, especially during scoring.

This chapter is about how to avoid these problems.

THE FOUNDATIONS OF ASSESSMENT QUALITY

To begin with, we need to think about two quality control factors that form the foundation of the appropriate use of essay assessment. First, certain realities of life in classrooms can and should contribute to your decision about when to use this option. You must know that the context is right.

Second, written response assessments represent the first of three assessment methods we will discuss over the next few chapters that are subjective, not just in their development, but this time, also in their scoring.

When to Use Essay Assessment

Essay assessment is not for every teacher and every classroom. First and most importantly, this method only works in situations where students are proficient in the English language (if that is the language of instruction) and as writers. Therefore, in the primary grades, when dealing with students with learning disabilities, or when students are not yet comfortable writing in English, for example, they will not be able to let you know whether they have mastered the material using this mode of communication.

In these cases, to gain access to accurate information, *you have no choice*—you need to change to another assessment method.

The other context factor to consider in applying essay assessment is time. Essay exercises are relatively easy to develop, as are scoring guides. But scoring takes time. For this reason, the more scorers you can involve, the easier it is to use this method. This becomes a factor in assessment FOR learning classrooms, where you can enlist your students as scorers of practice assessments while they are still learning. Of course, they must be trained to score accurately. But think about this. By engaging your students as partners in learning to apply practice scoring guides you are helping them master valued learning targets. Assessment for practice—assessment FOR learning. Just remember, at the end of the learning when a grade is to be assigned, it's not time for student involvement. You, or another qualified teacher, must be the evaluator.

Understanding Reliability: The Role of Judgment in Scoring

You will recall that reliable assessments produce consistent results. The danger here is that two teachers subjectively judging the same piece of student work could assign different scores. If this happens we see evidence of inconsistency; that is, of unreliability.

We all have heard of studies in which student essays are scored by many different teachers who assigned vastly different scores. Often this is used as an indictment of this method of assessment as inevitably producing unreliable results. This blanket condemnation is unjust. What these stories actually depict is a bad application of a potentially useful assessment option. When essay scorers are trained to apply high-quality scoring guides dependably essay scoring can be very reliable. Assessments that rely on teachers' professional judgments to evaluate student achievement can produce valid and reliable results leading to effective instruction if we anticipate potential problems and work to eliminate them. In other words, subjectivity of assessment need not be a source of inaccuracy.

In the case of essay assessment, as with any form of assessment, the responsibility for avoiding problems and for ensuring quality rests squarely with you, the teacher. Those who thoroughly comprehend the content and patterns of reasoning to be assessed are in an excellent position to plan exercises and scoring procedures that fit the valued learning targets. It is only through developing and using strong exercises and appropriate scoring criteria that you may avoid errors of measurement attributable to evaluator or rater bias. This chapter is about how to accomplish this.

MATCHING METHOD TO TARGETS

Remember, a valid assessment accurately reflects the desired learning. Essay assessments have a potential contribution to make in assessing key dimensions of student learning in all four categories of valued achievement targets—knowledge, reasoning, performance skills, and products.

Assessing Knowledge and Understanding

Most experts advise caution in using essay responses to assess student mastery of subject matter knowledge; that is, when the targets are specific facts or concepts students are to learn. The primary reason is that we have better options at our disposal for tapping this kind of target. Selected response assessment formats provide a more efficient means of assessment that, at the same time, allow for a more precise sampling of this particular kind of achievement.

Selected response test formats are more efficient than essays in this case for two reasons. First, as we have said previously, you can ask more multiple-choice questions than essay questions per unit of testing time because multiple-choice response time is so much shorter. So, you can provide a broader sample of performance per unit of time with selected response items than with essay exercises. Second, scoring selected response items is much faster than scoring essays.

Nevertheless, you can use the essay format for assessing student mastery of content knowledge in certain contexts. Let us explain.

Sometimes, the achievement standards we hold as important for students to master larger interrelated structures of knowledge. For example, we might want students to understand how the parts of a particular ecosystem in science interact with one another. It is the *relationships among ideas* that are key. An essay assessment can fit here. Or consider this exercise from a biology course final on the water cycle:

> *Describe how evaporation and condensation operate in the context of the water cycle. Be sure to include all key elements in the cycle and how they relate to one another. (20 points)*

One of the most common complaints about selected response assessment is that it compartmentalizes learning too much—students demonstrate mastery of discrete bits of knowledge but need not integrate them into a larger whole. Students familiar with and expecting essay assessments learn that such integration is important.

Assessing Reasoning

One very important strength of written responses resides in their ability to provide windows into student reasoning. At assessment time, we can present novel problems that ask learners to bring together their subject matter knowledge, understanding, and reasoning skills to find a solution. In instances where we cannot directly observe knowledge application or can't see the mental process of reasoning unfold, we can ask students to describe the results of their reasoning in their essays. From this, we infer the state of their understanding and their ability to use it in problem-solving contexts.

We can ask them to analyze, compare, draw and defend inferences, and/or think critically in virtually any subject matter area. Furthermore, we can pose problems that require integrating material from two or more subjects and/or applying more than one pattern of reasoning. The key question here would be, Do students know how and when to use the knowledge they have at their disposal to reason and solve problems? Here is an example from a "science, technology, and society" course taught by a middle school teacher:

> *Using what you know about the causes of air pollution in cities, propose two potentially useful solutions. Analyze each in terms of its strengths and weaknesses. (20 points)*

Remember, however, the keys to success in assessing student reasoning with essays are the same as the keys to success with selected response:

1. Assessors must begin with a highly refined vision of each relevant reasoning pattern.
2. Assessors must know how to translate that vision into clear, focused essay exercises and proper scoring criteria.

3. The exercises must present problems to students that are new at the time of the assessment (i.e., problems for which students must figure out a response on the spot).

Assessing Performance Skills

If our valued achievement target holds that students become proficient in demonstrating specific performance skills, then there is only one acceptable way to assess proficiency: performance assessment. We must observe actual demonstration and judge its quality. For instance, say we want to find out if students can perform certain complex behaviors, such as participating collaboratively in a group or reading aloud fluently in primary grades, communicating orally in a second language, debating a controversial issue in social studies, or carrying out the steps in a science experiment. In these cases, standards of sound assessment require that we give students the opportunity to demonstrate group participation skills, speak the language, debate, or conduct an actual lab experiment.

You cannot use essay responses to tap these kinds of performances. However, there are some related targets that we can tap with the essay format. For instance, we can use the essay to assess mastery of some of the complex knowledge, understanding, and even reasoning proficiencies prerequisite to performing the skill in question. For example, if students do not know and understand the functions of different pieces of science lab equipment, there is no way that they will successfully complete the lab work. We could devise an essay question to see if they have mastered that prerequisite knowledge and understanding. Thus, we could use the written response format to assess student attainment of some of the building blocks on their way up the scaffolding to skillful performance. Clearly these would represent assessments FOR learning.

Assessing Product Development Capabilities

In this case, if we wish to infer students' level of achievement based on the attributes of a complex achievement-related product that they create, the only high-fidelity way to assess the outcome is to have them actually create the product. Only then can we determine if it meets established standards of quality. This requires a product-based performance assessment.

However, as with skills, during the learning essay responses can provide insights into student mastery of prerequisite knowledge and reasoning targets that underpin the ability to create quality products. For instance, they can tell us whether students know and understand the attributes of or steps in the process of creating a quality product—fundamental prerequisite knowledge. The results of such an essay assessment will be useful in a classroom context where we are working on building the foundations of competence.

Assessing Student Writing as a Product

When we ask students to create samples of their writing, we can evaluate the quality of their work using several different performance criteria. It is important that you understand the differences among them to prevent confusion among your students.

For example, in the essay assessment context such as the one we are addressing in this chapter, we will focus on students' expression of ideas, where the *content* of the response that comes under the microscope. In this case, we establish exercise-specific criteria that reflect students' demonstration of content mastery and the quality of the reasoning presented.

In addition, however, we could evaluate students' writing proficiency with respect to matters of *form*. In this instance, our criteria reflect standards related to word choice, sentence fluency, organization, mechanics and the like. These would be important when instruction centers on the attributes of good writing.

Third, we can evaluate the quality of students' *reasoning* as depicted in their written product. If we were to do so, the rubrics associated with patterns of reasoning presented Chapter 3 would need to be brought to bear.

So in any essay context, you have choices. You can focus your evaluation on quality of content, quality of writing, or appropriateness of reasoning. Which you choose must be function of the focus of the standard or classroom learning target you are developing the assessment exercises and scoring guides to reflect. In any essay context, what's the name of your game? Content mastery, writing proficiency, reasoning proficiency or some combination? Your scoring guide(s) must reflect your answer and your students must know what counts from the very beginning of instruction. Make sure instruction helps them understand and learn to apply whichever standards of essay quality are relevant in that context.

Summary of Target Matches

On the whole, essay assessment is a very flexible option. It can provide useful information on a variety of targets. We can use it to evaluate student mastery of larger structures of knowledge, whether learned outright or retrieved through the use of reference materials. We certainly can tap student reasoning and problem-solving skills. We can assess mastery of the complex procedural knowledge that is prerequisite to skilled performance and/or the creation of quality products. Table 6.1 provides a quick summary.

TABLE 6.1
Essay Assessment of Achievement Targets

Target to Be Assessed	Essay
Knowledge & Understanding	Essay exercises can tap understanding of relationships among elements of knowledge
Reasoning Proficiency	Written descriptions of complex problem solutions can provide a window into reasoning proficiency
Performance Skills	Essays can assess mastery of the knowledge prerequisites to skillful performance, but cannot rely on these to tap the skill itself
Ability to Create Products	Essays can assess writing proficiency and mastery of the knowledge necessary to create other products

DEVELOPING ESSAY ASSESSMENTS

Designing and developing these assessments involves three steps:

1. Assessment planning
2. Exercise development
3. Scoring guide development

Test planning for this form of assessment is very much like planning selected response assessments. While exercise development is a bit easier, scoring preparation is much more challenging.

Preliminary Practice Exercise

Before we launch into this section on developing sound essay assessments please prepare for it by taking a few minutes to draft an essay exercise that could appear on a final exam on one of the first four chapters of this book—an exercise that asks respondents to describe the relationships among the keys to assessment quality, the link of assessment purpose to quality, the link of clear targets to quality, or target–method match. Also, draft a scoring guide for your exercise. Be sure both your exercise and scoring guide are as complete as you can make them. Please complete these tasks now, before reading on. If you try this before learning some of the intricacies of essay development, it will provide you with an experience base from which to understand the design suggestions offered. Keep these drafts handy and refer to them as we discuss procedures for developing and scoring essay assessments.

Assessment Planning

The challenge, as always, is to begin with clearly articulated achievement standards—in this case, key components of knowledge, reasoning, or writing. Consider this example from elementary literature:

> *The student will be able to analyze a piece of literature to understand its component parts and how they relate to one another.*

We can deconstruct this valued achievement standard into this set of classroom learning targets capturing and communicating to students from the beginning of instruction the meaning of academic success:

- Students will be able to describe the settings, characters, and plots of the stories (knowledge target).
- Students will be able to find similarities and differences in settings, plots, and characters (comparative reasoning).
- Students will be able to carry out a systematic evaluation of the quality of the stories (evaluative reasoning).

These, then, can be translated into student-friendly versions ("I can" statements) as needed and shared with learners as they begin their learning. And, of course, they can become the focus of essay exercises both for practice and accountability as we work through various pieces of literature. As is always the case, the starting place for clear expectations is high-quality achievement standards.

Exercise Development

One of Rick's graduate students once described an exercise he received on a final exam at the end of his undergraduate studies. His major was Spanish language, literature, and culture. His last final was an in-class essay exam with a 3-hour time limit. The entire exam consisted of one exercise, which posed the challenge in only two words: "Discuss Spain."

Many of us have had experienced questions like this. One of the advantages often listed for essay tests relative to other test formats is that exercises are much easier to develop. We submit that many users turn that advantage into a liability by assuming that "easier to develop" means they don't have to put much thought into it, as in the above example.

To succeed with this assessment format, we must invest thoughtful preparation time in writing exercises that challenge respondents by describing a single complete and novel task. Sound essay exercises do three things:

1. Specify the knowledge students are supposed to command in preparing a response. For example:

   During the term, we have discussed both the evolution of Spanish literature and the changing political climate in Spain during the twentieth century.

2. Identify any reasoning patterns or problem-solving strategies respondents are to carry out; that is, what respondents are to write about. For example:

   During the term, we have discussed both the evolution of Spanish literature and the changing political climate in Spain during the twentieth century. Analyze these two dimensions of life in Spain, citing three instances where literature and politics may have influenced each other. Describe the mutual influences in specific terms.

3. Point the direction to an appropriate response without giving away the answer. Good exercises literally list the key elements of a good response without cueing the unprepared examinee on how to succeed. For example:

   During the term, we have discussed both the evolution of Spanish literature and the changing political climate in Spain during the twentieth century. Analyze these two dimensions of life in Spain, citing three instances where literature and politics may have influenced each other. Describe the mutual influences in specific terms. In planning your response, think about what we learned about prominent novelists, political satirists, and prominent political figures of Spain. (5 points per instance, total = 15 points.)

Let's analyze the content of the following example:

Assume you are a French teacher with many years of teaching experience. You place great value on the development of speaking proficiency as an outcome of your instruction. Therefore, you rely heavily on assessments where you listen to and evaluate performance. But a problem has arisen. Parents of students who attained very high scores on your written tests are complaining that their children are receiving lower grades on their report cards. The principal wants to be sure your judgments of student proficiency are sound and so has asked you to explain and defend your procedures. Describe at least three specific quality standards that your oral proficiency exams would need to meet for you to be confident that your exams truly reflect what students can do; provide the rationale for each. (2 points for each procedure and rationale, total = 6 points.)

Here's the challenge to respondents in a nutshell:

Demonstrate understanding of:	Performance assessment methodology
By using it to figure out:	Proper applications of the method in a specific context
Adhering to these standards:	Include three appropriate procedures and defend them

Time for Reflection

Please return to the essay exercise you developed at the beginning of this section of the chapter. Did you specify the knowledge respondents must use, kinds(s) of reasoning they must employ, and standards they must apply? Adjust your exercise as needed to meet these standards.

Another excellent way to check the quality of your essay exercises is to try to write or outline a high-quality response yourself. If you can, you probably have a properly focused exercise. If you cannot, it needs work. Besides, this process will serve you well in your next step, devising scoring criteria.

Figure 6.2 presents a checklist of factors to think about as you devise essay exercises. Answering these questions should assist you in constructing effective, high-quality essay exercises—those that avoid bias and distortion.

In regard to the last point in Figure 6.2, don't offer choices: The assessment question should always be, "Can you hit the agreed-on target?" It should never be, "Which part of the agreed-on target are you most confident that you can hit?" This latter question creates a sampling problem. It will always leave you uncertain about whether students have in fact mastered the material covered in exercises not selected, some of which may be crucial to later learning. When students select their own sample of performance, it can be a biased one.

We have one final idea to offer for exercise development. Let's say you wish to use the essay format to assess reasoning skills, but you do not expect your students to learn the content outright. Turn to the interpretive exercise format here. Provide the knowledge needed to solve the problem as part of the exercise (as a chart, graph, table, or

_____ Do exercises call for brief, focused responses?

_____ Are they written at the lowest possible reading level? Double check at the time of administration to ensure understanding—especially among poor readers.

_____ Do you have the confidence that qualified experts in the field would agree with your definition of a sound response? This is a judgment call.

_____ Would the ingredients in your scoring criteria be obvious to good students?

_____ Have you presented one set of exercises to all respondents? Don't offer optional questions from which to choose.

FIGURE 6.2
Factors to Consider when Devising Essay Exercises

passage of connected discourse) and then see if they can use it appropriately by spinning an essay or essays out of the material presented.

Whether we seek extended or short answers to essay exercises, we must conduct our scoring with clearly articulated evaluative criteria in mind. We go there next.

Think Assessment FOR Learning

But before we do, remember, you can engage students in devising practice essay exercises like those that will appear on a future assessment of learning. This will help them learn to center on important content and will require that they become sufficiently comfortable with your valued patterns of reasoning so that they can build them into practice exercises. If they write such exercises, trade with classmates, and write practice responses, both you and they gain access to useful information on what they are and are not mastering on their journey to meeting standards.

Developing Essay Scoring Procedures

Some teachers score written responses by applying what we call "floating standards," in which you wait to see what responses you get to decide what you wanted. This represents the ultimate in unsound assessment practice.

In that regard, we hope you will adhere to the instructional and assessment philosophy that has guided everything we have discussed up to this point: *Students can succeed in reality and in their own minds only if they understand what it means to succeed.* State the meaning of success up front, design instruction to help students succeed, and devise and use assessments that reflect that vision of success. That includes formulating essay scoring criteria in advance and holding yourself and your students accountable for attaining those standards.

The scoring of an essay response represents a classic example of one of the most important reasoning patterns that we discussed in Chapter 3: evaluative reasoning. In evaluative reasoning, you will recall, one makes a judgment about something and defends it through the logical application of specified criteria. Theater critics evaluate plays according to certain (rarely agreed-on!) criteria and publish their reviews in the newspaper. Movie critics give thumbs up or down (an evaluative judgment) and use their criteria to explain why.

These are exactly the kinds of evaluative judgments teachers must make about responses to essay exercises. In all cases, the key to success is the clear articulation of appropriate evaluation criteria.

First, Evaluate What, Exactly?

When a student writes an essay, we established earlier, we can judge three different qualities of that work. We can evaluate whether the work conveys accurate knowledge and understanding, uses that knowledge in a manner that represents sound reasoning, or manifests the characteristics of effective written communication. The first two focus on substance, while the latter centers on matters of form. In this chapter, we will describe how one goes about evaluating the substance or content of essays: accuracy of knowledge and quality of reasoning. A rubric for evaluating the writing quality is provided in the next chapter on performance assessment.

A parallel way to think of essay scoring is to see that, when we judge the student's presentation of knowledge and understanding, the scoring guide will be task specific. That is, each essay task focuses attention on mastery of a particular segment of content.

The respondent demonstrates mastery of that domain. But when our criteria focus on the quality of student reasoning, we can apply generic scoring guides reflective of the proper representation of reasoning patterns regardless of content context. Comparative or analytical reasoning, for example, play out in a consistent form across applications. The Chapter 3 reasoning rubrics are descriptive of these.

The key to student success is to be sure they know which set of criteria will come into play in any particular essay assessment and that they be provided with lots of guided practice in hitting those targets during instruction leading up to the final assessment OF learning.

Scoring Options

Typically, we convey evaluative judgments about essay quality in terms of the number of points students attain. Here are two acceptable ways to do this, the checklist and scoring rubrics. Please note that scoring guides in essay assessment are exercise specific. That is, you create a separate and specific scoring guide for each new exercise, being sure to focus on keys to success in that specific context.

The Checklist. We award points when specific ingredients appear in students' answers. The previous French teacher example (expanded in Figure 6.3) provides an

---

Sample Essay Exercise:

Assume you are a French teacher with many years of teaching experience. You place great value on the development of speaking proficiency as an outcome of your instruction. Therefore, you rely heavily on assessments where you listen to and evaluate performance. But a problem has arisen. Parents of students who attained very high scores on your written tests are complaining that their children are receiving lower grades on their report cards. The principal wants to be sure your judgments of student proficiency are sound and so has asked you to explain and defend your procedures. Describe at least three specific quality standards that your oral proficiency exams would need to meet for you to be confident that your exams truly reflect what students can do; provide the rationale for each. (2 points for each procedure and rationale, total = 6 points.)

Score Responses as Follows:

2 points if the response lists any of these six procedures and defends each as a key to conducting sound performance assessments:

- Specify clear performance criteria
- Sample performance over several exercises
- Apply systematic rating procedures
- Maintain complete and accurate records
- Use published performance assessments to verify results of classroom assessments
- Use multiple observers to corroborate

Also award 2 points if the response lists any of the following and defends them as attributes of sound assessments:

- Specifies a clear instructional objective
- Relies on a proper assessment method
- Samples performance well
- Controls for sources of rater bias

All other responses receive no points.

FIGURE 6.3
Sample Essay Exercise and Scoring Guide

example of this kind of scoring. The scoring guide calls for respondents to cover certain material. They receive points for each key point they cover. Here is the scoring guide again:

2 points if the student's response lists any of these six procedures and defends each as a key to conducting sound performance assessments:

- Specify clear performance criteria.
- Sample performance over several exercises.
- Apply systematic rating procedures.
- Maintain complete and accurate records.
- Use published performance assessments to verify results of classroom assessments.
- Use multiple observers to corroborate.

Also award 2 points if the response lists any of the following and defends them as attributes of sound assessments:

- Specifies a clear instructional objective
- Relies on a proper assessment method
- Samples performance well
- Controls for sources of rater bias

All other responses receive no points.

Essay Scoring Rubrics. In this case, we define achievement in terms of one or more performance continua. For example, a 3-point rating scale might define three levels of mastery of the required material and we would apply that scale to each student's response. Here's an example:

3   The response is clear, focused, and accurate. Relevant points are made (in terms of the content expectations or kinds of reasoning sought by the exercise) with good support (derived from the content to be used, again as spelled out in the exercise). Good connections are drawn and important insights are evident.

2   The answer is clear and somewhat focused, but not compelling. Support of points made is limited. Connections are fuzzy, leading to few important insights.

1   The response misses the point, contains inaccurate information, or otherwise demonstrates lack of mastery of the material. Points are unclear, support is missing, and/or no insights are included.

Some teachers devise such scoring rubrics to apply in a "holistic" manner, as in this example. In this case, one overall judgment captures the teacher's evaluation of the essay. Other times teachers devise multiple "analytical" scales for the same essay, permitting them to evaluate the content coverage of the response separately from other important features. The idea is to develop as many such scales as needed to evaluate the particular material you are rating. Criteria for ratings, for example, might include these factors:

- Demonstrated mastery of content
- Organization of ideas
- Soundness of the reasoning demonstrated

Whether using holistic or analytical scoring, however, the more specific and focused the criteria, the more dependable will be the results.

- Set *realistic expectations and performance standards* that are consistent with instruction and that promise students some measure of success if they are prepared.
- Check scoring guides against a few real responses to see if any *last-minute adjustments* are needed.
- *Refer back to scoring guidelines* regularly during scoring to maintain consistency.
- *Score all responses to one exercise* before moving on to the next exercise. This does two things: It promotes consistency in your application of standards, and speeds up the scoring process.
- Score all responses to one exercise *in one sitting without interruption* to keep a clear focus on standards.
- Evaluate responses *separately for matters of content (knowledge mastery and reasoning) and matters of form (i.e., writing proficiency).* They require the application of different criteria.
- Provide feedback in the form of *points and written commentary* if possible.
- If possible, keep the *identity of the respondent anonymous* when scoring. This keeps your knowledge of their prior performance from influencing current judgments.
- Although it is often difficult to arrange, try to have *two independent qualified readers score* the papers. In a sense, this represents the litmus test of the quality of your scoring scheme. If two readers generally agree on the level of proficiency demonstrated by the respondent, then you have evidence of relatively objective or dependable subjective scoring. But if you and a colleague disagree on the level of performance demonstrated, you have uncovered evidence of problems in the appropriateness of the criteria or the process used to train raters, and some additional work is in order. When very important decisions rest on a student's score on an essay assessment, such as promotion or graduation, double scoring is absolutely essential.

FIGURE 6.4
Guidelines for Essay Scoring

In addition to these essay scoring guidelines, experts urge that you adhere to the additional principles outlined in Figure 6.4 as you develop and apply scoring procedures.

Time for Reflection

Please return to the scoring plan you developed for your exercise at the beginning of this discussion. Did you devise a clear and appropriate set of standards? Adjust them as needed.

Think Assessment FOR Learning

Because essay assessment scoring guides must be task specific—that is, unique to each exercise—we can't provide students with copies of those particular scoring guides in advance of a final exam, as that would defeat the purpose.

However, you can involve them with designing sample scoring guides for practice exercises like those that might appear on the final. Or, you can provide sample exercises and have students practice developing scoring guides for them. Further, they can practice scoring the content of each other's practice responses to those exercises. Further, we can provide students with lots of practice in applying generic reasoning or writing rubrics in writing essay responses and in evaluating their own and each other's practice responses.

Potential Sources of Problems	Counteraction
Lack of target clarity:	
• Underlying knowledge unclear	Carefully study the material to be mastered and outline the knowledge structures to assess.
• Patterns of reasoning unspecified	Define forms of reasoning to be assessed in clear terms.
Wrong target for essay	Limit use to assessing mastery of larger knowledge structures (where several parts must fit together) and complex reasoning.
Lack of writing proficiency on part of respondents	Select another assessment method or help them become proficient writers.
Inadequate sample of exercises	Select a representative sample of sufficient length to give you confidence, given your table of specifications.
Poor-quality exercises	Follow guidelines specified above.
Poor-quality scoring:	
• Inappropriate criteria	Redefine criteria to fit the content and reasoning expected.
• Unclear criteria	Prepare explicit expectations—in writing.
• Untrained rater	Prepare all who are to apply the scoring criteria.
• Insufficient time to read and rate	Find more raters (see Figure 6.6 for ideas), or use another method.

FIGURE 6.5
Anticipating and Countering Sources of Invalidity and Unreliability

By repeating this process as you proceed through a unit of study, you can provide students with opportunities to watch themselves improving. Assessment FOR learning. Then at final exam time, you can present them with novel reasoning or writing exercises to see if they can put their practice into action. Assessment OF learning.

BARRIERS TO SOUND ESSAY ASSESSMENT

To summarize, you can do many things to cause a student's score on an essay test to represent that student's real level of achievement with a high degree of accuracy. Potential sources of mismeasurement appear in Figure 6.5, along with action you can take to prevent or remedy them.

STUDENT INVOLVEMENT IN ESSAY ASSESSMENT

With all assessment methods, the first and most obvious way to integrate assessment into teaching and learning by making sure our students have the opportunity to learn what our standards expect and our assessments reflect. Beyond this essential perspective, Figure 6.6 summarizes and supplements our list of ways to integrate assessment with instruction by involving students as partners in assessing their own and each other's achievement. *Please study this list very carefully!*

- As with selected response assessment, develop a blueprint for an essay test before ever teaching a unit, share that plan with students, and keep track of how well instruction is preparing them to succeed on the exam.

- Present students with unlabeled essay exercises and have them practice fitting them into the content and reasoning cells of the table of specifications.

- Have students join in on the process of writing sample exercises. To do so, they will need to begin to sharpen their focus on the intended knowledge and reasoning targets—as they do this, good teaching is happening! Be careful, though; these might best be used as examples for practice. Remember, to assess student reasoning, the exercises that actually appear on a final test must present novel problems.

- Give students some sample exercises and have them evaluate their quality as test exercises, given the test blueprint.

- Have students play a role in developing the scoring criteria for some sample exercises. Give them, for example, an excellent response and a poor-quality response to a past essay exercise and have them figure out the differences.

- Bring students into the actual scoring process, thus spreading the work over more shoulders! Form scoring teams, one for each exercise on a test. Have them develop scoring criteria under your watchful eye. Offer them advice as needed to generate appropriate criteria. Then have them actually score some essays, which you double check. Discuss differences in scores assigned. Students find this kind of workshop format very engaging.

- Have students predict their performance in each cell in the table of specifications or objectives and then compare their prediction with the actual score. Were they in touch with their own achievement?

- Save essays and scoring criteria for reuse. A personal computer can help with this. If you keep information on student performance on each exercise (say, average score), you can adjust instruction next time to try to improve learning.

- Exchange, trade, or compare tables of specifications and/or exercises and scoring criteria with other teachers to ease the workload associated with assessment development.

FIGURE 6.6
Ideas for Student-Involved Assessment

But be advised that this list is intended merely to prime your mental pump. This list of ways to bring students into the assessment equation is as limitless as your imagination. Please reflect and experiment with other ways. These uses of essay assessment help make learning targets clear to learners, help learners make smart decisions about how to advance their own learning, keep students believing that success is within reach, and provide them and us with evidence of ultimate learning success. These strategies serve to remove the mystery surrounding the meaning of good performance on an essay and in the classroom. They put students in control of their own academic well-being.

Summary: Tapping the Potential of Essay Assessment

In this chapter, we have explored ways to tap the considerable power of essay assessment. We must avoid validity and reliability problems that can arise with naïve use. We began by exploring the prominent roles subjectivity and professional judgment play in essay assessment. This method carries with it dangers of bias. We studied specific ways to prevent these dangers from becoming realities. One is to connect essay assessment to appropriate kinds of achievement targets. These include mastery of complex structures of knowledge, complex reasoning processes, and some of the knowledge foundations of skill and product proficiencies.

However, the heart of the matter with respect to valid and reliable assessment is adherence to specific assessment development procedures. We studied these in three parts: assessment planning, exercise development, and preparation to score. In each case, we reviewed specific procedural guidelines.

In addition, we considered an array of strategies to engage students as full partners in assessment, from design and development of exercises, to scoring, to interpreting and using essay assessment results. These strategies connect assessment to teaching and learning in ways that can maximize both students' motivation to learn and their actual achievement.

Final Chapter Reflection

1. *What are the three most important new insights to come to you as a result of your study of this chapter?*
2. *Which of your previous questions about assessment can you now answer based on your study of this chapter?*
3. *What new questions have come to mind as a result of your study of this chapter—questions that you hope to have answered as your study continues?*

Practice with Chapter 6 Ideas

1. Critique for quality the following three essay examples:

Essay 1: Label the Graph

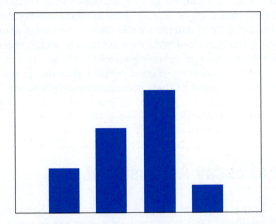

This question is intended for grades 3–12. It is one of six exercises using different content to assess problem solving in mathematics. Results will be used to track individual student progress toward mastery of state content standards. The scoring criteria have four traits, each scored separately by trained raters—conceptual understanding, mathematical procedures, strategic reasoning, and communication in mathematics. Students may or may not see the criteria, depending on the teacher.

1. What might this be the graph of? Put titles and numbers on the graph to show what you mean.
2. Write down everything you know from your graph.

Essay 2: Day and Night.*

The following task is intended for grade 2 to assess science understanding.

"Everyone knows about day and night. Write what you think makes day and night."

---

*Australian Council for Educational Research Ltd., *Exemplary Assessment Materials—Science*, 1996, p. 16. Available from The Board of Studies, 15 Pelham St., Carlton, Victoria 3053.

Essay 3: Emerson Quiz.[**]

This quiz is intended for grades 10–12 to assess mastery of content knowledge (knowledge of Emerson) and reasoning in literature. Results will be used as 10 percent of the final grade in a literature class. [One of the essay questions follows. No scoring mechanism is described.]

"Read each of the statements below and put a check if Emerson would most likely complete the activity or put an X if he would disagree or not do the listed activity. For each answer, find a statement from Emerson's work to support your check or X. Be sure to quote the statement directly and give the page number in parentheses. Use the introduction to Emerson, *Nature,* and 'Self Reliance.'"

1. _____ reject organized religion
2. _____ look to the past for guidance

[**]From Thomas Mavor, 1999, Brother Martin High School, 4401 Elysian Fields Ave., New Orleans, LA 70122.

3. _____ claim that religious truth comes from intuition
4. _____ rely on others for his success and happiness
5. _____ join a popular "civic organization"

2. Select a body of content you are learning as a student in another class or use the content of this chapter. Write three essay exercises that tap key content or reasoning dimensions of that material. When you have done so, review the list and defend your judgment that these represent the most important learnings from this chapter.

3. Devise scoring guides for each exercise, being sure they adhere to guidelines presented in this chapter.

4. Retrieve an example of an assessment that you have taken in the past that includes essay exercises. Using the rubrics found in Appendix B, along with the more specific guidelines provided in this chapter, evaluate the assessment for quality. Write a focused critique.

CHAPTER 7

Performance Assessment

CHAPTER FOCUS

This chapter answers the following guiding question:

> When and how do I use performance assessment most effectively?

When you are sure your assessment purpose is clear and the learning target in question is reasoning proficiency, performance skills, or product development capabilities you can turn to performance assessment as your method. But to do so, you will need to understand the following:

1. Performance assessments are developed in two steps: (1) define performance criteria, and (2) develop performance tasks or exercises.
2. This method can fall prey to problematic sources of bias that can distort results if users are not careful.
3. By involving your students in developing and using performance assessments, you can set them up for energetic and successful learning.

As we start this part of our journey, keep our big picture in mind. Figure 7.1 crosses our achievement targets with the four modes of assessment. In this chapter, we will be dealing in depth with the shaded areas.

ASSESSMENT BASED ON OBSERVATION AND PROFESSIONAL JUDGMENT

Performance assessments involve students in activities that require them actually to demonstrate performance of certain skills or to create products that demonstrate mastery of certain standards of quality. In this case, we observe their performance while it happens or examine their products.

As with essay assessments, we judge level of achievement by comparing each student's performance to predetermined levels of proficiency. Our goal is to make these subjective judgments as objective (free of bias) as possible. We accomplish this by devising and learning to apply clear and appropriate performance continuums that describe the range of quality from poor to very good.

Table 7.1 lists examples of achievement targets that lend themselves to performance assessment. Notice that nearly all academic disciplines include both skills and

	SELECTED RESPONSE	ESSAY	PERFORMANCE ASSESSMENT	PERSONAL COMMUNICATION
Knowledge				
Reasoning				
Performance Skills				
Products				
Dispositions				

FIGURE 7.1
Aligning Achievement Targets and Assessment Methods

products for which we might establish performance criteria in order to observe and judge proficiency. But to assess them accurately, we must be careful to zero in on the right standards of excellent performance. This chapter is about how to do this.

Our goals for this chapter are to describe and illustrate a basic performance assessment design structure and process and to reveal the power of student involvement in their use.

TABLE 7.1
Achievement Targets for Performance Assessment

Focus of Assessment	Process or Skill Target	Product Target
Reading	Oral reading fluency	
Writing	Cursive writing skill; keyboarding	Samples of writing
Mathematics	Manipulate objects to form sets	Model depicting math principle
Science	Lab safety procedures	Lab research report
Social Studies	Debate	Term paper
Foreign Language	Oral fluency	Sample of writing
Art	Use of materials	Artistic creation
Physical Education	Athletic performance	
Technical Education	Computer operation	Software system designed
Vocational Education	Following prescribed procedures	Effectively repaired machine
Teamwork	Each member's contribution	
Early Childhood	Social interaction skill	Artistic creation

The Promise and Perils of Performance Assessment

When we want to hear music in its truest form, we go to the hall where it is being performed. So it is with performance assessment. To evaluate achievement in its truest form, we ask students to perform live so we can observe and judge it. We evaluate public speaking proficiency, oral proficiency with a foreign language, musical performance, or writing proficiency, for example.

As with essay assessment, subjectivity brings the risk of biased judgments. So we must plan for thorough preparation and attention to detail to attain appropriate levels of performance assessment rigor. Adhere to the standards of assessment quality spelled out in earlier chapters when developing performance assessment and you can add immensely to the quality and utility of your classroom assessments. Begin assessment development with a clear purpose and clear learning targets. Devise a proper sample of performance tasks and develop quality scoring rubrics, while attending to relevant sources of bias. This chapter guides you down that path.

Time for Reflection

Can you think of instances in everyday life (outside of school) where performance assessment comes into play as a matter of routine, for example, when we observe and evaluate using criteria? Please share your examples with your classmates to see the diversity of applications. Across these various examples, what are the keys to doing this well?

THE FOUNDATIONS OF QUALITY

Once again in this case, as with selected response and essay assessment, we begin by identifying certain realities of life in classrooms that can and should contribute to your decision about when to use this option. The context must be right for appropriate application and we must understand the role of professional judgment in creating and using performance assessments.

By now it is clear to you that you will want to turn to performance assessment for certain kinds of achievement targets. We will review those connections in greater detail in the next section. For now, suffice it to say that the range of possible applications is as broad as the list of subjects we address in school. Table 7.2 illustrates this point with more examples.

Further, you must be sure all students have equal access to the resources and equipment needed to succeed. This may mean that each student has access to necessary materials provided at school or at home. If they don't, then circumstances beyond their control keep them from succeeding, and that's not helpful for learning or fair.

Consider performance assessment only when there is time to conduct it. It is a labor-intensive method. The more performance tasks you need to administer, the longer it will take to administer and score. One solution to a time crunch during the learning (formative assessment time) is to involve more observers and evaluators such as, for example, your students. Think assessment FOR learning—student involvement.

Use performance assessment when you need an active, hands-on way to engage your students. Student-involved performance assessment can take your students right inside their learning so they can self-assess and remain aware of and in control of their

TABLE 7.2
Examples of Learning Targets Assessable Using Performance Assessment

Reading	**Reasoning**: Evaluate the validity of what is read. **Skill**: Read at a rate of 110 words per minute by the end of grade 2.
Writing	**Product**: Vary form, detail, and structure of writing in accordance with intended audience and purpose. **Product**: Use language that is precise, engaging, and well suited to the topic and audience.
Communication	**Skill**: Communicate using different forms of oral presentation. **Skill**: Use effective listening and speaking behaviors.
Mathematics	**Reasoning**: Recognize when an approach is unproductive and try a new approach. **Skill**: Accurately measure temperature, distance, weight, and height. **Reasoning/Skill**: Support a conclusion or prediction orally and in writing, using information in a table or graph. **Product**: Create three-dimensional objects.
Physical Science	**Skill**: Choose and use laboratory equipment properly to design and carry out an experiment.
History	**Product**: Organize and record information.
Geography	**Product**: Use data and a variety of symbols and colors to create thematic maps and graphs (e.g., patterns of population, rainfall, or economic features).
Social Studies	**Reasoning and Skills:** Give examples of and exhibit the behavior of good classroom citizens, including respect, kindness, self-control, cooperation, sharing common resources, and good manners. **Skill:** Use maps and globes to locate places referenced in stories and real-life situations.
The Arts	**Reasoning:** Compare and contrast artwork in terms of elements of design. **Product:** Organize art elements to develop a composition and to change the impact of a composition.
Health/Fitness	**Skill:** Wrestle. **Product:** Create and implement a health and fitness plan.
Shop	**Reasoning:** Diagnose car engine problems. **Product:** Make a functional object out of wood or metal.

Source: Modified from *Classroom Assessment FOR Student Learning: Doing It Right—Using It Well* (p. 196) by R. J. Stiggins, J. A. Arter, J. Chappuis, and S. Chappuis, 2004, Portland, OR: Assessment Training Institute. Copyright 2006, 2004 by Educational Testing Service. Reprinted by permission of Educational Testing Service, the copyright owner.

own progress over time. As this chapter unfolds, we will offer several specific suggestions for how to do this.

Performance Assessment Is a Matter of Judgment

Professional judgment guides every aspect of performance assessment design, development, and use. These judgments must be made carefully if assessment results are to be dependable.

For instance, as the developer or user of this method, you establish the achievement target you will assess based on priorities expressed in state and local achievement standards and benchmarks, your text materials, and the opinions of experts in the field. You devise the performance criteria, formulate performance tasks, and observe and evaluate student proficiency. Every step is a matter of your professional and subjective judgment. Just be sure your decisions are based on the best current thinking of experts in the subjects you teach.

Over the past decade, we have come to understand that carefully trained performance assessors—those who invest the clear thinking and developmental resources needed to do a good job—can use this subjective assessment methodology very effectively.

Understanding Reliability: Inter-Rater Agreement

Because of the subjective nature of performance assessment, you, the rater, become a potential source of bias. If the performance criteria you apply in evaluating student work are incorrect, imprecise, or influenced by factors unrelated to the student's actual achievement (such as gender, prior performance, etc.), the filters through which you see and evaluate that work can lead you to inaccurate judgments about proficiency.

To prevent this, we must do our homework: establish sound performance criteria and learn to apply them consistently. The gauge of consistency that we apply in such assessment contexts is that of *inter-rater agreement*. Performance criteria are being applied consistently when two raters evaluate the same piece of work using the same criteria and, without conversing about it, draw the same conclusion about the level of proficiency demonstrated in that work. Surely you can see that, if they disagree, the judgment of student proficiency would be a function of who does the judging, not the actual level of achievement. That would be unfair. Our goal always is to be so clear about the attributes of good performance and so crisp and clean in our description of levels of proficiency in the performance continuum that consistency in judgment will always be within reach. This theme of inter-rater reliability will come up repeatedly through the rest of the chapter.

MATCHING METHOD TO TARGETS

Performance assessment can provide dependable information about student achievement of some, but not all, kinds of valued targets. Let's examine the matches and mismatches with our targets: knowledge, reasoning, performance skills, and products.

Assessing Knowledge

If the objective is to have students master content knowledge, observing and judging complex performance or products that call for the use of that knowledge may not be the best way to find out if they succeeded. It's not that we can't assess knowledge and understanding with this method. Under certain conditions, we can. But other times we cannot. Here's why:

Performance assessments—where it's the doing that counts, for example—typically ask students to carry out some kind of relatively complex operation; in effect, their challenge is to demonstrate more than that they merely "know and understand"—they must apply their knowledge to a complex cognitive operation (application). Here are three examples: (1) Use what you know about automobile engines to tune up this engine—final judgment will focus on the engine when the student is done; (2) Use what you know about Spanish to converse with another about a topic of mutual interest— final judgment will turn on the actual quality of language use; (3) Use what you know to write a term paper or science lab report demonstrating proper use of that form—final judgment will be based on the quality of the paper. Success in each case certainly does arise from a key foundation of knowledge.

But do you see how success also requires more? If students perform well, we can infer that they knew what they needed to succeed. But a problem arises when they do poorly—was it due to insufficient knowledge or inept use of their knowledge? We don't know. How do we find out? Probably we ask strategic questions to determine the cause of the failure—we would turn to another assessment method. This is my point! Why go through a complex performance when all we want to find out is if they "know" or not? We have three better (simpler) method options: selected response, written response, or personal communication.

Assessing Reasoning

Performance assessment can provide a means of assessing student reasoning and problem-solving proficiency. We rely on outward manifestations of having reasoned well to infer proficiency. For example, give chemistry students unidentified substances to identify and watch how they go about setting up the apparatus and carrying out the study. The performance criteria would have to reflect the proper order of activities for conducting such experiments—an example of analytical reasoning. In this case, the reasoning process is as important as getting the right answer—the reasoning process is what you're assessing.

Student products also can provide insight into their reasoning proficiency. Consider the example in which students are to carry out a science experiment calling for them to draw and defend an inference or take a position on a controversial science and society social issue and defend it (evaluative reasoning) and prepare a written report. You would evaluate these reports in terms of the standards of a good report, if those criteria have been clearly and completely articulated. But in addition, the resulting products would be evaluated in terms of the students' reasoning by using rating scales (rubrics) such as those presented in Chapter 3. You would rely on a two-part set of performance criteria, one reflecting the proper structure of a report including criteria reflective of the quality of the reasoning demonstrated.

Assessing Performance Skills

The great strength of this methodology lies in its ability to provide a dependable means of evaluating skills as students demonstrate them. Communication skills such as speaking and oral reading fall in this category, as do the performing and industrial arts, physical education, and oral proficiency in speaking a foreign language. Observing students in action can be a rich and useful source of information about their attainment of very important forms of skill achievement.

TABLE 7.3
Performance Assessment of Achievement Targets

Target to Be Assessed	Performance
Knowledge & Understanding	Not a good choice for this target—three other options preferred
Reasoning Proficiency	Can watch students solve some problems or examine some products and infer about reasoning proficiency
Performance Skills	Can observe and evaluate skills as they are being performed
Ability to Create Products	Can assess: (1) proficiency in carrying out steps in product development (skill), and (2) attributes of the product itself

Assessing Products

Herein lies the other great strength of performance assessment. There are occasions when we ask students to create complex achievement-related products. The quality of those products indicates the creator's level of achievement. If we develop sound performance criteria that reflect the key attributes of these products and learn to apply those criteria well, performance assessment can serve us as both an efficient and effective tool. We can evaluate everything from written products, such as term papers and research reports, to the many forms of art and craft products, and science exhibitions and models in this way.

Summary of Target–Performance Assessment Matches

Table 7.3 provides a simple summary of the alignments among performance assessment and the various kinds of achievement that we expect of our students.

DEVELOPING PERFORMANCE ASSESSMENTS

We initiate our creation of performance assessments just as we initiated the development of paper and pencil methods in the previous two chapters: with a plan or blueprint. The performance assessment plan includes just two specific parts. Each part asks the developer to make several specific design decisions. We start by defining the performance(s) we wish to evaluate. Then we prepare tasks or assignments that we will use to elicit student performance so we may evaluate it. Figure 7.2 presents an overview of the design decisions we must make as performance assessment developers. The immense potential of this form of assessment becomes apparent when we consider all of the design combinations available within this structure.

As we explore, we will examine how one group of teachers selected from among the array of possibilities to find the design they needed to serve their purposes. Remember Emily, the student who opened Chapter 1? We will explore the assessment challenges

Design Ingredient	Options
Remember to articulate your purpose: Specify user(s) and use(s). Then:	
Design Step 1: Define Performance	
A. Type of performance	Skill target, product, or both Individual, group achievement, or both
B. Develop performance criteria	Articulate the keys to successful performance
	Prepare to score holistically, analytically, or a combination
Design Step 2: Develop Performance Tasks	
A. Task specification	Define target and conditions
B. Selecting a sample	Decide how many tasks are needed to cover the terrain

FIGURE 7.2
Performance Assessment Design Framework

that her English teacher faced as she endeavored to put Emily and her classmates in touch with their emerging proficiency as writers.

Remember to Never Lose Track of Your Purpose

Remember, regardless of the assessment method, you must begin any developmental sequence with a clear sense of why you are assessing. Different assessment users need different information in different forms at different times to inform their decisions.

For example, as we discuss how Ms. Weathersby and her colleagues used performance assessments of writing proficiency, bear in mind that they assessed for two reasons, or to serve two purposes:

1. To help their students become better writers (assessment FOR learning: students and teacher are users; they seek to understand strengths and weaknesses)
2. To gather information on improvement in student writing as part of the faculty's demonstration of the impact of their new instructional program (assessment OF learning: verify achievement for accountability purposes)

Defining Performance

The first challenge we face as performance assessment developers is that of defining our vision of academic success. Ms. W. and the English faculty at Emily's high school, for example, needed to stipulate what it meant to be a "good writer" within their program. In specifying the target, we must make two design decisions: What type of performance are we assessing? Specifically, what does good performance look like? Let's consider these in a bit more detail.

Selecting the Type of Performance

This design decision asks us to answer the following basic question: How will successful achievement manifest itself? The answer might be in a particular set of performance skills—behaviors that students must demonstrate. Examples include oral reading proficiency, working well with classmates in the primary grades, development of motor skills in physical education, or proficiency at public speaking. In all these instances, success manifests itself in student actions.

Or, proficiency might be revealed in something the learner creates—that is, in a particular kind of product which we then examine to find evidence of achievement. Consider, for example, art or craft products, term papers, models, or effectively repaired machines.

Note also, that some performance assessments might focus both on skills and products that result, such as when we first assess a student's skill at writing a computer program and then assess the quality of the resulting program as it runs.

The English faculty in Emily's school wanted to evaluate their students' writing proficiency, so they needed to see and make judgments about the quality of actual samples of student writing (products).

Developing Scoring Guides or Rubrics

This is the part of the performance assessment design where we describe what "counts." The challenge is to not only describe what "outstanding" performance looks like, but also to map each of the different levels of performance leading up to the highest levels. We must do this with both descriptive language and with examples of student work illustrating each level of proficiency. In this sense, rubrics provide the vocabulary and illustrations needed to communicate with our students about the path to successful performance.

In one sense, accomplished teachers are connoisseurs of good performance, but in another sense, they are far more than that. Connoisseurs can recognize outstanding performance when they see it. They know a good restaurant when they find it. They can select a fine wine. They know which movies deserve a thumbs-up and which Broadway plays are worth their ticket price. Connoisseurs also can describe why they believe something is outstanding or not. However, because the evaluation criteria may vary somewhat from reviewer to reviewer, their judgments may not always agree. For restaurants, wines, movies, and plays, the standards of quality are, in part, a matter of opinion. But, that's what makes interesting reading in newspapers and magazines.

Teachers are very much like these connoisseurs in that they too must be able to recognize and describe outstanding performance. But for accomplished teachers, there is much more. Not only can well-prepared teachers visualize and explain the meaning of success, but they also can impart that meaning to others so as to help them become outstanding performers. *In short, they don't just criticize—they inspire and guide improvement.*

In most disciplines, the standards of excellence that characterize high-quality performance are always those held by experts in the field of study in question. Outstanding teachers/classroom assessors are those who have immersed themselves in understanding those discipline-based meanings of proficiency. It is this depth of understanding that we must capture in our performance expectations so we can convey it to students through instruction, illustration, and practice. Our rubrics cannot exist only in our minds. We must translate them into student-friendly language, with examples, for our students, their parents, school leaders, and the community to see and understand.

Many fields of study already have developed outstanding examples of sound rubrics for critical performances. Examples include writing proficiency, foreign language, mathematics, and physical education, and we use these as illustrations throughout this text.

As it turns out, the vision of good writing—the rubrics or scoring criteria—adopted by the English faculty at Emily's high school came from the summer professional development session they attended and included a set of rating scales reflecting six dimensions of effective writing. The faculty's first challenge was to understand these standards of writing excellence themselves. Then they had to transform the performance criteria into student-friendly language. They elected to bring their students in as partners. We'll explain later how they did that. But in the meantime, their transformation appears in Figure 7.3. Please read it.

Ideas

5. My paper is clear, focused, and filled with details not everybody knows.
   - You can tell I know a lot about this topic.
   - My writing is full of interesting tidbits, but it doesn't overwhelm you.
   - I can sum up my main point in one clear sentence: _____
   - You can picture what I'm talking about. I *show* things happening *(Fred squinted)*; I don't just *tell* about them *(Fred couldn't read the small print).*

3. Even though my writing grabs your attention here and there, it could use some spicy details.
   - I know *just* enough about this topic—but more information would make it more interesting.
   - Some "details" are things most people probably already know.
   - My topic is too big. I'm trying to tell too much. Or else it's too skimpy.
   - It might be hard to picture what I'm talking about. Not enough *showing.*
   - I'm afraid my reader will get bored and go raid the refrigerator.

1. I'm just figuring out what I want to say.
   - I need a LOT more information before I'm really ready to write.
   - I'm still thinking on paper. What's my main idea?
   - I'm not sure *anyone* reading this could picture *anything.*
   - I wouldn't want to share this aloud. It's not ready.
   - Could I sum it up in one clear sentence? No way! It's a list of stuff.

Organization

5. My paper is as clear as a good road map. It takes readers by the hand and guides them along every step.
   - My beginning hints at what's coming, and makes you want to read on.
   - Every detail falls in just the right place.
   - Nothing seems out of order.
   - You never feel lost or confused; however, there could be a surprise or two.
   - Everything connects to my main point or main story.
   - My paper ends at just the right spot, and ties everything together.

3. You can begin to see where I'm headed. If you pay attention, you can follow along pretty well.
   - I have a beginning. Will my reader be completely hooked, though?
   - Most things fit where I have put them. I might move *some* things around.
   - Usually, you can see how one idea links to another.
   - I guess everything should lead up to the most important part. Let's see, *where* would that *be?*
   - My paper has an ending. But does it tie up loose ends?

1. Where are we headed? I'm lost myself.
   - A beginning? Well, I might have just repeated the assignment . . .
   - I didn't know where to go next, so I wrote the first thing that came to me.
   - I'm not really sure which things to include—or what order to put them in.
   - It's a collection of stuff—kind of like a messy closet!
   - An ending? I just stopped when I ran out of things to say.

FIGURE 7.3
Analytical Writing Assessment Rating Scales

Source: From *Creating Writers Through 6-Trait Writing Assessment and Instruction,* 4th ed. (pp. 166–171) by Vicki Spandel, 2005, Boston: Allyn & Bacon. Copyright © 2005 by Pearson Education. Adapted by permission of the publisher.

Voice

5. I have put my personal, recognizable stamp on this paper.
- You can hear my voice *booming* through. It's *me*.
- I care about this topic—and it shows.
- I speak right to my audience, always thinking of questions they may have.
- I wrote to please myself, too.
- My writing rings with confidence.

3. What I truly think and feel shows up sometimes.
- You might not laugh or cry when you read this, but you'll hang in there and finish reading.
- I'm right on the edge of finding my own voice—so *close!*
- My personality pokes out here and there. You *might* guess this was my writing.
- It's pleasant and friendly enough, but I didn't think about my audience *all* the time. Sometimes I just wanted to *get it over with!*

1. I did not put too much energy or personality into this writing.
- It could be hard to tell who wrote this. It could be anybody's.
- I kept my feelings in check.
- If I liked this topic better or knew more, I could put more life into it.
- Audience? *What* audience? I wrote to get it done.

Word Choice

5. I picked *just* the right words to express my ideas and feelings.
- The words and phrases I've used seem *exactly* right.
- My phrases are colorful and lively, yet nothing's overdone.
- I've used some everyday words in new ways. Expect a few surprises.
- Do you have a favorite phrase or two in here? I do.
- Every word is accurate. You won't find yourself wondering what I mean.
- Verbs carry the meaning. I don't bury my reader in adjectives.

3. It might not tweak your imagination, but hey, it gets the basic meaning across.
- It's functional and it gets the job done, but I can't honestly say I stretched.
- O.K., so there are some cliches hiding in the corners.
- I've also got a favorite phrase lurking around here *someplace*.
- Verbs? What's wrong with a good old *is, are, was, were. . .?*
- I might have overutilized the functionality of my thesaurus.
- You can understand it, though, right? Like, nothing's really wrong.

1. My reader might go, "Huh?"
- See, I'm like this victim of vague wording and fuzzy phrasing.
- It's, you know, kind of hard to get what I'm talking about. *I* don't even remember what I meant and *I wrote this stuff*.
- Maybe I misutilized a word or two.
- Some redundant phrases might be redundant.
- I need verby power.

FIGURE 7.3
(continued)

Sentence Fluency

5. My sentences are clear and varied—a treat to read aloud.
   - Go ahead—read it aloud. You won't need to practice.
   - Sentence variety is my middle name.
   - Hear the rhythm? Smooth, huh?
   - Deadwood has been cut. Every word counts.

3. My sentences are clear and readable.
   - My writing is *pretty* smooth and natural—you can get through it all right.
   - Some sentences should be joined together. Others might be cut in two.
   - There's a little deadwood, sure, but it doesn't bury the good ideas too badly under extra verbiage, even though I must say it won't hurt to cut some unneeded words here and there and shorten things up just a bit.
   - I guess I did get into a rut with sentence beginnings. I guess I could use more variety. I guess I'll fix that.

1. I admit it's a challenge to read aloud (even for me).
   - You might have to stop or reread now and then it just feels like one sentence picked up right in the middle of another a new sentence begins and, oh boy, I'm lost. . . Help! Untangle me!
   - My sentences all begin the same way. My sentences are all alike. My sentences need variety. My sentences need work.
   - Some sentences are too short. They're too short. They're really short. Way short. Short.
   - Reading this is like trying to skate on cardboard. Tough going!

Conventions

5. An editor would fall asleep looking for mistakes in this paper.
   - Capitals are all in the right places.
   - Paragraphs begin at the right spots.
   - Great punctuation—grammar, too.
   - My spelling (even of difficult words) would knock your socks off.
   - I made so few errors, it would be a snap getting this ready to publish.

3. Some bothersome mistakes show up when I read carefully.
   - Spelling is correct on simple words.
   - Capitals are O.k. maybe I should look again, Though.
   - The grammar might be a little informal, but it's OK for everyday writing.
   - A few pronouns do not match what IT refers to.
   - You might stumble over my innovative! Punctuation.
   - It reads like a first draft, all right.
   - I'd definitely need to do some editing to get this ready to publish.

1. Better read it once to decode, then once again for meaning.
   - Lotsuv errers Mak? The going ruf.
   - I've forgotten some CAPS—otherS aren't Needed.
   - Look out four speling mysteaks.
   - To tell the truth, I didn't spend much time editing.
   - I'll really have to roll up my sleeves to get this ready for publishing.

FIGURE 7.3
(*continued*)

Imagine the clarity of understanding and foundation for success we create when we share this description of proficiency and accompany it with actual samples of student work demonstrating what proficiency actually looks like as it progresses from beginner to intermediate to highly competent writing.

Developing Performance Criteria (Think Assessment FOR Learning!)

To develop your own rubrics, you will need to carry out a thoughtful analysis of the performance skill or product you wish to evaluate. That means you must look inside the skills or products of interest to find the active ingredients. In most cases, this is not complicated. Do it on your own, work with colleagues, or partner with your students—it's all the same.

To illustrate, consider how Ms. W. led Emily and her classmates through the process of articulating the attributes of good writing resulting in the development of their student-friendly rubrics. Remember, this is not about students defining the attributes of good writing. Ms. W began with the department vision. What unfolds here is the process of her turning that vision over to her students lock, stock, and barrel.

As you follow the steps described, realize that these are the same steps teacher teams would take in developing their vision of academic success in reasoning, skill, or product contexts.

Also as you go, think about contexts where you might bring this process into play in your classroom. How might you use these steps to help your students understand rubrics for some form of their achievement you are evaluating? We once watched a class of third graders go through this same process to clarify criteria for assessing and improving upcoming dramatic presentations they were planning for their parents. A middle school social studies teacher we know used these steps to help his students see how to improve the research reports they were about to write. As you read on, see if you can see applications of this 5-step process that might be relevant in your classroom.

Step 1: Discover. The goal in this initial step is to help students begin to discover the keys to their own success. This requires that they become partners in the task analysis that will identify the active ingredients contributing to different levels of proficiency. As their teacher, you engage students in answering the question, How does a good task or product differ from a poor-quality one? To answer, students must have the opportunity to see examples. Regard Emily's experience as she describes it here.

"Ms. Weathersby gave us a writing assignment to complete on the first day of class. She said we were to write an essay about someone or something that we care deeply about. I wrote about my Mom. When we were done, she gave us each a folder and told us to put it in there and put the folder away.

"Then she gave us all copies of an essay that she had just written for a magazine. Our homework assignment was to read it and try to decide if it was any good. The tough part was that she said she didn't want us to try to please her. She wanted our honest reaction. If it's good, what makes it good? Be specific, she said. If it's not very good, tell me why.

"Some kids noticed some bad things. But mostly we just thought it was real good. I mean, she's a professional writer. What do we know? Besides who wants to tick off the grade giver?

"But then she did something very interesting. She gave us a copy of an essay that she had saved from her high school years, when she was first learning to write. She told us to read that one as our next homework assignment. Same deal: Come to class the next day ready to evaluate it. We all hoped that she meant it when she said that it's okay to be critical. We were! But she was cool. She made us be real specific about the problems we saw in that essay. She made us write 'em down, too. Then she took us back to her first essay—the real good one—and made us do the same thing. We brainstormed another list, this time of all the things that we thought made it good. We had to write those down, too, to take with us. This time our homework assignment was to study both essays and try to figure out the 10 most important differences between them. What are the things that one essay does well that are missing or done badly in the other? Then she told us to put our lists of differences in our folders along with the essay we had written. We'd return to them later.

"The next day, she gave us each a stack of essays—like, 10 or so. Our job was to tell the good from the not-so-good. She had us work in teams to sort them into four piles: Very Good, Good, So-so, and Pretty Bad. In my group, we each read each paper and then voted on which pile. Sometimes we disagreed. But not much—just about 2 or 3. Our homework that night was to get together to finish up the sorting if we didn't get done during class.

"The next day in class, she had us compare the Pretty Bad and So-so papers to figure out what made them different. Then we compared the So-so and Good papers, and then the Good and Very Good. Once again, we brainstormed lists of important differences. As I look back now, I see that she had us discovering how the quality of writing differs. When we finished figuring out the essential differences among those four stacks of papers, Ms. W. referred us back to our comparison of what was good and bad about her essays—you know, the list in our folders. The two lists were almost exactly alike!"

We'll return to this conversation with Emily. But first, notice the power of asking students to compare and contrast vastly different samples of performance—really good and really bad. It virtually always helps them zero in on and figure out how to describe performance keys in their own clear and understandable language.

Step 2: Condense. Next you help students begin to build a vocabulary that both you and they can use to converse with each other about performance. This is why it is important to engage students in understanding the rubric. When you share the stage with your students and involve them in defining success by having them analyze examples and choose the language to describe achievement, in effect you begin to connect them to their target. Emily continues:

"So now we're beginning to understand different levels of writing quality. Now Ms. Weathersby had us take our initial essays out of our folders and evaluate them. Which pile is our essay most like: Very Good, Good, So-so, or Pretty Bad? You know where mine was—thumbs down!! It was pretty bad. But she said, 'Just be patient. Improvement will come pretty quickly.' Since there wasn't a pile lower than the one my paper was in, I had to believe her.

"Ms. W. said that we had to start getting specific. We had long lists of attributes of different levels of performance, like 20 ingredients. We had to start boiling them down. We had to get to the important stuff. She asked things like, Can any of these be combined? Are some a lot more important than others? We actually read Ms. W.'s good essay again, this time out loud in class to see if it helped us zero in on keys to success. I don't remember all of our steps along the way. But this was when we had our first experience with the BIG SIX! Look! I put them on the cover of my writing portfolio:

Ideas and Content—you got something to say?

Organization—you have to have a plan

Sentence Fluency—rhythm, rhythm, rhythm

Word Choice—accurate and precise, always the right word, that's me!

Voice—speak right to your reader

Conventions—don't let errors distract your reader"

Step 3: Define. In this step, it is crucial to remember that the job is not merely to define successful, or high-level, performance. Rather, you seek to describe the full range of performance, so each performer can come to understand where they are now in relation to where you want them to be down the road. Only with that roadmap in hand can they watch themselves travel their own personal journey to excellence, feeling in complete control all along the way.

"Ms. Weathersby divided us up into collaborative teams—six teams. Then she placed the labels for our six categories in a hat and each team had to draw one out. Each team was to take the lead in helping the rest of the class learn to master their element of good writing.

"Each team had to write a definition of their element. But we couldn't just make it up. We had to go to the library and check in the dictionary and other reference materials. And we needed to review the essays we had been analyzing to find examples of strong and weak performance of our element. Then we had to prepare a presentation for the rest of the class to show them what we had learned—using the overhead projector or PowerPoint on the computer! Ms. W. encouraged us to question and argue with each other to be sure we all agreed on the final definitions. We really had good discussions. The illustrations really helped.

"As our next assignment, Ms. W. had us divide a piece of paper into three columns, labeled 'high,' 'middle,' and 'low.' Under the high column, we were to develop a list of words or phrases that we believed describe a piece of writing when it is of outstanding quality with respect to our particular element. Then under low, we were to describe a paper that is of poor quality on our assigned attribute. And finally, we were to describe the midrange, too. And once again, we had to find examples to illustrate different levels of writing and share with the class again.

"Each team presented and we listened and questioned. Ms. W. asked the best questions—really challenged us to see if we knew what we were talking about. She also showed us how to stretch our rating scales from 3 to 5 points. When we were all done, Ms. W. told us how proud she was of us and how much we had learned. She collected the results of each team's work and overnight put all of the rating scales on her computer and printed copies for all of us to use with our next assignments."

Again, refer back to Figure 7.3 to see the results of the work of Emily and her classmates.

Step 4: Learn to Apply the Rubric. The next step is to help your students learn to apply their performance criteria through practice. You accomplish this most effectively by providing them with varied examples of performance so they can analyze and evaluate quality. As this process unfolds, you can start your students down the road of discovering their own current level of performance using agreed-on rubrics. (When your students become trained raters, the scoring workload spreads over many shoulders.) In this way, you show them where they are now in relation to where you want them to be, so they can begin to take charge of their journey to excellence. Remember the assessment FOR learning strategies. Here's how Ms. W. did this, as Emily recounts it:

"First, she returned us to the stack of papers that we had sorted into piles. You know, Very Good, So-so, and so on. Then she had us pick one paper from each pile and rate it using our six 5-point performance criteria. We all rated the same four papers.

Then using a show of hands, she asked us how many of us rated each paper on each criterion at each level. We didn't all agree with each other exactly. But we were pretty close. And boy, those profiles sure revealed why we had put each paper in each pile originally. They were really different.

"Next, Ms. W. had us go to our files and pull out the essay that we had written at the very beginning and rate it using our scales. Mine was terrible. But she said that was okay. Low ratings are not a bad thing when you're first getting started. Low ratings don't mean you've failed. They only mean you're just starting to learn about something. But, you have to start improving.

"Then she gave us another writing assignment, promising that even now we probably would see improvement in the quality of our writing. As I wrote that night, I found myself thinking, Ideas and Content—Have I got anything to say?; Organization—I gotta have a plan; Sentence Fluency—rhythm, rhythm, rhythm; Word Choice—Am I telling my story accurately and precisely?; Voice—Am I speaking to my reader?; and Conventions—Don't let errors interfere.

"The next day in class, we worked in teams to read and evaluate each other's essays and we all found that this second effort was much better! Ms. W. was right.

"From then on we did more and more of the same. She shared samples of writing that she had found that did or didn't do something well. We dug up some, too, and shared them. We wrote a lot. Sometimes we just evaluated one or two of the six criteria. Ms. W. said, when we're working on Organization, that's what we evaluate. But, she said, eventually all of the pieces have to come together."

Step 5: Refine. Revising and refining performance criteria never stops. By evaluating lots of student work over time, you tune into the keys to success with increasing focus and precision. As new insights arise, revise your criteria to reflect your best current thinking. And remember, it is not uncommon for students who are involved in the process to "out think" their teachers and come up with criteria of excellence that you have not seen. When they do, honor their good thinking! Never regard performance criteria as "finished." Rather, always see them as works in progress.

Summary: Step by Step. When it comes down to devising your own performance assessment rubrics, do what Ms. Weathersby did. Her steps are listed in Table 7.4.

And remember, when students are partners in carrying out these steps, you and they join together to become a learning community. Together, you open windows to the meaning of academic success, providing your students with the words and examples they need to see that vision.

The Attributes of Good Rubrics

So how do we know if the performance criteria that make up your rubric are any good? Interestingly enough, we need a "rubric for rubrics"! Good rubrics for evaluating student proficiency in a performance assessment context just include two active ingredients: they specify the *important content* (what counts) with sharp *clarity* (everyone understands the criteria) (Arter & Chappuis, 2006).

"The *content* of a classroom rubric defines what to look for in a student's product or performance to determine its quality; what will 'count.' Teachers and students use this content to determine what they must do in order to succeed" (Arter & Chappuis, 2006, p. 34). The rubric needs to adequately reflect the target. There are three indicators for content quality:.

TABLE 7.4
Steps in Devising Performance Criteria

Step	Activity
Discover	Analyze examples of performance to uncover keys to success
Condense	Pool the resulting ideas into a coherent but concise and original set of key attributes
Define	Develop simple definitions of the key to success and devise performance continuums for each
Apply	Practice applying performance evaluation procedures until you can do so with consistency
Refine	Always remain open to the possibility that criteria might need to be revised

Indicator 1A: Covers the Right Content. A classroom rubric should (1) bear a direct relationship to the content standards and learning targets it is intended to measure, (2) cover all essential features that create quality in a product or performance, (3) leave out all trivial or unrelated features, and (4) support and extend your understanding about what you actually *do* look for when evaluating student work.

Indicator 1B: Criteria Are Well Organized. The attributes of features of quality performance need to be focused and well organized. Similar features are grouped together, and the relative importance of the various criteria to overall performance is noted.

Indicator 1C: Number of Levels Fits Targets and Uses. There needs to be enough levels to track student progress without so many that users can't distinguish among them. Levels need to be distinct.

"A classroom rubric is *clear* to the extent that teachers, students, and others are likely to interpret the statements and terms in the rubric the same way. A rubric can be strong on the criterion of *Coverage/Organization* but weak on *Clarity*—the rubric seems to cover the important dimensions of performance, but doesn't describe them very well. Likewise, a rubric can be strong on the criterion of *Clarity*, but weak on the criterion of *Coverage/Organization*—it's very clear what the rubric means, but it is not focused on the right criteria" (Arter & Chappuis, 2006, p. 39). There are two indicators for the criterion of *Clarity*.

Indicator 2A: Levels Defined Well. "The key with clarity is to define levels so transparently that both students and teachers can see precisely what features of work cause people to agree that work is Strong, Medium, or Weak. The instructional usefulness of any rubric depends on the clarity of level descriptions" (Arter & Chappuis, 2006, p. 40). If we can share and understanding of the path to success and the way we will know when we have arrived, then making that journey successfully will be difficult, if not impossible.

Indicator 2B: Levels Parallel. There needs to be consistency across levels of quality in the features that are evaluated. "For example, if you find that a rubric for playing the violin contains "lackadaisical bowing" as one descriptor of a low-level performance, then a statement about the quality of the bowing must be included at the strong and middle levels as well. If this descriptor is not referred to at other levels, the levels are not parallel" (Arter & Chappuis, 2006, p. 41).

Figure 7.4 presents a quality rating scale (rubric) for each of the attributes described here. Please study it now. Activities are provided at the end of the chapter for you to practice applying these criteria in evaluating some sample scoring guides.

Generalizable Rubrics Work Best. Remember when we were discussing scoring guides for essay questions where we were evaluating student mastery of content knowledge and we said that the criteria by which we would judge student success reflected the specific content of each item? The respondent's goal was to get as many of those points as possible. It only made sense in that the scoring guide for each exercise would need to focus only its own content.

In most performance assessment contexts, we seek to assess student mastery of general reasoning proficiencies, performance skills, and product development capabilities—that is, the scoring guide centers on academic capabilities we want students to be able to apply across a range of different contexts (tasks). We want students to develop generalizable oral reading, foreign language speaking, or writing proficiencies they can use in any reading, speaking or writing context. We want them to learn to transfer these proficiencies as needed to new situations. This expectation is noted at the very top of the rubric for rubrics (see Figure 7.4).

Devising Performance Tasks

Performance assessment tasks, like selected response test items and essay exercises, frame the challenge for students. Thus, performance assessment tasks clearly and explicitly reflect the achievement target(s).

We face two basic design considerations when dealing with tasks in the context of performance assessment. We must determine the following:

- The specific ingredients of the task, defining what performers are to do
- The number of tasks needed to sample performance

Let's delve into each in some detail.

Developing the Performance Task

Like well-developed essay exercises, sound structured performance assessment tasks specify and explain the challenge to respondents, while setting them up to succeed if they can, by doing the following:

- Identifying the specific kind(s) of performance to demonstrate
- Detailing the context and conditions within which proficiency will be demonstrated
- Reminding students of the criteria applied in evaluating performance

CRITERION 1: COVERAGE/ORGANIZATION

Strong	Medium	Weak
A. Covers the Right Content		
1. For reasoning, skills, and product learning targets, the rubric is general, not task-specific	1. Some parts of the rubric are task-specific when a general one would be better.	For reasoning, performance skill, and/or product targets, the rubric is task-specific, not general.
2. The content of the rubric represents the best thinking in the field about (a) what it means to perform well on the skill or product under consideration, or (b) how performance on the skill or product develops over time.	2. Much of the content represents the best thinking in the field, but there are a few places that are questionable.	You can't tell what learning target(s) the rubric is intended to assess, the learning targets don't seem important, or content is far removed from current best thinking in the field about what it means to perform well on the skill or product under consideration.
3. The content of the rubric aligns directly with the content standards/ learning targets it is intended to assess.	3. Some features don't align well with the content standards/learning targets the rubric is intended to assess.	The rubric doesn't seem to align with the content standards/learning targets it is intended to assess.
4. The content has the "ring of truth"—your experience as a teacher confirms that the content is truly what you *do* look for when you evaluate the quality of a student product or performance. In fact, the rubric is insightful; it helps you organize your own thinking about what it means to perform well.	4. Much of the content is relevant, but you can easily think of some important things that have been left out or that have been given short shrift, or it contains an irrelevant criterion or descriptor that might lead to an incorrect conclusion about the quality of student performance.	You can think of many important dimensions of a quality performance or product that are not in the rubric, or content focuses on irrelevant features. You find yourself asking, "Why assess this?" or "Why should this count?" or "Why should students have to do it this way?"
B. Criteria Are Well Organized		
The rubric is divided into easily understandable criteria as needed. The number of criteria reflects the complexity of the learning target. If a holistic rubric is used, it's because a single criterion adequately describes performance.	The number of criteria needs to be adjusted a little: either a single criterion should be made into two criteria, or two criteria should be combined.	The rubric is holistic when an analytic one is better suited to the intended use or learning targets to be assessed; or the rubric is an endless list of everything; there is no organization.
The details that are used to describe a criterion go together; you can see how they are facets of the same criterion.	Some details that are used to describe a criterion are in the wrong criterion, but most are placed correctly.	The rubric seems "mixed up"—descriptors that go together don't seem to be placed together. Things that are different are put together.
The relative emphasis on various features of performance is right—things that are more important are stressed more; things that are less important are stressed less.	The emphasis on some criteria or descriptors is either too small or too great; others are all right.	The rubric is out of balance—features of more importance are emphasized the same as features of less importance.
The criteria are independent. Each important feature that contributes to quality work appears in only one place in the rubric.	Although there are instances when the same feature is included in more than one criterion, the criteria structure holds up pretty well.	Descriptors of quality work are represented redundantly in more than one criterion to the extent that the criteria are really not covering different things.

C. Number of Levels Fits Targets and Uses

5—Strong	3—Medium	1—Weak
1. The number of levels of quality (or the number of developmental stages) used in the rating scale makes sense. There are enough levels to be able to show student progress, but not so many levels that it is impossible to distinguish among them. The levels are qualitatively different.	1. Teachers might find it useful to create more levels to make finer distinctions in student progress, or to merge levels to suit the rubric's intended use. The number of levels could be adjusted easily.	1. The number of levels is not appropriate for the learning target being assessed or intended use. There are so many levels it is impossible to reliably distinguish between them, or too few to make important distinctions.. Or, the levels don't seem to be qualitatively different.

Criterion 2: CLARITY

A. Levels Defined Well

5—Strong	3—Medium	1—Weak
Each level is defined with indicators and/or descriptors. There are examples of student work that illustrate each level of each trait. There is enough descriptive detail in the form of concrete indicators, adjectives, and descriptive phrases that allow you to match a student performance to the "right" level. A *plus:* If students are to use the rubric, there are student-friendly versions, and/or versions in foreign languages for ELL students. 3. If counting the number or frequency of something is included as an indicator, changes in such counts really *are* indicators of changes in quality. 4. Wording is descriptive of the work, not evaluative.	1. Only the top level is defined. The other levels are not defined. There is some attempt to define terms and include descriptors, but some key ideas are fuzzy in meaning. There is some descriptive detail in the form of words, adjectives, and descriptive phrases, but counting the frequency of something (when not appropriate) or vague quantitative words are also present. Wording is mostly descriptive of the work, but there are a few instances of evaluative labels.	No levels are defined; the rubric is little more that a list of categories to rate followed by a rating scale. Wording of the levels, if present, is vague or confusing, or the only way to distinguish levels is with words such as *extremely, very, some, little,* and *none;* or *completely, substantially, fairly well, little,* and *not at all.* Rating is almost totally based on counting the number or frequency of something, even though quality is more important than quantity. 4. Wording tends to be evaluative rather than descriptive of the work; e.g., work is "mediocre," "above average," or "clever."

Levels Parallel

5—Strong	3—Medium	1—Weak
The levels of the rubric are parallel in content—if an indicator of quality is discussed in one level, it is discussed in all levels. If the levels are not parallel, there is a good explanation why.	The levels are mostly parallel in content, but there are some places where there is an indicator at one level that is not present at the other levels.	Levels are not parallel in content and there is no explanation of why, or the explanation doesn't make sense.

FIGURE 7.4
Rubric for Rubrics

Source: Adapted from *Creating and Recognizing Quality Rubrics* (pp. 183–187), by J. A. Arter & J. Chappuis. 2006. Portland OR: Pearson Assessment Training Institute. Adapted by permission.

Here is a simple example of a performance task that frames clear and specific problems to solve in all three terms:

- *Identify Achievement*—You are to use your knowledge and understanding of how to convert energy into motion, along with your understanding of the principles of mechanics, to reason through the design for a mousetrap car. A mousetrap car converts one snap of the trap into forward motion. Then you are to build and demonstrate your car.
- *Specify Conditions*—Using materials provided in class and within the time limits of four class periods, design and diagram your plan, construct the car itself, and prepare to explain why you included your key design features.
- *Establish Criteria*—Your performance will be evaluated in terms of the specific standards we set in class, including the clarity and completeness of your diagrammed plan, the match between your plan and the actual quality of your car, and the quality of your presentation explaining its design features. Scoring guides are attached.

The Attributes of Effective Tasks. The bottom line for performance tasks is that they have to elicit from students the kind of response that will permit you to dependably assess proficiency. That means that each task must be on target.

Quality tasks address the right *content*. They elicit the correct response—a performance that reveals the proper proficiency. In other words, it is obvious that the response can be effectively evaluated using the scoring criteria or rubric. The two align. When the achievement target is simple in nature, the task reflects that simplicity: to assess oral reading fluency, have students read. When the target is more complex, so is the task: to assess ability to proficiency in preparing a science research paper, create the paper.

Quality tasks provide enough *evidence*—a sufficient number of examples of the desired performance—to lead to a confident conclusion about the student's proficiency.

Quality tasks are *feasible* for use in the classroom. They are practical given the realities of the context. Students have enough time to respond. Proper materials and equipment are readily available for all respondents. Time is available to examine and evaluate performance using the previously developed scoring criteria.

Finally, quality tasks are *free of bias* that can distort our evaluations of proficiency. This requires that tasks be specific in their instructions. There is no confusion—each student knows exactly what to do.

In short, there is nothing about the task set in its context that will give rise to an inaccurate picture of the student's proficiency. In this sense, it provides for a *fair and accurate* assessment of achievement.

In Figure 7.5, you will find a set of rating scales or rubrics you can used to judge the quality of your performance tasks.

Selecting a Sample

How do you know how many such exercises to include within any particular assessment to give you confidence that you or your students are drawing dependable conclusions about proficiency? In terms of our example, how many samples of Emily's writing must Ms. W. see to draw a dependable conclusion about her proficiency? The answer always involves tradeoffs between quality of resulting information needed and the cost of collecting it.

To understand this assessment challenge, let's say we are members of a licensing board charged with responsibility for certifying the competence of commercial airline

CRITERION 1: CONTENT OF THE TASK
What Information Do Students Need?

Strong	Medium	Weak
1. All requirements of the task are directly related to the learning target(s) to be assessed. The task will elicit a performance that could be used to judge proficiency on the intended learning targets.	1. Some requirements of the task are not related to the learning target(s) to be assessed. There is extra work in this task not needed to assess the intended learning targets.	1. Requirements of the task are not related to the learning target (s) to be assessed. The task will not elicit a performance that could be used to judge proficiency on the intended learning targets.
2. The task specifies the following: • The knowledge students are to use in creating the task • The performance or product students are to create—what form it should take • The materials to be used, if any • Timeline for completion	2. Some of the following information is clear; some is unclear or missing: • The knowledge students are to use in creating the task • The performance or product students are to create—what form it should take • The materials to be used, if any • Timeline for completion	2. The task does not specify the following: • The knowledge students are to use in creating the task • The performance or product students are to create—what form it should take • The materials to be used, if any • Timeline for completion
3. Tasks assessing a performance skill specify the conditions under which the performance or demonstration is to take place.	3. Tasks assessing a performance skill do not sufficiently specify the conditions under which the performance or demonstration is to take place.	3. Tasks assessing a performance skill do not at all specify the conditions under which the performance or demonstration is to take place.
4. Tasks taking more than one day to complete specify the help allowed from sources outside the classroom.	4. Although there is some reference to what kind of help is allowed for multi-day tasks, it could be misinterpreted.	4. Multi-day tasks do not specify the help allowed.
5. The task includes a description of the criteria by which the performance or product will be judged (see *Rubric for Rubrics*).	5. Although present, the mention of the criteria by which the performance or product will be judged is vague or unclear.	5. The task includes no reference to the criteria by which the performance or product will be judged.
6. The task description is sufficient to let students know what they are to do without giving so much information that the task will no longer measure level of mastery of the intended learning target. The content points the way to success without doing the thinking for the student.	6. Some parts of the task may give students too much help, compromising the results when they are intended to be used to measure the student's achievement of the learning target independently.	6. The task is over-scaffolded. If used for summative purposes, the task cannot measure students' ability to create the product or performance independently, because the content is so explicit that students can follow it like a recipe. Students can achieve a high score and/or satisfactorily complete the task without having mastered the intended learning target. The task measures only students' ability to follow directions.

(continued)

FIGURE 7.5
Rubric for Tasks

Source: From *Classroom Assessment FOR Student Learning: Doing It Right—Using It Well, Activities & Resources* (bundled CD-ROM) (n.p.) by R. J. Stiggins, J. A. Arter, J. Chappuis, and S. Chappuis, 2004, Portland, OR: Assessment Training Institute. Copyright 2006, 2004 by Educational Testing Service. Reprinted by permission of Educational Testing Service. Reprinted by permission of the copyright owner.

CRITERION 2: SAMPLING
Is There Enough Evidence?

Strong	Medium	Weak
1. The number of tasks or repeated instances of performance is sufficient to measure the intended learning target.	1. There are more tasks or repeated instances of performance than are needed to measure the intended learning target or to support the kind of judgment intended to be made.	1. The number of tasks or repeated instances of performance is not sufficient to measure the intended learning target or to support the kind of judgment intended to be made.

CRITERION 3: DISTORTION DUE TO BIAS
What Can Interfere with Accuracy?

Strong	Medium	Weak
1. The instructions are clear and unambiguous.	1. The instructions may leave room for erroneous interpretation of what is expected.	1. The instructions are likely to be confusing to students.
2. The task is narrow enough in scope to be completed successfully in the time allotted. It is clear that enough time has been allotted for successful completion of the task.	2. Some students will have difficulty completing the task to the best of their ability in the time allotted. The timeline will have to be extended or the task narrowed somewhat in scope.	2. Insufficient time has been allotted for students to complete the task to the best of their ability. Either the timeline or the task, or both, will have to be reworked considerably.
3. If the task allows students to choose different tasks, it is clear that all choices will provide evidence of achievement on the same learning targets. All choices ask for the same performance or product, with approximately the same level of difficulty, and under the same conditions.	3. If the task allows students to choose different tasks, some of the choices may relate to different learning targets, or there is some variation in performance or product called for, level of difficulty, or conditions.	3. If the task allows students to choose different tasks, none of the choices relate to the same learning target, or there is considerable variation in performance or product called for, level of difficulty, and/or conditions.
4. All resources required to complete the task successfully are available to all students.	4. Some students may have difficulty obtaining the necessary resources to complete the task successfully, or one or more of the resources required will be difficult for most students to obtain.	4. Many students will have difficulty accessing the resources necessary to complete the task successfully.
5. Successful completion of the task does not depend on skills unrelated to the target being measured (e.g., extensive reading required to complete a mathematics task).	5. Successful completion of the task may be slightly influenced by skills unrelated to the target being measured.	5. Successful completion of the task depends on skills unrelated to the target being measured.
6. The task is culturally robust. Successful completion is not dependent on having had one particular cultural or linguistic background.	6. Successful completion of the task may be influenced by having had one particular cultural or linguistic background.	6. The task is not culturally robust. Successful completion depends on having had one particular cultural or linguistic background.

FIGURE 7.5
(continued)

pilots. One specific skill we want them to demonstrate, among others, is the ability to land the plane safely. So we take candidates up on a bright, sunny, calm day and ask them to land the plane, clearly an authentic performance assessment. And let's say the first pilot does an excellent job of landing. Are you ready to certify?

If your answer is Yes, we don't want you screening the pilots hired by the airlines on which we fly! Our assessment reflected only one narrow set of circumstances within which we expect our pilots to be competent. What if it's night, not a bright, clear daylight? A strange airport? Windy? Raining? An emergency? These represent realities within which pilots must operate routinely. So the proper course of action in certifying competence is to see each pilot land under various conditions, so we can ensure safe landings on all occasions. To achieve this, we hang out at the airport waiting for the weather to change, permitting us to quickly take off in the plane so we can watch our candidates land under those conditions. And over the next year we exhaust the landing condition possibilities, right?

Of course not. Obviously, we're being silly here. We have neither the time nor the patience to go through all of that with every candidate. So what do we do? We compromise. We operate within our existing resources and sample pilot performance. We have each candidate land the plane under several different conditions. And at some point, the array of instances of landing proficiency (gathered under strategically selected conditions) combine to lead us to a conclusion that each pilot has or has not mastered the skill of landing safely.

This example frames the performance assessment sampling challenge in a real-world situation that applies just as well in your classroom. How many "landings" must you see under what kinds of conditions to feel confident your students can perform according to your criteria? The science of such sampling is to have thought through the important conditions within which you will sample performance. The art is to use your resources creatively to gather enough different instances under varying conditions to bring you and your students to a confident conclusion about proficiency.

You must consider the decision to be made in planning the size of your sample. Some decisions are very important, like promotion to the next grade, high school graduation, or becoming licensed to practice a profession. These demand assessments that sample both more deeply and more broadly to give all users confidence in the decision that results. An incorrect decision based on poor-quality assessment would have dire consequences.

But other decisions are not so momentous. They allow you to reconsider the decision tomorrow, if necessary, at no cost to the student. For example, if you mismeasure a student's ability to craft a complete sentence during a lesson on sentence construction, you are likely to discover your error in later assessments and take proper action. When the target is narrow and the time frame brief, you can sample more narrowly and not do great harm.

Figure 7.6 identifies six factors to take into account when making sampling decisions in any particular performance assessment context. Your professional challenge is to follow the rules of sound assessment and gather enough information to minimize the chance that your conclusions are wrong.

The conservative position to take in this case is to err in the direction of oversampling to increase your level of confidence in the inferences you draw about student competence. If you feel at all uncertain about the conclusion you might draw regarding the achievement of a particular student, you have no choice but to gather more information. To do otherwise is to place that student's well-being in jeopardy.

- *The Reason for the Assessment*—The more important the decision, the more sure you must be about the student's proficiency. The more sure you must be, the bigger should be your sample. Greater coverage leads to more confident conclusions about achievement.

- *The Scope of the Target*—The more narrowly focused the valued achievement target, the easier it is to cover it with a small sample. Targets broad in their scope require more exercises to cover enough material to yield confident conclusions.

- *The Coverage of Any One Exercise*—If the student's response is likely to provide a great deal of evidence of proficiency, you need not administer many such exercises. How many term papers must a student prepare to demonstrate that he or she can do it?

- *Time Available to Assess*—If you must draw conclusions about proficiency tomorrow, you have too little time to sample broadly. But as the time available to assess increases, so can the scope of your sample.

- *Consistency of Performance*—If a student demonstrates consistently very high or very low proficiency in the first few exercises, it may be safe to draw a conclusion even before you have administered all the exercises you had intended.

- *Proximity to the Standard*—If a student's performance is right on the borderline between being judged as competent or incompetent, you might need to extend the sample to be sure you know which conclusion to draw.

FIGURE 7.6
Practical Considerations in Performance Assessment Sampling

FINE TUNING YOUR USE OF PERFORMANCE ASSESSMENTS

Clearly, the first factor to consider in selecting and developing performance assessments is the learning target to be assessed. In addition, however, it is prudent to consider other practical questions when deciding if or how to use performance assessment in your classroom.

For example, we always face the danger of biased judgment with this methodology. Remember, we already have discussed many ways to ensure that your subjective assessment is as objective as it can be:

- Be crystal clear about the target—align tasks and rubrics precisely to it.
- Articulate the key elements of good performance in explicit performance criteria within the rubric.
- Share those criteria with students in terms they understand—provide practice in applying those criteria if they are to be among the judges.
- Learn to apply the rubrics in a consistent manner; remember the need for inter-rater agreement.

There is a simple way to check for bias in your performance evaluations. Remember, bias occurs when factors other than the kind of achievement being assessed begin to influence rater judgment, such as examinees' gender, age, ethnic heritage, appearance, or prior academic record. We already have established that you can determine the degree of objectivity of your ratings by comparing them with the judgments of another trained and qualified evaluator who independently observes and evaluates the same student performance with the intent of applying the same criteria.

Now, you may be saying, it's just not practical to determine inter-rater agreement in the classroom. It'll take too much time. Besides, where do I find a qualified second rater?

And how do I determine if the other rater and I agree in our judgments? This is a prime argument for not developing them alone. Team up. Help each other. Promote consistency in learning targets and performance ratings across classrooms in your school.

In fact, achieving inter-rater consistency among raters need not take much time. You need not find corroboration for every performance judgment you make. Just checking a few for consistency often will suffice. Perhaps a qualified colleague could double check a select few of your performance ratings to see if they are on target.

Further, it doesn't take a high degree of technical skill to do this. Have someone who is qualified rate some student performances you already have rated, and then sit down for a few minutes and talk about any differences in your ratings. If the performance in question is a product that students created, have your colleague evaluate a few. If it's a skill, videotape a few examples. Both you and your colleague apply your criteria to one performance and check for agreement. Do you both see it about the same way? If so, go on to the next one. If not, try to resolve differences, adjusting your performance criteria as needed.

Please understand that our goal here is not to have you carry out this test of objectivity every time you conduct a performance assessment. Rather, try to understand the spirit of my point. An important part of the art of classroom performance assessment is the ability to sense when your performance criteria are sufficiently explicit that another judge would be able to use them effectively, if called on to do so. Therefore, from time to time it is a good idea to actually check whether you and another rater really do agree in applying your criteria.

The more important the performance assessment (that is, the greater its potential impact on students, such as when it is used for promotion decisions, graduation decisions, and the like), the more important it becomes that you verify inter-rater agreement.

BARRIERS TO SOUND PERFORMANCE ASSESSMENT

By way of summary, many things in the design and development of performance assessments can cause a student's real achievement to be misrepresented. These potential problems and remedies are summarized in Figure 7.7.

THINK ASSESSMENT FOR LEARNING: INVOLVE STUDENTS IN PERFORMANCE ASSESSMENT

The intended purpose for the performance assessment will tell us who needs to be observing and evaluating student work. When the goal is to certify that students have met performance standards for important grading, promotion, or graduation decisions, then you, the teacher, must be the assessor. These are assessment OF learning contexts. The only acceptable alternative in these contexts is for you to bring into the classroom another adult rater (a qualified outside expert). Schools that ask students to do exhibitions and demonstrations, such as senior projects, science fairs, and music competitions, routinely do this. In all cases, it is essential that raters be fully trained and qualified to apply in a dependable manner the performance criteria that underpin the evaluation. High-stakes decisions hang in the balance. So you must do it right.

Potential Sources of Problems	Recommended Remedy
Inadequate vision of the achievement target	Seek training and advice or consult the professional literature to sharpen your focus; work with colleagues in this process
Mismatch of target and method	Performance assessment aligns well with complex reasoning, performance skills, and product assessments; use it only for these
Unclear performance criteria	Analyze samples of performance very carefully, working with qualified experts, if necessary, to sharpen your focus
Incorrect performance criteria	Compare and contrast samples of performance of vastly different quality for real keys to success; consult the professional literature for advice; work with qualified colleagues in the process of identifying criteria
Unfocused tasks	Seek help from qualified colleagues in task development
Biased tasks	Understand the social and linguistic backgrounds of your students; seek advice of qualified reviewers in revising and selecting tasks
Insufficient sample of tasks	Start with a clear definition of the desired achievement target; work with a team of qualified colleagues to devise new tasks and determine how many would be enough
Too little time to assess	Add trained raters . . . such as your students
Untrained raters	Train them and provide them with practice in applying criteria

FIGURE 7.7
Avoiding Problems

On the other hand, as we have established, you can use assessments as far more than simply sources of scores for report card grades and accountability. You can use them as teaching tools, as assessment FOR learning. You can accomplish this in one way by using performance assessments to teach students to evaluate their own and each other's performance. The very process of learning to dependably apply performance criteria helps students become better performers, as it helps them to learn and understand key elements of sound performance. So when the assessment is to serve instructional purposes, students can be raters, too. Table 7.5 summarizes assessment FOR learning strategies mentioned in the chapter, adding a few new suggestions and providing brief rationales for each.

Exploring the Social Context of Assessment

A teacher who "teaches the test" helps students literally learn the answers to the test and then has them take that very test. But when we do this we can't generalize from their test score to their mastery of the achievement domain the test represents. We don't know if they would do well on a parallel test of that domain using new items. Contrast this to "teaching to the test," where we provide practice in learning to do the things that an important upcoming assessment will require and then we have them take that assessment. Some object to this because it has the effect of narrowing the learning to just what is practiced—unanticipated dimensions of learning might be missed. In your opinion, is this bad practice, too? Why do you believe as you do? Discuss this with your classmates.

TABLE 7.5

Assessment FOR Learning—A Practical Performance Assessment Application

	Strategy	Rationale
1	Provide an understandable vision of the learning target. Teach students the concepts underpinning quality in your scoring guide by asking them what they already know (What makes a good _____ ?), then show how their prior knowledge links to your definition of quality.	Showing the connection between new information and knowledge students already have helps it all make sense and provides a link to long-term memory. It also lays the foundation for students understanding the upcoming learning.
2	Use models of strong and weak work. • Share anonymous strong and weak student work. Have students use the scoring guide to evaluate the samples, then share their reasons, using the language of the scoring guide. • Share published strong (and weak, if available) work. Let students comment on the quality of published examples and your own work, using the language of the scoring guide. • Share your own work. Show them how you revise work using a rubric.	Student performances improve when they understand the meaning of quality. This strategy teaches students to distinguish between strong and weak products or performances, and to articulate the differences. It also encourages teachers to share aspects of the beauty of their discipline. What does it look/sound/feel like when it's done especially well? Modeling the messy underside for students reassures them that high-quality work doesn't always start out looking like high-quality work. As teachers, we tend to smooth over this part, so when the going gets messy for students, they may infer they are "doing it wrong." What does high-quality work look like at its beginning stages? Model it.
3	Offer descriptive feedback instead of grades on practice work, pointing out what students are doing right as well as what they need to work on, using the language of the scoring guide.	Students need descriptive feedback while they're learning. It tells them how close they are to reaching the target, and it models the kind of thinking we want them to be able to do, ultimately, when self-assessing.
4	Teach students to self-assess and set goals. Ask them to identify their own strengths and areas for improvement, using the language of the scoring guide.	Periodic articulation about their understanding of quality and about their own strengths and weaknesses is essential to students' ability to improve. Self-assessment is a necessary part of learning, not an add-on that we do if we have time or the "right" students. Struggling students are the right students.
5	Design lessons around the elements of quality in the scoring guide. Focus on one aspect of quality at a time.	Novice learners cannot improve all elements of quality of a complex skill or product simultaneously. If your scoring guide represents a complex skill or product, students will benefit from a "mini-lesson" approach, wherein they are allowed to learn and master a portion at a time.
6	Teach students focused revision. Let students work in pairs to revise anonymous samples. Once they have evaluated a weak sample, ask them to use their reasons to go further: What could you do to make this receive a higher score?	Students need the opportunity to practice using the scoring guide as a guide to revision. That way, they, not their teachers, are doing the thinking about revision and the learning.

(continued)

Strategy	Rationale
7 Engage students in self-reflection. Let them keep track of and share what they know and how their capabilities are changing over time.	Any activity that requires students to reflect on what they are learning and to share their progress with an audience both reinforces the learning and helps them develop insights into themselves as learners. By reflecting on their learning, students are learning more deeply and will remember it longer.

Source: From *Classroom Assessment FOR Student Learning: Doing It Right—Using It Well* (pp. 241–242) by R. J. Stiggins, J. A. Arter, J. Chappuis, and S. Chappuis, 2004, Portland, OR: Assessment Training Institute. Copright 2006, 2004 by Educational Testing Service. Reprinted by permission of Educational Testing Service, the copyright owner.

Summary: Thoughtful Development Yields Sound Performance Assessments and Energized Students

This chapter has been about the great potential of performance assessment, with its array of design possibilities. Please refer to Table 7.1 on page 139 and consider once again the variety of classroom applications. However, we have tempered the presentation with the admonition to develop and use this assessment method cautiously. Performance assessment, like other methods, brings with it specific rules of evidence. We must all strive to meet those rigorous quality control standards.

To ensure quality, we discussed the conditions that must be present for performance assessment to be used effectively. We also discussed the need to understand the role of subjectivity. We analyzed the matches between performance assessment and the various kinds of achievement targets, concluding that strong matches can be developed for reasoning, skills, and products. We discussed key context factors to consider when selecting this methodology for use in the classroom, centering mostly on the importance of having in place the necessary expertise and resources.

Clearly, the heart of this chapter was our exploration of the two basic steps in developing performance assessments:

- Clarifying performance (dealing with the nature and focus of the achievement being assessed)

- Developing performance tasks (dealing with the way we elicit performance for observation and judgment)

As we covered each step, we framed the possibilities available to you as a classroom teacher, establishing standards for sound performance criteria and performance tasks. We will return to both of these in Part III of this book, where we study examples of each.

In our opinion, the most practical part of the presentation in this chapter occurred when we devised five steps for formulating your own sound performance criteria, urging collaboration with students and/or colleagues.

This is most practical because it affords you the best opportunities for bringing students into your performance assessment development and for teaching them the most valuable lessons. We began by comparing and contrasting examples of performance to discover the active ingredients of quality. From there, we began to boil those ingredients down to their essence: concise statements of the meaning of academic excellence. Once you and your students learn to apply those standards to evaluating student work, you are on the road to success.

As schools continue to evolve, we predict that we will come to rely increasingly on performance assessment as part of the basis for our evaluation of student achievement. Hopefully, we will find even more and better ways of integrating performance assessment and instruction. We feel strongly that, whatever those better ways are, they will have their foundation in student involvement. Let us strive for the highest-quality, most rigorous assessments our resources will allow.

Final Chapter Reflection

1. What are the three most important new insights to come to you as a result of your study of this chapter?
2. Which of your previous questions about assessment can you now answer based on your study of this chapter?
3. What new questions have come to mind as a result of your study of this chapter—questions that you hope to have answered as your study continues?

Practice with Chapter 7 Ideas

1. Two teachers fundamentally disagree on the performance criteria to apply to evaluating a particular kind of student work. How should they resolve their difference of opinion; that is, what collaborative process should they carry out to find the proper criteria?

2. A student and a teacher have a legitimate difference of opinion during learning about the standards of excellence to apply to evaluating a particular kind of student work. Should the teacher simply assert ultimate authority and evaluate accordingly? What are the assessment FOR learning alternatives that might permit the teacher to take advantage of this teachable moment?

3. Develop a rubric of an oral class presentation students will give. Do so by brainstorming keys to quality, condensing these into a few critical ingredients, defining each, and drafting a performance continuum for each key criterion. When you are done, compare the results of your work to the rubric offered in Table 7.6. Be disciplined here—don't consult the model until you have done your own thinking and drafting.

4. Following are three sample performance assessments. Evaluate them using the rubrics shown in this chapter, as appropriate for each example.

Example 1: Camping Trip—Grade 5

"Eight people are going camping for 3 days and need to carry their own water. They read in a guidebook that 12.5 liters are needed for a party of 5 people for 1 day. Based on the guidebook, what is the minimum amount of water the 8 people should carry all together? Explain your answer."

Responses were assessed using a rubric with three traits: conceptual understanding, problem solving, and communication in math. Each trait was scored on a five-point scale with points 1, 3, and 5 defined in Figure 7.8. Students received student-friendly versions early in the school year and practiced using the rubrics on many other problems.

TABLE 7.6
Oral Presentation Scoring Guide

Score	Language	Delivery	Organization
A = 5	Correct grammar and pronunciation are used. Word choice is interesting and appropriate. Unfamiliar terms are defined in the context of the speech.	The voice demonstrates control with few distractions. The presentation holds the listener's attention. The volume and rate are at acceptable levels. Eye contact with the audience is maintained.	The message is organized. The speaker sticks to the topic. The main points are developed. It is easy to summarize the content of the speech.
B = 4 C = 3	Correct grammar and pronunciation are used. Word choice is adequate and understandable. Unfamiliar terms are not explained in the context of the speech. There is a heavy reliance on the listener's prior knowledge.	The voice is generally under control. The speaker can be heard and understood. The speaker generally maintains eye contact with the audience.	The organization is understandable. Main points may be under-developed. The speaker may shift unexpectedly from one point to another, but the message remains comprehensible. The speech can be summarized.
D = 2 F = 1	Errors in grammar and pronunciation occur. Word choice lacks clarity. The speaker puts the responsibility for understanding on the listener.	The student's voice is poor. The volume may be too low and the rate too fast. There may be frequent pauses. Nonverbal behaviors tend to interfere with the message.	Ideas are listed without logical sequence. The relationships between ideas are not clear. The student strays from the stated topic. It is difficult to summarize the speech.

Source: Reprinted from *Toolkit98:* Chapter 3, Activity 3.3—Performance Criteria, Keys to Success. Reprinted by permission of Northwest Regional Educational Laboratory, Portland, Oregon.

Example 2: Tall Tales and Fables—Grade 2

The learning targets emphasized in this unit of instruction, as listed by the teacher, were "language arts, writing, reading, and spelling." The performance task and associated performance criteria were described in the following manner. (Students did not see the rubric or criteria ahead of time.)

> Unit Assessment List: Writing or retelling a tall tale or fable.
> Task Description: Develop and write a tall tale or fable.

Performance Criteria:
- Handwriting or word processing is neat and legible.
- Spelling on all core words is correct, and most other words are correct.
- *Sentence structure*—The student uses complete sentences.
- Capital letters are used appropriately to begin sentences and for proper names.
- Punctuation is used correctly.
- *Understanding*—The student demonstrates an understanding of the exaggeration and fictitious characters found in tall tales or fables.

Rubric:
- *Distinguished*— Writing shows creativity in plot and character development. Tall tale or fable uses exaggeration appropriately. Writing is correct in all mechanics.

Definitions

Mathematical Concepts and Procedures. A student demonstrates a grasp of the mathematical concepts, chooses and performs the appropriate mathematical operations, and performs computations correctly.

Problem Solving. A student demonstrates problem-solving skills and comprehension by framing the problem so that appropriate mathematical process(es) can be selected and used, by developing or selecting and implementing a strategy to find a solution, and by checking the solution for reasonableness.

Mathematics Communication. A student demonstrates communication skills in mathematics by explaining the steps and reasoning used in a solution with words, numbers, and diagrams.

Adult Rubric

Mathematical Concepts and Procedures

5 A strong performance occurs when the student demonstrates extensive understanding of the mathematical concepts and related procedures and uses them correctly. The student
- Understands mathematical concepts and related procedures.
- Uses all necessary information from the problem.
- Performs computation(s) accurately or with only minor errors.

3 A developing performance occurs when the student demonstrates general understanding of the mathematical concepts and related procedures, but there may be some gaps or misapplication. The student
- Partially understands mathematical concepts and related procedures.
- Uses some necessary information from the problem.
- May make some computational errors.

1 A weak performance occurs when the student demonstrates little or no understanding of mathematical concepts and related procedures. Application, if attempted, is incorrect. The student
- Does not appear to understand mathematical concepts and related procedures.
- Does not use information from the problem or uses irrelevant information.
- Does no computation, or does computation that is unrelated to the problem.

Problem Solving

5 A strong performance occurs when the student selects or devises and uses an efficient, elegant, or sophisticated strategy to solve the problem.
- The student translates the problem into a useful mathematical form.
- The student applies the selected plan(s) or strategy(-ies) through to completion; no pieces are missing.
- The plan or strategy may incorporate multiple approaches.
- Pictures, models, diagrams, and symbols (if used) enhance the strategy.
- The solution is reasonable and consistent with the context of the problem.

3 A developing performance occurs when the student selects or devises a plan or strategy, but it is partially unworkable.
- The student leaves gaps in framing or carrying out the strategy.
- The strategy may work in some parts of the problem, but not in others.
- The strategy is appropriate but incomplete in development or application.
- Results of computation, even if correct, may not fit the context of the problem.

1 A weak performance occurs when the student shows no evidence of a strategy or has attempted to use a completely inappropriate strategy.
- The student shows no attempt to frame the problem or translates the problem into an unrelated mathematical form.
- The strategy is inappropriate, misapplied, or disconnected.
- Pictures, models, diagrams, and symbols, if used, may bear some relationship to the problem.
- The solution is not reasonable and/or does not fit the context of the problem.

(continued)

FIGURE 7.8
Rubric for Camping Trip Mathematics Problem

Mathematical Communication

5 A strong performance occurs when a student clearly explains in words, numbers, and diagrams both the strategy used to solve the problem and the solution itself.
  • The problem could be solved following the explanation. It is clearly explained and organized.
  • The explanation is coherent and complete. There are no gaps in reasoning. Nothing is left out.
  • The student presents logical arguments to justify strategy or solution.
  • The explanations may include examples and/or counterexamples.
  • Charts, pictures, symbols, and diagrams, when used, enhance the reader's understanding of what was done and why it was done.
  • Few inferences are required to figure out what the student did and why.
  • Correct mathematical language is used.

3 A developing performance occurs when the student's problem solving is partially explained, but requires some inferences to figure out completely.
  • The student attempts to use mathematical language, but may not have used all terms correctly.
  • Some key elements are included in the explanation.
  • The student explains the answer but not the reasoning, or explains the process but not the solution.
  • Charts, pictures, symbols, and diagrams, if used, provide some explanation of the major elements of the solution.

1 A weak performance occurs when the student's explanation does not describe the process used or the solution to the problem.
  • Charts, pictures, symbols, and diagrams, when used, interfere with the reader's understanding of what was done and why it was done.
  • The explanation appears to be unrelated to the problem.
  • The reader cannot follow the student's explanation.
  • Little or no explanation of the thinking/reasoning is shown.
  • The explanation only restates the problem.
  • Many inferences are required to follow the student's work.
  • Incorrect or misapplied mathematical language interferes with the reader's ability to understand the explanation.

Student-Friendly Rubric

Mathematical Concepts and Procedures

5 I completely understand the appropriate mathematical operation and use it correctly.
  • I understand which math operations are needed.
  • I have used all of the important information.
  • I did all of my calculations correctly.

3 I think I understand most of the mathematical operations and how to use them.
  • I know which operations to use for some of the problem, but not for all of it.
  • I have an idea about where to start.
  • I know what operations I need to use, but I'm not sure where the numbers go.
  • I picked out some of the important information, but I might have missed some.
  • I did the simple calculations right, but I had trouble with the tougher ones.

1 I wasn't sure which mathematical operation(s) to use or how to use the ones I picked.
  • I don't know where to start.
  • I'm not sure which information to use.
  • I don't know which operations would help me solve the problem.
  • I don't think my calculations are correct.

Problem Solving

5 I came up with and used a strategy that really fits and makes it easy to solve this problem.
  • I knew what to do to set up and solve this problem.
  • I knew what math operations to use.

FIGURE 7.8
(*continued*)

- I followed through with my strategy from beginning to end.
- The way I worked the problem makes sense and is easy to follow.
- I may have shown more than one way to solve the problem.
- I checked to make sure my solution makes sense in the original problem.

3   I came up with and used a strategy, but it doesn't seem to fit the problem as well as it should.
- I think I know what the problem is about, but I might have a hard time explaining it.
- I arrived at a solution even though I had problems with my strategy at some point.
- My strategy seemed to work at the beginning, but did not work well for the whole problem.
- I checked my solution and it seems to fit the problem.

1   I didn't have a plan that worked.
- I tried several things, but didn't get anywhere.
- I didn't know which strategy to use.
- I didn't know how to begin.
- I didn't check to see if my solution makes sense.
- I'm not sure what the problem asks me to do.
- I'm not sure I have enough information to solve the problem.

Mathematical Communication

5   I clearly explained the process I used and my solution to the problem using numbers, words, pictures, or diagrams.
- My explanation makes sense.
- I used mathematical terms correctly.
- My work shows what I did and what I was thinking while I worked the problem.
- I've explained why my answer makes sense.
- I used pictures, symbols, and/or diagrams when they made my explanation clearer.
- My explanation was clear and organized.
- My explanation includes just the right amount of detail, not too much or too little.

3   I explained only part of the process I used, or I only explained my answer.
- I explained some of my steps in solving the problem.
- Someone might have to add some information for my explanation to be easy to follow.
- Some of the mathematical terms I used make sense and help in my explanation.
- I explained my answer, but not my thinking.
- My explanation started out well, but bogged down in the middle.
- When I used pictures, symbols, and/or diagrams, they were incomplete or only helped my explanation a little bit.
- I'm not sure how much detail I need to help someone understand what I did.

1   I did not explain my thinking or my answer, or I am confused about how my explanation relates to the problem.
- I don't know what to write.
- I can't figure out how to get my ideas in order.
- I'm not sure I used math terms correctly.
- My explanation is mostly copying the original problem.
- The pictures, symbols, and/or diagrams I used would not help somebody understand what I did.

FIGURE 7.8
(*continued*)

- *Proficient*— Tall tale or fable correctly uses plot and exaggeration. Characters may not be well developed. Few errors in mechanics are apparent.
- *Apprentice*— Tall tale or fable does not show exaggeration or fictitious characters. Errors in mechanics are common.

- *Novice*— Tall tale or fable is begun but not concluded. Writing shows lack of understanding of exaggeration. Several errors in mechanics are found.

Example 3: Math Portfolio—Grades 4 and 8

Students were asked to assemble a portfolio that demonstrated their mathematical problem-solving ability. Each portfolio was to contain 10–20 selections.

- 5–7 of these should be "best pieces" and must include: 1 puzzle, 1 investigation, 1 application, and no more than 2 pieces of group work.
- The student can select other pieces that demonstrate ability.
- The student should write a letter to the evaluator that describes what he or she has chosen for his or her portfolio and what it shows about the student.

The portfolios are assessed using this rubric:

Problem Solving: How well does the student understand the problem, how does the student solve the problem, why does the student solve it the way she or he did, and what observations, connections, and generalizations does the student make about the problem?

Communication: What terminology, notation, or symbols does the student use to communicate his or her math thinking, what representations (graphs, charts, tables, models, diagrams, pictures, manipulatives) does the student use, and how clear is the student's communication of mathematical thinking and problem solving?

PEARSON
myeducationlab™
Where the Classroom Comes to Life

Now go to www.myeducationlab.com to take a Pretest to assess your initial comprehension of chapter content, study chapter content with your individualized Study Plan, take a Posttest to assess your understanding of chapter content, practice your teaching skills with Building Teaching Skills exercises, and build a deeper, more applied understanding of chapter content with Homework and Exercises.

CHAPTER 8

Personal Communication as Assessment

CHAPTER FOCUS

This chapter answers the following guiding question:

> How can I best use direct personal interaction with my students during instruction to assess their achievement?

The context within which this option comes into play can be informal, sometimes spontaneous, and perhaps lightning quick. Your interaction with a student or a group of students during instruction may provide a brief glimpse into their current level of achievement or a flash of insight about what must come next in their learning. Indeed, it may offer the opportunity to teach, in effect, by asking a question that triggers new insights for learners. Other times the interaction may be as structured and purposeful as other assessments. In all cases, assessment quality matters. From your study of this chapter, you will understand the following:

1. Use personal communication–based assessments to tap knowledge and understanding, as well as reasoning and verbal performance skills.
2. This kind of assessment can take the form of instructional questions and answers, conferences and interviews, insights from class discussions, oral exams, and student journals and learning logs.
3. Using personal communication in conjunction with other methods can deepen our understanding of student learning.
4. As with the other methods, this one can fall prey to avoidable sources of bias that can distort results if we are not careful.
5. By involving our students in assessments that rely on personal communication, we can set them up for energetic and successful learning.

As we start this part of our journey, keep our big picture in mind. Look at Figure 8.1. Once again, we will be dealing in depth with the shaded areas.

	SELECTED RESPONSE	ESSAY	PERFORMANCE ASSESSMENT	PERSONAL COMMUNICATION
Knowledge				
Reasoning				
Performance Skills				
Products				
Dispositions				

FIGURE 8.1
Aligning Achievement Targets and Assessment Methods

TAPPING THE POWER OF CLASSROOM INTERACTION AS EVIDENCE OF LEARNING

Teachers gather a great deal of valuable information about student achievement by talking with them. We while we don't tend to think of this personal interaction as "assessment," it is. At different times during teaching and learning, we ask questions, listen to answers, and evaluate achievement.

Our intent in this chapter is not so much to provide precise detail on procedures as it is to describe the factors to be aware of in drawing inferences about students' achievement based on what they say. If our interactions are focused, characterized by active listening, and lead to cautious conclusions, then personal communications with and among students can provide a valid and reliable window into learning. We will address the following forms of personal communication: Questions and answers during instruction, conferences and interviews with students, student contributions during class discussions, oral examinations, and student journals and learning logs.

When we use these forms of assessment with care, we can tap dimensions of achievement not easily accessed through other means. For example, thoughtful questioners can effectively link assessment to instruction by using questions to uncover and immediately correct students' misconceptions or faulty reasoning.

Even as learning is progressing, a few strategically placed questions can help you to monitor and adjust your teaching. But even beyond this, personal communication affords you some special opportunities. For example, unlike some other forms of assessment, if you are startled, puzzled, or pleased by a student's response you can ask followup questions immediately to dig more deeply to reveal their reasoning. In other words, you can get beyond a particular response to explore its origins. For instance, let's say a student fails a performance assessment and you wish to discover why to help that student find success. You can follow up the assessment with a few carefully phrased questions to see if the student's performance was due to a lack of prerequisite knowledge or to poor-quality reasoning on their part.

Keys to Effective Use

As with the other three assessment methods we have studied, the validity and reliability of a personal communication–based assessment depend on its use in appropriate contexts and on your ability to manage effectively the subjectivity inherent in this method.

There are several contextual factors to consider in deciding when to turn to personal communication as a source of evidence of student learning.

Common Language and Cultural Awareness Are Fundamental

Teacher and student must share a common language for this mode of assessment to work effectively, for in its absence bias can creep in, rendering the evidence undependable. This factor has become increasingly important recently as ethnic and cultural diversity have increased in our schools.

By common language, we don't just mean a shared vocabulary and grammar, although these obviously are critical to sound assessment. We also mean a common sense of the manner in which a culture shares meaning through verbal and nonverbal cues. Ethnicity and cultural heritage may differ between student and teacher. For example, we must realize that, in some cultures where social emphasis is placed on the collective good, it is unseemly for a student to hold him or herself up publically as appearing to know more than others. This can give rise to a cultural reluctance to answer questions in class. Thus, the student may be proficient but not be willing to demonstrate that fact in this manner. Or similarly, in some cultures it is a sign of disrespect to one's elders (e.g., their teacher) for children to make eye contact with those of older generations. But sometimes, as teachers, we draw inferences about student learning based on such nonverbal signs. Just be sure you understand the social environment from which your students come before doing so. When you lack that understanding, you ensure mismeasurement.

Personality Can Be Important

Shy students simply may feel too vulnerable not reveal their achievement through direct interaction—especially under public circumstances. To make this work, some privacy may be in order. There also is the danger that students with very outgoing, aggressive personalities will mislead you with respect to their real achievement. But, this is a danger only when assessors permit themselves to be "snowed" or misled by factors other than achievement.

Create a Safe Environment

Personal communication works best as assessment when students feel they are in a safe learning environment. There are many ways to interpret this.

In its most general connotation, we create safe learning environments when we make it clear to our students that they are successful when they meet standards— when we tell them that we know they will grow at different rates, that it's okay, and that they will have time to grow at their own effective rate.

When considered in the context of personal communication–based assessment, we promote safety when we permit our students to succeed or fail in private, without an embarrassing public spotlight. As mentioned previously, in some cultures, it is unseemly to make public displays of competence—to call attention to one's self as standing above others. On the other side, it is always more embarrassing to fail in public than in private, especially for those students who lack social confidence. A safe environment provides private ways to excel or to grow.

Another kind of safety takes the form of a humane peer environment sensitive to the plight of those who perform less well. Still another kind of safety can arise from knowing that one will have the opportunity to learn more and perform again later with the promise of a higher level of success. Nowhere is this sense of personal safety more important to sound assessment than when that assessment is conducted through personal communication.

Exploring the Cultural Context of Assessment

For personal communication to work effectively as assessment FOR learning, students must understand and believe it's okay (in fact, essential) during their learning that they be honest about what they know and don't know—what they can and cannot do. Students must know that if they give you the "socially desirable" response to a question, a response that misrepresents the truth about their achievement, then you will be less able to help them. What specific things can you do in your classroom to promote their belief that "I don't know" is an acceptable answer while we are still learning? What can you do to make it okay for students to reveal their learning needs honestly during their learning?

Accurate Records May Be Important

Because, very often, there are no tangible assessment products (e.g., test papers or even scores or grades) resulting from assessments conducted via personal communication, records of achievement must be managed carefully. Sometimes information management is easy; when the interaction takes a few minutes, focuses on narrow targets for a few students, and the evidence is used immediately, extensive record keeping is unnecessary. Just rely on memory. But when the context includes many students, complex targets, and several samples of response you absolutely must maintain some record for later consideration. In such cases, do not rely on memory. Often, modern handheld digital technology can help with this. If you have no means or hope of securing such assistance, rely on some sort of recorded or written record. Or, revise your assessment plans to rely on another assessment method.

Figure 8.2 summarizes these practical keys to the effective use of assessment by means of personal communication by transforming them into seven quality control

---

Things to investigate:

- Do teacher and students share a common language?
- Have students attained a sufficiently high level of verbal fluency to interact effectively?
- Have you developed your own cultural awareness?
- Do students have personalities that permit them to open up enough to reveal true achievement?
- Do students see the environment as safe enough to reveal their true achievement?
- Do students understand the need to reveal their true achievement?
- Can accurate records of achievement be kept?

FIGURE 8.2
Factors to Consider When Using Personal Communication as Assessment

questions that you can ask about your assessments (the language/culture key is sub-divided into its three aspects).

Understanding Validity and Reliability Issues

Professional judgment, and therefore subjectivity, permeates all aspects of assessments that rely on personal communication. Consider the depth of your involvement: you set the achievement targets and criteria used to judge them, compose and store records of performance, summarize and interpret results, and make key instructional decisions based on what you see and hear.

This subjectivity makes it imperative that, as with other assessment methods, you know and understand your achievement target and know how to translate it into clear and specific questions and other probes to generate focused information.

Let's be specific about the three reasons not to take personal communication as assessment too lightly as a source of information and as a teaching strategy. These reasons are (1) the problem of forgetting, (2) the problem of "filters," and (3) the challenge of sampling.

The Problem of Forgetting

The first reason for caution is that we must remain mindful of the fallibility of the human mind as a recording device. Not only can we forget and lose things in there, but also the things we try to remember about a student's performance can change over time for various reasons, only some of which are within our control. This presents validity concerns. We must act purposefully to counteract this danger by conducting quality assessments and recording results before they get lost or are changed in our minds.

The Problem of "Filters"

We already have discussed this. We must remain aware of and strive to understand those personal and professional filters, developed over years of experience, through which we hear and process student responses. They represent norms, if you will, that allow us to interpret and act on the achievement information that comes to us through observation and personal communication. If not managed effectively, these filters hold the potential for harming assessment reliability. They can be the source of inappropriate bias.

If we set our expectations of a particular student, not on the basis of a clear understanding of the discipline and the student's current capabilities but rather on the basis of a gender or ethnic stereotype unrelated to real academic achievement, we risk doing great harm indeed.

The insidious aspect is that we can remain unaware of our own biases. We don't go around saying, "Boys who are athletes never study and don't learn," or "I have a feeling that Sarah can do this, even though she didn't demonstrate it this time." Biases are subtle and operate to reduce the objectivity of the evidence gathered.

We can avoid these problems only by striving to be aware of them and by adhering to sound assessment practices as described throughout this book.

Time for Reflection

As a student, have you ever been on the losing end of a biased assessment where, for some reason, your teacher's inappropriate personal or professional filters led to an incorrect assessment of your proficiency? What was that like? What effect did it have on your learning? Share your experiences with your classmates.

The Challenge of Sampling

As with other forms of assessment, we can make sampling mistakes that invalidate the assessment. One mistake is to gather incorrect information by asking the wrong questions, questions that fail to reflect important forms of achievement. We sample the wrong thing, for example, by asking knowledge recall questions when we really want to get at our students' ability to reason in a particular manner.

Another mistake is to gather too few bits of information to lead to confident conclusions about proficiency. Our sample can be too small.

Still another sampling error, paradoxically, can arise from spending too much time gathering too many bits of evidence. This is a problem of inefficiency. We eventually reach a point of diminishing returns, where collecting additional information is unlikely to change our conclusion about proficiency.

To avoid such sampling problems, we must be crystal clear about targets and purposes and gather just enough information. Remember, any assessment represents only a sample of all the questions we could have asked if the assessment could have been infinite length. The key to successful sampling in the context of personal communication is to ask a representative set of questions, one that is long enough to give you confidence in the generalizations you draw to the entire performance domain.

Example of an Easy Fit. Mr. Lopez, an elementary teacher, tells this story illustrative of a time when sampling challenges were relatively easy to meet:

"I was about to start a new science reading activity on fish with my third graders. As a pre-reading activity, I wanted to be sure all my students had sufficient background information about fish to understand the reading. So I checked the story very carefully for vocabulary and concepts that might be stumbling blocks for my students. Then I simply asked a few strategic questions of the class, probing understanding of those words and ideas and calling on students randomly to answer. As I sampled the group's prior knowledge through questions and answers, I made mental notes about who seemed not to know some of the key material. There were only three or four. Later, I went back and questioned each of them more thoroughly to be sure. Then I helped them to learn the new material before they began reading."

In this scenario, the performance arena is quite small and focused: vocabulary and concepts from within one brief science story. Sampling by means of personal communication was simple and straightforward, and there are no real record-keeping challenges presented. Mr. Lopez simply verified understanding on the part of the students before proceeding. After that, most records of performance could go on the back burner. Mr. Lopez did make a mental note to follow up with those students who had the most difficulty, but decided that all other records could be "deleted."

Example of a More Challenging Fit. Now here's a scenario in which the assessment challenges are more formidable: A high school health teacher wants to rely extensively on small- and large-group discussions of health-related social issues to encourage student participation in class discussions. To accomplish this, she announces at the beginning of the year that 25 percent of each student's grade will be based on the extent and quality of their participation in class. She is careful to point out that she will call on people to participate and that she expects them to be ready.

This achievement target is broader than that of Mr. Lopez in two ways: It contains many more elements (the domain is much larger), and it spans a much longer period of time. Not only does the teacher face an immense challenge in adequately sampling each individual's performance, but also, her record-keeping challenge is much more complex

Attribute of Quality	Defining Question
Arise from a clear and specific achievement target	Do my questions reflect the achievement target I want my students to hit?
Serve clear purposes	Why am I assessing? How will results be used?
Assure a sound representation of that target	Can the target of interest to me be accurately reflected through personal communication with the student?
Sample performance appropriately	Do I have enough evidence?
Minimizing bias	Am I in touch with potential sources of bias, and have I minimized the effects of personal and professional filters?

FIGURE 8.3
Defining Issues of Quality for Personal Communication as Classroom Assessment

and demanding. Consider the record-keeping dilemma posed by a class schedule that includes, say, four sections of eleventh-grade health, each including 30 students! Mental record keeping is not an option: When we try to store such information in our gray matter for too long, bad things happen. Besides, this qualifies as an assessment OF learning. So the pressure is on to do it right. These are not unsolvable problems, but they take careful preparation to assess. In this sense, they represent a significant challenge to the teacher.

These two scenarios capture the essence of the quality control challenge you face when you choose to rely on personal communication as a means of assessing student achievement. You must constantly ask yourself, Is my achievement target narrow enough in its scope and short enough in its time span to allow for conscientious sampling of the performance of an individual student or students as a group? If the answer is yes in your opinion, proceed to the next question: Is the target narrow enough in its scope and short enough in its time span to allow me to keep accurate records of performance? If the answer again is yes, proceed. *If the answer to either question is no, choose another assessment method or abandon the target.*

Summary: Avoiding Validity and Reliability Problems

We can avoid problems due to the fallibility of the human mind and bias only by attending to those five ever-present, important, basic attributes of sound assessment as they apply in the context of personal communication. Whether we plan or are spontaneous in our personal communication with students, we must bear these quality standards in mind. Figure 8.3 reviews these standards as they apply to personal communication as assessment.

MATCHING METHOD TO TARGETS

Personal communication–based assessments can provide direct evidence of proficiency in three of our four kinds of targets and can provide insight into the student's readiness to deliver on the other. This is a versatile assessment option.

Assessing Knowledge and Understanding

This can be done with personal communication, but you need to be cautious. Obviously, you can question students to see if they have mastered the required knowledge or can retrieve it through the effective use of reference materials. To succeed, however, you must possess a keen sense of the limits and contents of the domain of knowledge. Once again, since you cannot ask all possible questions, especially using this labor-intensive method, your questions must sample and generalize in a representative manner. And remember, knowing and understanding are not the same thing. So you will want to query both.

Assessing Reasoning

Herein lies a real strength of personal communication as a means of assessment. Skillful questioners can probe student reasoning and problem solving, both while students are thinking out their answers and retrospectively, to analyze how students reached a solution. But even more exciting is that you can use questioning to help both of you understand and enhance each other's reasoning.

For example, you can ask students to let you in on their thought processes as they analyze events or objects, describing component parts. You can probe their abilities to draw meaningful comparisons, to make simple or complex inferences, or to express and defend an opinion or point of view. There is no more powerful method for exploring student reasoning and problem solving than a conversation while students are actually trying to solve the problem. By exploring their reasoning along with them, you can provide students with the kinds of understanding and vocabulary needed to converse with you and with each other about what it means to be proficient in this performance arena.

Asking students to "think out loud" while they're learning can provide a window into their reasoning. For example, mathematics teachers often ask students to talk about their thinking while proceeding step by step through the solution to a complex math problem. This provides a richness of insight into students' mathematical reasoning that cannot be attained in any other way. Further, as students talk through a process, you also can insert followup questions: Why did you take (or omit) certain steps? What would have happened if you had . . . ? Do you see any similarities between this problem and those we worked on last week? When students are unable to solve the problem, tactical questioning strategies can tell you why. Did they lack prerequisite knowledge? Analyze the problem incorrectly? Misunderstand the steps in the process? If assessments FOR learning, these probes permit you to find student needs and link your assessment to instruction almost immediately—there is no need to wait for test score reports to be returned!

In a different context, one popular way of assessing reading comprehension is to have students retell a story they have just read. As the retelling unfolds, you are free to ask questions as needed to probe the student's interpretation.

Assessing Performance Skills and Products

In the previous chapter, we established that the only way to obtain direct information about student performance skills or proficiency in creating quality products is to have them actually "do" or "create" so we and they can compare their work to established standards of quality.

The great strength of direct personal interaction with students in this category is in the assessment of their oral communication skills—their ability to use the language to convey their ideas. Whether we endeavor to talk with them in English or a foreign language, that interaction can provide evidence of essential performance skills.

But even in other performance areas, a skilled teacher of "doing" or "creating" (i.e., a teacher who possesses a highly refined vision of relevant skill or product targets), can ask students to talk through a hypothetical performance, asking a few key questions along the way, and know with a certain degree of confidence whether they are likely to be proficient or less than proficient performers. While admittedly an approximation of actual performance, this can save assessment time in the classroom and focus instruction.

In this same performance-related sense, you can ask students strategic questions to examine the following:

- Prior success in performing similar tasks
- Their sense of certainty or uncertainty about the quality of their work
- Knowledge and understanding of the criteria used to evaluate performance (i.e., key skills to be demonstrated or key attributes of quality products)
- Awareness of the steps necessary to create quality products

Based on the results of such probes, you can draw cautious inferences about student competence and learn how to help them grow.

Summary of Target Matches

Personal communication in its many forms can supply useful information to teachers about a variety of important educational outcomes, including mastery of subject matter knowledge, reasoning and problem solving, and procedural knowledge that is prerequisite to skill and product creation proficiency. Table 8.1 presents a summary of matches.

To create effective matches between this method of assessment and these kinds of targets, however, you must start with a clear vision of the outcomes to be attained. In addition, you must know how to translate that vision into clear, focused questions,

TABLE 8.1
Personal Communication Assessment of Achievement

Target to Be Assessed	Personal Communication
Knowledge & Understanding	Can ask questions, evaluate answers, and infer mastery, but a timeconsuming option
Reasoning Proficiency	Can ask students to "think aloud" or can ask followup questions to probe reasoning
Performance Skills	Strong match when skill is oral communication proficiency; also can assess mastery of knowledge prerequisite to skillful performance
Ability to Create Products	Can probe procedural knowledge and knowledge of attributes of quality products, but not product quality

share a common language, open channels of communication with students, and understand how to sample performance representatively. But none of these keys to success is powerful enough to overcome the problems that arise when your interpretive filters predispose you to be inappropriately biased in deciphering communication from students.

THE MANY FORMS OF PERSONAL COMMUNICATION AS ASSESSMENT

As with the other three modes, this one includes a variety of assessment formats: questioning, conferences and interviews, class discussions, oral examinations, and journals and logs. We will define each format and identify several keys to its effective use in the classroom.

Instructional Questions and Answers

This has been a foundation of the education process forever. As instruction proceeds, the teacher poses questions for students to answer. They gather evidence and adjust instruction accordingly. This activity can promote thinking and learning, and drive up achievement. The teacher listens to answers, interprets them in terms of internally held standards, infers the respondent's level of attainment, and proceeds accordingly.

The following keys to successful use will help you take advantage of the strengths of this as an assessment format, while overcoming weaknesses:

- Plan key questions in advance of instruction, so as to ensure proper alignment with the target and with students' capabilities.
- Ask clear, brief questions that help students focus on a relatively narrow range of acceptable responses.
- Probe various kinds of reasoning, as appropriate.
- Ask the question first and then call on the person who is to respond. This will have the effect of keeping all students on focus.
- Call on both volunteer and non-volunteer respondents. This, too, will keep all students in the game.
- Acknowledge correct or high-quality responses; probe incorrect responses for underlying reasons.
- After posing a question, wait for a response. Let respondents know that you always expect a response and will wait for as long as it takes.

While this last suggestion, allowing time for students to respond, turns out to be surprisingly difficult to do, research reviewed and summarized by Rowe (1978) reveals major benefits for student learning, especially for low-achieving students.

The Nature of Questions
If our objective is to determine what our students know and understand, direct questioning of content will suffice. But if we want to help our students become active strategic reasoners, using their new insights to make meaning, the questions we pose for

TABLE 8.2
Triggers for Reasoning Questions

To Tap	Begin the Question with . . .
Analysis	How do the parts of a _____ work together? How does _____ break down into its parts? What are the components of _____ ? What are the active ingredients in _____?
Synthesis	Given what you know about _____ and _____, what would happen if you _____? What two sources of knowledge do you need to combine to solve this problem? What do _____ and _____ have in common?
Comparison	How are these alike? Different? Define the similarities between … (differences)? How does this correspond to that?
Classification	Into which category does each of the following fit? Group the following and label each category. Match each entry below with its classification.
Induction & Deduction	If this were to happen, then what would result? Using what you know about _____, solve this problem. What would be the consequences of _____? The central idea or theme of the story is what?
Evaluation	State your position on this issue and defend it. Is this a good quality piece of work, in your opinion? Why? Argue in favor of or against _____.

them are crucial to their success. Table 8.2 suggests some triggers for questions that ask students to apply the various patterns of reasoning described in previous chapters.

Think Assessment FOR Learning

Questions need not always flow from teacher to student. Students can ask themselves key questions and then discuss their answers with you, their teacher. For example, here are some questions that can focus student reflection on their reading experiences:

Understanding	Did I understand what I read?
Ease	Was the reading easy or difficult for me?
Meaning	Did I learn anything from this? If so, what?
Evaluation	Was it well written?
Pleasure	Did I like what I read?

Johnston (2004, pp. 13–59 passim) suggests ways to use questions in what certainly could be described as assessment FOR learning ways to promote learning:

To help students notice and learn:	"Did anyone notice that . . . .?"
	"Remember how you used to . . . . Now you . . . Notice the difference?" (Helps students attend to changes)
	"What kind of . . . is this?" (Notice characteristics to classify)
	"What . . . surprised you?"
To establish student control:	"How did you figure that out?"
	"What problems did you come across today?"
	"How are you planning to go about this?"
	"What parts are you sure (not sure) about?"
To help students transfer:	"How else . . .?"
	"What's that like?"
	"What if things changed . . . ?"
To help students confirm knowing:	"How do you know we got this right?"
	"I hadn't thought about it that way. How did you know?"
	"How could we check?"
	"Would you agree with that?"

These and similar questions can provide an excellent basis from which to encourage students to think aloud in conversation with you about their reading.

Conferences and Interviews

Some student-teacher conferences serve as structured or unstructured audits of student achievement, in which the objective is to talk about what students have learned and have yet to learn. Teachers and students talk directly and openly about levels of student attainment, comfort with the material the students are mastering, specific needs, interests, and desires, and/or any other achievement-related topics that contribute to an effective teaching and learning environment. In effect, teachers and students speak together in the service of understanding how to work effectively together.

Remember, interviews or conferences need not be conceived as every-pupil, standardized affairs, with each event a carbon copy of the others. You might meet with only one student, if it fills a communication need. Remember, you can accomplish a lot in 3 minutes one-on-one with some preparation. Also, interviews or conferences might well vary in their focus with students who have different needs. The following are keys to your successful use of conference and interview assessment formats:

- Carefully think out and plan your questions in advance. Remember, students can share in their preparation.
- Plan for enough uninterrupted time to conduct the entire interview or conference.
- Be sure to conclude each meeting with a summary of the lessons learned and their implications for how you and the student will work together in the future.

One important strength of the interview or conference as a mode of assessment lies in the impact it can have on your student–teacher relationships. When conducted in a context where you have been up front about expectations, students understand the achievement target, and all involved are invested in student success, conferences have the effect of empowering students to take responsibility for at least part of the assessment of their own progress. Conducted in a context where everyone is committed to success and where academic success is clearly and openly defined, interviews inform and motivate both you and your students.

Class Discussions

When students participate in class discussions, the things they say reveal a great deal about their achievements and their feelings. Discussions are teacher- or student-led group interactions in which the material to be mastered is explored from various perspectives. Teachers listen to the interaction, evaluate the quality of student contributions, and infer individual student or group achievement. Clearly, class discussions have the simultaneous effect of promoting both student learning and their ability to use what they know.

To take advantage of the strengths of this method of assessment, while minimizing the impact of potential weaknesses, follow these keys to successful use:

- Prepare questions or discussion issues in advance to focus sharply on the intended achievement target.
- Be sure students are aware of your focus in evaluating their contributions. Are you judging the content of students' contributions or the form of their contribution— how they communicate? Be clear about what it means to be good at each.
- Remember, the public display of achievement or lack thereof is risky in the eyes of some students. Provide those students with other, more private, means of demonstrating achievement.
- In contexts where achievement information derived from participation in discussion is to influence high-stakes decisions—assessments OF learning—keep dependable records of performance. Rely on more than your memory of their involvement.

Think Assessment FOR Learning

As always, remember to consider the learning potential of student involvement in classroom discussion when used as assessment:

- Involve students in preparing for discussions, being sure their questions and key issues are part of the mix.
- Rely on debate or other team formats to maximize the number of students who can be directly involved. Pay special attention to involving low achievers.
- Formalize the discussion format to the extent that different roles are identified, such as moderator, team leader, spokesperson, recorder, and so on, to maximize the number of students who have the opportunity to be deeply involved and thus present evidence of their achievement.

In addition, Figure 8.4 provides an illustration of a student-friendly scoring guide for self-assessment of one's own performance in class discussion situations—that is, a performance assessment in a personal communication assessment context.

Trait 1: My Understanding of the Topic
I Do This Well—I completely understand what we're discussing.
- I understand the meaning of the "technical" words being used.
- I know exactly which pieces of information I need to make a point.
- I can give good examples of what I mean.
- I can give evidence to support what I say.

I'm On My Way—I think I understand most of what we're discussing.
- I understand some of the ideas, but not all of them.
- I understand many of the "technical" words, but not all of them.
- I can sometimes give examples of what I mean.
- I picked out some of the important information, but I might have missed some.

I'm Just Starting—I'm not sure I understand what we're discussing.
- I'm not sure I understand what everyone else is talking about.
- I don't understand many of the "technical" words being used.
- I'm unsure which examples or information to use to make a point.
- I'm not sure that the information I use is correct.

Trait 2: My Understanding of What Group Work Is About
I Do This Well—I understand the reasons for working in a group and how to get group work done.
- I try to make sure I understand the reasons for the group work—what the group is supposed to accomplish.
- I help make sure that the discussion stays on the topic.
- I understand various ways to get group work done efficiently. For example, I know when it is useful to summarize the discussion, when the group needs additional information or help, when the group needs a leader, when the group needs to make sure all ideas are expressed, and when ideas need to be clearer.
- I know just what information is needed to contribute to the discussion.
- I know when the job of the group is done.
- I try to help make sure the group gets its work done.
- I know when it's useful to work in a group and when it is not.

I'm On My Way—I'm learning the reasons for working in a group and how to get group work done.
- I sometimes understand the goals of group work and sometimes I don't.
- I participate in the group when asked to by others, but I usually don't without being asked.

I'm Just Starting—I'm not sure I understand the reasons for working in a group, nor how to get group work done.
- I don't think I understand why we sometimes work in groups. I don't understand what working in a group is supposed to accomplish.
- I don't understand how to get group work done in an efficient manner.
- I usually don't follow what is going on.
- I get distracted and don't pay attention.
- I let others take responsibility for making sure the work gets done.

Trait 3: How I Interact with Others
I Do This Well—I know just how to get along with others when working in a group.
- I listen to what others have to say. I don't interrupt.
- When I disagree with someone, I know how to do it so that I don't hurt anyone's feelings.
- I make sure that everyone who wants to has a chance to talk.
- I'm polite.

FIGURE 8.4
Self-assessment Rubric for Group Discussion

I'm On My Way—I sometimes get along well with others when working in a group.
- I generally listen to others, but sometimes I get distracted.
- I sometimes interrupt.
- I try not to hurt others' feelings, but I think I sometimes do anyway.
- I understand how to be polite, but sometimes I'm not.

I'm Just Starting—I'm not sure how to get along with the others in a group.
- I think I hurt people's feelings when I disagree with them, but I'm not sure.
- I try to do all the talking.
- I try to never do any talking.
- I don't listen to what others have to say.
- I don't understand what to do to be polite to others.
- I don't understand why everyone needs a chance to talk.

Trait 4: The Language I Use During the Discussion
I Do This Well—I know just how to say things so that others will understand.
- I say things in a way that others in the group will understand.
- I don't use more words than I need to. I know just how much to say to be clear.
- I try to use words that others will understand. I know when I need to use different words to be clear.

I'm On My Way—I sometimes say things in ways that others understand.
- I think I sometimes use more words than needed to make a point.
- I think I sometimes use words that others don't understand.

I'm Just Starting—I'm unsure if I say things in ways that others will understand.
- I try to use big words to impress others.
- I'm not sure how to say things in ways others will understand.
- I didn't realize that I need to pay attention to how I say things.

FIGURE 8.4
(continued)

Oral Examinations

In this case, teachers plan and pose exercises for their students, who reflect and provide oral responses. Teachers listen to and interpret those responses, evaluating quality and inferring levels of achievement.

In a very real sense, this is like essay assessment, discussed in Chapter 6, but with the added benefit of being able to ask followup questions.

Although the oral examination tradition lost favor in the United States with the advent of selected response assessment during the last century, it still has great potential for use today, especially given the increasing complexity of our valued educational targets and the complexity and cost of setting up higher-fidelity performance assessments.

You can take advantage of the strengths of this format by adhering to some simple keys to its successful use, in effect the quality control guidelines listed in Chapter 6 for developing essay assessments:

- Develop brief exercises that focus on the desired target.
- Rely on exercises that identify the knowledge to be brought to bear, specify the kind of reasoning students are to use, and identify the standards you will apply in evaluating responses.

- Develop written scoring criteria in advance of the assessment.
- Be sure criteria separate content and reasoning targets from facility with verbal expression.
- Prepare in advance to accommodate the needs of any students who may confront language proficiency barriers.
- Have a checklist, rating scale, or other method of recording results ready to use at the time of the assessment.
- If necessary, record responses for later reevaluation.

Clearly, the major argument against this assessment format is the amount of time it takes to administer oral exams. However, you can consider assessment FOR learning applications in which you can alleviate part of this problem by bringing students in as partners. If you adhere to the guidelines listed here and spread the work of administering and scoring over many shoulders, you may derive great benefit from oral assessment as a teaching and learning aid.

Journals and Logs: Naturals as Assessments FOR Learning

Sometimes personal communication–based assessment can take a written form. Students can share important learnings, views, experiences, and insights by writing about them. You can derive clear and useful information by assigning writing tasks that cause students to center on particularly important achievement targets. Further, you can then provide them with descriptive feedback.

Four particular forms bear consideration: response journals, personal writing journals or diaries, dialogue journals, and learning logs. These are infinitely flexible ways of permitting students to communicate about their learning, while at the same time practicing their writing and applying valued patterns of reasoning. In addition, because these written records accumulate over time, you can use them to help students reflect on their improvement as achievers—the heart of assessment FOR learning.

Response journals are most useful in situations where you ask students to read and construct meaning from literature, such as in the context of reading and English instruction. As they read, students write about their reactions. Typically, you would provide structured assignments to guide them, including such tasks as the following:

- Analyze characters in terms of key attributes or contribution to the story.
- Analyze evolving storylines, plots, or story events.
- Compare one piece of literature or character to another.
- Anticipate or predict upcoming events.
- Evaluate either the piece as a whole or specific parts in terms of appropriate criteria.
- Suggest ways to change or improve character, plot, or setting, defending such suggestions.

Teachers who use response journals report that it is an excellent way to permit students to practice applying reasoning patterns, and to increase the intensity of student involvement with their reading. Further, it can provide a means for students to keep track of all the things they have read, building in them a sense of accomplishment in this facet of their reading.

Personal writing journals or diaries represent the least structured of the journal options. In this case, you would give students time during each instructional day to write in their journals. The focus of their writing is up to them, as is the amount they write. Sometimes you evaluate the writing, sometimes it is merely for practice. When you evaluate it, either you, or the student, or both, make judgments. Often young writers are encouraged to use their journals to experiment with new forms of writing, such as dramatic dialogue, poetry, or some other art form. Some teachers suggest to their students that they use personal journals as a place to store ideas for future writing topics. This represents an excellent way to gain insight into the quality of student writing when students are operating at typical levels of motivation to write well. Because there is no high-stakes assessment under way, they do not have to strive for excellence. They can write for the fun of it and still provide both themselves and you with evidence over time of their improvement as writers.

Dialogue journals capture conversations between students and teachers in the truest sense of that idea. As teaching and learning proceed, students write messages to you conveying thoughts and ideas about the achievement expected, self-evaluations of progress, points of confusion, important new insights, and so on, and periodically give you their journals. You then read the messages and reply, clarifying as needed, evaluating an idea, amplifying a key point, and so on, and return the journals to the students. This process links you and each of your students in a personal communication partnership.

Learning logs ask students to keep ongoing written records of the following aspects of their studies:

- Achievement targets they have mastered
- Targets they have found useful and important
- Targets they are having difficulty mastering
- Learning experiences (instructional strategies) that worked particularly well for them
- Experiences that did not work for them
- Questions that have come up along the way that they want help with
- Ideas for important study topics or learning strategies that they might like to try in the future

The goal in the case of learning logs is to have students reflect on, analyze, describe, and evaluate their learning experiences, successes, and challenges, writing about the conclusions they draw.

STUDENT-INVOLVED ASSESSMENT FOR LEARNING

Because instruction is conducted in large part through personal interaction between teacher and student, in a very real sense students are always partners in personal communication–based forms of assessment. Nevertheless, we can list a variety of concrete strategies for helping this partnership reach its full potential. Consider the ideas listed in Figure 8.5.

- Turn leadership for discussion over to students; they can ask questions of each other or of you (put your own reasoning power on the line in public once in a while).
- Ask students to paraphrase each other's questions and responses.
- Ask students to address key questions in small groups, so more students can be involved.
- Offer students opportunities to become oral examiners, posing questions of each other.
- Ask students to keep track of changes in the depth of their own questions over time, such as through the use of tally sheets and diaries.
- Designate one or two students to be observers and recorders during discussions, noting who responds to what kinds of questions and how well; other teachers can do this too.
- Engage students in peer and self-assessment of performance in discussions.
- Schedule regular interviews with students, one-on-one or in groups.
- Schedule times when your students can interview you to get your impressions about how well things are going for them as individuals and as a group.

FIGURE 8.5
Ideas for Student-involved Assessment While They're Learning

Summary: Person-to-Person Assessment

The key to success in using personal communication to assess student achievement is to remember that, just because assessment is sometimes casual, informal, unstructured, and/or spontaneous, this does not mean we can let our guard down with respect to standards of assessment quality. In fact, we must be even more vigilant than with other forms of assessment, because it is so easy to allow personal filters, poor sampling techniques, and/or inadequate record keeping to damage quality.

When we attend to quality standards, we use our interactions with students to assess important achievement targets, including mastery of knowledge, reasoning, and dispositions. We also can assess student mastery of knowledge and reasoning prerequisites to performance skills and product development capabilities. But remember, to tap the skills and products themselves, performance assessment is required.

Thus, like the other three modes of assessment, this one is quite flexible. Even though we typically don't refer to personal communication as assessment, if we start with a clear and appropriate vision, translate it into thoughtful probes, sample performance appropriately, and attend to key sources of bias, we can generate quality information in this manner.

So can students. Whether in whole-class discussions, smaller collaborative groups, or working with a partner, students can be assessors, too. They can ask questions of each other, listen to responses, infer achievement, and communicate feedback to each other. Beware, however. The ability to communicate effectively in an assessment context is not "wired in" from birth. Both you and your students must practice it, to hone it as an assessment skill.

Final Chapter Reflection

1. What are the three most important new insights to come to you as a result of your study of this chapter?
2. Which of your previous questions about assessment can you now answer based on your study of this chapter?
3. What new questions have come to mind as a result of your study of this chapter that you hope to have answered as your study continues?

Practice with Chapter 8 Ideas

1. Draw a concept map that shows your current understanding of how the topics shown randomly in Table 8.3 link together.

2. Referring to the text of this chapter as needed, fill in the cells of Table 8.4 in your own words.

TABLE 8.3
Interrelated Assessment Topics

Selected Response	Essay	Assessment Methods
Performance assessment	Products	Fill in the blank
Constructed response	Dispositions	True/False
Reasoning	Learning targets	Personal communication
Skills	Matching	Knowledge/Understanding
Sampling	Unclear tasks	Sources of bias & distortion
English language learner	Unclear criteria	Problems with test administration

TABLE 8.4
Personal Communication Format Strengths and Weaknesses

Assessment Format	Strengths as a Source of Evidence of Learning	Weaknesses
Instructional questions and answers		
Conferences and interviews		
Class discussion		
Oral examination		
Journals and logs		

Now go to www.myeducationlab.com to take a Pretest to assess your initial comprehension of chapter content, study chapter content with your individualized Study Plan, take a Posttest to assess your understanding of chapter content, practice your teaching skills with Building Teaching Skills exercises, and build a deeper, more applied understanding of chapter content with Homework and Exercises.

CHAPTER 9

Assessing Dispositions

CHAPTER FOCUS

This chapter answers the following guiding question:

> Why, when, and how might I assess the dispositions of my students?

From your study of this chapter, you will understand the following:

1. In school, the students' dispositions that are of interest to us are feelings that motivate students to behave in academically productive ways.

2. Dispositions take many forms, many of which can contribute to academic success or failure.

3. Primary among these is a student's sense of academic self-efficacy, or sense of control over her or his academic well being.

4. Dispositions vary in their focus, direction, and intensity, and can be assessed in these terms in the classroom.

As we start this part of our journey, keep our big picture in mind. Refer to Figure 9.1. In this chapter, we will be dealing in depth with the shaded areas.

	SELECTED RESPONSE	ESSAY	PERFORMANCE ASSESSMENT	PERSONAL COMMUNICATION
Knowledge				
Reasoning				
Performance Skills				
Products				
Dispositions				

FIGURE 9.1
Aligning Achievement Targets and Assessment Methods

STUDENTS WHO ARE PREDISPOSED TO SUCCEED

In our opening scenario in Chapter 1, Emily became more than just a good writer. She became a confident writer. She came to believe in herself as a writer. The early improvements in her writing gave her the feeling that she could succeed if she kept trying. The direction of this effect was critical. When students experience what they believe to be real and important academic success that they believe they have earned, the result can be a strong desire to want more of that feeling. From the beginning, we have contended that we can succeed as teachers only if we help our students *want* to learn. Ms. Weathersby succeeded with Emily and her classmates. Motivation and desire represent the very foundations of learning. If students don't want to learn, there will be no learning. If they feel unable to learn, there will be no learning.

Desire and motivation are not academic achievement characteristics. They are *affective* characteristics. Feelings. Emotions. We have established that we can assess achievement. But can we assess these feelings or dispositions? Yes. And, from time to time, it may be helpful to your students to assess them and use the results to support their learning.

When we assess mastery of subject matter knowledge, we seek to know how much of the material students have learned. When we assess reasoning, we seek to know how effectively students can use that knowledge to solve problems. When we assess performance skills, we evaluate demonstrated proficiencies. When we assess products, we evaluate whether students can create things that meet certain standards of quality. These are things you already know.

When we assess dispositions, we tap student feelings about school-related things, the inner motivations or desires that influence their thoughts and their actions. In this case, we center, not on what students know and can do, but on the attitudes, motivations, and interests that predispose students to behave in academically productive ways. Our assessment challenge in this case is easy to understand. Students' feelings about school vary in their focus (feelings about what, exactly), in their direction (from positive through neutral to negative) and in their intensity (from very strong to moderate to very weak). Our assessment task is to specify the focus and ask about direction and intensity.

With these features in mind, we can share why we have adopted the label *dispositions* in this chapter. Our goals for developing student feelings are not value neutral. Often, we hope for strong, positive or negative, feelings in our students when it comes to learning. We strive to develop learners predisposed to behave in certain academically productive ways in school. Often, we seek a strong positive work ethic, positive motivation, intense interests, positive attitudes, and a positive academic self-concept; that is, we want them to have a strong sense of internal control over their own academic success; that is, a strong sense of academic self-efficacy. Indeed, assessment FOR learning is entirely about helping students develop these very feelings.

ASSESSMENT FOR LEARNING ENGAGES STUDENT DISPOSITIONS

We have advocated student involvement in classroom assessment throughout this book because research tells us it can lead to greater student learning. It is imperative that you understand how this works. When applied effectively, the principles of assessment

FOR learning help students *feel* like capable learners, feel in control of their own success. They enhance students' confidence and desire to learn.

Our point is that we cannot separate dispositions and achievement from one another in the classroom. As teachers, we must know how to help students develop academically empowering dispositions and must be ready to teach them how to use those dispositions to promote their own success. Very often, students fail, not because they cannot achieve, but because they choose not to achieve. Often, they have given up and are not motivated to learn. Why? There can be many reasons: They don't understand the work, find it too hard to do, lack prerequisite achievement, and so on. And so they fail, which in turn robs them of (1) the prerequisites for the next learning and (2) a sense that they could succeed if they tried. This can become a vicious cycle, a self-fulfilling prophecy. They feel academically powerless and thus become so. This negative sense of oneself as a learner drives out of students any motivation to try. This downward spiral can result from the complex interaction between achievement and dispositions. These students become predisposed to fail.

But this spiral also can take a very positive direction. Right from the time students arrive at school, they look to us, their teachers, for evidence of the extent to which they are succeeding. If that early evidence (from our classroom assessments) suggests that they are succeeding, what can begin to grow in them is a sense of hope for the future and expectation of further success down the road. This, in turn, fuels their motivation to strive for excellence, which spawns more success and results in the upward spiral of positive dispositions and academic achievement that every parent and teacher dreams of for their children. These students become predisposed to succeed.

Clearly, many forces in a student's life exert great influence on attitudes, values, interests, self-concept, and indeed on dispositions to try to achieve excellence. Chief among these are family, peer group, church, and community. But schools are prominent on this list of contributors, too, especially when it comes to dispositions to invest the energy required to learn. To the extent that we wish to help students to take advantage of dispositions as driving forces toward greater achievement, it will be important for us to understand and apply the principles of assessment FOR learning (Chappuis, 2009):

1. Show them where their learning is headed by
   - Revealing achievement targets to them using student-friendly language.
   - Providing examples of good- and poor-quality work so students can see the range.

2. Show students where they are now in relation to that vision of academic success by
   - Providing focused practice relying heavily on descriptive feedback that they can use to see how to do better the next time.
   - Teaching them to monitor their own progress along the way and be partners in setting learning goals.

3. Help them close the gap between where they are now and where we want them to be by
   - Planning lessons that focus on one key attribute of achievement at a time.
   - Teaching them focused revision: how to improve their work one attribute at a time.
   - Teaching them to reflect on, track, and communicate with others about changes in their work over time.

In these ways, student-involved assessment can fuel a strong sense of hope for success on every student's part, predisposing them to pursue academic excellence.

Time for Reflection

From a personal point of view, which of your school-related feelings (positive or negative) seem to have been most closely associated with your achievement successes in school? Were there subjects you liked or disliked? Instructors who motivated or failed to motivate you? Positive or negative values that you held? How have your dispositions toward school-related things impacted to your achievement?

A Crucial Difference between Achievement and Affect

There is one very important difference between student achievement and student affect that bears directly on differences in the manner in which we *use* assessment. It has to do with the reasons for assessing.

It is perfectly acceptable to hold students accountable for mastery of knowledge, reasoning, skill, and/or product targets. In assessment OF learning contexts, where students are responsible for learning, we assess to verify that students have met our academic achievement standards.

However, it is rarely acceptable to hold students accountable in the same sense for their dispositions. It is never acceptable, for example, to lower a student's grade because they have a negative attitude about the subject. Evidence of learning or the lack of it must speak for itself at grading time, regardless of attitudes expressed in class. Nor, conversely, is it acceptable to raise a student's grade just because of a positive attitude or other disposition, regardless of achievement.

Rather, we assess dispositions in the hope of finding positive, productive attitudes, values, sense of academic self, or interest in particular topics so we can take advantage of these—build on them—to promote greater achievement gains.

If our assessments should reveal academically inappropriate or counterproductive feelings, then we are obliged to strive to create educational experiences that will turn those around and result in the productive dispositions we hope for. In fact, such experiences may or may not succeed in producing the positive motivational predisposition we desire. But if we do not succeed in this endeavor, we cannot place sanctions on students with negative affect in the same way we can for those who fail to achieve academically.

In fact, we believe responsibility for school-related student dispositions should rest with *us*, their teachers. We hold myself accountable for your dispositions regarding assessment. If we don't help you feel strongly about the critical importance of quality assessment, if you don't leave our classes or complete this book feeling a strong sense of responsibility to create accurate assessments and if you don't feel a strong desire to use them to benefit your students, then *We regard that as our fault*. We must strive to find better ways to motivate you, our students, to act responsibly with respect to the quality of your classroom assessments. We believe you have that same responsibility with your students.

TWO VERY IMPORTANT GROUND RULES

Before we define and discuss ways to assess dispositions, let us lay out two critically important ground rules for dealing with dispositions in the classroom. Note them well; violate them at your own peril and that of your students.

Ground Rule 1: Remember, This Is Personal

Always remain keenly aware of the sensitive personal nature of student feelings and strive to promote appropriate dispositions through your assessment of them. Delving into student school-related emotions and feelings can be risky on both sides. When you assess, you ask students to risk being honest in an environment where an honest response has not always been what their teacher is looking for. They may be reticent to express honest feelings because of the risk that you may somehow use the results against them. It takes a teacher who is a true master of human relations to break through these barriers and promote honest expression of feelings in classrooms. One good avenue to honest response is to find ways for students to tell you their true feelings anonymously. We will offer specific instructions regarding how to foster honesty later in the chapter.

For your part, you risk asking for honesty in a place where the honest response just may not turn out to be the one you had hoped to hear. Positive feedback is wonderful to receive, but negative feedback is never easy to hear and act on. Many avoid this danger by simply not asking. If you ask how students are feeling about things in your classroom, listen thoughtfully to the answers, and act on the results in good faith—the reward will be worth the risk you take. The result can be a more productive student–teacher relationship, a working partnership characterized by greater trust.

Time for Reflection

Under the best of circumstances, as teachers, we can become anxious when the time comes to ask students what they think about the instruction they are experiencing. Can you think of specific actions you might take to minimize your personal risk when preparing for, conducting, and interpreting the results of such an assessment? List as many ideas as you can.

Ground Rule 2: Stay in Bounds

Know your limits when dealing with student feelings. There are two important interrelated limits you should be aware of. First, as you come to understand and assess student feelings, you will occasionally encounter students who are troubled, personally and/or socially. Be caring but careful in these instances. These are not occasions for you to become an amateur psychologist. *If you find yourself in a situation where you feel uneasy with what you are learning about a student or about your ability to help that student deal productively with feelings or circumstances, get help.* The most caring and responsible teachers are those who know when it is time to contact the principal, a counselor, a school psychologist, or a physician to find competent counseling services for students. Do not venture into personal territory for which you are not trained.

The second set of limits is corollary to the first. We urge you to focus your attention on those classroom-level dispositions over which you are likely to (and in fact should) have some influence. When assessing and evaluating student dispositions, stick with those feelings as they relate to specific school-related objects: dispositions toward particular subjects or classroom activities, academic interests students would like to pursue in school, personal dispositions as learners in an academic setting, and so on. These have a decidedly school-oriented bent, and they represent values families and school communities are likely to agree are important as parts of the schooling experience. You need not go too far over those classroom-related limits before members of your community may begin to see your actions on behalf of positive, productive affect as invading their turf. Some families and communities are very protective of their responsibility to promote the development of certain strongly held values and will not countenance interference from schools. This is their right.

Exploring the Cultural Context of Assessment

As we all know, the attitudes, values, and so on we individually hold are influenced by our home culture. Sometimes, these can spill over into school in ways that require thoughtful accommodation. For example, in some cultures, humility is valued as an interpersonal characteristic. One doesn't behave in ways that call attention to oneself as being superior to others. What might be the classroom assessment implications of such a value? How might you keep such a value from biasing your assessments of the achievement of such a student? Are there other cultural attitudes or values of which you are aware that require careful attention in our classrooms?

DEFINING *AFFECT* AS IT RELATES TO DISPOSITIONS

To help you make sense of the range of relevant student dispositions, We will follow Anderson and Bourke (2000) and note several kinds of affect that can come into play in the school setting:

- school-related attitudes
- school-related values
- academic self-efficacy
- academic interests
- academic aspirations
- assessment anxiety

These represent significant dimensions of classroom affect that bear directly on students' motivation to learn. They represent students' attributes that predispose them to behave in academically and socially productive ways. In addition, each has been clearly defined in the professional literature, is relatively easy to understand, and can be assessed in the classroom using relatively straightforward procedures.

School-Related Attitudes

An *attitude* is a favorable or unfavorable feeling about someone or something. Very simply, if a student likes a particular teacher, that student holds a positive attitude about that teacher. If one dislike a school subject, one has learned a negative attitude about it. One does not learn the feeling itself, one learns rather the association between the feeling and a particular focus. And once ingrained, the feeling is consistently experienced in the presence of that object. The focus might be a person, a school subject, or a particular method of instruction. However, attitudes can be unstable in the sense that they can change quickly, especially among young people.

Attitudes vary in direction (favorable to unfavorable) and intensity (strong to weak). The stronger the favorable or unfavorable attitudes, the greater is the likelihood that they will influence behavior.

Obviously, the range of attitudes within any individual is as broad as the array of experiences or objects to which that person reacts emotionally. In schools, students might have favorable or unfavorable attitudes about each other, teachers, administrators, math, science, reading, writing, instructional activities, and so on. It is our hope as educators that success breeds positive attitudes, which then fuel the desire for greater achievement, which in turn breeds more positive attitudes. Thus, certain attitudes predispose students to academic success.

School-Related Values

Our *values* are our "beliefs about what should be desired, what is important or cherished, and what standards of conduct are . . . acceptable. Second, values influence or guide behavior, interests, attitudes, and satisfactions. Third, values are enduring. That is, they tend to remain stable over fairly long periods of time" (Anderson & Bourke, 2000, p. 32). Values also are learned, tend to be of high intensity, and tend to focus on enduring ideas.

The following are among those values related to academic success:

● Belief in the value of education as a foundation for a productive life
● Belief in the benefits of strong effort in school
● A strong sense of the need for ethical behavior at testing time (no cheating)
● The belief that a healthy lifestyle (for example, no drugs) underpins academic success

These, then, are among the values that influence behavior and predispose students to succeed in school.

Academic Self-Efficacy

No affective characteristic is more school related than this one. It is the evaluative judgment one makes about one's possibility of success and/or productivity in an academic context. In essence, it is an attitude (favorable or unfavorable) about one's self when viewed in a classroom setting. Academic self-concept, Anderson and Bourke (2000) instruct us, is a learned vision that results largely from evaluations of self by others over time. Quite simply, those who see themselves as capable learners are predisposed to be capable learners.

There is one part of academic self-concept that is sufficiently important to justify its consideration here. In this case, the characteristic of interest is students' attributions or beliefs about the reasons for academic success or failure (this is referred to in the literature as *locus of control*). One kind of attribution is defined as *internal*: "I succeeded because I tried hard." Another possible attribution is *external,* where chance rules: "I sure was lucky to receive that A!" Yet another external attribution assigns cause to some other person or factor: "I performed well because I had a good teacher." At issue here are students' perceptions of the underlying reasons for the results they are experiencing. These, too, are learned self-perceptions arising from their sense of the connection of effort to academic success.

Consider the contrasting experiences, emotions, and implications for students who are on academic winning versus losing trajectories, as depicted in Figure 9.2. In school, our aspiration must be to seek to imbue students with a strong internal sense of academic control and well-being (the winning streak profile in Column 1). This is the basis of our intense belief in the principles of assessment FOR learning. Students who perceive themselves as being in control of their own academic destiny and who, at the same time, see learning success as being within their reach, are predisposed to do the things that will result in that success. Please spend some time reading this table—it captures the emotional dynamics of the assessment experience from the student's point of view better than anything presented so far.

As with other affective characteristics, self-efficacy varies in direction (can do, can't do) and intensity (weak to strong) and is learned. "The learning takes place over time as the student experiences a series of successes or failures" (Anderson & Bourke, 2000, p. 35). At the risk of being repetitive, once again we say that through their involvement in assessment, record keeping, and communication, we hope to help students develop a "can do" perspective in the classroom.

Academic Interests

Let's define an *interest* as a learned preference for some activity, skill, idea, or understanding. This preference influences behavior in that it causes us to pursue its object. Feelings range from a high level of excitement to no excitement about the prospect of engaging in a particular activity.

A student might be very interested in drama, but completely disinterested in geography. Strong interests, like positive attitudes, can link students to their greater potential for success. In this sense, they too relate to student dispositions. Students learn most effectively and efficiently when they are interested in what we expect them to learn.

Academic Aspirations

In this case, we refer to the desire to learn more—the intent to seek out and participate in additional education experiences. Thus, Anderson and Bourke (2000) write, "We would suggest that aspirations are moderately high intensity affective characteristics . . . the direction of which is 'more' or 'no more'" (p. 30). Aspirations emerge from students' history of academic success or the lack thereof, feelings of self-efficacy or control over that level of success, interests in the topic(s) they are studying, and attitudes about school.

Assessment Anxiety

Hall and Lindsay (1970) define *anxiety* as "the experience of [emotional] tension that results from real or imagined threats to one's security" (p. 145). This feeling varies from a sense of relaxed safety on one end to extreme tension on the other. When faced with the prospect of having their achievement evaluated, students will experience varying levels of this kind of anxiety, depending on their record of success or the lack thereof and the extent and nature of their preparation to succeed on the assessment.

Students on Winning Streaks	Students on Losing Streaks
What assessment results consistently say:	
Continuous evidence of success	Continuous evidence of failure
Likely effect on the learner:	
Hope rules; remain optimistic	Hopelessness dominates
Success fuels productive action	Initial panic gives way to resignation
What the student is probably thinking in the face of these results:	
It's all good; I'm doing fine	This hurts; I'm not safe here
See the trend? I succeed as usual	I just can't do this either . . . again
I want more success	I'm confused; I don't like this—help!
We focus on what I do well	Why is it always about what I can't do?
I know what to do next	I have no idea what to do next; nothing seems to work . . .
Move on, grow, learn new stuff	Defend, hide, get away from here
Feedback helps me	Feedback hurts me—scares me
Public success feels very good	Public failure is embarrassing
I can make the difficult make sense	I can't make this make sense
Actions likely to be taken by the learner:	
Take risks—stretch, go for it!	Trying is too dangerous—retreat, escape
Seek what is new and exciting	Can't keep up—can't handle new stuff
Seek challenges	Seek what's easy
Practice with gusto	Don't know how to practice
Take initiative	Avoid initiative
Persist	Give up
Likely result of these actions:	
Lay foundations now for success later	Can't master prerequisites needed later
Success becomes the only reward	No success, no reward
Self-enhancement	Self-defeat, self-destruction
Positive self-fulfilling prophecy	Negative prophecy
Extend the effort in face of difficulty	Give up quickly in face of difficulty
Acceptance of responsibility	Denial of responsibilty
Make success public	Cover up failure
Self-analysis tells me how to win	Self-criticism is easy given my record
Manageable stress	Stress always remains high
Curiosity, enthusiasm	Boredom, frustration, fear
Resilience	Yielding quickly to defeat
Continuous adaption	Inability to adapt

FIGURE 9.2
Contrasting Profiles of Student Dispositions Based on Academic Record

In the classroom, we can conceive of ways in which anxiety can affect students' behavior. One is as a driving force. It can supply positive energy, motivating students to work hard. This happens when their judgment of the chances of success are high. Alternatively, anxiety can serve as a source of debilitation, fear, and frustration, causing students to give up in hopelessness or cynicism. The systematic application of the principles of assessment FOR learning promotes the expectation of success, reducing evaluation anxiety.

Anxiety also can be a source of feelings of vulnerability, leading students to feel at risk of harm in the face of an assessment. Be advised that, depending on the strength of that anxiety, it can (1) inhibit clear thinking and thus performance on the assessment, thus leading to biased results, or (2) overwhelm the student with a sense of hopelessness, thus inhibiting learning itself. Both are effects to be avoided at all cost.

VARIATIONS IN DISPOSITIONS

As mentioned earlier, the various kinds of dispositions vary along three important dimensions: focus, direction, and intensity. They focus on our feelings about specific aspects of the world around us. Some, such as attitudes and values, can focus outside of ourselves. Others, such as academic self-concept and locus of control, focus on our inner views.

Affect also can vary in direction, stretching from a neutral point outward in both directions along a continuum to differing anchor points. Table 9.1 lists those end points.

And finally, feelings vary in their intensity, from strong to moderate to weak. As you visualize the continuum for each type of affect and move further and further away from neutral, think of feelings as increasing in intensity. In the extremes, feelings become strong.

Bear in mind also that some feelings can be volatile, especially among the young. Such student dispositions as attitudes, interests, and anxiety can quickly change both in direction and intensity for a large number of reasons, only some of which are rational or understandable to adults. On the other hand, values, self-concept dimensions, and aspirations may be more enduring. We mention this to point out that it may be important to sample volatile dispositions repeatedly over time to keep track of them. The results of any one assessment may have a very short half-life.

Given our discussion so far, we're sure you can understand why our assessment challenge is to gather information on the direction and intensity of school-related feelings. We capture the essence of student dispositions about success in school when we focus on the right-hand column of Table 9.1. It is quite possible to determine how closely students approximate these desired feelings, if we understand and apply some relatively straightforward assessment strategies.

MATCHING METHOD TO TARGETS

So how do we assess the focus, direction, and intensity of feelings about school-related things? Just as with achievement, we rely on standard forms of assessment: selected response, open-ended written response, performance assessment, and personal communication with students.

TABLE 9.1
The Range of Dispositions

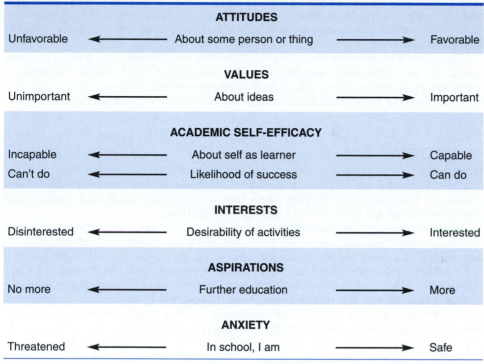

	ATTITUDES	
Unfavorable ←	About some person or thing	→ Favorable

	VALUES	
Unimportant ←	About ideas	→ Important

	ACADEMIC SELF-EFFICACY	
Incapable ←	About self as learner	→ Capable
Can't do ←	Likelihood of success	→ Can do

	INTERESTS	
Disinterested ←	Desirability of activities	→ Interested

	ASPIRATIONS	
No more ←	Further education	→ More

	ANXIETY	
Threatened ←	In school, I am	→ Safe

Source: From *Assessing Affective Characteristics in Schools*, 2nd ed. (p. 38) by L. W. Anderson, & S. F. Bourke, 2000, Mahwah, NJ: Lawrence Erlbaum & Associates. Copyright © 2000 by Lawrence Erlbaum & Associates. Adapted by permission.

In this case, let's group selected response and essay into a single paper and pencil assessment form because the two options represent different ways that questions can appear on a basic affective assessment tool: the *questionnaire.* We can ask students questions about their feelings on a questionnaire and either offer them a few response options to select from, or we can ask them open-ended questions and request brief or extended written responses. If we focus the questions on affect, we can interpret responses in terms of both the direction and intensity of feelings. Examples are coming right up. But first, let's see the other options.

Performance assessment of affective targets is like performance assessment of achievement targets. We *observe* of student behavior and/or products with clear criteria in mind and from them infer the direction and intensity of students' dispositions. So once again, as with open-ended questionnaires, professional judgments form the basis of our affective assessment.

Assessments of dispositions via personal communication typically take the form of *interviews,* either with students alone or in groups. In addition, we can interview others who know the students. These can be highly structured or very casual, as in discussions or conversations with students. The questions we ask and the things we talk about reveal the direction and intensity of feelings.

Each method for tapping student dispositions can be cast in many forms and each carries with it specific advantages, limitations, keys to success, and pitfalls to avoid. Let's examine these, then review a few tips for your effective development and use of each. As we go, we will try to illustrate how you can use the various forms of questionnaires, performance assessments, and personal communications to tap the different kinds of dispositions.

We will now consider procedural guidelines that can enhance the quality of questionnaires, performance assessment, and interview planning and design. The remainder of this chapter examines each of these basic assessment options and explores how each can help tap the various kinds of dispositional targets defined previously.

Questionnaires

Questionnaires represent one of the most convenient means of tapping important student dispositions if we can find ways to help students provide complete and honest responses. That means focusing on topics that students care about and making sure they know we will act on results in ways that benefit them.

Whenever we develop a questionnaire, we strive to combine all of these ideas in a way that enlists respondents as allies, as partners in generating useful information, information that promises to help us all. Sometimes that means permitting responses to be offered anonymously, to reduce the risk to respondents. Sometimes it means promising to share results or promising to act purposefully and quickly based on those results. Sometimes it just means urging them to take the questionnaire seriously, to care as we do about the value of the results for making things better for all. In any event, we try to break down the barriers between us.

Selected Response Questionnaires

The major strengths of selected response questionnaires is their ease of development, administration, and processing of results. We have a variety of selected response formats to choose from as we design questionnaires. For example, we can ask students the following:

- If they agree or disagree with specific statements
- How important they regard specific things
- How they would judge the quality of something
- How frequently they feel certain ways

To illustrate the first option, Figure 9.3 includes the eight items that make up the "The Way I See School" questionnaire that Jim Popham and Rick developed for use in elementary classrooms. Its items ask students about their feelings about two aspects of their classroom experience that relate directly to assessment FOR learning processes: *academic self-efficacy* and *eagerness to learn*, as well as two classroom practices that might influence those feelings: their sense of the *clarity of the learning targets* and availability of information to allow them to *self-monitor* their progress. The form includes two items for each of these four foci.

Time for Reflection

Please read the items in the Figure 9.3 questionnaire and identify which two items relate to each of the four dimensions of affect identified in this text as foci.

Directions: Please indicate how you feel about each statement as follows:

SA = Strongly Agree A = Agree   U = Undecided   D = Disagree SD = Strongly Disagree

1.   I usually understand what I am supposed to learn.

     SA   S   U   D   SD

2.   If I'm asked to learn new things, even if it's difficult, I know I can learn it.

     SA   S   U   D   SD

3.   Typically, I don't know if I'm making progress as fast as I should.

     SA   S   U   D   SD

4.   I'm excited about learning new things in school.

     SA   S   U   D   SD

5.   Very often, I'm not certain what I'm supposed to be learning.

     SA   S   U   D   SD

6.   Lots of the time, I don't look forward to learning new things in school.

     SA   S   U   D   SD

7.   Even if I get lots of help and plenty of time, it is hard for me to learn new things.

     SA   S   U   D   SD

8.   I get plenty of information to help me keep track of my own learning growth.

     SA   S   U   D   SD

Thank you for completing this form.

FIGURE 9.3
Assessment FOR Learning Affect Questionnaire
Source: From *Assessing Student Affect Related to Assessment FOR Learning* (n.p.), by
R. J. Stiggins and W. J. Popham (n.d.). Washington DC: Council of Chief State School Officers
FAST SCASS. Public Domain.

So, if a teacher was to administer this questionnaire anonymously, summarize the results across students by tallying responses and find low levels of academic self-efficacy and/or eagerness to learn, along with feelings that learning targets were not clear to students and/or students lacking information needed to keep track of their own progress, then adjusting the latter practices might be in order. This teacher might follow up making such changes with a later administration of the questionnaire to see if dispositions have improved.

But remember, agree/disagree items are only one option. Questions also can determine perceived frequency of occurrence of a particular event:

How frequently do you feel you understand and can do the math homework assignments you receive in this class?

  a. Always
  b. Frequently
  c. Occasionally
  d. Rarely
  e. Never

One of the most common forms of selected response questionnaire items asks students to choose between or among some forced choices. The following examples are designed to help us understand students' locus of control:

If I do well on a test, it is typically because

  a. My teacher taught me well.
  b. I was lucky.
  c. I studied hard.

Or

I failed to master that particular standard because

  a. I didn't try hard enough.
  b. My teacher didn't show me how.
  c. I was unlucky.

Yet another kind of selected response format is a scale anchored at each end by polar adjectives and offering direction and intensity options in between. Here's an example focused on student interest and motivation:

Use the scales provided to describe your interest in learning the school subjects listed. Place an X on the blank that best reflects your feelings:

Mathematics

Very Interested ____ ____ ____ ____ ____ Completely Uninterested

Very Motivated ____ ____ ____ ____ ____ Completely Unmotivated

Science

Very Interested ____ ____ ____ ____ ____ Completely Uninterested

Very Motivated ____ ____ ____ ____ ____ Completely Unmotivated

An easy adaptation of the selected response format can provide a means of tapping the attitudes of very young students. Rather than using words to describe feeling states, we can use simple pictures:

Given school-related events or activities about which to express their feelings, such as free reading time, for example, you would instruct the students to circle the face that tells how they feel about it.

Using these kinds of scales, students can easily reveal their attitudes, interests, school-related values, academic self-concept, and the like. Further, it is usually easy to summarize results across respondents. The pattern of responses, and therefore the feelings, of a group of students is easily seen by tallying the number and percent of students who select each response option. This can lead to a straightforward summary of results.

Open-Ended Written Response

Another way to assess affect is to offer open-ended questions, to which respondents are free to write their responses. If we ask specific questions eliciting direction and intensity of dispositions about specific school-related issues, we may readily interpret responses:

> Write a brief paragraph describing your reaction to our guest speaker today. Please comment on your level of interest in the presentation, how well informed you thought the speaker was, and how provocative you found the message to be. As you write, be sure to tell me how strong your positive or negative feelings are. I will use your reactions to plan our future guest speakers.

Or here's an interesting option—consider combining assessment of affect with practice in evaluative reasoning:

> As you think about the readings we did this month, which three did you find most worthwhile? For each choice, specify why you found it worthwhile.

A thoughtful reading of the responses to these kinds of questions will reveal similarities or differences in students' opinions and can help you plan future instruction.

To maximize the value of questionnaire results, always anticipate how you can connect your questions to direct action. By this, we mean ask only those questions that will provide you with the specific and significant information you need to make your decisions. For each question you pose, you should be able to anticipate the course of action you will take given each possible response: "If my students respond this way, I will do. . . . If they respond the other way, I should instead do. . . ." Discard any query that leaves you wondering what you'll do with the results.

Here is must issue one more critical reminder: *If you promise respondents that you will gather information anonymously, stick with that promise under all circumstances.* Never try to subvert such a promise with invisible coding or other identification systems. Students need to be caught in that trap only once to come to believe they can trust neither teachers nor administrators.

Performance Observations as Assessments of Dispositions

Student behavior has always been a standard indicator of dispositions. Adhering to classroom rules, for example, is often cited as evidence of a "positive attitude." Tardiness is seen as evidence of a lack of respect for school or as evidence of poor attitude. It has been almost a matter of tradition that teachers observe and reflect on their interactions with students, such as when students appear not to be trying or when they just don't seem to care. Our almost automatic inference is that they are "unmotivated" and "have a bad attitude."

While these inferences may be correct, they also can be dangerous. What if our casual observations and intuitive inferences about the underlying causes of the behavior we see are wrong? What if adhering to the rules comes from a sense of personal vulnerability and reflects a low willingness to take risks? What if tardiness is due to some factor at home that is beyond the student's control, or the apparent lack of motivation is not a result of low self-esteem, but rather an indication that we were not clear in helping that student understand the task to be completed? If our inferences are wrong, we may well plan and carry out remedies that completely miss the point, and that do more harm than good.

This leads us to a very important note of caution: The cavalier manner in which some observe and draw inferences about student attitudes, values, interests, and the like very often reflects a lack of regard for the basic principles of sound assessment. The rules of evidence for observing and judging don't change just because the nature of the target changes. Vague targets, inappropriately cast into the wrong methods, that fail to sample adequately or control for bias lead to incorrect assessments of dispositions just as they lead to incorrect inferences about achievement. The rules of evidence for sound assessment are *never* negotiable.

For this reason, developing performance assessments of dispositions requires that you follow exactly the same basic design sequence used for performance assessment of achievement. You must specify the performance you will evaluate, devise scoring criteria, select a context and task within which to observe, and record and store results dependably.

This does not mean spontaneous observations and judgments are unacceptable. But you must remain vigilant, for many things can go wrong with such on-the-spot assessments. That awareness can make you appropriately cautious about making snap judgments.

When developing affective performance assessments, you face the same design decisions that we spelled out in detail in Chapter 7. They are translated into design questions for the assessment of dispositions in Figure 9.4.

This list of design questions looks imposing in this context. You might read it and ask, Why be so formal? It's not as if we're conducting an assessment for a final grade or something! In fact, many regard it as instinctive for teachers to observe some behavior and infer almost intuitively about student attitudes, motivations, school-related values, and so on. But this is exactly our point. If you disregard the rules of evidence in conducting assessments based on observation and judgment whether assessing attitudes or writing proficiency, your assessment will almost always produce undependable results. For this reason, it is always important to strive for quality assessment.

And finally, remember, neither performance assessment or personal communication (addressed next) permit anonymity.

Personal Communication as a Window to Student Feelings

Direct communication is an excellent path to understanding student feelings about school-related topics. We can interview students individually or in groups, conduct discussions with them, or even rely on casual discussions to gain insight about their attitudes, values, and aspirations. In addition, if we establish a trusting relationship with students that permits them to be honest with us, we can understand their sense of self-efficacy and even the levels of anxiety that they are feeling.

This method offers much. Unlike questionnaires, we can establish personal contact with respondents, and can ask followup questions. This allows us to more completely understand students' feelings. Unlike performance assessment, we can gather our information directly, avoiding the danger of drawing incorrect inferences. This assures a higher level of accuracy and confidence in our assessment results.

1. How shall we define the disposition to be assessed?

    What shall we focus on to evaluate student feelings?

    - A behavior exhibited by the student?

    - A product created by the student?

    What specific performance criteria will guide our observations and inferences about student affect?

2. How shall we elicit performance to be evaluated in terms of the disposition it reflects?

    What will we tell students to do under what conditions, according to what standards of performance?

    How many instances of performance will we need to observe to make confident generalizations about student feelings?

3. What method will we use to record results of our observations?

    Which do we wish to obtain?

    - A single holistic judgment about student affect?

    - Analysis of several aspects of student feelings?

    What record will we create of student affect?

    - Checklist?

    - Rating scale?

    - Anecdotal record?

FIGURE 9.4
Designing Performance Assessments of Dispositions

Keys to Success

One key to success in tapping true student dispositions is trust. We cannot overemphasize its critical importance. Respondents must be comfortable honestly expressing the direction and intensity of their feelings. Respondents who lack trust will either tell us what they think we want to hear (i.e., give the socially desirable response) or they will shut us out altogether. For many students, it is difficult to communicate honest feelings in an interview setting with the real power sitting on the other side of the table, because all hope of anonymity evaporates. This can seem risky to them.

Another key to success is to have adequate time to plan and conduct high-quality assessments. This is a labor-intensive means of soliciting information.

In many ways, the remaining keys to success in an interview setting are the same as those for questionnaires:

- Prepare carefully.
- Make sure respondents know why you are gathering this information.
- Ask focused, clear, brief questions that get at the direction and intensity of feelings about specific school-related topics.
- Act on results in ways that serve students' best interests.

In other ways, this assessment format brings with it some unique challenges. Figure 9.5 offers guidelines to help you meet those challenges.

- *Don't overlook the power of group interview.* Marketing people call these *focus groups.* Sometimes students' feelings become clear to them and to you by bouncing them off or comparing them to others. Besides, there can be a feeling of safety in numbers, allowing respondents to open up a bit more.

- *Rely on students as interviewers or discussion leaders.* Often, they know how to probe the real and important feelings of their classmates. Besides, they have credibility in places where you may not.

- *Become an attentive listener.* Ask focused questions about the direction and intensity of feelings and then listen attentively for evidence of the same. Sometimes interviewers come off looking and acting like robots. Sometimes just a bit of interpersonal warmth will open things up.

- *Be prepared to record results if needed.* We can use tape recorders in interview contexts, but this is certainly not the only way to capture student responses. For example, you could create a written questionnaire form but ask the questions personally and complete the questionnaire as you go. Or, you could just take notes and transcribe them into a more complete record later. In any event, students will appreciate that you asked how they felt, but only if you seem to remember what they said and take it into consideration in your instructional planning.

FIGURE 9.5
Guidelines for Conducting Interviews to Assess Dispositions

Summary: Dispositions That Boost Achievement

Our aspiration for students is that they develop positive dispositions about learning and negative dispositions about those things that interfere with it. Our assessment questions are these:

1. Are students developing the positive attitudes, strong interests, positive motivations, positive school values, positive academic self-concept, and the "can do" sense of internal locus of control needed to succeed in school and beyond?

2. Are students feeling safe in school and are they experiencing levels of anxiety appropriate to fuel productive learning but not so high as to be debilitating?

These are affective targets influencing student tendencies to behave in academically productive ways. They vary both in intensity and direction, ranging from strongly positive to strongly negative. Our assessment challenge is to track their intensity and direction.

There are two basic reasons why we should care about student dispositions. First, they have value in their own right. They represent personal characteristics that we value as a society. We want all citizens to feel as though they are in control of their own destinies. Second, student attitudes, motivation, interests, and preferences are closely related to achievement. Those who experience academic success are far more likely to develop appropriate attitudes and values that, in turn, provide the impetus to take the risks associated with seeking further academic success. Thus, we know that affect and achievement support each other in important ways.

Our assessment options in this case are the same as those we use to track student achievement: selected response, open-ended written response, performance assessment, and personal communication. Selected response and open-ended written alternatives take the form of questionnaires. We reviewed several different question formats for use in these instruments. Performance assessments have us observing student behaviors and/or products and inferring affective states. Careful development of these observation-based assessments may help us draw strong inferences about dispositions. Personal communication using interviews, discussions, and conversations can clarify student attitudes and often give us the clearest insights.

We began the chapter with two specific ground rules intended to prevent misuse of assessment in this arena. They bear repeating as final thoughts on this topic.

1. Always remain keenly aware of the sensitive personal nature of student feelings and strive to promote productive dispositions through your assessment of these outcomes.
2. Know your limits when dealing with student affect. Assess school-related dispositions only and get help when appropriate.

Final Chapter Reflection

1. *What are the three most important new insights to come to you as a result of your study of this chapter?*
2. *Which of your previous questions about assessment can you now answer based on your study of this chapter?*
3. *What new questions have come to mind as a result of your study of this chapter—questions that you hope to have answered as your study continues?*

Practice with Chapter 9 Ideas

1. In your own words, explain the relationship between student dispositions and achievement which, if it is developed for students, can lead them to ultimate achievement success. Explain how that relationship can go awry in ways that damage student learning.
2. Listed here are some cultural perspectives that have implications for how, when, or if we assess student dispositions. For each, what are the implications and what would be the proper course of action in contexts where these perspectives emerge?
   a. In some cultures, the public expression of private attitudes and concerns is viewed as inappropriate.
   b. When assessing dispositions through nonverbal behaviors that occur naturally in the classroom (e.g., assuming that student eye contact with the teacher represents interest in the content of a lesson), cultural differences among students can interfere with the accuracy of our judgments. In some cultures, a raised eyebrow signifies agreement and interest. In others, eye contact with one's elders is considered disrespectful. In still others, silence is a sign that one is in agreement with perspectives being expressed.
   c. Young people in some cultures are expected to express only positive dispositions to those in authority—in the classroom, in the home, and in the community. Inviting such students to fill out a scaled attitude survey is likely to result in high ratings regardless of the student's feelings. It is thought disrespectful of those in authority to do otherwise.

3. Answer the questions and fill in the blanks for each of the kinds of disposition listed in Table 9.2 to reveal how dispositions might be expressed.

4. Let's say you want to tap student attitudes about a particular textbook you are using. Your challenge is to assess the direction and intensity of their most important feelings

TABLE 9.2
Disposition Questions

What might a student say that would indicate a negative attitude about science?	**ATTITUDES**	What comment from a student might reflect a positive attitude about science?
How might a student whose culture favors individual achievement above group accomplishment act when taking a test?	**VALUES**	How might a student whose culture favors collaborative good above individual accomplishment act when taking a test?
Incapable: How might a student with a negative view of herself as a learner act when faced with learning challenging content? *Can't do:* What actions or words would indicate that a student believes s/he is unlikely to succeed? Might telling words or actions be different in a culture where humility is valued?	**ACADEMIC SELF-EFFICACY**	*Capable:* How might a student with a positive view of himself as a learner act when faced with learning challenging content? *Can do:* What actions or words would indicate that a student believes s/he is likely to succeed? Might these words or actions be misleading in a culture which requires public expressions of confidence and discourages public admission of uncertainty?
Disinterested: In what ways does a student indicate disinterest? What nonverbal cues do you look for? Is our mental set of "interest" cues limited by our cultural experiences?	**INTERESTS**	*Interested:* How might a teacher interpret a child's interest in reading if, when asked "Darren, would you like to read the next paragraph?", the child declines? How would this interpretation change if the teacher knew that the child is from a culture where such a question such as the teacher asked is viewed as an invitation not a request, and that it is okay to decline invitations?
Low: When asked about their future academic goals, what are likely responses from students whose aspirations for themselves are low?	**ASPIRATIONS**	*High:* What are some of the things that students with high academic aspirations are likely to say and do?
Threatened: How might a student act who is anxious about speaking in front of a group?	**ANXIETY**	*Safe:* How might a student act who is comfortable with speaking in front of a group?

about the text. Create 5 to 10 bipolar scales for a questionnaire that focus on aspects of the book students might have an opinion about. Here are two examples:

Instructions: Place an X on the space on each scale that best describes your feeling:

Well organized __ __ __ __ Very disorganized
Well written __ __ __ __ __ Not well written

Once you have written and administered your questionnaire, how might you use the results in your decision making to benefit students' learning?

Now go to www.myeducationlab.com to take a Pretest to assess your initial comprehension of chapter content, study chapter content with your individualized Study Plan, take a Posttest to assess your understanding of chapter content, practice your teaching skills with Building Teaching Skills exercises, and build a deeper, more applied understanding of chapter content with Homework and Exercises.

PART III

Communicating Assessment Results

We can deliver accurate information about student mastery of important achievement targets (as described in Chapter 3) into the hands of important decision makers to serve important purposes (as outlined in Chapter 2) only if we understand how to assess those targets accurately (as discussed in Chapters 4 to 9) and then communicate the results effectively. Next we add that final component to our big picture—effective communication of results. Remain constantly aware of the fact that the highest-quality assessment is wasted if its results are miscommunicated.

The chapters of Part III introduce the keys to making sure our communication about student achievement works to support student learning when it is the purpose and to certify learning when that is appropriate.

Chapter 10 sets the stage by offering concrete suggestions for collecting and managing information about student achievement. Once again in this case, you will see the differences between assessment OF and FOR learning coming into play, as they have direct implications for record keeping in preparation for information sharing to support or to judge the sufficiency of student learning.

Chapter 11 delves into report card grades as communication intended to certify learning. We will explore what should be factored into report card grades and what should not. Sound grading practices are spelled out in specific detail, as are other forms of report cards that provide more detailed descriptions of student mastery of standards.

Chapter 12 details a truly effective way to communicate the detail of student achievement using portfolios with their unlimited potential to support student learning. We will establish that portfolios can be structured in a number of ways to serve different purposes. The key is to know what story the collection of work is to tell.

Chapter 13 explores the strengths, weaknesses, and keys to success found in using a variety of conferences to tell the story of students' in journeying to and arrival at academic success. In this context, of course, we offer a major role for the student as the storyteller.

Chapter 14 deals with standardized test scores as a means of conveying summative information about student achievement. You will learn where these scores come from and how to interpret them, as well as their strengths and limitations.

In each chapter, we will consider opportunities for student-involved communication of assessment results. Involving students in assessment development during learning helps them understand the terms of their own success. If we involve students in repeated assessment of their own achievement over time, we provide them with the opportunity to watch themselves grow. This permits them to feel in control of their own success and can motivate them to strive for excellence. So it is with student-involved information management and communication. We involve students in collecting and presenting evidence of their own success in order to sustain within them the belief that they will succeed if they keep trying.

CHAPTER 10

Record Keeping: The Foundation of Effective Communication

CHAPTER FOCUS

This chapter answers the following guiding question:

> How can we keep records of achievement that will help us communicate effectively about student learning success?

From your study of this chapter, you will understand the following:

1. Why clear and appropriate learning targets form the foundation for good record keeping.
2. How to separate records of assessments intended to support learning from those of assessments intended to judge and report its sufficiency.
3. The role of quality assessment in promoting good record keeping for effective communication.
4. How to turn achievement records into useful information that can be effectively communicated to support or certify learning.

GOOD RECORDS UNDERPIN GOOD COMMUNICATION

In this information age, we know how to communicate effectively. We communicate well when dependable information coming from the message sender gets through to the intended recipient in a timely and understandable way. Only then can the recipient act in an informed manner based on the information conveyed. Keep in mind that the most valid and reliable assessment in the world is wasted if its results are miscommunicated. In this chapter, we will argue that the starting place for effective communication in the classroom is the effective management of the achievement information that is the basis for that communication.

In standards-driven schools classroom assessment, record keeping, and communication about student learning must focus on student mastery of the established academic achievement standards. This necessity compels us to confront another paradigm shift—another deviation from our classroom assessment legacy. Our tradition has been to keep records of achievement evidence according to the manner in which it was collected: quiz scores, unit test scores, grades on homework assignments, and so on over the grading period. Then teachers assign weights to each, combine them, and convert the composite to the report card grade. The problem with this procedure in standards-driven schools is that it prevents us from communicating about how *each student* did in mastering *each achievement standard* for that grading period. Without that level of detail communication about student learning success cannot be completed effectively. In this chapter, we will consider how to keep records that help us make that concrete link.

Also in standards-driven schools, as established throughout this text, we must always remain aware of why we are communicating about student achievement, because purpose varies with context. Sometimes we communicate to support learning, other times to report our judgments of the sufficiency of a student's learning. Both communication purposes are important, but the requirements they impose for effective communication are different. We will consider how accurate record keeping can help us do both well.

In this chapter we ask, How do we prepare for effective standards-based communication OF and FOR learning with productive record keeping? The answer unfolds in four parts. They will be familiar given the values expressed in our journey so far.

1. Keep achievement records by standard or classroom learning target
2. Keep records separately by purpose
3. Keep accurate records of evidence of achievement
4. Transform records into useful information

The subsequent chapters of Part 3 offer ways to do the actual information sharing—report card grades, portfolios, conferences, and test scores. This chapter helps you get ready.

Time for Reflection

Anticipate what may be coming in this chapter. If we are going to differentiate between record keeping in the service of supporting learning and in the service of reporting about that learning, in which context might students play a role in record keeping? Why?

1. Keep Records by Achievement Target

Throughout this presentation, we have used a particular vocabulary and set of definitions to describe achievement expectations. In response to the priority of developing standards-based schools focused on state and local learning priorities, we have referred to the highest or broadest level of curricular aims as academic achievement *standards*. Quality standards, we have said, satisfy the following criteria. Standards that are ready for prime time

- Reflect the best current thinking of the field of study they describe.
- Are so clearly defined that independent interpretations of them by qualified educators reflect agreement on their meaning.
- Are ordered to unfold over time within and across grade levels in a manner consistent with current understanding of needed prerequisites.
- Are in priority order in case resources for their teaching and learning become limited; in other words, are manageable in number given available resources.

- Are accompanied by samples of student work reflecting levels of proficiency from poor to outstanding quality.
- Are mastered by the teachers who are assigned responsibility for helping students master them.

Within the context of a balanced assessment system described in Chapter 2, including annual, interim/benchmark, and classroom levels of application, sometimes we assess to gather evidence of student mastery of the standards themselves.

But other times, especially during learning, we need to track student ascent of the scaffolding leading to each standard. In these instances, we assess their mastery of the foundations of *knowledge* needed to attain the standard, and whatever patterns of *reasoning*, *performance skills*, or *product development* capabilities are appropriate. These map the route up the scaffolding to mastery. We have referred to those consistently as *classroom learning targets*.

The criteria by which we judge the quality of these classroom curricular aims are mostly the same as those just listed. They must lead naturally to mastery of the standard; be clearly defined, classified, and articulated; transformed for student understanding; and mastered by those charged with teaching them. In the context of a balanced assessment system, then, teachers must be qualified and ready to assess, keep records on, and, when appropriate, report (1) ongoing student success in mastering the classroom learning targets as each student ascends the scaffolding leading to success, and (2) each student's ultimate success in mastering each relevant standard. Used thoughtfully, both sets of records can serve to inform instructional decisions that support student leaning and that can certify achievement for accountability purposes on report cards.

One key to good record keeping is to identify in advance what we need to keep records about as learning unfolds. In standards-driven schools, as stated, ultimately our records need to tell us and others how each student did in mastering each relevant standard or classroom learning target, depending on the context. At accountability time, we summarize evidence of mastery across standards to form a single index of achievement, such as when assigning a report card grade. Other times, while students are still learning, effective communication requires that we maintain and share evidence of learning standard by standard, such as when we need to figure out what comes next in a particular student's learning; that is, when diagnosing student needs. In either case, the basis of good communication is the record of each student's mastery of each relevant standard. This leads directly to our next guideline.

2. Keep Records According to Purpose

We have established that we assess for two purposes: to support student learning and to verify and certify learning success. When assessing to help students learn more, we must communicate results in a manner calculated to inform and encourage. When we assess for accountability purposes, we must communicate in ways that judge the sufficiency of student learning. These two contexts require different kinds of communication. As a foundation for your ability to communicate in each mode, we therefore suggest separating achievement records by purpose.

Effective record keeping starts with an assessment plan for an upcoming grading period that anticipates (1) when each assessment FOR learning will take place during learning, and (2) when each assessment OF learning will be conducted to record mastery of a standard. Your assignment, then, is to start each reporting period or unit of study with these assessments mapped out. To do this, you need a roadmap of what you will assess, when, and why.

When keeping records to be used to support learning, because of the intent, evidence might take any of a number of forms. For example, you might engage your students as record-keeping partners in accumulating actual samples and descriptions of their work in growth portfolios, revealing to you and to them changes in their capabilities over time. Emily built such a record of achievement, you will recall from our Chapter 1 opening vignette. In this learning context, it is in everyone's best interest to maintain the detail in each record so as to be able to watch the quality of work improve over time. This will enable you to provide students with (or help students generate on their own) the kind of descriptive feedback needed to see how to do better the next time. This amount and kind of record-keeping work becomes more manageable the more you involve students as partners sharing responsibility for maintaining their own records during their learning. Those records are, after all, first and foremost for and about them to support their improvement.

But at assessment OF learning time, students must understand that they are to be held accountable for their learning. Periodic assessments will occur after learning is supposed to have been attained during which you will evaluate the sufficiency of their mastery of each relevant standard. Those results typically will take the form of summary judgments you typically record in a gradebook. At certain established intervals, you will report those summaries either (1) by standard on a standards-based report card, or (2) as a report card grade reflective of the extent of each student's mastery of the relevant set of standards that guided instruction.

3. Keep Accurate Records

In standards-driven schools, the order of activities is, first, to use assessment and record keeping to maximize success, and to then use them to judge and report how each student has done in mastering each relevant standard or learning target. We can do these things well only if achievement records are derived from assessments that accurately reflect student achievement. Misinformation about student learning due to faulty classroom assessment places student well-being in jeopardy. Remember, quality assessments do all of the following:

- Rely on assessment method(s) capable of reflecting the learning target(s)
- Sample student achievement in a manner that leads to a confident inference about achievement
- Rely on high-quality assessment items, tasks, or exercises and scoring schemes
- Minimize bias that can distort assessment results

The method of choice, we have established, is a function of the kind of learning target in question. We addressed keys to effective method selection, good items, and sources of bias in Part II.

But the matter of sound sampling deserves a bit of attention in the context of this chapter on effective record keeping and communication. You will recall that, to sample student achievement well in any particular assessment, we need to define and set limits on the target in question so we can decide the range of items or tasks needed to lead us to a confident conclusion about student success. Our assessment sampling traditions have had us sampling broad domains of achievement. To illustrate, our standardized achievement batteries often sample and yield scores labeled as reading, mathematics, social studies, and so on—all labels for broad domains of academic proficiency. At middle and high school levels, our courses of study and thus our classroom assessments sample domains within history, such as the Civil War; science, such as chemistry; or math, such as intermediate algebra. During a given grading period, we commonly build our sample using evidence of homework performance with scores on unit tests and final exams. These we average and convert to semester grades. The achievement domains sampled carry labels such as English, Algebra, Physics, and so on.

Classroom assessment in standards-driven schools exchanges such broad domain sampling, from which we infer student mastery of large bodies of achievement, to sampling standards within these domains. That is, our assessments must provide enough evidence—enough demonstrations of competence—to allow us to infer how each student did in mastering each established standard. This is why we must anticipate in our assessment and record-keeping plans from the beginning of the learning how we intend to sample mastery by standard.

To illustrate, let's say you have established the guiding standards for a given grading period, and have analyzed each standard to determine the classroom-level learning target for the scaffolding students will climb to get there. That is, you have anticipated the knowledge, reasoning, skill, or product targets that build over time to success. During the learning, your classroom assessments FOR learning must sample (i.e., inform you and your students about) how each did on each scaffolding target so you may know at any point in time what comes next in their learning and to accommodate differences in each student's pace of learning. You and they need evidence by learning target. As students ascend the scaffolding to a place where you hope they have mastered the standard, your preplanned assessments OF learning must document that fact. These might document (sample) mastery of each standard as achieved or mastery of a set of standards in the same assessment. You decide. But your sampling frame must center on each standard.

4. From Records to Useful Information

The kind of information that is likely to be helpful to the user of assessment results will vary depending on the context (target and purpose—what you are assessing and why). Our record keeping and communication must anticipate this.

Regardless of the context (target and purpose), assessment records can translate into useful information *only* when they do the following:

- Reflect achievement expectations that are familiar to all engaged in the communication
- Address achievement expectations that are or have been the focus of instruction—that is, that students are having or have had the opportunity to learn
- Accurately reflect student learning because they arise from quality assessments
- Translate into inferences about how each student did in mastering each standard

In other words, achievement records can lead to effective communication when they reflect and keep everyone informed about and aware of student mastery of standards and their corresponding learning targets. Regardless of the context, communication works best when progress is apparent to all decision makers—when they know at all times what students have learned and what comes next.

Record keeping can fail us and communication can break down regardless of context when the learning targets are unclear, activities or assessments are not to be aligned with desired outcomes, or results fail to discriminate clearly where a student is in the mastery of standards or ascension of the scaffolding leading to each standard.

On the other hand, research tells us that achievement records can underpin effective communication to *support* learning when they contribute to communication that does the following:

- Focuses on specific attributes of the student's work, not on attributes of the student as learner—i.e., to improve writing, provide feedback on characteristics of the student's writing, don't merely encourage the student to try harder
- Is descriptive, informing the learner how to do better the next time—making sure there is a next time so the learner gets a chance to act on that feedback
- Is clearly understood by the message receiver, in this case, the student—students without the capacity to map the evidence shared back onto a performance continuum are likely to have some difficulty acting on it in productive ways
- Is at an appropriate level of detail and is presented in amounts that the learner is likely to be able to act productively on at that time, as opposed to being so complex or broad in scope as to overwhelm
- Arrives in a timely manner, giving the student time to learn from it and act productively on it before being held accountable for the learning

These help communication serve useful purposes of informing important instructional decisions during learning.

On the accountability side, achievement records support effective communication when they help teachers focus communication on student mastery of each individual standard and summarize such evidence across standards, when appropriate, into a meaningful report card grade.

Record Keeping Illustrated

Depending on the learning target and the kind of assessment used, records can take the form of scores or ratings. For example, selected response and essay test evidence typically yield test scores, while performance assessments produce profiles of ratings based on rubrics. But in some situations, especially during learning, students and teachers might wish to accumulate actual samples of student work to be stored as evidence of achievement. Personal communication–based assessments tend to yield impressions, anecdotal notes, and professional judgments.

When the evidence anticipated takes the form of scores or performance ratings, the classroom record-keeping process can be very straightforward. Table 10.1 provides an illustration of one teacher's classroom record system that differentiates by achievement target and purpose. Within each target, records can be kept both about the date and nature of the assessment, whether it is a formative assessment (for practice) or summative (for grading), and each student's performance.

When the achievement record takes the form of actual samples of student work with student or teacher reflections on the quality of the work collected, then portfolios

TABLE 10.1
Elementary Gradebook Arranged by Learning Target

Number Sense					
	Identifies place value to 10,000s	Reads, writes common fractions	Reads whole numbers through 4 digits	Writes whole numbers through 4 digits	Orders and compares whole numbers through 4 digits
Date					
Task					
F/S					
Students					
1.					
2.					
3.					

Computation						
	Addition	Subtraction	Multiplication		Division		Uses calculator to + or −4 or more digits	Estimation Skills
	+ with 3 or more digits	− with 3 or more digits	Facts to 10	Fact Families	Facts to 10	Fact Families		
Date								
Task								
F/S								
Students								
1.								
2.								
3.								

Task: SR = Selected Response; PA = Performance Assessment; O = Oral;
HA = Homework Assignment; Q = Quiz

F/S: F = Formative; S = Summative

Source: Adapted from the work of Ken O'Connor, Scarborough, Ontario. Personal communication, June 1, 2004. Adapted by permission.

must come into play. Think about growth portfolios with deep student involvement here. We address portfolios in just this way in Chapter 12.

A Note on Gradebook Software
Many educational software companies have developed record-keeping and grading software products designed to both (1) help teachers store evidence of achievement, and (2) help standardize grade reporting across classrooms and schools within school

districts (or in a very few cases entire states!). These systems vary widely in the nature of the records they can store and receive as well as in what they permit the user to do by way of summarizing evidence for grading purposes. For example, many permit teachers to assign weights to evidence according to its importance in determining grades.

One important thing to remember when considering these systems is that, during learning, when assessment is for practice—FOR learning—it is *not* for grading. But that doesn't mean we wouldn't want to keep records of evidence derived from practice assessments. Such records can provide productive encouragement for learners as they grow, as well as information about what instruction is working or not. But, as you will learn in the next chapter, these practice records have no place in determining report card grades. They're merely for practice—to help students get better at "it" before being held accountable for it. Thus, you will want to use systems that permit the user to assign weight of zero to practice evidence during grade computation so it doesn't get factored into the grade.

Summary: Going for the Record

The quality of our communication about student learning is only as good as the information that forms the foundation of the message being delivered. The quality of that information, in turn, will be determined by the records of achievement that feed it. In standards-driven schools, those records need to arise from assessments that reveal how each student has done, or is doing, in mastering each relevant achievement target. Therefore, we recommend keeping records separately by classroom learning target or standard, depending on the context, and by purpose such as whether to support or report learning, while always being sure to rely on quality assessments to generate accurate evidence that is transformed into useful information appropriate for the intended purpose. Table 10.2 provides a concise summary of these points.

TABLE 10.2
Summary of Achievement Record-Keeping Priorities

Recommendation	Communication to *Support* Learning (FOR Learning)	Communication to *Report* Learning (OF Learning)
Keep records by achievement target	Reflect mastery of classroom learning targets leading to standards—maintain details	Reflect mastery of standards—summarize details into judgments
Keep records by purpose	Reveal changes in student achievement to student and teacher as students learn	Reveal sufficiency of student achievement to the teacher
Keep accurate records	Maximize quality of evidence of mastery of learning targets	Maximize accuracy of evidence of mastery of standards
Transform into useful information	Provide descriptive feedback in bite-size pieces suggesting what comes next in the learning	Provide judgmental information by standard or summary grade

Final Chapter Reflection

1. What are the three most important new insights to come to you as a result of your study of this chapter?
2. Which of your previous questions about assessment can you now answer based on your study of this chapter?
3. What new questions have come to mind as a result of your study of this chapter that you hope to have answered as your study continues?

Practice with Chapter 10 Ideas

1. If you were to develop a rubric for evaluating the quality of a teacher's record-keeping system, what would it look like? Define three points on the performance continuum: Still needs work, Well on its way, and Ready to use.

2. If you were to develop a rubric depicting the levels of student involvement in classroom record keeping, what might that look like? Define the same 3-point continuum as in question 1.

Now go to www.myeducationlab.com to take a Pretest to assess your initial comprehension of chapter content, study chapter content with your individualized Study Plan, take a Posttest to assess your understanding of chapter content, practice your teaching skills with Building Teaching Skills exercises, and build a deeper, more applied understanding of chapter content with Homework and Exercises.

CHAPTER 11

Report Cards: Summarizing Assessments OF Learning

CHAPTER FOCUS

This chapter answers the following guiding question:

> How can I communicate effectively about student achievement using report cards?

From your study of this chapter, you will understand the following:

1. In standards-driven schools, reports must be based on how each student did in mastering each relevant standard.
2. Grades represent just one of several ways to communicate using report cards. Other options include report achievement in terms of standards attained, narrative reporting, and continuous-progress reporting.

REPORT CARD GRADING

We begin our exploration of reporting options with a comprehensive treatment of grading issues. The key issues revolve around the following:

- What student characteristics should we factor into determining a student's report card grade?
- What sources of achievement evidence are appropriate to tap in determining a student's grade?
- How should we combine evidence gathered over time into the composite achievement index and convert that composite picture into a grade?

Each issue hides challenging dilemmas within it, and thus poses real dangers to students' dispositions and, therefore, to their ultimate academic success.

Report card grades are by no means the only way to share information about student achievement using. Some report forms convey much greater detail about student achievement. Sometimes that detail is crucial to sound decision making. So, after we address grades, we will explore useful alternatives.

Understanding Our Current Grading Environment

To answer questions such as those just posed, we have to think about the evolving school environments within which we grade students. Four key dimensions of those environments present profound challenges and so warrant our careful reflection:

1. The changing mission of schools
2. Grades as communicators versus motivators
3. A continuing expectation of grades
4. Wide-ranging student needs

1. The Changing Mission of Schools

The mission of schools used to be merely to produce a dependable rank order of students at the end of high school. As long as there was a valedictorian and everyone had a "rank in class," few questioned the effectiveness of the school's functioning. Grades formed the basis of this sorting and selecting social function.

Recently, however, as the demands of both our society and the economy changed, we have come to understand the inadequacy of this definition of effective schools. The demand for higher levels of competence for larger proportions of our students brought about a demand for schools driven by expectations of high achievement for all, not merely a rank order. Society now demands that all students be made ready for college and the workplace. Society now expects, indeed demands, that all students leave school having mastered the essential lifelong learner proficiencies in reading, writing, and math problem solving. But beyond these basics, we expect dropout rates to decline rapidly, and want a far higher proportion of our students to graduate from college. The consensus is that our collective prosperity hinges on our success in meeting these demands. We must think about grading practices in light of this social priority.

2. Grades as Communicators versus Motivators

We must also think about what we want to and can accomplish with report card grades. Traditionally, we have wanted to use report card grades as our primary means of communication about achievement and as our system of rewards and punishments to manage (meaning motivate and control) student behavior. But what if those two purposes come into direct conflict with one another?

Here's how that happens: Let's say a teacher uses homework grades as a motivator to compel students to practice because this teacher believes that those who do the work learn more—a reasonable position, to be sure. So he warns students that failure to turn in any homework assignment will be entered as a failure in the gradebook. All incomplete assignments turn into Fs when it's time to compute that final grade.

Now let's say there are two students in this class, both of whom have developed a very high level of mastery of the material. Each has an outstanding record on all tests, quizzes, and projects. Yet one student has consistently failed to complete practice assignments and so has accumulated many Fs for homework in the gradebook.

At report card grading time, the message sender (the teacher) sends out word (via grades) that one student has been assigned an A, while the other is assigned a D (the result of averaging in all those Fs). The resulting communication problem becomes apparent when we realize that both students learned the same amount. The message receivers (parents, other teachers, etc.) have no basis on which to distinguish the differences in the meaning of the messages. They won't know or understand the subtleties of meaning hidden within the message and may draw inappropriate conclusions about each student's achievement. Thus a reporting process designed to promote greater effort yields miscommunication about this student's achievement.

This is precisely why we argue that, when it comes to grades, we must choose one purpose or the other. One simple set of five letter grades (A through F) cannot shoulder the responsibility for being both (1) our primary way of judging and sharing information about student achievement, and (2) our primary means of motivation.

3. A Continuing Expectation of Grades

For the foreseeable future, parents and communities still expect their children to be assigned report card grades in school, especially at high school levels. They know, as we should too, that grades will play a key role in decisions that influence students' lives. This may not remain true forever, because we are constantly struggling with the limitations of grades as a communication system. But it is true now. This means our challenge is to do the very best job we can of assigning accurate, interpretable grades.

To be sure, we are currently experiencing greater freedom to explore other communication options at primary, elementary and, sometimes, middle school or junior high levels. We will consider many alternatives, including portfolios, checklists, rating scales, narratives, and student-led conferences, in the following chapters.

In the meantime, we must address grades and grading in all of their various forms. Elementary teachers often say to us, "We don't grade our students. We use check, check plus, and check minus." Or, "We use O for outstanding, S for satisfactory, and U for unsatisfactory. So we don't have to worry about grades." Of course, in a very real sense, these are grading symbols too and the ideas covered in this chapter apply in these contexts also. *Grading* is the process of condensing a great deal of information into a single symbol for ease of communication. The only things that change in the instances just cited are the symbols used; the underlying issues remain the same.

4. Wide Ranging Student Needs

As we strive to communicate effectively about achievement to support and certify learning, we also must deal with the grading issues that arise from mainstreaming special needs students and accommodating the learning pace of gifted students. The typical teacher is facing a much broader range of academic abilities and achievement today than ever before. We must plan and conduct assessments and assign grades in classrooms where individual students are working toward attaining fundamentally different achievement targets. If each student succeeds at a personally appropriate level, each deserves an "A." But how do we communicate the differences in the underlying meaning those As? Is it even conceivable to individualize these communication systems to promote understanding and sound decision making? This reality places immense pressure on our traditional report card grading practices. We will consider how to deal with this issue in this chapter.

COMMUNICATE ABOUT WHAT?

If we are to devise report card grading approaches that meet our communication needs in achievement-driven schools and that contribute to a supportive, productive, and motivating environment, the first issue we must confront is, What do we wish to use grades to communicate about? We must decide which student characteristics should be factored into report card grades.

Traditionally, teachers may have considered a variety of factors, among them the following five:

- *Achievement*—Those who learn more receive higher grades than those who learn less.
- *Aptitude*—Those who "overachieve" in relation to their aptitude, intelligence, or academic ability receive higher grades than those who fail to work up to their "potential."

- *Effort*—Those who try harder receive higher grades.
- *Compliance*—Those who follow school and classroom rules (i.e., those who behave) receive higher grades than those who don't.
- *Attitude*—Those who demonstrate more positive attitudes receive higher grades than those with negative attitudes.

Teachers address these factors in different ways. It is troubling to speculate on the interpretability of letter grades when those who assign them don't agree on (1) which of these elements should be considered, (2) how to define them, (3) how or how well to assess them, and (4) what weight to assign each factor in grade computation. If we expect to communicate effectively about student achievement via grades, we must regard all of these potential differences of opinion as very problematic. But this is just the tip of the iceberg when it comes to describing the challenge of communicating through grades.

To illustrate what we mean, join us now in a thoughtful analysis of the role of each of these factors in the grading process. Here are the issues in a nutshell:

There would be no debate about whether achievement should be a grading factor. It is what school is about and so it is what we what to communicate about—judgments about the sufficiency of student learning in relation to teacher expectations. Those who learn more receive higher grades.

That leaves us with some compelling questions:

Should you consider students' *aptitude, intelligence,* or *academic ability* when grading? That is, let's say two students have demonstrated exactly the same level of achievement, and let's say that level is right on the line between two letter grades. But you regard one as an overachiever in relation to ability and the other an underachiever who has not worked up to potential. Is it appropriate to assign them different grades?

Is it appropriate to consider a student's level of *effort,* seriousness of purpose, or motivation in grading? That is, let's say two students have demonstrated exactly the same level of achievement and, again, that level is right on the line between two letter grades, but you regard one as having tried very hard while the other has not tried hard at all. Is it appropriate to assign them different grades?

If you establish rules and deadlines with which you expect students to *comply,* should students who violate them be assigned lower grades? For instance, say you have two students, both of whom demonstrate the highest level of achievement on major tests and assignments, but one is delinquent in completing work. Should that student's grade suffer?

Is it proper to factor students' *attitudes* into the grade? Again, given two students equal in actual achievement and on a grade borderline, one of whom has exhibited a positive attitude in class and one a distinctly negative attitude, is it appropriate to assign them different grades?

Time for Reflection

Please Take Special Note: The reflections in this chapter represent particularly critical aspects of your learning. We are going to make some very provocative assertions in the following discussion. They are intended to elicit a response from you. You need to be a critical consumer of the ideas that we offer. Please take time to think through each reflection and take a personal position before moving on.

To figure out the keys to effective grading, let's conduct an analysis of arguments for and against weaving each of these factors into a grade. Then let's draw conclusions regarding which should win out, arguments for or against, given that our purpose is to communicate effectively.

Achievement as a Grading Factor

If we use achievement as a basis for determining students' report card grades, in effect, our contract with students says that those who learn more (that is, master a larger amount of the required material, hit a larger proportion of the valued standards or produce higher-quality work) will receive higher grades than those who learn less. This has long represented the foundation of grading.

One obvious reason this factor has been so prominent in grading is that schools exist to promote student achievement. In that sense, it is the most valued result of schooling. If students achieve, they are being set up for future success and schools are seen as working effectively. Grades have represented our index of success.

Besides, students are expected to achieve in life after school. School is an excellent place to learn about this fundamental societal expectation.

These are all compelling reasons why we traditionally have factored achievement into the report card grade, most often as the most prominent factor. Who would question the wisdom of grading in this way? No one, as long as the assessments of achievement are accurate and the process of summarizing evidence is carried out in a professional manner.

Aptitude as a Grading Factor

Remember the issues here: Assume two students demonstrate exactly the same level of achievement, and that level happens to be right at the cutoff between two grades. If you judge one student to be an overachiever in relation to ability, aptitude, or intelligence, and judge the other to be an underachiever, is it appropriate to assign them different grades? In other words, is it appropriate to factor a judgment about students' academic aptitude into the grading equation?

Arguments For

If we consider intelligence, ability, or academic aptitude in the grading equation, we hold out the promise that every student will reach her or his highest potential. It is the American way. Those who can learn more and faster are expected to attain a higher level of achievement and to get a good grade. They advance quickly. What teacher is not energized by the promise of individualized achievement targets set to match the capabilities of individual students, thus ensuring each aspires to do their best?

Besides, if we can identify those underachievers, we can plan the special motivational activities they need to begin to work up to their fullest potential. This is a win-win proposition!

These are compelling arguments indeed. Factoring aptitude or ability into the grading process makes perfect sense. Who could argue against it?

Arguments Against

In this case, there are important counterarguments. For example, the definition of *aptitude* or *intelligence* is far from clear. Scholars who have devoted their careers to the study of intelligence and its relationship to achievement do not agree among themselves as to whether each of us has one of these or many, whether this is a stable or volatile human characteristic, or whether it is stable at some points in our lives and unstable at others. Not only do they disagree fundamentally about the definition of these characteristics, but they also are at odds regarding how to assess them (Gardner, 1993; Sternberg, 1996).

Given these uncertainties among experts, how can we, who have no background whatever in the study of intelligence, presume to know any student's true potential? That is not to say that all students come to school with the same intellectual tools. We know they do not. But it is one thing to sense this to be true and quite another matter to assume that we possess enough refined wisdom about intelligence to be able to measure it dependably, turn it into a single quantitative index, and then factor it in when computing report card grades.

But even if teachers were to come up with a dependable definition (which they cannot), then they would face the severe difficulty of generating the classroom-level aptitude and achievement data needed to classify students according to their potential and thus categorize them as over- or underachievers. That is, each teacher would need a formula for deciding precisely how many units of achievement are needed per unit of aptitude to be labeled an over- or underachiever, and that formula would have to treat each and every student in exactly the same manner to assure fairness. *We do not possess the conceptual understanding and classroom assessment sophistication to enable us to do this.*

A brief comment is in order about aptitude as something separate from achievement. It is tempting to use students' records of prior achievement as a basis from which to infer ability, intelligence, or aptitude. But achievement and aptitude are not the same. Many things other than intellectual ability influence achievement, such as home environment, school environment, and dispositions. *Inferring level of ability from prior achievement is very risky. Resist this temptation.*

Besides, what if you label a student as an underachiever on the record and you are wrong? That student may be misclassified for years and suffer dire consequences. Such a wrong label may well become a self-fulfilling prophecy.

Even if the label is justified, is there not a danger of backlash from the student labeled as being a bright high achiever? At some point, might this student ask, How come I always have to strive for a higher standard to get the same grade as others who have to do less? Consider the motivational implications of this!

And then there is the possibility, if we consider aptitude when grading, that the same level of achievement attained by two students in the same class could deserve different grades, especially in borderline cases. We know of no one who wants to try to explain *this* one to those students or their parents.

And finally there is the "signal–noise" dilemma. Because different teachers define intelligence or ability or aptitude differently, assess it differently, and factor it into the grade computation equation differently, those who try to interpret the resulting grade later cannot hope to sort out those teachers' intended messages. This adds only confusing noise to our communication system.

Resolution

There are compelling arguments for and against factoring this student characteristic called aptitude into report card grades. Which shall win?

Time for Reflection

How do you sort out the arguments for and against? Take a position and articulate your defense before reading on.

The standards by which we judge the appropriateness of factoring academic aptitude into grades are the same as those we used for achievement. To justify incorporating it, we must be able to take concrete and specific action to overcome all arguments against it. Can we devise a definition of *academic aptitude* that translates into sound assessment and that promises to treat each student equitably? Perhaps someday, but not today. We lack a defensible definition and the measurement tools needed to know students' aptitude. We can't even say for sure whether it's a stable human characteristic. There is no place for aptitude, ability, or intelligence in the report card grading equation. For now, these problems are insurmountable.

But, you might ask, what about all of those compelling arguments in favor of this practice? What about our desire to individualize so students and teachers can be motivated by the potential of success? What about the hope this practice seems to offer to perennial low achievers? Must we simply abandon these hopes and desires?

The answer is a clear and definite, No! We must individualize on the basis of a student characteristic that we can define clearly, assess dependably, and link effectively to learning. We submit there is a far better candidate, a candidate that meets all requirements while not falling prey to the problems we experience in struggling with aptitude or intelligence. That individualizing factor is students' *prior achievement*.

Think of it this way: If we know where a student stands along the continuum of ascending levels of competence, then we know from our carefully planned continuous-progress curriculum what comes next for that student. Thus, we can tailor instruction to help that student move on to that next step in mastery of knowledge, demonstration of reasoning proficiency, performance of required skills, and/or creation of required products. Each student's success in hitting those next targets, then, becomes the basis for the report card grades we assign. Think of it as a contract between teacher and student where all agree on targets at the outset and then monitor progress continually together, until success is achieved.

Effort as a Grading Factor

Remember that, in this case, the issue is framed as follows: Assume two students demonstrate exactly the same level of achievement, and that level happens to be right on the borderline between two grades. If one student obviously tried harder to learn, demonstrated more seriousness of purpose, or exhibited a higher level of motivation than did the other, is it appropriate to assign them different grades? Does level of effort have a place in the report card grading equation?

Arguments For

Many teachers factor effort into their grading for apparently sound reasons. They see effort as being related to achievement: Those who try harder learn more. So by grading on effort, in effect, they believe that they are driving students toward greater effort and by extension greater achievement.

Besides, as a society, we value effort in its own right. Those who strive harder contribute more to our collective well-being. School seems an excellent place to begin teaching what is, after all, one of life's important lessons.

A subtle but related reason for factoring effort into the grade is that it appears to encourage risk taking, another characteristic we value in our society. A creative and energetic attempt to reach for something new and better should be rewarded, even if the striving student falls short of actual achievement success. And so, some think, it should be with risky attempts at achievement in school.

This may be especially important for perennial low achievers, who may not possess all of the intellectual tools and therefore may not have mastered all of the prerequisite knowledge needed to achieve. The one thing within their control is how hard they try. Even if students are trapped in a tangle of inevitable failure because of their intellectual and academic history, at least they can derive some rewards for trying.

Thus, there are compelling reasons, indeed, for using effort as one basis for grades. Could anyone argue against such a practice?

Arguments Against

In fact, we can. One such argument is that definitions of what it means to "try hard" vary greatly from teacher to teacher. Some definitions are relatively easy to translate into sound assessments: Those who complete all homework put forth effort. But other definitions are not: Trying hard means making positive contributions to the quality of the learning environment in the classroom. To the extent that teachers differ in their definition, assessment, and manner of integrating information about effort into the grading equation, we add noise to our grade interpretation. Message receivers simply have no way to uncover the subtleties of the teacher's intended message.

Besides, some teachers may say they want students to participate in class as a sign of their level of effort. But who most often controls who gets to contribute in class? The teacher. How, then, do we justify holding students accountable for participating when they don't always control this factor?

Further, students can manipulate their apparent effort to mislead us. If, as students, we know you grade in part on the basis of our level of effort and we care what grade we receive, we promise that we can behave in ways that make you believe that we are trying hard, whether we are or not. How can you know if we're being honest?

From a different perspective, effort often translates into assertiveness in the learning environment. Those who assertively seek teacher attention and participate aggressively in learning activities are judged to be motivated. But what about naturally quieter or more timid students? Effort is less likely to be visible in their behavior regardless of its level. And this also may carry with it gender and/or cultural differences, yielding the potential of systematic bias in grades as a function of factors unrelated to achievement. Members of some groups are enculturated to avoid competition. Gender, ethnicity, and personality traits have no place in the report card grading equation.

And finally, factoring effort into the grade may send the wrong message to students. In real life, just trying hard to do a good job is virtually never enough. If we don't deliver relevant, practical results, we will not be deemed successful, regardless of how hard we try.

Besides, from the perspective of basic school philosophy, what is it we really value, achieving, or achieving and knowing how to make it look like we tried hard? What if it was easy?!

Resolution

The balance scale tips in favor of including effort in the computation of report card grades only if we can eliminate all arguments against including it.

Time for Reflection

Given the arguments of both sides, what is your position? How does the scale tip and why?

First, as a matter of general principle, we must decide what we value. If we value learning, then we must define it and build our reporting systems to share information about student success in learning. If we value effort too, then again we must arrive at a mutually acceptable definition and must devise appropriate assessment tools and procedures. If we value both, why must we combine them into the same grading equation? It's not complicated to devise reporting systems that present separate information on each.

Continuing the theme of what we value: As noted previously, what do we care about, learning, or learning and making it look hard? What if it's easy for some students? What if I don't need to put forth much effort to learn? What if I don't have to practice anymore because I've got it? What if I can demonstrate mastery without doing hours of homework assignments? Why am I to be penalized for this? *However we define and assess effort, there can be no penalty for those who need little effort to learn.* Besides, what do you think will happen to their motivation (desire to learn) if we do?

Let's examine the other side as well. Let's say, as a student, I do need to practice a lot to learn and I don't take responsibility for doing so. Will that fact (my lack of effort) be reflected in my lack of achievement? Certainly it will. I won't learn much. If you factor my level of effort into the report card grade in addition to achievement, are you not in effect counting effort twice?

After we define effort, we must assess it well. As we have established, the assessment must arise from a clear target, rely on a proper method of assessment, sample effort in a systematically representative manner, and control for all relevant sources of bias that can distort our assessment and mislead us. But if we use behavioral indicators of students' level of effort and most of the "trying hard" behaviors take place outside of our presence (i.e., at home), how can we know that we are sampling well or controlling for bias?

For example, here's one form of bias that is hard to overcome: When students set out purposely to mislead us with respect to their real level of effort, they can seriously bias our assessment. This may be impossible to eliminate as a problem. If we see 30 students per day all day for a year and some are misleading us about their real level of effort, we may well see through it. But as the number approaches and exceeds 150 students for one hour a day and sometimes only for a few months, as it does for many middle and high school teachers, there is no way to confidently and dependably determine how hard each student is trying.

Think about that issue of student motivation. Let's say that you gather undependable evidence and conclude that a student is not trying hard and, in fact, this is incorrect. That is, in the truth of the world, that student is giving maximum effort but you conclude the opposite. What message does that send to the student? What effect is this turn of events likely to have on her desire to try hard and learn? Also, consider the other error. What if you say that a student is trying hard and, in fact, he is not? What message does this send and what impact is that message likely to have?

Moreover, if effort influences the grades of some, equity demands that it have the same influence on all. The assessment and record-keeping challenges required to meet this standard are immense, to say the least.

But a more serious challenge again arises from the personality issue. Less outgoing people are not necessarily trying less hard. Quiet effort can be diligent and productive. As teachers, we really do have difficulty knowing how much effort most students are putting forth. And we have few ways of overcoming this problem, especially when most of the effort is expended outside the classroom.

If you can define effort clearly, assess all students consistently, and meet the standards of sound assessment, then gather your data and draw your inferences about each student's level of effort. Just be very careful how you use those results at report card grading time. This is a minefield that becomes even more dangerous when you combine effort and achievement data in the same grade. *We urge you to report them separately,* if your report effort outcomes at all.

Assessment FOR Learning: A Better Way to Motivate

We grade on effort to motivate students to try hard. We feel that if they try hard, they will learn more. For those students who care about their grades and feel that success in those terms is within reach, this may work. But these aren't our only students. We must also consider those cases in which grades simply don't motivate. How shall we motivate those students who could not care less what grade we assign them, those who have given up and who are just biding their time until they can get out? If you think they are going to respond to admonitions that they try harder so they can raise their grade, you are being naïve.

Time for Reflection

Say you live in a hypothetical land where the ruler sent out a decree that you could no longer use grades and report cards as a source of reward and punishment to control students. What strategies would you use to encourage students to come to school and participate with you in the learning experiences you have designed for them? How would you draw them in? List your ideas. Then read on.

Consider these options: We might strive to learn students' needs and interests and align instruction to those. We might work with students to establish clear and specific targets so they would know that they were succeeding. In short, we could try to take the mystery out of succeeding in school. Chronic failure to learn would discourage them and they'd leave. We'd have to promise and deliver success. But we're just getting started. We would want to be sure instructional activities were interesting and provocative, keep the action moving, always keep agreed targets in mind. We would share decision-making power to bring students into their learning as full partners, teaching them how to gauge their own success. In short, we would strive to establish in our students a feeling of internal control over their own academic well-being. If they participate, they benefit, and they know this going in. Research suggests that this kind of motivation beats threatening Fs and promising As in producing learning success.

Compliance as a Grading Factor

The question in this case is, What role should adherence to school and classroom rules play in determining students' report card grades? If two students have demonstrated exactly the same level of achievement, but one disobeys the rules, should that student's grade be lowered?

Arguments For

Of course it should. Consider the kinds of compliance that we absolutely must demand. What if students fail to come to school? The law says they must attend. If they're not in school, how can they learn? The threat of reduced or failing grades can compel attendance, as well as punctuality. Students are expected to learn important lessons of personal responsibility. Fail to show up on the job after school and you get fired. We can use grades to teach this lesson.

Another problematic behavior that we can control with the threat of grade reduction is cheating. If you cheat on a test, you get a zero. When averaged in at the end of the term, this will have the effect of radically reducing the final average and grade. This punishment will deter cheating and, again, teach another important life lesson.

Besides, without factoring compliance into grading, how do we manage the classroom? Deadlines would mean nothing. If students thought they didn't have to get homework in on time, they'd never do it. Then we'd have no evidence on which to base their grade. Or they'd hand it in late all at once and our grading workload would become overwhelming. If we can't issue sanctions for misbehavior by connecting compliance with the rules to their grade, students would be out of control. We're talking about one of the teacher's most powerful classroom management tools here.

In real life, society expects us to follow the rules—to obey our agreed-on laws. It's the way we preserve the social order. Schools are supposed to be conveying to young people the lessons of behavior in a civil culture. Connecting grades to behavior helps us in that effort.

Compliance with the rules leads to greater student learning in at least two ways. First, as teachers, we know better than our students do what is best for them. Learning is maximized when they follow our plan—comply with our wishes. If they deviate, learning suffers. Second, a well-managed, compliant class permits everyone to benefit the most. If one or two students fail to follow the rules, everyone's learning suffers. We should not permit that to happen. It's not fair to the others.

Finally, although students are not in control of the academic ability that they bring to school, they are in complete control of whether they follow the rules and meet deadlines. If they wish to influence the grades they receive, this is one concrete way for them to do it.

Arguments Against

Before citing the counterarguments, we need to establish that it is very important for students to obey school and classroom rules. Not only can those rules affect student learning, but they can protect their safety and well-being.

But surprising as it may seem, that's not the issue in this case. When behaviors such as truancy, tardiness, cheating, and the like come up, they inflame the rhetoric. We mentioned them in citing "arguments for" for just that reason. We wanted to show you how easy it is to draw your attention away from the essential issue. These behaviors are counterproductive and need to be addressed. But the question is, How? If our desire is to punish students in the hope that we can extinguish the undesirable behaviors, then what is the most appropriate way to punish? Is lowering report card grades the best way?

If we do issue sanctions in the form of lowered grades, then the accuracy of the information about student achievement contained within the grade suffers and miscommunication is assured. Let us explain how. Let's say a student has taken four of five exams during a grading period and averaged 93 percent correct across all of them. Then this student is accused of cheating on the fifth exam and is given a zero in the gradebook. To add to the intrigue of this case, let's say that this student had mastered the material of that last exam and could have attained another very high score. If we wanted to communicate accurately about the achievement of this student we would assign an A on the report card to deliver a message to all message receivers of almost total mastery of the material.

However, when we factor the zero into the average, the result is 74 percent (93 times 4 on the first four exams plus zero on the fifth exam equals 374, divided by 5 equals 74), or a C on the report card. The effect is a misrepresentation of the student's actual level of achievement—intentional miscommunication. We have no way to let the various message receivers know the subtle message hidden in this grade. Is it wise to completely sacrifice any hope of accurate communication simply to punish alleged dishonest behavior? Are there other punishment options that don't result in such a profound communication breakdown?

Besides, once again we must consider the noise that is introduced into our communication system if every teacher defines standards of compliance differently, gathers evidence of different sorts, and gives compliance issues different weight when determining their particular grades. The message receiver will always have difficulty determining what the report card grade is supposed to mean. Miscommunication will result.

Finally, we have to be very careful about the messages our grading practices send to our students. Sometimes adult life presents us with situations where it might be wise to challenge established rules. While we would never advocate violation of accepted codes of behavior, if our nation's forefathers and foremothers had merely obeyed the prescribed rules, where would our country be today? Obviously, we are not encouraging rebellion. But we must help our students keep perspective regarding the meaning and role of compliance.

Time for Reflection

How do you sort out these arguments for and against? Take a position and articulate your defense before reading on.

Resolution

To be sure, as mentioned previously, violation of some school or classroom rules is unacceptable. Sometimes, stiff penalties should be imposed.

However, we believe that the decisions that will be made based on the achievement information contained in report card grades are too important to permit that information's accuracy to be sacrificed by lowering grades as punishment for behaviors unrelated to actual achievement. Besides, there is strong legal precedent for this perspective. Many states have passed laws that disallowed grading policies that, for example, permit grade reduction for poor attendance. You should check for such laws in any state in which you practice. When the use of grade reduction as punishment has the effect of distorting the student's academic record, we violate the student's constitutional guarantees to equal access to future educational opportunities (Bartlett, 1987).

Let us hasten to add that the courts also have upheld the school's right to administer punishment for violating truancy laws. It's just that the punishment cannot lead to a distortion of the student's record of achievement. The courts compel us to separate the punishment, whatever that is, from our achievement records.

In the case of cheating cited here, the school is justified in administering fair punishment. But that punishment cannot cause a distortion of the student's academic record. The only acceptable action is to administer another fifth exam, average the resulting score with the other four, and assign the grade indicated by that average.

We have many appropriate punishment options at our disposal that don't distort the record and violate student rights, including detention, limiting access to desirable activities, community service, and so on. There is no need to sacrifice the accuracy of the academic record.

Attitude as a Grading Factor

You understand the problem: Two students attain exactly the same level of achievement. Their semester academic average is on the cutoff between two letter grades. One has constantly exhibited a positive attitude, while the other has been consistently negative. Are you justified if you assign them different grades?

Arguments For

A positive attitude is a valued outcome of school. Anything we can do to promote it is an effective practice. People with positive attitudes tend to secure more of life's rewards. School is an excellent place to begin to teach this lesson.

Besides, this just may be the most effective classroom management tool we teachers have at our disposal. If we define *positive attitude* as treating others well, listening to the teacher, interacting appropriately with classmates, and the like, then we can use the controlling leverage of the grade to maintain a quiet, orderly learning environment.

And, once again, this represents a way for us to channel at least some classroom rewards to perennial low achievers. As with effort, attitude is within students' control. If they're "good," they can experience some success. Sounds good, let's make it part of the grading equation!

Arguments Against

It is seldom clear exactly which attitudes are supposed to be positive. Are students supposed to be positive about fellow students, the teacher, school subjects, school in general, or some combination of these? Must all be positive or just some? What combinations are acceptable?

How shall we define a positive attitude? As teachers, we value different human characteristics. Is it positive to accept an injustice in the classroom compliantly, or is it positive to stand up for what you think is right? What is the important value here? Is it positive to act as if you like story problems in math, when in fact you're frustrated because you don't understand them? The definition of "positive attitude" is not always clear.

Further, if students can manipulate their apparent effort, so can they manipulate their apparent attitude. Regardless of my real feelings, if I think you want me to be positive and if I care about that grade, you can bet that I will exhibit whatever behavior you wish. Is dishonest game-playing a valued outcome of education?

Assessment also can be a source of difficulty in this case. It takes a special understanding of paper and pencil assessment methodology, performance assessment methods, and personal communication to evaluate affective outcomes such as attitudes, as you saw in Chapter 9. The rules of evidence for quality assessment are challenging, as you will recall from our earlier discussion of the assessment of affect. So mismeasurement is a very real danger.

Oh, and as usual, to the extent that different teachers hold different values about which attitudes are supposed to be positive, devise different definitions of positive, assess attitudes more or less well, and assign them different weights in the grading equation, we factor even more noise into our communication system.

Some pretty tough problems . . .

Time for Reflection

Once again, are you for or against? Make your stand and then read on.

Resolution

To decide which side of the balance sheet wins out here, we must determine which use of attitude information produces the greatest good for students. Let's say we encounter an extremely negative attitude on the part of one student about a particular school subject. Which use serves that student better: Citing your evidence of the attitude problem (gathered through a good assessment) and telling that student they had better turn it around before the end of the grading period or their grade will be lowered? Or, accepting the attitude as real and talking with the student honestly and openly about the attitude and its origins (using high-quality assessment of this disposition through personal communication) in an honest attempt to separate it from achievement and deal with it in an informed manner?

If we enlist students as partners, they are likely to be even more honest with us about how they feel about their learning environment, thus providing us with even more ammunition for improving instruction. But if you think for one moment students are likely to be honest with us in communicating attitudes if they think the results might be used against them at grading time, you are being naïve.

Although we might be able to overcome the difficulties associated with defining attitudes for grading purposes, and can overcome the assessment difficulties attendant to these kinds of outcomes, we contend it is bad practice to factor attitudes into report card grades.

Summary of Grading Factors

In an era of standards-driven schools, if report card grades are to serve decision makers, they must reflect student attainment of the specific knowledge, reasoning, skill, and product creation achievement targets leading up to state or local standards. Only then can we teachers, for example, know where students are now in relation to where we want to take them. For this reason, grading systems must include indicators of student achievement unencumbered by other student characteristics, such as aptitude, effort, compliance, or attitude (see O'Connor, 2007, for a detailed treatment of this issue's nuances). This is not to say that we should not report information about factors other than achievement, if definition and assessment difficulties can be overcome, which is no small challenge. But under any circumstances, aptitude or intelligence or ability have no place in grade reporting.

Grades can help us communicate effectively about student success in meeting our achievement expectations only if we do the following:

- Clearly define these expectations in each grading context for a given grading period.
- Develop sound assessments for those outcomes.
- Keep careful records of student attainment of the achievement expectations over the grading period.

In the next section, we explore these procedures in detail.

GATHERING ACHIEVEMENT EVIDENCE FOR GRADING PURPOSES

If report card grades are to inform students, parents, other teachers, administrators, and others about student achievement, then we must clearly and completely articulate and assess the actual achievement underpinning each grade. To be effective, we must spell out the valued achievement standards before the grading period begins. Further, we must lay out in advance an assessment plan to systematically sample those standards. While it sounds like a great deal of preparation to complete before teaching begins, it saves a great deal of assessment work during instruction.

Let's analyze an effective and efficient 4-step plan for gathering sound and appropriate achievement information for grading purposes. Figure 11.1 summarizes these key steps.

Step 1: Spelling Out the Big Achievement Picture

To complete a picture of the valued achievement targets for a given subject over a grading period, gather together all relevant background information: appropriate state or local achievement standards, the local written curriculum, and text materials for your intended units of instruction. From these, make a list of your priority standards for that grading period. Some will be knowledge standards, some knowledge and reasoning, others performance skill standards and finally product development expectations.

Build your grading period-long instructional plan around these by putting your achievement expectations, standards, and their corresponding learning targets into the order in which they will unfold, instructional unit by unit.

By the way, we do not list disposition targets here, not because they are unimportant, but because, as discussed, they should not play a role in report card grading decisions.

The standards you select for students obviously will form the basis of your actual assessments and instruction. For now, simply create a general outline of the important elements of your big assessment picture, spelled out in your own words, across units. In short, immerse yourself in this and force yourself to set priorities within and to impose limits on it.

---

1. Begin the grading period with a comprehensive set of achievement expectations.

2. Transform that "big picture" into an assessment plan describing evidence-gathering tactics.

3. Develop and administer the specific assessments as instruction unfolds.

4. Summarize assessment results into a composite index of achievement for each student.

FIGURE 11.1
Steps in Report Card Grading

As you prepare to present each unit of instruction, you will need to provide your students with (1) student-friendly descriptions of your standards as needed to set them up for success, and (2) the opportunity to learn to hit each of the achievement targets you have set out for them. There should be one-to-one correspondence between targets and instruction. For each target, you should be able to point to its coverage in your instructional and evidence collecting plans.

Step 2: Turning Your Big Picture into an Assessment Plan

At this point, it is imperative that you reaffirm that your classroom assessments need to serve two purposes: some support learning—the assessments FOR learning, while others certify or verify learning. The former are about learning, not grading. The latter feed into the report card grading decision. So in Chapter 10 we recommended separate records for these.

Once you are clear about your standards of instruction, your assessment and report card grading challenge is clearly drawn. The next question is, How will you assess to accumulate evidence of each student's attainment of those standards? Remember, report card grading is an assessment OF learning decision-making context. Taken together, the assessments that you use over time must help you determine, with confidence, what proportion of the total array of those achievement standards each student has met. In other words, what specific assessments (selected response, essay, performance, personal communication) will provide you with an accurate estimate of how many of the required standards each student has mastered? You need an assessment plan to determine this.

You don't need the assessments themselves, not yet. Those come later, as each unit of instruction unfolds. But you do need to know how you will take students down the assessment road, from "Here are my achievement standards" to "Here is your grade," making sure both you and they know how they are progressing all along that road. The assessment plan that you start the grading period with needs to satisfy certain conditions:

- It must list each assessment you will conduct for grading (assessment OF learning) purposes within each unit of instruction, detailing the expected achievement target focus of each, approximately when you expect the assessment to take place, and what assessment method(s) you will use.
- Each assessment listed in the plan needs to supply an important piece of the puzzle with respect to the priority standards of the unit and grading period within which it occurs.
- Each assessment must accurately represent the particular target(s) it is supposed to depict (i.e., each must be a sound assessment according to our agreed quality standards).
- The full array of assessments conducted across units over the entire grading period must accurately determine the proportion of your expectations that each student has attained.
- The entire assessment plan must involve a reasonable assessment workload for both you and your students.

A Reality Check

These conditions will be easier to meet than they appear. The report card grading challenge is to gather just enough information to make confident *grading* decisions and no more. Ask yourself: How can I gather the fewest possible assessments for grading and still generate an accurate estimate of achievement? We believe that most teachers spend entirely too much time gathering and grading too many assessments. Some feel they must grade virtually everything students do and enter each piece of work into the record to assign accurate report card grades. This is simply not true. With planned, strategic assessments, you can very economically generate accurate estimates of performance.

Also many teachers seem to operate on the shotgun principle of grading: Just gather a huge array of graded student work over the course of the grading period, and surely somewhere, somehow, some of it will reflect some of the valued targets. While this may be true in part, this approach is at best inefficient. Why not plan ahead and minimize your assessment work?

If you can zero in on the key targets and draw dependable inferences about student mastery of them with a few unit assessments and a final exam or project assignment, that's all you need to produce report card grades that reflect student achievement.

Remember Assessments FOR Learning, but Not for Grading

Remember, assessment is no longer merely about grading. We also assess to diagnose student needs, provide students with practice performing or evaluating their own performance, and track student growth as a result of instruction. In fact, sometimes we assess just to boost student confidence by helping them see themselves growing.

Generally, it's a bad idea to factor into the report card grade student performance on assessments intended for purposes of providing students with practice. Self-assessment can be used for diagnosing needs and to help learners see how to do better the next time. We don't grade students when they are evaluating their own needs or trying to discover the keys to their own success. Practice assessments are for mastering targets skills, identifying and overcoming problems, and fine tuning performance. We shouldn't grade students when they are trying to learn from their mistakes. Students need time simply to explore new learnings, time to discover through risk-free experimentation, time to fail and learn from it without the shadow of evaluative judgment.

Experienced teachers who read this might say, "If I don't assign a grade and have it count toward the report card grade, students won't take it seriously, they won't do it!" Trust us. Once students come to understand that practice helps, but performance on previously announced assessment of learning determine grade, they will practice if they need to. If they don't need the practice because they already have mastered the standard, evidence at assessment time will speak for itself. If they do need to practice and don't do so, again, the evidence speaks for itself. They ignore it at their own peril. They must take responsibility for controlling their success—that's life. This is exactly the point we have made repeatedly when speaking of developing an internal sense of responsibility for one's own success.

While it might take some time to break old dependencies, once students come to understand that good grades are not the rewards for doing work but rather for the learning that comes from doing the work effectively, they will practice as needed, especially if that practice can take place in a supportive, standards-based and success-oriented classroom.

Step 3: From a Plan to Actual Assessments

So, you begin the grading period with your assessment plan in hand. What next? You then need to devise or select the actual assessments for each unit, being sure to follow the development guidelines specified in earlier chapters. You will need to create and conduct each assessment, evaluating and recording the results as you go. Those that are assessments OF learning (vs. FOR) are for grading.

In each case, specifically spelled out in earlier chapters, where you have knowledge and reasoning targets to assess via selected response or essay assessments, you need to devise those specific assessments around precisely defined categories of knowledge and reasoning. You can capture these in lists of objectives, tables of specifications, propositions, and finally the test exercises themselves, which you may assemble into assignments, quizzes, and tests.

When assessing skill and product outcomes, you need to assemble performance criteria, tasks to elicit performance, and rating scales or checklists. Each component assessment fills in part of your big picture.

All assessments must align exactly with a specific part of your vision of student competence. Although you may develop some in advance, to save time later, you may develop others during instruction. We know this sounds like a great deal of work, but remember five important facts:

1. This sharply targeted grading approach is not nearly as much work as the shot-gun approach.
2. It affords the conscientious teacher a great deal more peace of mind. When your students obviously are succeeding, you will know that you have been successful.
3. In between your periodic assessments OF learning for grading purposes, your students can play key roles in your assessments FOR learning, thus turning nearly all of that assessment time and energy into productive learning time and energy.
4. Student motivation to learn is likely to increase; "no surprises, no excuses" leads to a success orientation.
5. The plans you develop now remain intact for you to use or adapt the next time you teach the same material, and the time after that. Thus, development costs are spread out over the useful life of your plan and its associated assessments.

Step 4: Summarizing the Resulting Information

At the end of the grading period, your records should tell you how well each student mastered the standards that made up your big picture. The question is, how do you get a grade out of all of this information?

We urge you to rely on a consistent compositing process for all students that you can reproduce later should you need to explain the process or revise a grade. Such a sequence helps to control for your personal biases, which may either inappropriately inflate or deflate a grade for reasons unrelated to actual achievement.

Please note that we are not opposed to a role for professional judgment in grading. As we established in earlier chapters, that role comes in assessment design and administration. We need to minimize subjectivity when combining indicators of achievement for grading purposes. Let the evidence speak for itself.

Combining Achievement Information

To derive a meaningful grade from records of achievement, again, *each piece of information gathered should contribute to your inference about student mastery of the standard(s) to which that assessment relates*. If we combine them all for standards within a grading period, we should obtain an estimate of the proportion mastered for that grading period. To do this, convert each student's performance on each contributing assessment into a percentage of total standards mastered.

In this case, the computation is *not* on the percentage of points attained on assessments averaged to determine a composite index of achievement, as has been our tradition. It is on the percentage of preestablished standards mastered. To be sure, the points attained on an assessment of a particular standard will help you judge the sufficiency of learning and whether a student has mastered that standard. But the composite judgment of sufficiency must relate directly back to the extent of student mastery of the set of standards upon which instruction focused. So, for example, mastery of 90 percent of standards or more might be assigned an A, 80 percent a B, etc. You get to decide about the cutoffs, or there might be district policy set in this matter. In any event, the interpretive link to preset standards must be clear, specific, and consistent.

To be sure, you can give greater weight to some standards and their assessment results than to others based on your priorities, if you wish. Accomplish this very simply by counting higher priority standards more than once in determining the percent of standards mastered. Just be sure to advise students of these priorities from the very beginning of the grading period.

Time for Reflection

Under what conditions might you assign some assessment results a greater weight than others in your grading?

With this system of record keeping and grade computation based on percentages, everyone involved can know at any particular point in time how they are doing in mastering your preset, announced standards. At any point in time, we can keep students informed of standards assessed to date and their achievement record for each. This permits students to remain aware of and in control of their success.

Some Practical Advice

Unless you carefully develop and summarize assessments, the result may be misleading about the proportion of the total achievement picture that students have mastered. Let us illustrate.

Using Gradebook Software. You may want to select your own computer software to help you maintain your achievement records for grading or the district in which you work may have selected an application for all faculty to use. In either case, it is important that its systems permit you to keep records by standard or learning target and by purpose (formative or summative). This will permit you to report achievement to the student on a standard-by-standard basis so they can track their own success as the learning unfolds. Then you can summarize the achievement evidence in the summative fields to assign periodic report card grades.

Using the Most Current Information. Let's say your strategic assessment plan includes five unit assessments focused on particular standards and a comprehensive final exam that covers the entire set of standards for the grading period. A particular student starts slowly, scoring very low on the first two unit assessments, but gains momentum and attains a perfect score on the comprehensive final exam, revealing, in effect, subsequent mastery of the standards covered in those first two unit assessments.

The key grading question is this: Which piece of information provides the most accurate depiction of that student's real achievement at the end of the grading period, the final exam score or that score averaged with all five unit tests? If the final is truly comprehensive, averaging it with those first two unit assessments will produce a misleading result.

If students demonstrate achievement at any time that, in effect, renders past assessment information inaccurate, then you must drop the former assessment from the record and replace it with the new—even if the new information reflects a lower level of achievement. To do otherwise is to misrepresent that achievement.

Grades and Heterogeneous Grouping. Here is one of the most difficult challenges teachers face in grading: How do we grade different students in the same classroom who are striving to attain fundamentally different targets? As we mainstream special needs students and students from diverse cultural and linguistic backgrounds, as well as students of exceptional talent, this becomes a critical issue.

In a classroom of mixed achievement, for instance, one student might be working on basic math concepts, while another is moving toward pre-algebra. If both hit their respective targets, each deserves an A. But those A's mean fundamentally different things. How is someone reading the report cards of these two students to be made aware of this critical difference?

To begin with, let's talk about how to determine these grades, then we can discuss how to report and interpret them. Remember in Chapter 3 when we discussed the need to map the curriculum as it unfolds in learning progressions over time within and across grade levels? We need our standards to be arrayed in the order in which they will be mastered—an order consistent with the way learning happens, noting that which is prerequisite to that which follows from it in a natural learning sequence. These progressions provide the key to sound grading in achievement-diverse classrooms.

To grade effectively, one must determine from the beginning of the learning where academically challenged or gifted students are on each relevant progression. From there we must determine what comes next in their learning and where each student must be at the end of the learning (that is, what standards they must have mastered) to have earned an A, B, etc.

The only viable solution to this grading dilemma in standards-driven schools is the use of learning contracts for each student, each anchored in the standards that are the focus of their instruction. The alternative is to hold all students accountable for hitting the same target. But, if a student lacks the prerequisites needed to succeed (i.e., is not there yet in the learning progression) this would doom them to inevitable failure. That's not fair—not ethical. Accommodation through individual educational plans is required, as is the individual determination of grades.

But how can others interpret such grades if we report those grades alone? They cannot. In our opinion, this single problem renders purely letter grade–based communication systems inadequate to meet our communication needs in a standards-driven educational environment. The grade must be accompanied by information about the standards it is based on. Without this detail, we cannot communicate about individual differences in the grades assigned within the same classroom.

Grading on Status versus Improvement. Remember, assessment FOR learning is all about helping students watch themselves grow. We want them always to be in touch with where they are now in relation to where we want them to be so they can watch themselves ascending the scaffolding.

But report card grading is all about accountability. It is assessment OF learning time—show what you know. We want to report achievement status at a particular point in time—the end of the grading period. What proportion of achievement expectations did each student master?

First, we use assessment to support learning, then we use it to verify learning. Report card grading represents an instance of the latter.

The best practice, we believe, is to connect back to the previous section on diversity in the classroom and set expectations based on actual starting points for students; that is, on the standards reflected in the IEP of students with special needs and on relevant preset standards for all other students. Then base report card grades on each student's mastery of those expectations at the end of the grading period. This is entirely about grading on individual academic improvement—that is, in terms of standards mastered and advancement along the learning progression.

Grading in a Cooperative Learning Context. In brief: Don't. The rule is this— report card grades must provide dependable information about the actual achievement of the student to whom they are assigned. This means that, even in contexts where students cooperate during learning, assessments must yield a clear and unencumbered indication of how well each individual student mastered the desired learning target. These are assessments OF learning that happen after learning is supposed to have occurred. Only evidence derived in this way should contribute to determining each student's report card grade.

Dealing with Cheating. Let's say student cheats on a test and, as punishment, is given a zero in the gradebook for a particular standard or set of standards.

The problem in this instance is that the zero misrepresents that student's real achievement. *This is not acceptable under any circumstances.* Consequently, you must separate the grade and the discipline for cheating. You should retest the student to determine real level of achievement and enter that retest score into your gradebook. Cheating should not be punished via grade reduction if we seek to communicate effectively.

Awarding "Extra Credit." Some teachers try to encourage extra effort on the part of their students by offering extra credit opportunities. You must be very careful of the message you send here. If grades are to reflect achievement, you must deliver the consistent message that *the more you learn, the better your grade.* If extra credit work provides dependable evidence that students have learned more, then it should influence your grading judgment. In other words, the message to students must be, You don't get higher grades merely by doing extra work—you get it for the extra leaning that results from doing that work. To communicate effectively, grades must reflect the amount learned.

The Matter of Unsound Grading Policies. Sometimes, district policy can cause serious grading problems. For instance, some districts permit grades to be influences by nonachievement factors such as attendance. Or local policies might rigidly require a certain number of assessments for grading over a given time period regardless of the learning targets in question or time span. These happen because those in leadership positions have not been given the opportunity to understand sound grading practices. While you are obliged to do your best to be in compliance with all district policies, it also is acceptable to call inappropriate grading policies to the attention of your supervisor, being sure to suggest a more defensible alternative.

Prior Notice. One final critically important guideline to follow is to be sure all students know and understand in advance the procedures you will use to compute their grades. What assessments will you conduct, when, and how will you factor each into your grading? What are students' timelines, deadlines, and important responsibilities? If students know their responsibilities up front, they have a good chance of succeeding.

The Bottom Line

In developing sound grading practices for use in communicating about achievement, logic dictates that you start with a clear vision of targets, translate it into quality assessments, and always remain mindful of that big achievement picture for a given grading period. Then you must follow this simple rule (another part of the art of classroom assessment): *Grades must convey an accurate a picture of a student's real achievement at the time that grade is assigned. Any practice that has the effect of misrepresenting actual achievement of agreed standards is unacceptable.* Figure 11.2 presents a summary of guidelines for avoiding the problems we have discussed here.

- Grade on achievement of prespecified targets only, not intelligence, effort, attitude, or personality.

- Always rely on the most current information available about student achievement.

- Devise grades that reflect achievement status at the time of grading rather than improvement over time.

- Decide borderline cases with additional information on achievement.

- Keep grading procedures separate from punishment for bad behavior.

- Change all policies that lead to miscommunication about achievement.

- Advise students of grading practices in advance.

- Add further detail to reports when needed to promote understanding.

- Expect individual accountability for learning even in cooperative environments.

- Give credit for evidence of extra learning—not for doing extra work if it fails to result in extra learning.

FIGURE 11.2
Practical Guidelines for Avoiding Common Grading Problems

As a practical matter, if you consider the purchase and use of gradebook software, keep the list in Figure 11.2 close at hand as you evaluate options. These software packages vary greatly in their adherence to recommended grading practices.

REPORT CARDS THAT DELIVER GREATER DETAIL

As schools evolve into standards-driven institutions interest has increased on reporting achievement results in greater detail. Here are two examples of how local educators are making that interest operational.

Standards-Based Reporting

One currently popular way to report greater detail about student achievement in preparation for conferences is to assemble an extended list of specific achievement standards or competencies and to indicate the extent to which students have mastered each. An example from the Lincoln, Nebraska, Public Schools primary grade reporting appears in Figure 11.3. Note that each academic discipline is allocated one section of the report. Then each of these is subdivided into statements about expectations. The teacher uses the rating schemes at the top to report each student's level of achievement by standard. This form extends to a second page to include achievement domains such as art, music, and physical education. In addition, for each standard, the faculty has collaborated to develop detailed rubrics depicting each level of student attainment reflected in the rating scale for that standard. All of this available for message receivers to see and understand if they wish.

An elementary version of this same kind of reporting is provided in Figure 11.4 from the Winchester, Virginia, public schools. This one goes on to report special accomplishments in learning and goals for future learning for each reporting quarter.

This kind of reporting, backed up, for example, by a growth portfolio replete with samples of student work and student reflections on changes in their academic capabilities over time, could provide an excellent basis for student-led parent/teacher conference. We'll learn about these communication options in the following chapters.

For those who teach at middle and high school levels, we offer a strong recommendation about this kind of more detailed communication (especially for high school). To ensure complete understanding from the beginning, as we have said before, start any course of study by providing students with a list of the achievement standards that will guide instruction and for which they will be held accountable. Then at the end of the grading period, when a grade is assigned and delivered to the student, accompany that grade with that same list of standards with specific indications for which standards were and were not mastered. This will connect each student's achievement directly to the meaning of the grade in standards terms. This kind of reporting is so important in our opinion that we believe it should be required in every high school classroom.

Dealing with the Practicalities
As you consider these options, remember that their successful implementation requires that teachers collaborate in developing the achievement targets, creating the performance rating system, and implementing the communication system. It must

REPORT CARD
3rd Grade
Lincoln Public Schools

Student_____

Student ID_____

Year_____

	Q1	Q2	Q3	Q4
Absences				

	Q1	Q2	Q3	Q4
Tardies				

ACADEMIC ACHIEVEMENT
4=Exceeds district standards 3=Meets district standards 2=Approaches but does not meet district standards 1=Does not meet district standards •=Not taught/assessed this quarter

WORK/STUDY HABITS
4=Exceeds expectations 3=Meets expectations 2=Approaches expectations 1=Does not meet expectations

Indicators: Listens, Follows oral and written directions, Is on task, Participates in class, Strives for quality work, Seeks help as necessary, Completes assignments on time.

The descriptions below reflect the Lincoln Public Schools standards for this grade level. The marks given reflect quarterly performance.

CHARACTER DEVELOPMENT

	Q1	Q2	Q3	Q4
Selects and Uses Age-Appropriate Behavior • Accepts consequences for actions taken • Demonstrates self-discipline/control • Follows school and classroom rules				
Selects and Uses Age-Appropriate Coping Skills • Demonstrates decision making skills • Demonstrates organizational skills • Acts on the need for help				
Demonstrates Confidence in Self • Recognizes and accepts own abilities • Demonstrates a positive attitude toward self • Expresses personal feelings and ideas				
Interacts with Others Appropriately • Develops and maintains friendships • Demonstrates respect for individual rights • Works cooperatively with others				

Teacher(s)_____

MATHEMATICS

MATHEMATICS CONTENT	Q1	Q2	Q3	Q4
Numeration and Number Sense • Reads, writes, and compares whole numbers through 10,000 • Writes fractions • Rounds numbers to nearest 10 or 100 • Compares and orders decimals to hundredths				
Computation and Estimation • Adds and subtracts 3-digit numbers • Knows multiplication and division facts to 10				
Measurement • Tells time • Finds elapsed time • Finds perimeter				
Geometry • Uses properties of lines and angles • Plots ordered pairs				
Data Analysis and Probability • Collects, organizes, and interprets data • Interprets graphs • Uses probability to make predictions				
Algebra • Writes addition and subtraction sentences • Solves addition and subtraction word problems				

MATHEMATICAL PROCESSES	Q1	Q2	Q3	Q4
Problem Solving				
Develops Conceptual Understanding				
Work/Study Habits				

Teacher(s)_____

LANGUAGE ARTS

READING	Q1	Q2	Q3	Q4
Word Analysis/Spelling • Uses knowledge of advanced phonics patterns and multi-syllable word structures to read, write, and spell words				
Fluency • Reads grade level text accurately with appropriate phrasing, expression, and rate				
Vocabulary • Builds knowledge of literary, content, and academic words • Applies context clues and text features to infer meanings • Identifies word relationships (e.g., synonyms, antonyms, multiple meanings)				
Comprehension • Identifies author's purpose • Retells information from narrative text including characters, setting, and plot • Summarizes main ideas from informational text • Uses prior knowledge to connect text to self, to other texts, and to the world. • Monitors understanding and self-corrects when appropriate				
Multiple Literacies • Identifies, locates, and evaluates print and electronic resources to find and share information				
Work/Study Habits				

WRITING	Q1	Q2	Q3	Q4
Writing Process • Applies writing process to plan, draft, revise, and edit • Writes strong sentences using correct spelling, grammar, punctuation, and capitalization				
Writing Genres • Writes for a variety of purposes and audiences • Writes considering characteristics of a specific genre				
Handwriting/Publishing • Writes legibly and fluently • Publishes using electronic resources				
Work/Study Habits				

SPEAKING/LISTENING	Q1	Q2	Q3	Q4
Conversations and Presentations • Communicates ideas in classroom activities • Demonstrates presentation techniques and conversation strategies				
Listening • Listens in formal and informal settings for a variety of purposes				
Work/Study Habits				

Teacher(s)_____

FIGURE 11.3
Reporting Specific Competencies Attained

Source: Copyright © 2005 by Lincoln Public Schools. Reprinted with permission.

Winchester Public Schools   Elementary Report Card

ACADEMIC CODE

MS = Mastered Skills. The student is using this skill or concept independently.
LS = Learning Skills. The student is developing use of the skill or concept.
AC = Area of Concern. The student has been introduced to the skill or concept, is receiving instruction, and continues to experience difficulty. NA = Not Assessed. The student's work is not being assessed for mastery at this time.

READING	1	2	3	4
Applies knowledge of sounds, letters, and word patterns				
Reads and demonstrates comprehension of fiction and/or nonfiction using appropriate strategies				
Reads accurately and fluently with expression				
Uses a variety of skills and strategies to achieve word recognition and meaning				
Uses a variety of resources to collect, organize, and understand information				

WRITING	1	2	3	4
Writes clearly and effectively				
Understands and uses the steps in the writing process				
Writes in a variety of forms for different audiences and purposes				
Analyzes and revises written work				
Uses correct punctuation, capitalization, and spelling				

ORAL LANGUAGE	1	2	3	4
Communicates ideas clearly and effectively				
Communicates ideas clearly and effectively in oral presentations				

MATHEMATICS	1	2	3	4
Number and Number Sense: Understands counting, classification, whole numbers, place value, fractions, number relationships, and effects of single step and multi-step computations				
Computation and Estimation: Understands the skills involved with addition, subtraction, multiplication, and division to develop strategies for solving problems				
Measurement: Understands the concept of a measurement unit—standard and nonstandard				
Geometry: Identifies solid objects and plane figures by observing, comparing, and contrasting attributes				
Probability and Statistics: Understands the methods of data collection and graphing Understands the concept of chance				
Patterns, Functions, and Algebra: Understands various types of patterns and functional relationships by sorting, comparing, and classifying				

SCIENCE				
Uses scientific investigation appropriately to research, predict, observe, record, analyze data, and draw conclusions with selected tools				
Defines and applies scientific terms and concepts				

HISTORY and SOCIAL STUDIES				
History: Identifies important historical people and events and their significance				
Geography: Uses maps and globes and identifies features of the earth				
Economics: Defines and applies economic terms and concepts Civics: Demonstrates an understanding of rules, law, and citizenship				

FIGURE 11.4

Reporting by Standard

Source: Reprinted with permission from Winchester Public Schools, Department of Instruction.

represent the collective wisdom and teamwork of many experienced professionals. This backing and commitment is required to make such a system work.

Another important key to successfully using this communication system is that teachers must be trained to make dependable ratings of student performance. This training takes time and effort. Resources must be allocated to make it possible. However, these costs are minimized to the extent that the teachers who are to use the system play a role in its development.

This system provides a high level of detail about student achievement. Although users report that the performance criteria become second nature and easy to rate with practice and experience, we would be naïve to think such records are easy to create and deliver at conference time. Because the report is detailed, communicating results can be time consuming.

Narrative Reporting

Another way to forge a strong communication link between school and home is to use narrative descriptions of student learning. Narrative descriptions of student achievement must be carefully crafted to reflect a clear vision of achievement, clear criteria and standards, and a vivid sense of how this student relates to those expectations. Such written descriptions and samples of student work, in addition to grades and scores, communicate a great deal about student achievement.

Dealing with the Practicalities

The major drawback of these reports, obviously, is the time required to prepare them. High student–teacher ratios may render this option impractical for many teachers. However, if the narrative is intended for delivery to parents, could students and teachers work as partners to compose the letter? Shared work results in positive achievement for the student; shared planning and preparation of the narrative assists the teacher; open and effective student-involved communication goes to families; and everyone shares credit for doing a good job! Sounds like a win-win-win situation.

In addition, as always, we must center the narrative message on the relevant achievement targets. We must take care to transform those targets into rigorous assessments and write about specific achievement results. In other words, we must maintain a clear focus on achievement. To use this option productively, users must regard these reports as far more than "free writing time," when they can say whatever comes to mind about the student. The issues in narrative reports are, What does it mean to be academically successful, and how did this student do in relation to those expectations?

The only way this communication can become practical for a teacher is with careful planning and record keeping. At the time of the writing, all relevant information to be factored into the report must be readily available. The framework for the report must be completely spelled out. And to the extent possible, modern information processing technology should be brought to bear. For example, you might develop a template for narrative reporting on your personal computer. Within this general outline, then, you might merely need to enter essential details.

Remember, however, that narrative reporting places a premium on being able to write well. Teachers or students who have difficulty communicating in writing will find a narrative system frustrating to use and will not use it well.

Summary: Communicating with Report Cards

The key to effective communication with report cards is for you, the teacher, to be master of the material your students are to learn. This permits you to translate your clear and appropriate targets into rigorous, high-quality assessments, which, in turn, you can convert to information that you may report in detail or combine into fair and equitable grades.

The reference point for interpreting a report card grade should always be the specific material to be learned. Students deserve to know in advance how you will accomplish this in their class, and they need to know the standards you expect them to meet. If you are assessing characteristics other than achievement, you must follow appropriate rules of sound assessment, and should report results separately from achievement grades.

Teachers must carefully plan to gather accurate information for report card grading. We need to produce meaningful communication about student attainment of ascending levels of ever-more-advanced competencies.

This requires a clearly stated set of grading standards. These achievement expectations are most productively set when a faculty meets across grade levels and across classrooms within grade levels to determine the building blocks of ultimate competence and to integrate them into their classrooms, systematically dividing up responsibility for learning.

You must, however, take responsibility for assembling a strategic assessment plan for generating the information to determine which of your students attain the desired targets. You must then translate that plan into quality assessments throughout the grading period.

As you conduct assessments and accumulate results, you must take care to record as much detail about student achievement as is available. To be sure, nearly all of this useful detail ultimately will be sacrificed in our obsession to describe the rich complexity of student achievement in the form of a single letter grade. But don't give up the detail until you absolutely must. And when report card grading time arrives, share as much of the detail as you can with your students, so they understand what is behind the single little symbol that appears on the report card. Then boil the richness of your detail away only grudgingly.

Remember two final guidelines: (1) You need not assign a grade to absolutely everything students produce. It's acceptable to sometimes simply use words and pictures to convey your judgment. Allow time to learn (explore and grow) in between grades—assessment FOR learning. (2) Your challenge is not to rank students in terms of their achievement. Although not all students will learn the same amounts or at the same rates and a ranking may naturally result from your work, the student's next teacher needs more information than the student's place in the rank order to understand what to do next to assist that student. Remember, as teachers, our goal is to communicate in ways that help students learn and feel in control of their own success.

When you need to communicate greater detail when using a report card–based communication system, consider the alternatives of sharing your information about student achievement via a checklist of standards attained or a written narrative report.

Final Chapter Reflection

1. *What are the three most important new insights to come to you as a result of your study of this chapter?*
2. *Which of your previous questions about assessment can you now answer based on your study of this chapter?*
3. *What new questions have come to mind as a result of your study of this chapter—questions that you hope to have answered as your study continues?*

Practice with Chapter 11 Ideas

1. Consider the entries in the gradebook from Chris Brown's science class shown in Table 11.1.

   a. Given the guidelines of sound practice outlined in this chapter, is Chris in compliance? If not, what's wrong?

   b. What grading issues arise from this case, both with respect to sound grading practices and the principles of effective communication?

   c. What should Chris do in the future to avoid these problems?

2. Please read the following newspaper story. Using the principles and guidelines discussed in this chapter, identify as many apparent violations in achievement reporting referenced in this editorial as you can. What remedy would you recommend for each suspected violation?

Report Card Stew—Case Study

By Linda Cagnetti, *Cincinnati Enquirer*, Forum, Sunday, November 30, 1997[*]

If men are from Mars and women are from Venus, the men and women who create report cards must be from a more distant galaxy. As some of the report cards reviewed in our Forum section today demonstrate, schools and parents are sometimes not on the same planet at grading time.

First of all, they're no longer called report cards; they're "progress reports." Students don't pass or fail they are now "recommended for promotion" or "assigned to the same level." Ds and Fs are replaced with "areas of concern" or "needs more time to develop." Behavior is now "social habits."

Most of these kinder-gentler report cards are computer generated, with check-marked "comments" such as "pleasure to have in class," or "uses self control." None look alike; each district and sometimes each school, designs its own.

Reactions from parents vary. Some say they're much better than the old-fashioned, too-simple ABC versions. Others find them ridiculous. Most parents are simply bewildered.

"I don't have a clue what half of this means," one parent told us. "I'm not sure how my child is doing, but, hey, they say this is progress."

Kentucky Enquirer columnist Karen Samples recently wrote about the [recently]-reformed report cards from a dozen or so districts in [several] counties, along with [traditional] ones. It's quite a smorgasbord. Some cards are easy to understand with both letter and number grades; others are overwhelming and mystifying.

Schools are working hard to communicate more to parents about new standards. Good idea. But more doesn't automatically translate to better. For example, the common-sense alarm buzzes when you read that an elementary student is graded on 72 different skills, and the explanations are so fuzzy that a college-educated parent is befuddled.

Smoke-and-mirror report cards are another example of the gap between what education reformers believe is important and what ordinary people want. No wonder Joe and Jane Public don't feel public schools belong to them anymore.

Student report cards are the most basic and precious link between schools and parents. When they're reduced to meaningless symbols and babble, educators deserve an old-fashioned, unequivocal F for failure.

3. A group of teachers, school administrators, and parents attended a workshop on grading. A parent asked if the educators in the room would explain what a letter grade of B

---

[*]Copyright © 1997 Cincinnati Enquirer. Reprinted by permission.

TABLE 11.1
Gradebook Page

NAME	LAB REPORTS										TOTAL LABS	TEST/EXAMS			TOTAL TESTS	MISCELLANEOUS*					TOTAL MISC.	FINAL TOTAL		FINAL GRADE
																1	2	3	4	5				Letter
Out of	10	10	10	10	10	10	10	10	10	10	100	50	50	10	200	20	20	20	20	20	100	400	%	
Robin	6	6	6	5	6	6	7	6	6	6	60	33	39	81	153	15	15	12	0	10	52	265	66	C
Kay	2	3	5	5	6	6	7	8	9	10	61	11	29	86	126	15	13	18	10	10	66	253	63	C
Marg	10	10	A	10	10	10	A	10	A	A	60	50	A	100	150	0	0	0	0	15	15	225	56	D
Jim	9	8	8	9	10	9	10	8	8	9	89	24	24	49	97	20	17	17	20	20	94	280	70	B
Peter	10	10	9	9	8	8	7	7	6	5	79	45	36	32	113	20	10	15	10	5	60	252	63	C
Lorna	10	10	10	10	10	10	10	10	10	10	100	32	29	59	120	20	20	20	20	20	100	320	80	A
John	8	8	7	9	9	8	7	9	10	8	84	32	30	57	119	20	8	7	0	5	40	243	61	C

A = Absent = 0 (for Lab Reports and Tests/Exams)

*Miscellaneous:1–Attendance; 2–Care of Equipment; 3–Attitude/Participation; 4–Notebook; 5–Reading Reports (4 X 5 marks)

Letter Grade Legend (in Ontario): A = 80%–100%; B = 70%–79%; C = 60%–69%; D = 50%–59%; F = 0%–49%

Source: From *How to Grade for Learning: Linking Grades to Standards,* by Ken O'Connor. © 2002 by SkyLight Professional Development. Reprinted by permission of LessonLab, a Pearson Education Company, *www.lessonlab.com.*

on a report card means and how it differs from an A or C. Participants were asked to answer the following specific questions:

- What should a grade tell us about students?
- What are the factors that are actually used to determine students' grades?

Here are the brainstormed answers of the educators present:

What should grades tell us about students?

* What things they know and can do
* Why they have improved during the marking period
* What their strengths are and the things they need to work on
* Whether they can solve real-world problems
* What level their work is
* How well they behave
* Whether they are ready to move on
* How they help one another
* Whether they've reached a standard
* How well they can apply what they know

What factors are actually included in grades?

* Attendance and lateness
* Behavior/attitude
* End of marking period test scores
* Homework
* Family status
* Ability
* Appearance
* Personality
* Teacher attitude toward the student
* Portfolios

Given these lists, please answer the following questions:

1. Do you agree with the first list—what grades should tell us? If not, what's wrong or missing?

2. Would this list of factors actually provide the information needed to tell us what these educators believe grades should tell us? Think particularly about sound assessment practices, sound grading practices, and effective communication as you answer.

3. What changes are needed in each list to form a foundation for effective communication about achievement? Why?

PEARSON

Now go to www.myeducationlab.com to take a Pretest to assess your initial comprehension of chapter content, study chapter content with your individualized Study Plan, take a Posttest to assess your understanding of chapter content, practice your teaching skills with Building Teaching Skills exercises, and build a deeper, more applied understanding of chapter content with Homework and Exercises.

CHAPTER 12

Portfolios as Rich Communication

CHAPTER FOCUS

This chapter answers the following guiding question:

> How can my students and I communicate effectively with each other and with others about their achievement using portfolios—that is, collections of their work?

From your study of this chapter, you will understand the following:

1. The power of portfolios resides in their potential for student involvement in record keeping and communication in ways that promote learning.
2. Portfolios can take many forms, all of which can serve us well if we keep our purpose in mind as we select from among the options.

STUDENT-INVOLVED COMMUNICATION PART 1: PORTFOLIOS

A *portfolio* is a collection of student work assembled in a way that tells a story about student achievement. The story it tells will be a function of the context: the purpose for assessing and the achievement target(s) about which we wish to communicate. Thus, the range of possible applications of portfolios in the classroom is wide indeed.

Arter & Spandel (1992) set up portfolios for use in assessment FOR learning classrooms:

> The portfolio's communication potential and instructional usefulness are enhanced when students participate in selecting content; when the selection of material to include follows predetermined guidelines; when criteria are available for judging the merit of the work collected, and when students regularly reflect on the quality of their work. (p. 36)

Just as artists assemble portfolios of their work to convey their talents and journalists assemble collections of their writings to represent their capabilities, so too can students collect examples of their work to tell their school achievement story.

Portfolios Provide the Details

Based on our discussion of report cards in Chapter 11, it should be clear to you that we condense a great deal of information into one single little symbol when we assign grades. Over an entire semester or year, as teachers, we gather a great deal of detail about student achievement. Visualize a large vessel full of information on student mastery of content knowledge, reasoning proficiencies, performance skills, and product development capabilities. To assign a grade, we must force the contents of that big container through a narrow-diameter funnel. When it comes out the other end as an A, B, or C, all of the detail is gone.

The problem is some decision makers need that detail to do their jobs—to make their decisions. For instance, let's say we are teachers receiving new students on their journey to excellence as math-problem solvers and all we receive from their previous teacher is a letter grade next to the word "Math" on a report card. That level of specificity tells us nothing about each student's strengths or weaknesses. Based on the report card grade alone, we have no idea what comes next in the student's learning. We need greater detail in this communication.

Or say we are parents. Our ability to understand, appreciate, and support our child's growth is enhanced if we have access to details regarding that growth, or its lack. A single report card grade tells us only a small part of a very large story. If we are to support the learning of our child, we need to know where that child's strengths and weaknesses reside.

This is where portfolios can help. Typically, they contain details in the form of examples of student work with feedback about and student reflections on the quality of that work. As teachers or parents, if we can study those work samples, read the student's reflections, and have that student talk us through the portfolio, describing growth during the period covered by the work, we get a clear view of that individual's growth and current needs. Besides, imagine the pride students might feel when their portfolios illustrate the real growth they have experienced.

In this chapter, we will explore this option, with the goal of having you know and understand why portfolios have become so popular as a record-keeping option to underpin effective communication.

Benefits for Teachers and Students

If done well, portfolios permit teachers to do the following:

- Track student achievement over time to reveal improvement or the lack thereof. In this sense, they can be continuously diagnostic.
- Provide a context within which to teach students to take responsibility for maintaining and tracking their own files and records of achievement. This assessment FOR learning application represents a critical life skill.
- Help students learn to reflect on and see their own improvement as achievers in preparation for communicating with others about this. This involvement, as we have established previously, encourages students to keep trying.
- Provide important insights into students' academic self-efficacy, academic interests, and sense of their own needs. Obviously, this can facilitate our planning.
- Provide excellent opportunities for students to practice their reasoning proficiencies by analyzing their own work, comparing samples of their work over time, drawing inferences about their growth or needs, and learning to evaluate productively.
- Document student attainment of required district or state standards in an assessment OF learning context.

For all of these reasons, teachers experienced in using portfolios find them to be engaging for both themselves and their students.

Portfolios Assessment? No

As portfolios have increased in popularity in recent years, unfortunately some have begun to speak of "portfolios assessment" when referring to their use. Portfolios are correctly thought of as collections of assessments, not as an assessment method in and of themselves.

Similarly, some have linked portfolios inexorably to "performance assessment." There is precedent for this. When artists assemble portfolios of their work, they collect the artistic products they have created. When journalists collect samples of their articles, they too gather their work into a coherent whole. These are products. As you know, they can serve as the basis for product-based performance assessments. Thus, it is tempting to think of portfolios as relying only on performance assessments as the source of their information of student achievement. Resist this temptation. We have four forms of assessment at our disposal—selected response, essay, performance assessment, and personal communication. Each can contribute to the story of student achievement. So they all can appear in portfolios. Additionally, portfolios can hold many other types of artifacts, such as photos, letters, rough drafts, schedules, lists (such as of books read), and other evidence relevant to telling a complete story of achievement status or growth.

Time for Reflection

If you were to develop a portfolio that told the story of who you are as a candidate for a teaching position—say, for the purpose of serving as a job application portfolio—what would you include?

Keys to Successful Use

The effective use of portfolios requires that we apply them in a disciplined way. We have come in contact with several local and even state education agencies that like the portfolio idea so much that they simply order teachers to start one for each student—without ever asking or answering the question, "Why?" Envision what we might call the universal, all-encompassing "mega-portfolio." Starting in primary grades, teachers accumulate evidence of achievement. Then each teacher along the way adds more, as the child's school story unfolds. Visualize a file folder that then becomes a file drawer, then a file cabinet, and then a closet full of material. Soon we've evolved to a room-sized collection, leading ultimately to the student driving a tractor-trailer across the stage at high school graduation!

Sound foolish? Of course. And we can take little comfort from technology buffs who tell us not to worry about volume of "stuff" because we can digitize it all and place it on a computer chip the size of your thumbnail. Imagine an "electro-mega-super-portfolio," still completely devoid of purpose. This lack of focus arises from a lack of understanding or discipline on the part of those who would conceive of such plans. If we start with no focus, no story to tell, no purpose, no clear achievement targets, we end up with a useless and unmanageable mass of evidence, whether on paper or in electrons.

Consider a different scenario. We must begin each portfolio application with a clear sense of context. During their schooling, students develop and use many portfolios for various purposes, each focusing on a different achievement target. Some will reflect math competence for the purpose of helping students grow, some verify reading and writing competence for accountability, and others center on science skills for other purposes. Some will be more structured, some less. Some will be more student involving, some less. Some will deal with knowledge targets, others with reasoning, still others with skills or products. Their contents will vary depending on the learning context. But we hope what will remain in students' minds is a sense that they are in control of their increasing academic competence—a strong and growing academic self-concept. We should feel free to use portfolios flexibly and opportunistically to gather and communicate information about student achievement and develop a sense of academic well-being. Over the years, most of these portfolio collections will end up in students' hands after serving their purpose. But every one of them will focus on its own unique and crystal clear set of achievement expectations.

Accurate Assessments

By this point in our journey, we don't need to add detail about how quality assessments form the foundation of an effective communication system. We have long since defined our quality control criteria and discussed how to meet those standards. As we accumulate evidence of student achievement in a portfolio, we and our students must collect solid evidence.

We know of a school in which teachers record students struggling to speak a new language in early grades and then continue to collect recorded segments over the years as each student's proficiency increases. They wrap the CDs as gifts and present them to their students at graduation along with their diploma. If they have developed high-quality, student-involved assessments, students not only hear themselves improving over time, but also can articulate precisely what it is that makes each new addition to the recording better than those that preceded it. Quality assessments placed in student hands will encourage learning.

Form Follows Function

To merge effectively into instruction, portfolios must tell a particular story. We must plan to collect materials that can tell that story. These plans provide students and teachers with specific guidelines for selecting work for the portfolio. Spandel and Culham (1995) provide a productive way to think of this by suggesting several structures for portfolios. These are not mutually exclusive categories, and you may blend them to fit the occasion. These structures are the celebration portfolio, the growth portfolio, the project portfolio, and the achievement status portfolio.

Celebration Portfolio. A portfolio can be used as a keepsake, which you invite students to create as a personal collection of favorite works and special academic mementos. They might use this to communicate to families the things they are most proud of or to show positive examples of their learning experiences or classroom activities.

In this case, students' guidelines for portfolio selection are driven by this question: What do I think is really special about my work and why? This is a wonderful place for young students to begin their portfolio development experience by just collecting favorite pieces of work. They may then begin to categorize and cull for the really special works. The only evaluations are made by the students, according to their own vision of what's "special." No one else's standards have a place here. This is critically important.

Students can use this experience to begin to identify the attributes of special classroom work and to generate personal insights about their own meaning of quality.

Over time and through interaction with their teachers and classmates, they can begin to connect these elements of quality into a growing framework that ultimately helps them understand their own sense of what represents "good work." In this sense, the celebration portfolio can begin to put students in touch with their own strengths and interests and can help them learn to make choices.

Growth Portfolio. Another reason to build a portfolio is to highlight changes or accomplishments in a student's academic performance over time. Two classroom applications of this idea warrant discussion, the growth portfolio and the project portfolio.

In the growth portfolio, the creator (storyteller) collects samples of work over time to show how proficiency has changed. When this is the purpose, guidelines for selection dictate assembling multiple indicators of the same proficiency, such as samples of writing or selections of artwork. As you recall from the opening scenario in Chapter 1, Emily shared a sample of her writing from the beginning of the year for the school board to review and critique. Then she wowed them with another sample from the end of the year that revealed how much more proficient she had become. These writing samples came from her writing portfolio—a growth portfolio.

In this case, the evaluation criteria need to be held constant over time. Emily was able to discuss specific improvements in her work included in her portfolio over the year because the writing criteria—word choice, organization, sentence structure, voice, and so on—remained the same for each writing activity. This gave her a yardstick by which to see her writing progress to higher levels of competence. The motivational power of a growth portfolio can be immense when students get to see their own improvement.

Project Portfolio. Alternatively, the storyteller might depict the completion of steps in a project conducted over time. When this is the purpose, guidelines for selection dictate that the storyteller provide evidence of having completed all necessary steps in a quality manner. For example, students completing a major science project might show how they arrived at a hypothesis, how they assembled the apparatus for gathering the needed data, how they conducted the tests, the test results, and the analysis and interpretation of those results. A project portfolio is an ideal format to use to describe such work carried out over an extended period.

The evaluative judgments made in this case are based on two sets of performance criteria. The first reflects the steps students must have completed within a specified time frame. These typically provide highly structured guidelines for what to collect as proof of work completion. They teach students lessons about the necessity of planning a task and sticking to a timeline. You might also hold students accountable for periodically reviewing progress with you.

The second set focuses on the quality of work completed at each step along the way. These, of course, demand that students not merely provide evidence of having done the activity, but also provide evidence that they did it well.

One final comment regarding growth and project portfolios: The span of time covered can range from a brief project lasting only a few days to one lasting a full year or longer, depending on the context. These are very flexible.

Achievement Status Portfolio. Yet another use of portfolios can be to prove students have met certain established academic standards. Here, either we or our students must make a case within the portfolio for having attained certain levels of proficiency depending on the context. Therefore, the intended achievement targets determine the guidelines for content selection.

Several applications of this kind of portfolio are relevant in school. As students move through the learning progression of the math curriculum, for example, we might maintain portfolios depicting their current achievement status. So at any point in time, decision makers could check this record and know what comes next. In this case, when a sample of student work is collected that reveals a new high level of achievement, then the old evidence previously held in the portfolio—now outdated—would be discarded. If there is any portfolio format that might accompany a student across grade levels over the years, this is it.

In another kind of application, in some districts, students present a portfolio of evidence of having attained certain essential proficiencies in order to qualify for graduation. Indeed, some states require such evidence to earn a certificate of mastery.

In a much simpler context, we might ask students to assemble evidence of having mastered all requirements for completing a particular course. Or, we might review an achievement status portfolio to make a course placement decision, such as when we select the next natural course in a student's progression of math instruction.

In all of these cases, the guidelines for selecting material will probably be highly structured and driven by specific academic requirements that provide evidence that students have mastered prerequisites and are ready to move on.

Exploring the Social Context of Assessment

When the idea of portfolios first arrived on the educational assessment scene, several states explored their application as an alternative to their large-scale statewide selected response testing. Why do you think they did this? In fact, the idea was abandoned after several attempts. Why do you think that happened? Does this mean portfolios are without value? Where can their value be shown to best advantage?

Portfolios as Assessment FOR Learning Tools

As you well know by now, we need to establish criteria by which to evaluate students' progress, whether judging the merit of writing, charting the expansion of scientific knowledge, or recording increased proficiency in speaking a foreign language. Portfolios can handle a range of target possibilities, relying on a variety of assessment formats.

To illustrate, if we were to decide that the best evidence of student attainment of a particular target is a score on a multiple-choice test, then the criteria used to judge merit is a high score on the test. If an essay test most accurately reflects the target, then once again, a traditional test score provides the needed information. However, with performance assessments, the criteria applied must reflect proficiency on the skills of interest or reflect the extent to which the student has met quality product standards.

Consequently, we must decide in advance and share with our students how we and they will judge merit. We continue to press the point that students can hit any target that they can see and that holds still for them. Obviously, this is equally important with portfolios and is the essential way to link assessment and instruction.

Involving Students in Selecting Portfolio Entries

Let's say you were assembling a job application portfolio. Clearly it would be important for you to take responsibility for selecting the material to be included for two reasons. First, you know yourself best and can best ensure the telling of a complete and accurate story. Second, selecting the content allows you to present yourself in the most positive light called for in this competitive situation.

Our students are driven, Covington (1992) tells us, by a desire to maintain and to present to the world a sense that they are academically capable. We support and encourage that positive self-image by involving students in recording their own story through their portfolios. But to make this work, they must also actively participate in selecting the work for the portfolio.

In the celebration portfolio described previously, the story is essentially the student's to tell. But there also is much room for student involvement in the growth, project, and achievement status options. Notice that we are not saying that the student selects everything, nor does their teacher. We're talking partnership here. Here's how one teacher friend of ours handles this: Her sixth graders maintain files of all work completed, one for each discipline. When it comes time to assemble a growth portfolio in preparation for a student-led parent conference (discussed in Chapter 13), for example, students and teacher work as a team to select work.

Davies, Cameron, Politano, and Gregory (1992) advise us that we can maximize the benefits of student involvement in selection by having them describe what they selected and why they selected it. They recommend using a cover sheet for each portfolio entry to capture this information. Figure 12.1 presents an example.

Periodic Student Self-Reflection

One of the truly important ingredients in a productive portfolio is periodic student self-reflection. If we are to keep students in touch with their emerging academic successes, we must do the following:

- Share our vision of what it means to succeed in understandable terms
- Provide them with a vocabulary to use in communicating about it
- Keep them in touch with the accumulating evidence of their own proficiency

As you know, we apply principles of assessment FOR learning to do these things. But another way to help them maintain a clear sense of themselves as learners is to have them write or talk about that accumulating evidence and what it says to and about them.

Clearly *students who learn to evaluate their own achievement become better achievers through that process*. They maintain contact with their own evolving strengths and weaknesses. Figure 12.2 provides an example in two parts, a student essay, "Visions of Hope," and the author's reflection on the quality of her work. In this essay, she assumes the persona of a prisoner who uses her art to maintain perspective. Please read the essay carefully first, then the self-reflection. Note that the author applies the six analytical writing assessment score scales presented in the chapter on performance assessment. This represents compelling evidence that she is in touch with her own writing proficiency.

Helping Students Learn to Reflect

Sometimes it's helpful to initiate students into self-reflection by posing some simple questions for them to reflect about, such as the following (adapted from Arter & Spandel, 1992):

When I chose to include this example of my writing in my portfolio
I remembered that . . .

FICTION	NON-FICTION
• has a good story	• gives information
• uses interesting language	• groups information under main headings
• has a beginning, a middle, and an end	• has a table of contents
• uses a variety of sentences, both simple and complex	• has diagrams or pictures to give additional information

I also know that it is important that my work is neat and that it has been
edited for spelling and sentence structure.

The piece of work I have chosen is . . .

It shows . . .

I want you to notice . . .

Please give me one compliment and ask me
one question after you read my selection . . .

I put this in my portfolio on _____   _____

                               [date]   [signature]

FIGURE 12.1
Summary Sheet for Student Use in Describing Portfolio Selections
Source: From *Together Is Better: Collaborative Assessment, Evaluation and Reporting* (p. 79) by A. Davies, C. Cameron, C. Politano, and K. Gregory, 1992. Winnipeg, MB: Peguis. Reprinted by permission.

VISIONS OF HOPE

I call my picture "Visions of Hope." If I'm caught with this picture, I'll be killed. But it's worth it if people outside see it. I want them to know what life was like in the camp and how we kept our hopes up.

You may be wondering how I got the materials I used in this picture. It wasn't easy. I got the materials for the prisoner figures from old pieces of uniforms that had been torn off. This was one of the easier things to get. Uniforms get torn all the time from hard work. All the people look alike because to the Nazis it doesn't matter what you look like—only what you can do. To the Nazis we are all just numbers, without faces and without names.

The buildings in the picture are black to represent evil and death. Most of the buildings, aside from the barracks, you would enter but never come out again alive. I got this cloth from an old blanket that had worn thin from overuse. The Germans didn't care if we were cold or uncomfortable, so they didn't make any real effort to mend things. Everything in our world badly needs mending, too, including our spirits.

Inside the smoke of death coming out of the smokestacks you will see the Star of David. This star represents hope. Hope for life and for living. We will never totally die as long as our hope lives on.

My picture has two borders. One is barbed wire. It symbolizes tyranny, oppression, and total loss of freedom. The barbs are shaped like swastikas to represent the Nazis, Hitler and hate. This is a symbol of true evil.

The other border, outside the barbed wire, represents all the hope and dreams that are outside the camp. The flowers, sun, moon and bright colors were all things we took for granted in our old world. Even though we can see the sun through the clouds and smoke, we can't enjoy it anymore. The feathers represent the birds we barely see or hear inside the camp. We miss the cheeriness of their voices. The tiny brown twigs are as close as we come to the trees we remember. I got the bright cloth from a dress. When new prisoners come to the camp they must take off their own clothes and put on the hated prison outfits. All the nice clothes are sent to Germans outside the camps. My job is to sort through the clothes and pick out the nice things that will be sent away. When I saw this beautiful cloth, I tore off a piece and saved it for my picture.

I hope someone finds this and remembers that we always kept our hopes alive even when they took away everything else. They could never take our hope.

REFLECTION

This piece has always been one of my favorites. It shows not only what I can do as a writer, but as an artist as well. I knew very little of the Holocaust before working on this project. It was almost impossible for me to believe how brutal people could be. It both frightened and horrified me. In my written piece and my picture, I tried to capture that horror but also the courage which kept many people going. I also tried hard to imagine how it would really feel to be imprisoned, locked away from the things and the work and the people I loved. I don't know if anyone can really imagine this without living it, but this project made me think.

In **Ideas and Content,** I gave myself a 5. I thought my ideas were clear, and I thought I created a vivid picture of an artist trying to keep his work alive.

I would also give myself a 5 in **Organization.** My opening does a good job of leading the reader into my paper, especially with the dramatic and honest statement: "If I'm caught with this picture I'll be killed." I want the reader to know right away what is at stake.

My **Voice** is not as strong as I would have liked it to be. It is hard to take on the voice of another person. I am pretending to be someone else, not myself. I guess I just haven't had enough practice at this. Also,

FIGURE 12.2
Sample of Student Writing and Author's Self-Reflection
Source: "Visions of Hope," a sample of writing and self-reflection by N. Spandel. Reprinted by permission.

my natural voice tends to be humorous, and clearly, this is the most serious of topics. Anyway, I just did not find quite the voice I wanted, and I gave myself a 4.

I gave myself a 5 in **Word Choice.** The language is simple and natural. I did not try to impress the reader with words they might not understand. Also, I tried to capture the mood of what it would be like to live in a concentration camp and think how the people who lived there might talk. What words would they use? My **Sentence Fluency** was pretty strong. You will notice that I vary my sentence beginnings a lot. That's one of my strengths. It's smooth, whether you read it silently or aloud. I think a few sentences are a little short and choppy, though. Some sentence combining would help. So I rated myself a 4 on this trait. In **Conventions** I would rate myself a 5. I have always been strong in this trait. Conventions are fairly easy for me, if I think about them, especially with the aid of a computer. I can catch most grammatical errors, and I use a spell checker. I also read through my paper when it's finished to make sure it sounds just right. Rating myself on these traits is very helpful. It allows me to see how I'm doing as a writer and to see my work as it really is. I think the traits give you a way of teaching yourself.

FIGURE 12.2   (*continued*)

- Describe the steps you went through to complete this assignment. Did this process work and lead to successful completion or were there problems? What would you change next time?
- Did you receive feedback along the way that permitted you to refine your work? Describe your response to the feedback offered—did you agree or disagree with it? Why? What did you do as a result of this feedback?
- What makes your most effective piece of work different from your least effective? What does your best work tell you about where you have improved and where you need further work?
- What are the strengths of your work in this project (or this series of works)?
- What aspects still need more work? What kind of help will you need?
- What impact has this project had on your interests, attitudes, and views of this area?

It's human nature to find it difficult to be constructively analytical and self-critical, at least at first. As we established earlier, this is risky business for most, especially for those with a history of academic failure. Research reminds us that students will go to great lengths to maintain a positive internal sense of academic ability, even to the point of denying or being unable to see, let alone face, the flaws in their work (Covington, 1992). For this reason, guided practice is a necessity.

It may help for students to see you model the process by analyzing and self-evaluating some of your own work. Or, consider having the whole class collaborate as a team to compose a hypothetical self-reflection on a particular project. This is the best way we know to show students that your classroom is a safe place within which to risk trying. Either success or problems point the direction not to a judgmental grade, but to a specific path to each student's improvement.

Dealing with Some Practicalities

As we work with teachers exploring classroom applications of portfolios, several questions seem to come up over and over. Jan recently discussed portfolios with a teacher who knows and has extensive experience with them. That conversation unfolds here.

Time for Reflection

As you read down through this conversation, make a list of the specific pieces of advice this teacher offers in discussing her particular portfolio applications. Then compare your list with those of a classmate or your study team.

"How does your district or school use portfolios?"

"We start small," she replied, "with simple celebration portfolios in primary grades, as teachers ease their students into the process. We ask them to answer questions like, what do you like about this piece? What do you think you might be able to improve?

"In the elementary grades, we have them begin growth portfolios, keeping the targets simple and the criteria very clear, student-friendly, and constant. Then in middle and high school we introduce the status report portfolio. I use growth, but our students must assemble a status report, too, as they progress through the high school."

"The long-term experience with different applications must help students become comfortable with the practice," I inferred.

"It makes the process much easier for them to learn and manage. I've noticed a difference in my students when they come to my class with prior portfolio experience. Those students plunge in with confidence."

"What got you started?"

"We wanted to do student-led parent conferences. We needed the portfolio to help students get ready—to gather evidence of their growth and achievement to share with parents. I have my students build a writing growth portfolio."

"How much time does it take?"

"It varies," she said. "It depends on coverage. As the scope of the target and time span of the portfolio increase, so does the time commitment. But as students mature and gain experience, they learn to handle most of the work and to enjoy it. The bigger the students' role, the easier it is for me. They do a lot of the work while they're learning. That allows me to tailor their use of portfolios to fit their available time."

"You teach high school and face 150 students a day in different classes, yet the idea really is feasible for you?"

"You bet! But it has to be a partnership, with students shouldering most of the load. Without them, I couldn't do it."

"Can students really manage their own portfolios? What if they cheat?" I asked.

"They can manage it, as long as I provide clear directions and insist on those timelines.

"Cheating always becomes an interesting point of conversation in my classes. In other classrooms, students can copy someone else's test paper, sneak in a crib sheet, have someone else do their homework for them, and even change grades on assignments before returning them to the teacher. I've seen it all.

"But you know what really minimizes cheating? The weekly written self-reflections I require. Students share these with their study teammates, then put them in their portfolios, where I get to read them. If you don't know where you are in your own development and don't know what you're talking about, it shows. It's impossible to bluff this."

"You've made cheating irrelevant, in effect," I observed.

"My students know that I expect to see increasing quality over time on their part. It's as if each self-reflection is more demanding than the one preceding it. Everyone seems to acknowledge that there are no excuses in this classroom. It may sound crazy, but I think you're right. They really get it that cheating makes no sense in here.

"Besides, my students quickly learn through the grapevine that they simply can't bluff in their conference with their parents and me, where any attempt to misrepresent their own achievement will be obvious to everyone. I ask tough questions in front of their families. They know they're responsible for providing solid answers. And you know, I can see the pride in their eyes when they deliver quality."

"How do you convert portfolio work to a grade?," I asked.

"We work as a class to devise a set of grading rules," she replied. "Before anyone starts, I share examples of good and bad work from past classes, and we work as a team to identify the differences between them. We establish and define our keys to success, and formulate performance rating scales.

"I base their grade on the quality of the final few products at the end of the grading period. We agree on the target in advance, and we define levels of proficiency that equate to different grades—you know, what their profile of ratings must look like to earn an A, a B, and so on. No one gets credit for just doing work. It's the learning that comes from doing the work that counts."

Next I asked, "Who owns the portfolios?"

"My students keep the growth portfolio. When our purposes have been served, they take them home."

"Where do you store all of these portfolios?"

"With their owners—my students. They can be responsible for this. If they wish, they can use a file cabinet in my room. But, the agreement is that each portfolio is private property.

"I have heard that there are some electronic portfolio software packages coming on the market. We've begun to investigate this option for the district for the future."

"Thanks for sharing your experiences."

Electronic Portfolios

As this teacher points out, there are some promising new developments afoot for storing student portfolios. A number of computer software developers have created and are refining packages that permit classroom teachers to help students develop electronic portfolios. These purport to allow easy entry of traditional academic records (student background, grades, etc.), as well as actual examples of student work, including everything from written products to color videos with sound. Easy retrieval also is possible using networked personal computers.

Summary: Communication with Portfolios

Portfolios offer ways to communicate about student achievement in much greater detail than is permitted by report card grades. In these cases, the communication arises from and focuses on actual examples of student work. Unlike grades, portfolios can tell a more detailed story of a student's achievement. This does not mean that they should replace grades, but rather that we should see them as serving different purposes—different users and uses.

Portfolios have gained popularity in recent years because of their potential as a teaching tool that offers many opportunities for student involvement. They can help us diagnose student needs and reveal improvement over time. They can encourage students to take responsibility for their own learning, track that learning, and gain an enhanced sense of academic progress and self-worth. Portfolios help students learn to reflect on their own work, identify strengths and weaknesses, and plan a course of action—critically important life skills. And finally, they give students opportunities for practicing important and useful reasoning and problem-solving skills.

But with all these pluses, these ways of communicating take very careful planning and dedication to use well. The hard work can pay off with immense achievement and motivational dividends if we implement them in calculated small steps. See the big picture, but move toward it in baby steps, one step at a time. Unfortunately, many have drowned in the sea of student papers collected to serve a policy maker's mandated "mega-portfolio" system. We can avoid such problems by preparing carefully.

Specifically, this means the following:

- Collect evidence of student attainment of clearly articulated student- and family-friendly achievement targets.
- Gather dependable evidence so as to create an accurate picture with students as partners in that process.
- Use portfolios in a communication environment that lends itself to open sharing.

- Provide plenty of opportunities to inter-act with students about their evidence of achievement.
- Regularly check to be sure students are in touch with and feeling in control of their own progress.

The possibilities of student involvement in this kind of communication are bounded only by the imagination of the users, meaning you and your students. The methods of conveying information explored in this chapter hold the promise of allowing students to tell their own story of academic success. They can play key roles in identifying the story to be told, devising guidelines for the selection of work to go into the portfolio, devising criteria for judging merit, applying those criteria, reflecting on their own achievement status or growth over time, and communicating to others about their success in learning. This, in and of itself, represents one of the most powerful learning experiences we can offer them.

Final Chapter Reflection

1. *What are the three most important new insights to come to you as a result of your study of this chapter?*
2. *Which of your previous questions about assessment can you now answer based on your study of this chapter?*
3. *What new questions have come to mind as a result of your study of this chapter—questions that you hope to have answered as your study continues?*

Practice with Chapter 12 Ideas

1. Create a chart, labeling each line with one of the four types of portfolios discussed in this chapter: celebration, growth, project, and achievement status. Add four columns headed by these questions: What story will the portfolio tell? What kinds of evidence must it contain? How will we evaluate the information? How does this portfolio type connect to our instruction? Referring to the text, within each cell of this four-by-four chart, briefly answer each question for each portfolio type.

2. Compare and contrast report card grades and portfolios as means of communication about student achievement. How are they alike? How are they different? What do those similarities and differences tell you about the information users each is likely to serve well?

3. Listed below are some possible contexts for portfolios. Classify each as calling for a celebration, growth, project, or achievement status portfolio:

Student-led parent-teacher conference

Certify competence for high school graduation

Collect personal favorites

Science fair

Tracking progress toward math standards

College admissions

Encourage students to keep reading

Identify academically challenged or gifted students

4. Assume that you are an educator applying for a teaching job. However, instead of completing the normal application form, you decide to submit a portfolio as your application. Identify a position in a context that would be right for you. What would you put in your portfolio? Identify each entry and your rationale for its inclusion. What story do you want to tell about yourself and why? When you have completed this task, please answer the following questions:

a. Of the four kinds of portfolios described in this chapter, which kind is this?

b. In the job application and candidate selection process, who sets the scoring criteria? Therefore, in preparing your story, with whom would you like to speak in advance? Why?

c. What would you do if they wouldn't tell you what you wanted to know? What if they told you they really hadn't identified selection criteria? Or what if you spoke to several members of the selection committee and they each identified different performance criteria? How would you feel in each of these cases and what would you do?

d. What if the purpose for your portfolio was different? For instance, what if the purpose was for you to build your own personal celebration portfolio of your career as an educator? Would you include different ingredients? Why?

Now go to www.myeducationlab.com to take a Pretest to assess your initial comprehension of chapter content, study chapter content with your individualized Study Plan, take a Posttest to assess your understanding of chapter content, practice your teaching skills with Building Teaching Skills exercises, and build a deeper, more applied understanding of chapter content with Homework and Exercises.

CHAPTER 13

Conferences as Productive Communication

CHAPTER FOCUS

This chapter answers the following guiding question:

> How can my students and I communicate effectively with each other and with others about their achievement using conferences?

From your study of this chapter, you will understand the following:

1. How portfolios can feed productively into a variety of conference formats involving students, parents, and teachers.
2. As with report cards, certain conditions must be satisfied for conferences to facilitate our communications about student achievement.

STUDENT-INVOLVED COMMUNICATION PART 2: CONFERENCES

In the previous chapter's discussion of portfolios as collections of student work with frequent student self reflection of their learning we established that students need to understand the target and have the vocabulary needed to talk about achievement expectations. In addition, they need to have played a role in gathering the evidence of their learning that will be the focus of the meeting—they need to be in close touch with their own academic development. With all of this collection of evidence and development of student capacities to do their own communicating we have put in place the key ingredients in what we think of as the biggest breakthrough to happen in communication in the classroom: student-led parent conferences, one of several conference formats we will address in this chapter. Let us begin the chapter with a true story illustrating this communication option.

A Productive Experience for All

"The tablecloths are out, cookies arranged, lemonade cooling, and I'm eating supper—frozen yogurt." Terri Austin, a sixth-grade teacher from Fairbanks, Alaska, begins to tell us what it's like in her classroom the evening of student-parent conferences. Let's listen to the rest of her story.

It's 5:45. Will they come? No matter how many times I do this, I always wonder if families will show up.

At 5:50, Frank and his mom arrive early. He's all polished, clean shirt and hair combed. As she sits at a table by the window, he quickly finds his portfolio, joins her and begins.

At 6:00, the room fills quickly, Ruth and her mother drink lemonade while looking at the class photographs on the bulletin board.

Chuck says, "Pick a table, Mom." She picks one with a purple tablecloth. Chuck smiles and says, "Oh yeah, you like purple. Would you like some refreshments?" After his mother and brother are seated, Chuck goes to pick up cookies and drinks.

Dennis and his father come in. Dennis's father is still in his military uniform. They find a table by the window. As Dennis shares his work, his father smiles. The father leans closer to Dennis, so they see the paper at the same time.

With his mother sitting across from him, Chuck goes over each paper very carefully. Occasionally, she looks over Chuck's head and smiles at me. Greg and his mom speak Spanish as they look at the papers together.

Darrin's father rushes in with his family trailing behind. His father asks, "Mrs. Austin, what time are we?" "I scheduled the time wrong," Darrin apologizes. I say, "It's OK. There are no set times. Just find a table and begin." They stop at the refreshment table as Darrin finds his portfolio.

I hear Greg explaining his summary sheet in Spanish.

Steve, his mom, and an unknown lady and child arrive. At the end of the conference, I find out the woman is a neighbor who heard about "Steve's portfolio" and wanted to see it. So Steve invited her to his conference. Darrin's mom catches my eye and smiles. She listens to Darrin read [one of his papers].

On their way out the door, I talk with Hope's family. They are very pleased with Hope's work. Her mom has tears in her eyes as she tells me how proud she is of Hope. (Austin, 1994, pp. 66–67)

Thus, Terri introduces us to the idea of student-led parent conferences. In this case, we combine the strengths of student-teacher conferences and parent-teacher conferences into a rich and engaging learning experience for students. Terri and her students spend a great deal of time both preparing information about student achievement and preparing to share it with parents. These personal conferences with families add a depth of communication about student growth and development over time that is unattainable with any of the other communication options.

After the conferences, Terri checked with her students to see if they thought the hard work and preparation were worth it for them. She was startled at the strength of student feelings. Virtually all of the students reported that they felt this method of holding conferences was both beneficial and empowering. The students felt more at ease in discussing their grades and their reasons for their answers on assessments. They also gained a better awareness of what their results meant and how they could use them to assume greater ownership of both their learning and their evaluation of their own performance and progress. The experience was so positive for them that they unanimously agreed to continue to use this sort of conference going forward. Further, they felt their parents also received a clearer picture of their child's progress from these conferences, and this made everyone feel more involved and better informed in the learning process.

Any doubt about the power of Terri's way of setting clear goals, compiling evidence of goal attainment in portfolios, and preparing students to share information about their own achievement is erased when we read this kind of comment from a parent:

The transformation of Jason as a student has been remarkable, from an F and C student to an A and B student. We cannot help but believe that a great deal of the credit must go to the manner in which class materials are presented and the curriculum is organized. Jason certainly has become more focused on his capabilities rather than his limitations. The general emphasis on responsibility for one's own actions and performance has also been most beneficial. Jason was a very frustrated young man in [his former school] and has had a tendency to place blame on others rather than accepting responsibility for his own choices. The last portion of this year has brought welcome changes in this respect. Though not always the most conscientious student, he puts forth serious effort on his studies and assumes responsibility for the results of his efforts. We believe that the "writing classroom" environment has been crucial to Jason's educational development, self-examination and personal growth. (Austin, 1994, p. 48)

Be advised that student-involved ways of sharing information do not represent panaceas that promise to deliver us from our communication challenges. Each option presents its own unique strengths and challenges. And, to be sure, each requires every bit as much work. However, we believe that teachers can markedly increase our positive impact on students' achievement by using conference formats intelligently.

Necessary Conditions

Before we delve into the topic of conferences, let's review the keys to effective communication. If conferences are to be conducted in a productive manner, the following conditions must be satisfied:

We must be crystal clear and up front with our students about the achievement expectations we hold for them. Those expectations should fit into a continuous-progress vision of student growth, both within and across grade levels. And we ourselves must be confident, competent masters of the targets that they are supposed to hit. Without this, we can neither assess nor communicate.

Our assessments of student achievement must be accurate. Dependable information lays a solid foundation for effective communication. Inaccurate information lays a foundation of shifting sand.

To communicate effectively, the interpersonal environment must be right. That is, *all who are involved* must

- Understand what we are trying to accomplish by means of our communication about student achievement.
- Use a common language to share information.
- Take time to tune in and be in the moment when information is being shared.
- Check back with each other to be sure everyone understood and felt able to use the achievement information shared.

Our students must be deeply involved in assessing their own achievement over time, so they can understand the meaning of success, watch themselves grow, and develop the vocabulary needed to communicate effectively about their own success.

It is only with these pieces in place that we can meet with each other to share insights into individual students' learning.

Conference Formats That Enhance Communication and Learning

We're going to explore three practical conference formats:

- Student-teacher conferences
- Traditional parent-teacher conferences
- Student-led parent conferences

In the first format, *teacher and student* share a common vision and definition of academic success that allows them to share focused discussions of the student's progress. Some teachers are using these strategies to transform their classrooms into workshop settings. We'll share an example.

The second format brings *parents and teacher* together to share information on student achievement. While this kind of conference has long been a standard part of schooling, we'll put some new spins on the idea to bring students into the process.

The third, *student-led parent* conferences, takes advantage of the benefits of the other two formats, adding some special pluses of its own. It represents the capstone of an assessment FOR learning environment. Further, it overcomes many of their weaknesses, although it brings its own challenges. With this approach, as we learned from Terri Austin at the beginning of this chapter, the primary responsibility for communicating about expectations and progress shifts from teacher to student. We'll explore some practical guidelines for using this option, review benefits to students and parents, and share some reactions from users.

Student-Teacher Conferences

A classroom learning environment turns into a workshop when the teacher shares the vision of achievement with students and then sets them to work individually or in small groups in pursuit of the designated target. In this setting, the teacher becomes a consultant or coach, working one on one or with groups to improve students' performance. This permits individualization that works very well when students are at different levels of achievement, such as in the development of their math or writing proficiencies. Much of the communication between teacher and student occurs in one-on-one conferences.

These conferences give students personal attention. Besides, students who are reticent to speak out in class often will come forth in a conference. As a result, that two-way communication so essential to effective instruction can take place. Finally, the conference provides an excellent context in which to provide specific descriptive feedback. Teachers can provide commentary on student performance and students can describe what is and is not working for them.

To understand the dialogue that can emerge from this idea, read the example of student writing shown in Figure 13.1. A conference is about to take place between the teacher, Ms. Weathersby, and the student focusing on this work. Ms. W. has been holding conferences with her students since the beginning of the school year. It is now January. She tries to confer with each student every 2 to 3 weeks, and although it takes a fair amount of time, she feels that the payoff is worth it. The dynamics of the conferences are changing a bit. In the beginning, she had to ask lots of questions. Now, students usually come to a conference with things to say.

Jill, the student, has never been an exceptional writer. Until recently, she didn't like to write and wrote only when forced. She didn't like talking about her writing, and her most frequent comment was, "I can't write."

At first, she didn't want to speak about her writing. The last two conferences, however, have been somewhat different. Jill is beginning to open up. She is writing more on her own. She keeps a journal. She is still, however, reluctant to voice opinions about her own writing; she looks to her teacher for a lead. (Be sure to read Figure 13.1 before continuing.)

My Dog

Everyone has something important in their lives and the most important thing to me, up to now, has been my dog. His name was Rafe. My brother found him in an old barn where we were camping in a field near my grandpa's house. Somebody had left him there and he was very weak and close to being dead. But we nursed him back to health and my mom said we could keep him, at least for a while. That turned out to be for ten years.

Rafe was black and brown and had a long tail, floppy ears, and a short, fat face. He wasn't any special breed of dog. Most people probably wouldn't of thought he was that good looking but to us he was very special.

Rafe kept us amused a lot with funny tricks. He would hide in the shadows and try to spook the chickens but they figured out he was just bluffing so he had to give up on that one. When Rafe got hit by a truck I thought I would never stop crying. My brother misses him too, and my mom, but no one could miss him as much as I do.

FIGURE 13.1
Sample of Jill's Writing

Source: From *Creating Writers: Linking Assessment and Writing Instruction* (p. 105) by V. Spandel and R. J. Stiggins; 1990. Published by Allyn & Bacon, Boston, MA. Copyright © 1990 by Pearson Education. Adapted by permission of the publisher.

"Pretty terrible, huh?" Jill asks Ms. Weathersby.

"What do you think of it?" Ms. W. asks, tossing the question back to her. She doesn't answer right away, but her teacher doesn't break the silence. The seconds tick by. Ms. W. waits.

"I don't like the ending," Jill volunteers at last.

"Tell me why."

"Well, it just stops. The whole thing just doesn't tell how I really feel."

"How do you feel?"

She thinks for a minute. "Oh, it isn't like I miss him all the time. Some days I don't think about him at all. But then—well, it's like I'll see him at the door, or I'll see this shadow dashing around the side of the barn. Sometimes when we cook out, I think about him because he used to steal hot dogs off the grill, and one time my dad yelled at him when he did that and he slipped and burned one of his feet real bad."

"Now there's the real Jill and Rafe story beginning to come out! You're telling me about Rafe in your real personal voice and I sense some of your feelings. When you wrote about Rafe, did you speak like that? Let's read part of your writing again."

After doing so, Jill comments, "Pretty blah, not much me!"

"If you did write like you were speaking, how do you think it might read?"

"Like a story, I guess."

"Try it and let's see what happens. Talk to me about Rafe in your own personal voice. Besides, stealing hot dogs off the grill conjures up a funny picture, doesn't it? Those are the kinds of mental pictures great stories tell. When I can picture what you're saying, that's 'ideas.' You're giving the story some imagery and focus that I like very much. What kind of imagery do you see in this writing?"

They scan the piece again. Jill says in a low voice, "No images here—just facts."

"How about if you think up and write about some of those personal things you remember about Rafe?"

"Do you think I should?"

"Well, when you were talking, I had a much better sense of you in the story—of how much you missed your dog and how you thought about him."

"I think I could write about some of those things."

"How about if you give it a try, and we'll talk again in about a week?"

"How about the spelling, punctuation, and sentences? Were those okay?" Jill asks.

"Let's leave that 'til later. Think about the ideas, the organization, the voice. We'll come back to the other."

"I don't want any mistakes, though," Jill confesses.

"But is this the right time to worry about that?"

"I don't know; I just don't want to get a bad grade."

"Okay," Ms. W. nods. "Suppose we agree that for now, we'll just assess the three traits I mentioned: ideas, organization, and voice."

"That's all?"

Ms. W. nods again. "And if you decide you want to publish this paper in the school magazine, then we'll work on the rest."

"We can fix the other stuff then, right?"

"You will have time to fix it, yes."

Time for Reflection

In your opinion, what are the keys to making conferences like this work? What are some of the barriers to effective conferences? How might you remove these barriers?

Dealing with the Practicalities

Those who have turned classrooms into workshops tell us that conferences need not be long. We can communicate a great deal of information in just a few minutes. However, thoughtful preparation is essential. It is best if both students and teacher examine student work beforehand with performance criteria in mind and prepare focused commentary.

Good listening is essential. If you prepare a few thoughtful questions in advance, you can draw insight out of students, triggering their own self-reflection. Effective conferences don't rely on traditional, one-way communication. Rather, they work best when teachers share both the control of the meeting and the responsibility for directing the communication.

Over time, and with experience in conferences, it will become easier to open the dialogue because both you and your students will become more at ease with each other. Over time, students also will become more familiar with your expectations. They will develop both the conceptual frameworks and vocabulary needed to communicate efficiently with you about their progress. So begin with modest expectations and let the process grow.

Parent-Teacher Conferences

We would be remiss if we failed to insert the traditional parent-teacher conference into our discussion of effective ways to communicate. During our school years, most of us became the "odd person out" of these meetings. We were left wondering, What did they say about me? Further, many experienced teachers who have been on the other side of the desk and who obviously know what was said, wonder if they said the right things and if they were understood.

Exploring the Benefits

Parent-teacher conferences offer three specific advantages over report card grades as means of communication. They permit us to do the following:

1. *Retain and share a sufficiently high level of detail to provide a rich picture of student achievement.* In effect, they provide a personal way to share the checklists, rating scales, and narratives discussed previously.
2. *Ask followup questions to determine if we have succeeded in communicating.* We can provide additional detail and explanation as needed to be sure the message gets through. Parents can ask questions to eliminate uncertainty.
3. *Plan jointly with families to blend school and home learning environments for maximum productivity.* In some cases, that means we can find out what may be going wrong with a student's home environment and urge adjustments in that environment.

But these advantages should not lead us to infer that conferences should replace report cards or any other record-keeping or communication option. Rather, we can use our various communication options in combination, where part of our conference time is used to explain grades, checklists, ratings, or other symbols, for example.

Anticipating the Challenges

Of course, challenge number one is time. Parent-teacher conferences take a great deal of time to prepare for and to conduct. Every family must get its share of one-on-one time with you. For junior high and high school teachers working with large numbers of students, again, this option may not be feasible, especially given the number of courses students take at one time.

Challenge number two is that of devising a jargon-free, family-friendly vocabulary and interpersonal manner to use in describing student achievement to parents. If we pile on a great deal of technical language delivered in an aggressive style, we will have difficulty connecting.

Challenge number three is encouraging parental participation in the conferences. Some families care more about their children's learning than others. Some have busy lives, and competing priorities always seem to win. Some parents feel vulnerable in parent-teacher conferences, especially if things aren't going well in school for their child. There is always the chance in their minds that you might accuse them of failing to support your teaching efforts. Even though you know you would never do that, they don't know it for sure.

Challenge number four is helping students to come through conference time with academic self-concepts intact. This can be risky stuff for our students. If they're left wondering what was really said about them—as they usually are—the effect can be uncertainty, frustration, and even anger. At the very least they may be left with the impression that they aren't important enough in this communication equation to warrant a role.

For any one or all of these reasons, if we use parent-teacher conferences as our means of message delivery, we can be in danger of failing to communicate effectively with students and with some families.

Dealing with the Practicalities

We can meet these challenges and take maximum advantage of this conference format if we follow some simple, straightforward procedures:

STEP 1:   Establish a clear and complete set of achievement expectations.

STEP 2:   Transform those expectations into quality assessments and gather accurate information.

STEP 3:   Carefully summarize that information for sharing via grades, checklists, rating scales, narrative, portfolios, or test scores.

STEP 4:   Conduct a student-teacher conference to review all of this material before conducting the parent-teacher conference. This permits students to understand the message to be delivered. In fact, imagine a classroom in which this step was unnecessary because steps 1 to 3 were carried out with full student involvement. With targets clarified and shared, students involved deeply in accumulating achievement evidence, and students as partners in developing the portfolio that will be the topic of discussion at the parent-teacher conference, everyone shares. The motivational and achievement benefits of such a partnership are considerable.

STEP 5:   Schedule and conduct the parent-teacher conference. By the way, imagine the ongoing communication link that we might forge with parents if we had our continuous progression of achievement targets written in family-friendly terms that we had shared with parents from the beginning of the learning. We'd have put in place concrete ways to show parents both how their children are doing with respect to our expectations and, if necessary, in relation to other students of like age or grade.

STEP 6:   Ask for a written followup reflection from parents presenting their impressions of the achievement and progress of their children.

Student-Led Parent Conferences

Of all the communication possibilities available to us, this one excites us the most because it places students at the heart of the process. Notice immediately that we did not label this "student-involved parent-teacher conferences." We used the label "student-led" to emphasize the need to both give students the opportunity to tell, and to hold students accountable for telling, at least some of the story of their own achievement.

This is a more complex communication option than either of the other two conference formats. However, the payoff for the added work can be impressive, to say the least. This conference format offers us the most potential for comprehensive, satisfying communication among all parties about student achievement.

Exploring the Benefits

Among the positive effects reported by teachers who use this idea are the following:

1. *A much stronger sense of responsibility for their own learning among students.* When students understand that, down the road, they (not you) will be telling their own success (or lack of success) story, they realize that there is no escaping accountability. They realize very quickly that, if they have nothing to share at that meeting by way of success, they are going to be very uncomfortable. This can be a strong motivator. And once they have some positive experience with this process and develop confidence in themselves, they become even more motivated to do well at it.

2. *A much stronger sense of pride when they do have a success story to share at conference time.* It feels good to be in charge of a meeting in which you're the star of a winning team.

3. *A different and more productive relationship between students and their teachers.* When that conference takes place, if the student has nothing by way of success to share, the student won't be the only one who will be somewhat embarrassed. In this sense, students and teachers become partners in the face of a common challenge. Both must succeed together. This alliance can boost student achievement.

4. *Improved student–parent relationships.* Many families report that their conversations about student achievement extend far beyond the conference itself—sometimes weeks beyond. Often what emerges from the meeting is a sense of mutual interest in student projects, along with a shared language that permits ongoing interaction. School–family partnerships can flourish under these circumstances.

5. *An active, involved classroom environment built on a strong sense of community.* Students take pride not only in their own accomplishments and their ability to share them, but also in the opportunity to help each other prepare for and succeed at their conferences. A team spirit, a sense of community, can emerge and this can benefit the motivation and achievement of all.

6. *A reduction in relevance or value of cheating.* Not only is it difficult to misrepresent one's achievement when concrete evidence will be presented at the conference, but also, students seem less interested in cheating. What can emerge is a greater sense of honor and honesty related to their heightened sense of responsibility for and pride in actually achieving.

7. *The development of important leadership skills.* Coordinating and conducting a student-led parent conference requires that the student schedule the meeting, invite participants, handle the introductions, organize and present information to the group, and follow up to discern meeting results. These are important life skills.

8. *Greater parental participation in conferences.* Virtually all schools report that a far higher percentage of parents show up to be part of conferences when students are the leaders. You can probably anticipate why this might be the case. If you are a parent, which invitation is more likely to bring you to a meeting: a standardized note from your child's teacher stuck to the refrigerator with a date and time filled in, or your child standing in front of you looking up with those eyes reminding you that the conference is tomorrow and she will be in charge and "You're going to be there, right?"

Also, remember that some parents' school experiences were less than positive and, for some, things may not be going well in their adult lives. In their minds, there is a danger that, if they come to a parent-teacher conference, you might accuse them of being a bad parent. For this reason alone, they might avoid the meeting. When they know that their child is to lead the meeting, this risk seems to be reduced in their minds. For this reason among others, virtually all users of this conference format report a major jump in the proportion of parents who participate.

Facing the Challenges

At the same time, this idea of student-led conferences is not without its downside risks. For example, it's not easy for some teachers to share this level of control with students. This requires a trust teachers traditionally have not granted to their students. When we give up control in this way, we cannot always be absolutely sure what will happen. If difficulties arise, they arise in a fishbowl and some pretty important people will see them. That's scary.

Further, it should be clear that the presentation of student-led conferences is just the tip of a pretty big iceberg. *You buy the whole idea or none of it.* Effective communication is possible only if the conference arises from a student-involved classroom assessment FOR learning environment. We cannot simply plug in student-led parent conferences in a traditional teacher-centered assessment environment, where students have little idea what the expectations are or how they are doing with respect to those targets. Rick recently spoke with a parent whose third-grade daughter "got caught" between two adults talking about her. The child was scared before and during the event, according to her mom. She had no idea what was happening, was given no responsibility in planning for the meeting, was asked to answer questions she was totally unprepared to address, and had a completely negative experience. This was a good idea badly implemented and one mother was left very cold about the whole concept. *We must set students up to succeed at the conferences or such conferences will do far more harm than good.*

Another challenge is finding the time to prepare for and manage such conferences. Most teachers plan for at least 30-minute conferences. This is especially difficult for junior high or high school teachers, who might face 150 students a day. First, be careful about how you think about time used in this context. There is a strong tendency to think of it as time lost to instruction. Nothing could be further from the truth. The time spent preparing to confer turns into highly focused teaching and learning time.

Beyond this, we need to creatively manage the logistics of holding conferences. Many teachers report that they can have students conducting several at one time, once those students have experience running conferences. In addition, high school teachers we know limit conferences to one or two courses per grading period, thus spreading them across four quarters of the year. In fact, one teacher we know asks that conferences last at least one hour, with only the first 30 minutes taking place in the classroom. The remainder is to take place at home, and students are responsible for reporting back in writing about how the rest of the conference went. Every student reported that conferences stretch far beyond the required hour.

But perhaps the most difficult challenges faced by those who would place students in charge of these conferences arise when the student comes from a dysfunctional family. The easiest version of this problem occurs when parents simply fail to show up. More difficult versions have parents showing up and becoming abusive in any of a number of ways.

Time for Reflection

How might we plan conferences in collaboration with our students in ways that maximize the chances that parents will show up? Further, if parents or other invited guests fail to arrive for the conference, how might we handle this in a manner that keeps the student's ego intact? Think about this for a moment before reading on.

Some teachers we know cover the very rare occurrence of parents failing to show up by having a backup "listener" available on conference day. It might be a former teacher, the principal, a custodian, or counselor. The only requirement is that the listener be someone the student knows and whose opinion the student cares about. When this condition is satisfied, students can present enthusiastically and take pride in their achievements. It's okay to reschedule too, if the listener scheduled cannot make it.

Keys to Success

We overcome these challenges only by attending to some simple fundamental conditions. To make this idea work, we need the following:

- Students who feel confident, safe, and trusting enough to take the risk of describing their own growth to their parents
- Students who have had time to learn about, to prepare for, and to practice their leadership roles
- Teachers who are willing to take the risk of stepping aside and letting their students take charge, just as a coach helps players learn the game and then places them on the field or court to play the game themselves
- Achievement targets that have been clearly and completely defined, woven into instruction, and used as the basis for an open and honest ongoing communication system
- Accurate, student-involved assessments filling the portfolios that tell the story
- Both teacher and students who share a common language for talking about attainment of each important achievement target

When these conditions are satisfied and students take the lead in evaluating their learning, many good things occur. For example, because students and teacher must work closely together to prepare for the conference, it builds a greater amount of individual attention into instruction. As evidence of success is compiled, a sense of being in control emerges for students, spurring them to greater heights—especially in the hope that they might be able to achieve those last-minute gains that will impress their parents even more. Parents acquire new understanding of their children, and of the teacher. This gives students a greater sense of their own importance in the classroom.

Time spent planning and preparing for student-led parent conferences becomes high-quality teaching and learning time. Students work to understand the vision of success, master the language needed to communicate about it, learn to describe their achievements, and evaluate their own strengths and weaknesses. Is this not the essence of a productive learning environment? Besides, as they prepare for the meeting, students might organize demonstrations, set up exhibitions, and/or develop other documentary evidence of success. It is difficult to envision more engaging student learning experiences.

Dealing with the Practicalities

Here are the steps in conducting a student-led parent conference:

STEP 1: Establish the relevant achievement targets, be sure all students and parents are aware of them, and plan instruction around their achievement.

STEP 2: Convert those expectations into quality assessments and use those assessments to help students build portfolios of quality evidence of their own achievement. Note that these can be either growth or status report portfolios, depending on your wishes. You don't have to rigorously control the evidence gathering. Your students can take the lead—if they're prepared.

STEP 3: While the evidence is building, keep the channels of communication open with the student's family. This might involve the use of a "take-home" portfolio or journal that students use to keep their parents informed of progress during instruction. Ask parents to respond to you in writing about their impressions of the progress or about any concerns they may have.

STEP 4:   As conference time approaches, convene a student-teacher conference to assemble the conference portfolio. Work as a team to select the samples of student work that you will use to tell the desired story.

STEP 5:   Model a student-led conference for your students. Role play a good one and a bad one, so they can see what makes them work well. Be absolutely sure students know their role (as leader), your role (as coach), and their parents' role (as interested listeners and questioners). Be sure your students understand that we strive for a natural conversation among conferees—an interaction about accomplishments that includes examples, questions, answers, and sharing.

You might consider engaging your students in collaborating to develop performance criteria for a good conference. Remember from performance assessment design?

- Brainstorm important elements of a good conference.
- Cluster them into major categories.
- Label and define the categories.
- Analyze and compare conferences of vastly different quality (have your students role play good and bad conferences).
- Devise rating scales or checklists to capture the essential differences between the two.

Your students can be partners with you in building criteria for good student-led conferences. Then you can team up to plan conferences that meet your agreed standards of excellence.

STEP 6:   Provide opportunities for students to practice their conference presentations in teams using the performance criteria developed in step 5 to provide feedback and offer suggestions for improvement.

STEP 7:   Establish the time period during which the conferences are to take place. Permit students to select their own specific presentation time. Make them responsible for inviting participants, and for following up the invitation to be sure all are informed.

STEP 8:   When the event happens, be sure students welcome all participants, handle introductions, review the objectives of the meeting, coordinate meeting events, handle followup communications, and summarize results. If you have prepared carefully, conferences should unfold productively with few surprises.

STEP 9:   Offer parents an opportunity for an additional one-on-one meeting with you, the teacher, if they wish—just in case there are any personal, family, or risky issues that need attention. In our experience, virtually all parents will decline, but it is good to offer. Incidentally, one teacher we know frames the conference this way: It will last 30 minutes, with the student leading the first 20 minutes. The final 10 minutes is intended for teacher and parents alone, unless the parents invite the student to remain. Almost all do.

STEP 10:   Solicit a followup written review from parents. You might develop a simple questionnaire to help them. Such a questionnaire might, for example, offer them the opportunity to suggest future learning targets for their child. Students can take responsibility for collecting this feedback and can be partners in its interpretation and use.

STEP 11:   Debrief your students on the entire experience. Discuss it as a group or have students evaluate the experience by writing about it. What facets worked? What needs improvement? Be sure you and they learn the important lessons this process teaches both about academics and students' personal reactions.

With a combined 35 years of teaching experience, we have rarely found a more valuable educational process than student-led conferences. During preparation the students experienced goal setting, reflected upon their own learning, and created a showcase portfolio.

Once underway, the conferences seem to have a life of their own. We, the teachers, gave up control and became observers, an experience that was gratifying and revealing. It validated our growing belief that students have the ability to direct their own learning and are able to take responsibility for self-evaluation. For many of our students, we gained insights into individual qualities previously hidden from us in the day-to-day classroom routine.

Students blossomed under the direct and focused attention of their parents. In this intimate spotlight, where there was no competition except that which they placed on themselves, they stepped for a moment into the adult world where they took command of their own convergence as well as their own development. Parents were surprised and delighted at the level of sophistication and competence their children revealed while sharing personal accomplishments.

In order to refine and improve this process, we surveyed both students and parents. Parents were emphatic in their positive response to student-led conferences, with most requesting that we provide this type of conference more often. Students, even those at risk and with behavior problems, overwhelmingly responded with, "We needed more time; a half an hour was not enough."

FIGURE 13.2
Teacher Commentary on Experiences with Student-Led Conferences
Source: By Harriet Arnold and Patricia Stricklin, 1993, Central Kitsap School District, Washington. Reprinted by permission of the authors.

Virtually every teacher we have spoken with across the continent who has carefully prepared for and conducted student-led parent conferences has found it to be a compellingly positive experience. In fact, a surprising number have told us that it was a career-altering and powerfully rejuvenating experience. Figure 13.2 shares the thoughts of two sixth-grade teachers on their experiences with student-led conferences. Figure 13.3 presents a concise summary of the key points made in this section about student-led parent conferences.

COMMUNICATION FOR LEARNING

If we want our students to use feedback about their achievement as the basis for academic improvement, they need to have continuous access to timely and understandable information about the quality of their work. When that evidence affirms improvement, confidence and effort grow. But the problem comes when it reveals a lack of success in learning or even worse when the student begins to feel that it always reveals failure to grow. This is when acceptance of the message can be difficult. Students can and often do find ways to brush these messages aside, to rationalize them, to discredit the source, or to find some other way to escape. Call this human nature. The problem is, however, that such avoidance is counterproductive.

Be mindful of conditions you must satisfy for students to really listen to and accept important feedback about the quality of their work. You must find ways to help your students learn to respond in a productive manner to the results even when they reveal a

Benefits
1. Stronger sense of accountability among students
2. Stronger sense of pride in achievement among students
3. More productive student-teacher relationship
4. Improved student-parent relationship
5. Stronger sense of classroom community
6. Reduced cheating
7. Development of leadership skills among students
8. Greater parental participation in conferences

Challenges
1. The uncertainty of sharing control with students
2. The need to adopt a completely student-involved philosophy
3. The amount of time required to prepare and present conferences
4. The logistical challenges of organizing for conferences
5. The difficulties that can arise with dysfunctional families

Keys to Success
1. Students willing and able to risk
2. Teachers willing and able to step aside
3. Clear targets known to all
4. Accurate student-involved assessments
5. A shared language for talking about targets and their achievement
6. A commitment of time to learn, prepare, and practice

FIGURE 13.3
Student-Led Parent Conference in a Nutshell

lack of success. Steady application of principles of assessment FOR learning—student-friendly targets, work samples, descriptive feedback, self-assessment, goal setting, and reflection of their own growth over time—will help students see themselves as key players in the search for information about their own achievement. In addition, students will come to see themselves as having a sufficiently strong sense of their own academic self-efficacy to acknowledge their shortcomings and not feel defeated. In other words, they must always believe that success is within reach if they keep trying. Someone once said, "Confidence gives us the freedom to be patient with our failures." Confidence comes only from some level of success in learning. It is your responsibility to help students find that success.

Further, students must see the provider of the feedback as credible, honest, and helpful. The feedback must be descriptive and must reflect attributes of their academic performance—not attributes of them as learners. Only then can they see how to do better the next time.

And finally, they must come to see the benefits of the message very quickly, so they can muster the resources needed to act purposefully. They must see how acting on the feedback they receive will move their work closer to the desired level of quality.

From the other point of view, the giver of the feedback (you, classmates, their parents . . .) must be able to present it constructively, delivering a clear and focused message using understandable language. You must be able to communicate your acceptance of students while critiquing their achievement. They must know that you are evaluating their achievements, not them as people. Even more importantly, you must help students understand that you have a common mission: to raise their confidence as learners and ensure their academic success.

Summary: Student-Involved Communication

Like portfolios, conferences offer ways to communicate about student achievement in greater detail than is permitted by report cards. In these cases, the communication arises from and focuses on actual examples of student work. Unlike report cards, conferences can afford students the opportunity to explain their own rich, complete story.

The idea of student-led conferences is gaining recognition as a key component of a complete assessment FOR learning experience. That experience begins with student-friendly versions of achievement targets. These form the foundation for the creation of a continuous array of classroom assessments that we use over time in collaboration with our students to reveal their own growth to them. They accumulate that evidence, along with the vocabulary needed to tell the story of their own journey to academic success.

As with portfolios, discussed in the previous chapter, conferences take careful planning and dedication to succeed. Specifically, this means the following:

- Provide plenty of opportunities to interact with students about their achievement.

- Structure conferences so students feel comfortable with and able to express their own growth and achievement.
- Schedule conferences to maximize parental participation.

However, remain aware of the fact that this represents just one of several conferencing formats that permit not just the exploration of student learning today, but the further assessment (via personal communication) and development of that learning. Conferences also afford opportunities for students to reflect on where they want to be, where they are now, and what comes next in their learning. In all conference contexts the keys to success are starting a specific reason for the conference (assessment OF or FOR learning), making sure the learning targets are clear to all involved, and factoring in quality assessment results whose meaning is clear to all involved. When these conditions are satisfied, as you will see, the power of conferences resides in their ability to bring concrete evidence to bear in telling rich stories of learning that can advance that learning.

Final Chapter Reflection

1. *What are the three most important new insights to come to you as a result of your study of this chapter?*
2. *Which of your previous questions about assessment can you now answer based on your study of this chapter?*
3. *What new questions have come to mind as a result of your study of this chapter—questions that you hope to have answered as your study continues?*

Practice with Chapter 13 Ideas

1. If you were to replace your parent-teacher conferences with student-led parent conferences (see Chapter 12), what type of portfolio would you have students develop? Why?

2. Reread the conference in this chapter (pp. 274–275) between Jill and Ms. W. about Jill's piece on Rafe. Then answer the following questions:

   - What conditions of effective communication as described in Chapter 10 were demonstrated by this interaction?
   - What was Ms. W. doing well?
   - What questions would you like to ask either participant about their communication and why?
   - How might this communication have been improved, if at all?

3. Here is a case study in student-led conferences. Please read it and then respond to the questions that follow.

The High School Faculty Debate on Student-Led Conferences

A high school principal has just returned from a national conference on assessment full of excitement about an innovative new idea—student-led parent conferences—and he has put the topic on the agenda for the next faculty meeting. After introducing it and discussing some of its positive aspects, the principal invites the faculty to comment.

One teacher was negative about the idea based on his experience at a previous school. There, students assembled portfolios that included all subjects and met with their parents in homeroom at year's end to review their achievement. Conferences were 20 minutes, so it took a long day and evening to complete them all.

For this teacher, such conferences just didn't work. First, 20 minutes was not enough time to cover six different subjects. Further, students didn't know what work to place in their portfolios or how to share it, so the meetings turned out to be very brief

discussions of the report card grades—completely from the student's point of view. Finally, homeroom teachers were not equipped to answer parents' questions in subjects other than their own, so parents' needs were not satisfied. All in all, it was a disaster and was abandoned after one try.

Another teacher offers a different experience. She had one student who seemed full of academic potential but didn't seem to care about school. Her only comment was, "If my parents don't care, why should I?" When the teacher called the parents it became obvious that there had been a severe breakdown in communication in the family.

In a risky move, the teacher bet the student that her parents did care and that she could prove it. During the next grading period, the two of them assembled a growth portfolio showing the student's improvement. Further, the teacher asked her to think about how she might present herself as an improving student and to write biweekly self-reflections about the work in her portfolio. As the term ended, the teacher requested the student to invite her parents in for a special student-parent-teacher conference. The conference was a success for all.

In response to these comments, the principal makes a proposal: The faculty could institute student-led conferences to bolster three initiatives already in place. First, twelfth graders are required to complete special senior projects. Second, the guidance staff has all college-bound students assemble "college admissions portfolios." Finally, students are required to complete a certain number of community service hours and assemble evidence of the productivity of their work. All three might provide an excellent basis for a school- and communitywide end-of-year acknowledgement of a productive school year.

Specifically, he proposes a three-day "School Success Celebration." Senior projects might culminate in "showcase" student-led conferences in which students present their work for review and discussion. College admissions portfolios might be shared with parents or review boards. Community service portfolios might be presented in a group session.

The principal asks for volunteers to see if this is feasible and useful.

Please answer the following questions about this case:

1. Analyze each of the teachers' experiences with student-led conferences applying the standards of effective communication. Why did some work and some not?

2. What do you think is motivating the principal here? How good is the celebration idea from the perspectives of the students, teachers, and community? What would it take for this idea to play out in a successful manner?

3. Make a two-by-two chart crossing students and teachers on one dimension with benefits and problems on the other. Use it to evaluate the pluses and minuses of this idea. What judgment does this analysis lead you to? Go or no go? Why?

Now go to www.myeducationlab.com to take a Pretest to assess your initial comprehension of chapter content, study chapter content with your individualized Study Plan, take a Posttest to assess your understanding of chapter content, practice your teaching skills with Building Teaching Skills exercises, and build a deeper, more applied understanding of chapter content with Homework and Exercises.

CHAPTER 14

Communicating with Standardized Test Scores

CHAPTER FOCUS

This chapter answers the following guiding question:

> What role should large-scale annual standardized tests play in the classroom in communicating about student achievement?

From your study of this chapter, you will understand the following:

1. The scores these tests produce can provide valuable information to some very important decision makers, although they are of limited value day to day in the classroom.

2. As professional educators, it is our responsibility to see that standardized tests are administered and used appropriately.

As you read this chapter, continue to keep in mind our big assessment picture. Annual standardized tests represent one way to gather and communicate information about student achievement to some assessment users. Typically, they meet the once-a-year information needs of school leaders, policy makers, and instructional program planners.

TESTS THAT PRODUCE COMPARABLE RESULTS

Thus far, we have focused on assessments teachers develop or select for use in their particular classrooms or sometimes across classrooms. In this chapter, we veer away from that track to explore the world of large-scale standardized achievement tests. We will study their purposes, the complex array of forms they can take, and how to interpret and use test results. As background, we will consider the techniques test developers use to create quality assessments. But more importantly, we'll compile a list of responsibilities that teachers and administrators who administer, interpret, and use standardized testing must fulfill.

These once-a-year tests will be of value to you as classroom teachers when the results you receive help you identify standards your students have succeeded in mastering and those your students struggle to master. This kind of information can assist in long-term program improvement to meet more needs of more of your students. But most often we use these tests in an assessment OF learning role, basing judgments of the sufficiency of student achievement on the results. Both applications are important. So we have included this chapter specifically to address the classroom teacher's primary standardized testing question: As a classroom teacher, what should I do in response to community expectations that schools "raise those test scores"?

The purpose of this chapter is to provide you with enough background information about large-scale annual standardized assessment to permit you to understand how such assessments fit into the big assessment picture in general and into your classroom in particular.

Background Information

First, it is important to understand that the educational system in the United States has included a strong standardized test tradition for nearly a century. The idea is to have large numbers of students respond to the same or similar sets of test items under approximately the same conditions. Thus, the test itself, the conditions under which it is administered, scoring procedures, and test score interpretation are the same, or "standardized," across all examinees. As a result, users can interpret the scores to mean the same thing for all examinees. The benefit is that scores can be compared across students and compiled over students to compare classrooms, schools, districts, states, and even nations, depending on the context.

Such comparable scores can inform some important decisions. For example, special education teachers can use them to identify relatively strong or weak students, so limited resources can be channeled to them. Scores on some standardized tests, averaged across students within schools or districts, can help evaluate and identify strong and weak programs. Here again, the objective is to funnel resources to those places where they are most needed to improve the quality of schools.

Although standardized tests are developed and published to assess both students' achievement and their aptitude or intelligence, this chapter is limited to the consideration of achievement tests only. Fundamental and deep-seated disagreements among learned scholars about the definition of intelligence, as well as their concern over the dangers of intelligence testing, cause us to exclude them from this book. If you wish to accommodate individual differences in student learning, we recommend individualizing on the basis of *prior achievement*, not intelligence.

Often, school districts participate in several layers of standardized achievement testing, from districtwide testing to statewide to national and sometimes even to international programs. Some districts may administer a dozen or more different standardized testing programs in a given year for different purposes involving different students.

Some standardized tests produce scores that are *norm referenced*; they communicate in a manner that permits us to compare a student's achievement to that of other students who took the same test under like conditions. Scores on these tests can communicate information about how students rank in achievement.

Other standardized tests yield scores that are *criterion referenced*; they communicate how each student's test score compares, not to other students, but to a preset standard of acceptable performance. These kinds of scores permit us to detect which specific achievement standards students have and have not met; that is, to determine individual strengths and weaknesses in achievement. Clearly, these kinds of results are of greatest value to classroom teachers.

Professional test publishers develop standardized tests, either to sell directly to schools or under contract for a local, state, or national educational agency. Tests are available to cover virtually all school subjects across all grade levels. Further, they can involve the use of any of our four basic forms of assessment, although historically most have relied on selected response formats because they can be automatically scanned and scored with great efficiency. This permits relatively inexpensive scoring of very large numbers of tests. Recently, we have seen an increase in reliance on very brief written response assessment formats too, as test publishers strive to align their tests with more complex forms of achievement targets.

The Various Layers of Annual Testing

From the beginning of our testing traditions in the United States in the first part of the twentieth century, we have evolved into a school culture that has increasingly relied on centralized assessment of student achievement, resulting in the layers of annual testing programs that we see in place today.

College Admissions Testing

This level of testing began modestly early in the twentieth century with a few local scholarship testing programs, which relied on essay tests to select winners. Thus, right from the outset, quality tests were those that could differentiate among levels of student achievement. These differences would serve to rank examinees for the award of scholarships.

These local applications were so effective that they gave rise to our first national college admissions testing programs, the College Boards (also known as the SATs). While the earliest tests relied on essay assessment, in the 1930s the huge volume of national testing soon forced a change as the College Board turned to multiple-choice testing technology as a more efficient format. With this change dawned the era of selected response testing for sorting purposes. Then in the 1940s, the second college admissions test appeared on the scene, the ACT Assessment Program. Some selective postsecondary institutions continue to include scores on these tests in their admissions selection processes.

Districtwide Testing

In the 1940s, several test publishers began selling standardized versions of selected response tests to schools for use at all grade levels. The test user guides were careful to point out that scores on these tests were intended to serve as one additional piece of information for teachers to use to supplement their classroom assessments and help sort students into proper instructional treatments. Remember this purpose; it is a critical issue in the whole historical picture.

The most commonly used form of assessment in districtwide programs is the commercially published, norm-referenced, standardized achievement test battery. Test publishers design, develop, and distribute these tests for purchase by local users. Each battery covers a variety of school subjects, offering several test forms tailored for use at different grade levels. Users purchase test booklets, answer sheets, and test administration materials, as well as scoring and reporting services. It is not uncommon these days for districts with their own response sheet scanning technology to also purchase test scoring software from the publisher to analyze their own results. Further, some tests are administered and scored online.

The unique feature of these tests is the fact that they are nationally "normed" to facilitate test score interpretation. This simply means that the designers administered the tests to large numbers of students before making them available for general purchase. Test results from this preliminary administration provide the basis for comparing each subsequent examinee's score. We explain exactly how this is accomplished later in this chapter.

In addition, however, most test publishers report at least some criterion-referenced information on score reports. Items in the battery that test the same achievement standard are collected into a small test within a test, allowing the publisher to generate a score for each student reflecting that student's mastery of each specific standard. Again, we will show you such scores later in the chapter.

Statewide Testing

In the 1960s, in the midst of a time of international competition and social upheaval in the United States, society began to raise serious questions about the effectiveness of schools. There emerged the sense that schools (and the educators who run them) should be held accountable for more than just providing quality opportunities to learn, for more than just sorting students according to achievement. Rather, they should also be held responsible for producing real student learning and for ensuring that all students attain certain specified levels of achievement.

In response to the challenge that schools might not be "working" (that is, to evaluate their programs) administrators turned to their only source of objective, "third party"—and thus believable—student achievement data: scores from commercially available standardized objective paper and pencil achievement tests.

This represented a profoundly important shift in society's perceptions of these tests. They would no longer be seen as just one more piece of information for teachers. Now they would be seen as standards of educational excellence. Understand that the underlying testing technology did not change. These were still tests designed to sort students based on assessments of very broad domains of content. All that changed was our sense of how the tests should be used. They came to be seen as the guardians of our highest academic expectations, a use their original developers had never intended. Educational policy makers began to believe that standardized tests could drive major improvements in school effectiveness. We moved rapidly from districtwide testing to statewide testing applications and beyond.

We began the decade of the 1970s with just a handful of such tests and ended with a majority of states conducting their own testing programs. Now virtually every state conducts its own program. Significantly, many states opted to develop their own tests to be sure they focused on important academic standards in that state. They tended to move from tests designed to sort to tests reflecting student attainment of specific achievement targets (that is, from norm-referenced to criterion-referenced tests).

National Assessment

Beginning in the late 1970s, we added the National Assessment of Educational Progress (NAEP) in the hope that testing achievement at ever more centralized levels would somehow lead to school improvement in ways that other tests had not.

NAEP is a federally funded testing program that periodically samples student achievement across the nation to track the pulse of changing achievement patterns. These biannual assessments gauge the performance of national samples of 9-, 13-, and 17-year-olds, as well as young adults, reporting results by geographic region, gender, and ethnic background. Results are intended for use by policy makers to inform decisions. Since its first test administration in 1969, NAEP has conducted criterion-referenced assessments of valued outcomes in reading, writing, math, science, citizenship, literature, social studies, career development, art, music, history, geography, computers, life skills, health, and economics. NAEP assessment procedures have used all four assessment methods, with selected response methods dominating.

International Assessment

Periodically, the United States, Canada, and other nations around the world collaborate in competitive assessments specifically designed to determine the relative standing of nations with respect to student achievement. Content and assessment experts from around the world meet for the following purposes:

- Define achievement targets common to the participating nations' collective curricula.
- Design exercises that pose problems that make sense in all particular cultures.
- Translate those exercises into a range of languages.
- Devise scoring criteria reflecting differing levels of proficiency.

Given the cultural and linguistic diversity of the world, you can anticipate the challenges in conducting such an assessment.

State Consortium Assessment of Common Core Standards

At the time of this writing, as mentioned previously, steps are being taken by the U.S. Department of Education in collaboration with the Council of Chief State School Officers and the National Governor's Board to refine common core achievement standards in literacy and mathematics. Those standards are being adopted by states to guide their curricula and instructional programs. In addition, at the behest of the USDOE, many states are entering into collaborative consortiums to develop common assessments of student mastery of the core standards. It is anticipated that the assessment systems developed will inform users of how each student has done in mastering each of the common standards. The specific scoring and reporting schemes have yet to be developed and implemented.

The Result: Troubling Contradictions

Over the decades in the United States, conventional wisdom has held that, if we just find the right level at which to test and exert the proper level of intimidating consequences for low test scores, schools will improve. Throughout this evolution, standardized testing has been troubled with apparent contradictions arising out of a general lack of understanding of these tests, both within and around our school culture among both teachers and school leaders. Let us illustrate.

As a society, we have placed great value on standardized test scores. They attract great political visibility and power at local, state, national, and international levels. The paradox is that, as a society (*both within and outside schools*), we seem to have been operating on blind faith that educators are using them appropriately. As a society, almost to a person, we actually know very little about college admission testing, national assessment, state testing, or local annual testing programs. It has been so for decades. This blind faith has prevented us from understanding either the strengths or the important limitations of standardized tests. As a result, the discrepancy is immense between what most educators and the public think these tests can do and what they actually are capable of delivering.

We have tended to ascribe a level of precision to test scores that belie reality. Many believe we can use standardized test scores to track student acquisition of new knowledge and skills so precisely as to detect month-to-month growth in student learning; so precisely that we can use them to predict success at the next grade level, in college, or in life after school. But standardized tests typically have not been the precise tools or accurate predictors most think they are. Typically, they have not been designed to produce high-resolution portraits of student achievement. Rather, they have been designed to produce broad general indicators of that achievement. This has been their often-misunderstood heritage.

Over the decades, some have noticed these problems and concluded that we should do away with standardized tests, arguing that the problems meant that the tests were of poor quality. In fact, standardized tests can do a good job of assessing a limited range of kinds of achievement—those that can be tapped with multiple-choice test items and very brief essays. This includes only mastery of content and some reasoning patterns. So their coverage has been very limited—they have not tapped complex reasoning, performance skills, or product development capabilities.

Our long-term societal habits of assigning great power to standardized tests, ascribing unwarranted precision to the scores they produce, striving to make them instructionally relevant, and generally misunderstanding them even while attacking them have conspired to create a major dilemma in education today. We have permitted these tests to form the basis of a school accountability system that is incapable of contributing to much-needed school improvement efforts. Sadly, our general lack of understanding of these tests has prevented us from achieving the real accountability that we all desire.

Addressing the Problems: A Guiding Philosophy

Because of this pervasive lack of understanding, one challenge we face as a school culture and as a larger society is to keep these standardized tests in perspective in terms of their potential impact on student learning. They do inform policy- and institutional-level users once a year in productive ways. But the plain and simple fact is that *large-scale assessment results will have much less impact on student learning than will your classroom assessments*. Yet our allocation of resources, media attention to scores, and political emphasis on standardized tests would lead one to believe just the opposite is true. In this regard, our priorities have been grossly out of balance for quite a long time.

Another pervasive problem has been the fact that scores have tended to represent broad domains of achievement; that is, test items have sampled domains such as math, reading, language usage, and so on. But these tests are evolving, with developers paying far more attention to standards-based assessment. Current and future generations of these tests will provide criterion-referenced evidence indicating how each student has done in mastering each standard assessed; that is, they will sample student mastery of the standards within broad domains. This kind of information (level of precision) is likely to enhance the utility of results for productive instructional decision making.

Also as assessment is evolving today, we are balancing our assessment priorities by giving greater attention to (1) promoting communitywide understanding of the limitations of standardized tests to ensure their proper use, and also (2) establishing the importance, and maintaining the quality, of classroom assessments. A balanced perspective encourages effective use of all assessment tools we have at our disposal. This includes standardized tests. In the hands of informed users who know and understand both the strengths and limitations of these tests, they can contribute useful information to educational decision making. Besides, they are so deeply ingrained in our educational fabric that our communities have come to expect periodically to see scores from these tests.

STANDARDIZED TEST DEVELOPMENT

While standardized tests may differ in coverage from context to context, they all are developed in roughly the same way regardless of context. Some are developed by test publishers for their own proprietary use—to sell to schools. Others are developed under contract for clients, such as state departments of education for state assessments. We explore the typical test development process here, so you may understand the work developers must do.

Step 1: Clarify Targets

Typically, standardized test developers begin with the thoughtful study of the valued achievement targets they wish to assess—the academic achievement standards that students are to master. In terms of our five attributes of sound assessment, therefore, these tests typically arise from very clear targets.

Step 2: Translate Targets into Assessments

Developers of large-scale standardized tests know how to match their target with a proper assessment method. In the past, they have relied on selected response formats; of late, very brief essay responses have become more common.

The most popular mode of assessment in this context by far is and always has been selected response. It is relatively easy to develop, administer, and score in large numbers. When the achievement targets are content mastery and/or certain kinds of reasoning and problem solving, its great efficiency makes this the method of choice for large-scale test developers. Its major drawback, as you know, is the limited range of targets test developers can translate into these formats.

Historically, essay assessment has been infrequently used in standardized testing in the United States. Recently, however, this has begun to change. Short answer essays have begun to appear in the content-area exams, such as science and social studies, of state assessments. This popularity arises directly from the fact that, these days, state proficiency standards typically include reasoning and problem-solving targets. Document scanning technology and computer-driven paper management systems have permitted test scoring services to evaluate written work with great dependability and efficiency. These services can now have students respond on their computers or may scan student essays so trained raters can read and score them electronically.

The assessment research and development community is exploring performance assessment applications in writing, mathematics problem solving, science, reading, foreign languages, the arts, interdisciplinary programs, and other performance areas. The great strength of this methodology is its ability to capture useful information about student performance on complex targets. Its limitations are the cost of sampling and scoring. This is a labor-intensive option (that is, expensive) when large numbers of examinees are involved.

Personal communication is almost never used in large-scale standardized testing due to cost. One-on-one standardized testing is simply too expensive.

Step 3: Develop Test Items

When assessment plans are ready, test construction begins. Some developers use their own in-house staff of item writers; others recruit qualified practicing teachers to create exercises. In either case, item writers are trained in the basic principles of sound item construction. Further, once trained, item writers must demonstrate an appropriate level of proficiency on a screening test before being asked to contribute to test development.

Step 4: Assemble Test and Evaluate for Appropriateness

Once items have been assembled into tests that sample the content in a representative manner, that test is reviewed by qualified test development experts, content-area experts, and members of minority groups review the exercises for accuracy, appropriateness, and bias. Poor-quality or biased exercises are replaced. This review and evaluation removes possible extraneous sources of bias and distortion.

To uncover and eliminate other potential problems, the next step in test development is to pretest or pilot test the items. Developers recruit classrooms, schools, or districts to administer the exercises under conditions as similar as possible to those in which the final test will be used. Their objectives are to find out if respondents interpret exercises as the authors intended and to see how well the exercises "function." Test developers also want to know how difficult the items are and how well they differentiate between those who know and do not know the material. All of this helps them retain only the most appropriate exercises for the final test.

Step 5: Administer Test to Establish Norms (Norm-Referenced Tests)

When a test is created for national sale and distribution by a test publisher (not under contract to a client), the next step typically calls for administering the final test as a whole for further quality control analysis and, in the case of norm-referenced tests, to establish norms for score interpretation.

As soon as a test is ready, the publisher launches a national campaign to recruit school districts to be part of the "norming sample." The aim is to involve large and small, urban and rural districts in all geographic regions, striving to balance gender and ethnicity; in short, to generate a cross-section of the student population in the United States.

Even though thousands of students may be involved, these norm districts are volunteers. For this reason, they cannot be regarded as systematically representative of the national student population. Thus, when we compare a student's score to national norms, we are *not* comparing them with the actual national student population, but rather to the norm group recruited by that test publisher for that particular test.

Norm-referenced standardized tests are revised and renormed regularly to keep them up to date in terms of content priorities, and to adjust the score scale. This is necessary because, as the test remains on the market, districts align their curricula to the material covered. This is how they meet the accountability challenge of producing high scores. Over time, more and more students will score higher on the test. To adjust for this effect and to accommodate changes in the student populations, test publishers renorm their tests to adjust the score scale downward.

Setting Standards of Acceptable Performance (Criterion-Referenced Tests)

As states have established statewide achievement standards and transformed them into criterion-referenced state assessments, an important issue has come to the fore: How do we decide if a student's score is "high enough" to be judged competent? This is a critically important issue when decisions such as grade-level promotion, high school graduation, or the award of certificates of mastery hang in the balance.

Typically, these "cutoff scores" are established by pooling the collective opinions of teachers, administrators, parents, representatives of the business community—a cross-section of society within that state. The processes employed to accomplish this are too complex to describe here. But suffice it to say that this test scoring technology is very well developed and is very precise when carried out by experts.

Once those cutoff scores are established, then each new test developed for use in subsequent years can be "equated" to the original to ensure comparability of score meaning, even though it might use different test items. This is important to ensure equity of opportunity for students regardless of the year when they happen to be tested. Again, for our purposes, it's not important that you know how this is done. We just want you to know that it *is* done.

INTERPRETATION OF COMMONLY USED TEST SCORES

Standardized tests that rely on selected response items can report any of a variety of kinds of scores. We will review these in this section by explaining how each score is derived and suggesting how educators may use each score to understand and interpret test performance. Standards referenced scores are typically used in statewide testing programs and in some district testing programs. Norm referenced scores tend to be used in districtwide testing programs.

It is imperative that you understand what these different kinds of scores mean and do not mean because it will be your responsibility to interpret them to the parents of your students or to your students themselves. It is *your* responsibility to promote clear understanding.

Scores Reported on State Assessments

State assessments typically are designed to reflect student mastery of specific academic achievement standards. State departments of education hire professional test developers to translate their standards into test items that yield evidence of student mastery of those standards. This process can yield either of two kinds of scores: evidence of student mastery of each standard or a composite score reflective of student mastery of an array of standards.

Mastery of Each Standard

When the evidence is to take this form, the test developer will include enough items on the test for each standard to permit a determination of each student's mastery of it. The number of items will vary as a function of the scope of the standard. Simple, focused standards will require a smaller sample of performance to yield a dependable result. The student must answer a certain number or percentage right to be judged to have mastered that standard. In any event, interpretation is straightforward and criterion referenced: Did each student provide evidence of having met each standard? We prefer this kind of score to the one we discuss next because it is more precise.

Composite Mastery Score

Our standardized testing traditions have focused on assessing student mastery of material in broad domains. You will see in the next subsection, for example, commercial tests report scores labeled "reading," "mathematics," and so on. Each test includes a set of items that samples these domains broadly.

This kind of thinking also has carried over into many state assessments. Test developers will pool all of the individual academic achievement standards into a broad set and build the test to lead to a conclusion about student mastery of that "domain"—reading, math, and so on. Then a cutoff score is established, identifying the number of items the student must answer correctly to be judged to have mastered this domain of standards. In fact, often, multiple cut scores are calculated: mastered, nearly mastered, and clearly did not master or words to that effect. The contention is that, because standards drove test development, this represents a standards-referenced examination.

Scores Reported on Norm-Referenced Tests

In this case, you can encounter five different kinds of scores. Each provides a different perspective on student achievement.

Raw Score

This is the easiest score to explain and understand. When students take a test, the number of items they answer right is called their *raw score*. In the standardized test context, this forms the basis of all the other scores. In other words, all other scores are derived from it, as you will see. It is the foundation of any communication arising from a standardized test.

Percent Correct

This score is as familiar and easy to understand as the raw score. *Percent correct* reflects the percent of test items the examinee answered correctly: raw score divided by total test items. This is the kind of score we use in the classroom to promote a common understanding and interpretation of performance on classroom tests. As the total number of items changes from test to test, we can always convert raw scores to percent correct and obtain a relatively standard index of performance.

There are two reasons why this kind of score is important in the context of standardized tests. First, this is the kind of score large-scale test developers use to determine mastery of objectives for a criterion-referenced score report. Score reports often label these *objective mastery scores* or something similar. This is exactly like the state assessment score described previously. Examinees are judged to have mastered the objective if they answer correctly a certain percentage of the items covering that objective. The exact cutoff varies at around 70 to 80 percent correct across standardized tests.

The second reason for addressing this kind of score is to differentiate it from percentile score or percentile rank. Very often, test users confuse percent correct with percentile scores. *They are fundamentally different kinds of scores bringing completely different interpretations to the meaning of test performance.* To understand the differences, we must first understand each.

Percentile Score

The *percentile score* (sometimes called *percentile rank*) represents the essence of a norm-referenced test score. This score tells us what percent of the norm group a student with any given raw score outscored. A student with a percentile rank of 85 outscored (scored higher than) 85 percent of the examinees in that test's original norm group. They allow us to see how each student's score ranked among others who have taken the same test under the same conditions. Did the student score higher than most? Lower? Somewhere in the middle?

You can see why the percentile is a norm-referenced score. It provides a straightforward comparison of student-to-student performance as the basis for score interpretation.

It also should be clear how percent correct and percentile differ. The former refers scores back to the number of items on the test for interpretation, while the latter compares the score to those of other examinees for interpretation. Their points of reference are fundamentally different.

Refer to Appendix C for more details on how percentile scores are derived from actual test scores.

Stanine

A student may also be assigned a stanine score based on percentile rank. *Stanine* simply represents a less precise score scale, each point of which can be interpreted quite easily (Table 14.1). In this case, the percentile scale is divided into nine segments, each of which represents a "standard nine" or, abbreviated, stanine. When interpreted in terms of the general descriptors listed in the right-hand column on Table 14.1, this score is easy to understand. A student who attains a stanine of 3 on a test is interpreted to have scored below average in terms of the performance of the norm group.

TABLE 14.1
Understanding Stanines

Stanine	Percent of scores	Percentile range	Descriptor
9	4	96–99	well above average
8	7	89–95	
7	12	77–88	above average
6	17	60–76	
5	20	40–59	average
4	17	23–39	
3	12	11–22	below average
2	7	4–10	
1	4	1–3	well below average

Grade Equivalent Scores

This score scale represents yet another way to describe the performance of a student in relation to that of other students. The basis of the comparison in this case is students in the norm group at specified grade levels. A student with a grade equivalent of 3.5 in reading is said to have scored about the same as students in the norm group who were in the fifth month of third grade. Those whose grade equivalent is below their current assigned grade are said to have scored below grade level. Those whose grade equivalent score is higher are said to be performing above grade level. For details on how these scores are derived from actual test data, see Appendix C.

The strength of this kind of score is its apparent ease of interpretation. But this very strength also turns out to be its major flaw. Grade equivalent scores are easily misinterpreted. They don't mean what most people think they mean. Here is an example of what can go wrong:

Let's say a very capable fifth-grade student attains a grade equivalent score of 8.5 in math. An uninformed parent might see that and say, "We must start this fifth grader using the eighth-grade math book at once!"

This is an incorrect conclusion for two reasons. First of all, no information whatever was gathered about this student's ability to do seventh- or eighth-grade math content. All that was tested was fifth- and sixth-grade math content. No inference can be made about the student's proficiency at higher-level work. Second, eighth graders have probably never taken the test. The score represents an extrapolation on the part of the test score analyst as to how eighth graders would be likely to score if they had taken the test of fifth- and sixth-grade math. Thus, again no reliable conclusion can be drawn about any connections to eighth-grade math.

The bottom line is that grade equivalent scores are not criterion-referenced scores. There is no sense in which the grade equivalent score is anchored to any body of defined content knowledge or skill mastery. It is only a comparative score referring a student's performance back to the typical performance of students at particular grade levels in the norm group. Our fifth grader is just very good at fifth- and sixth-grade math—probably a whole lot better than most fifth and sixth graders.

Table 14.2 provides a concise summary of the various kinds of scores we have discussed.

IMPLICATIONS FOR TEACHERS

So what does all of this mean for those concerned primarily with classroom assessment? As a teacher, it means understanding that you have a three-part responsibility with respect to standardized tests.

Above All, Protect the Well-Being of Your Students!

Your primary responsibility is to keep your students free from harm. First, make sure they have the opportunity to learn to hit the achievement targets reflected in whatever standardized tests they take. Second, ensure that the scores reported for your students are accurate—that they reflect each student's real level of achievement. Third, you must do everything you can to be sure all students come out of large-scale assessment experiences with their academic self-concepts intact. Let's consider several specific things you can do to fulfill these professional obligations.

TABLE 14.2
Test Score Summary

Score	Meaning	Strength	Caution
Raw	Number of items answered correctly; range = 0 to number of items (points) on the test	Provides the basis of all other scores	Difficult to interpret by themselves in a norm referenced context; can't be used to compare scores across tests
Percent correct	Percent of total test items answered correctly; range = 0% to 100%	Easy to understand; can communicate mastery of specific objectives	Sensitive to test length—short tests yield huge % jumps between scores. Can't compare across tests
Percentile	Percent of students in norm group that an examinee outscored; range = 0 to 99 percentile	Permits clear comparison to other similar students; can serve to compare scores across tests in same test battery	Often confused with percent correct; cannot be averaged
Stanine	Divides scores into 9 broad categories	Permits a broad grouping of students by score	Too imprecise to detect small differences in achievement; cannot be averaged
Grade equivalent	Compares performance on the test to that of students at various grade levels who took the same test	Provides interpretive reference to grade levels	Often misinterpreted; does not refer to grade-level competencies. Cannot be averaged

Prepare Your Students by Providing Opportunities to Learn

Do all in your power to gather information about and to understand the achievement targets to be assessed in upcoming standardized tests. If a state assessment is pending that reflects state standards, it is your job to know what those standards are and how they apply to your students. Remember the very important lesson you learned in Chapter 3 on achievement targets. Deconstruct each state standard into the enabling knowledge, reasoning, performance skill, or product development targets that form the scaffolding leading up to that standard. Plan instruction and assessment FOR learning to bring students up that scaffolding in ways that let you and them know they are progressing appropriately over time.

If a published test is to be administered, consult the teacher's guide or the user's materials for that test to know precisely what knowledge, reasoning, performance skill, or product targets it will be assessing. Again, make these the focus of instruction.

Another lesson from Chapter 3 needs reaffirming here: Be sure you yourself are a master of the achievement targets your students will be expected to master. Be sure you have the vision of success, then share that vision with your students in terms they can understand.

Strive for Accurate Results

When asked to administer standardized tests, take the responsibility seriously and follow the prescribed instructions. This contributes to the quality of the results. You must follow accepted standards of ethical practice. Anything you may do to cause students to misrepresent their real levels of achievement has the potential of doing harm to them, to you as a professional, and to the integrity of the educational community as a whole. If you are opposed to a particular set of standardized testing practices, bring all of your assessment literacy tools to bear during the debate. That is your right and your responsibility. But when assessment begins, adhere to prescribed procedures so users can accurately interpret the results.

Sometimes ensuring accuracy demands more than merely following prescribed test administration procedures. Some students bring physical or intellectual handicaps to the testing environment that require you to adjust test administration procedures to obtain accurate scores for them. Most often these days, test publishers or state testing agencies will issue guidelines for such accommodations. One such list is presented in Figure 14.1. Note that adjustments can be made in setting, timing, scheduling, presentation, and response. As a general rule of thumb, accommodations allowed at testing time are the same as accommodations made during instruction as listed in the student's individualized education program (IEP).

Is it clear to you why such adjustments are necessary in some cases? If some students take the test under standard conditions, the result may well be a score that misrepresents what they know and can do. These accommodations permit us to get past those physical or intellectual challenges to use their strengths to permit us to see students' real achievement more clearly. But we have to be sure that such accommodations don't alter the target being assessed, thus leading to inaccurate measurement.

Encourage Student Self-Confidence

Prepare your students to participate productively and as comfortably as possible in large-scale testing programs. Take time to be sure they understand why they are taking these tests and how the results will be used. Our next suggestion may startle you, but take it seriously. If the scores are complex or technical in nature, such as percentiles or state assessment mastery scores, and students are likely have difficulty understanding, do not report them to students. If the scores can't help students in any purposeful way to make productive decisions about their own learning do not give them the scores. Under these circumstances, the scores will do more harm than good. But if you do report them, be sure students know what the scores mean and do not mean—how they will and will not be used. Provide practice with the kinds of test item formats they will confront, so they know how to deal with and feel confident with those formats. This includes practice with accommodations in place for special education students.

Communicate with parents about the importance of keeping these tests in perspective. Be sure they know the meaning of the scores. And above all, be positive and encouraging to all before, during, and after these assessments and encourage parents to do the same. All of these steps help students become "test wise." Positive talk can send students into uncomfortable testing circumstances knowing that you are on their side—and that helps.

Also, Build Community Awareness

As a classroom teacher, you can and should strive to promote understanding within your community of the role of standardized testing and the meaning of test results. Members of the school board, parents, citizens, and members of the news media may

Examples of Setting Accommodations

Conditions of Setting	Location
Minimal distractive elements (e.g., books, artwork, window views) Special lighting Special acoustics Adaptive or special furniture Individual student or small group of students rather than large group	Study carrel Separate room (including special education classroom) Seat closest to test administrator (teacher, proctor, etc.) Home Hospital Correctional institution

Examples of Timing Accommodations

Duration	Organization
Changes in duration can be applied to selected subtests of an assessment or to the assessment overall Extended time (i.e., extra time) Unlimited time	Frequent breaks, even during parts of the assessment (e.g., during subtests) Extended breaks between parts of the assessment (e.g., between subtests) so that assessment is actually administered in several sessions

Examples of Scheduling Accommodations

Time	Organization
Specific time of day (e.g., morning, midday, afternoon, after ingestion of medication) Specific day of week Over several days	In a different order from that used for most students (e.g., longer subtest first, shorter later, math first, English later) Omit questions that cannot be adjusted for an accommodation (e.g., graph reading for student using Braille) and adjust for missing scores

Examples of Presentation Accommodations

Format Alterations	Procedure Changes	Assistive Devices
Braille edition Large-print version Larger bubbles on answer sheet One complete sentence per line in reading passages Bubbles to side of choices in multiple-choice exams Key words or phrases highlighted Increased spacing between lines Fewer number of items per page Cues on answer form (e.g., arrows, stop signs)	Use sign language to give directions to student Reread directions Write helpful verbs in directions on board or on separate piece of paper Simplify language, clarify or explain directions Provide extra examples Prompt student to stay focused on test, move ahead, read entire item Explain directions to student anytime during test Answer questions about items anytime during test without giving answers	Audiotape of directions Computer reads directions and/or items Magnification device Amplification device (e.g., hearing aid) Noise buffer Templates to reduce visible print Markers to maintain place Dark or raised lines Pencil grips Magnets or tape to secure papers to work area

FIGURE 14.1
Example of Assessment Accommodations to Meet Students' Special Needs

Source: Adapted from *Testing Students with Disabilities* (pp. 47–58) by M. L. Thurlow, J. I. Elliott, and J. E. Ysseldyke, 1998. Thousand Oaks, CA: Sage Publications. Copyright 1998. Adapted by permission of Sage Publications.

Examples of Response Accommodations		
Format Alterations	**Procedure Changes**	**Assistive Devices**
Mark responses in test booklet rather than on separate page	Use reference materials (e.g., dictionary, arithmetic tables)	Word processor or computer to record responses
Respond on different paper, such as graph paper, wide-lined paper, paper with wide margins	Give response in different mode (e.g., pointing, oral response to tape recorder, sign language)	Amanuensis (proctor/scribe writes student responses)
		Slantboard or wedge
		Calculator or abacus
		Brailler
		Other communication device (e.g., symbol board)

FIGURE 14.1
(*continued*)

need basic assessment literacy training to participate productively in the proper use of results. Only when they, too, understand the meaning of sound assessment will they be in a position to promote the wise use of these tests.

Finally, Maintain Perspective

Be constantly mindful of when standardized tests are likely to contribute useful information and when they are not. You can do this only if you understand the meaning of test results and how that meaning relates to the reasons for testing. In our opinion, we have entirely too much standardized testing being conducted merely as a matter of tradition, with no sense of purpose. Always insist on attention to purpose: What are the specific decisions to be made, by whom, and what kind(s) of information do they need? Will the test provide useful information?

We must all constantly urge those who support, design, and conduct standardized testing programs to keep these tests in perspective in terms of their relative importance in the larger world of educational assessment. We must constantly remind ourselves and others that these tests represent but a tiny fraction of the assessments in which students participate and that they have relatively little influence on day-to-day instruction.

Exploring the Social Context of Assessment

At the time of this writing (late 2010), a proposal has been advanced by the U.S. Department of Education that teachers be evaluated, in part, through analysis of their performance as indicated by student achievement. Those in favor argue that this is the job they are hired to do and they should be able to prove they've done it. Opponents argue that many factors beyond teachers' control influence student learning success. Still others contend that annual test scores should be the index of teacher impact; disagreeing are those who contend that currently available annual tests are incapable of detecting the impact of a single teacher on students. Is this a good proposal in your opinion or not? Defend your perspective.

Summary: Productive Standardized Testing

Our purpose in this chapter has been to understand and learn to negotiate the challenges presented by standardized testing to teachers and those in positions of instructional support.

We reviewed the array of assessment purposes introduced in Chapter 2, emphasizing again the place of standardized testing in the larger context of educational assessment. These tests serve both policy and instructional support functions. They tend to be of little specific value to teachers, because classroom demands require greater frequency of assessment and higher-resolution pictures of student achievement than the typical standardized test can generate. The one part of the score report teachers are likely to find useful are the criterion-referenced scores reflecting student mastery of specific objectives. While once a year is not frequent enough to be comprehensive, at least teachers get some detail with these scores.

We studied the various levels of standardized testing, from local to state to national to college admission testing, pointing out that all four assessment methods are used at various levels. We discussed their history and the mechanics of their development.

Next, our attention turned to understanding and interpreting commonly used standardized test scores: raw scores, percent correct, percentile, stanine, and grade equivalent. These and other such scores are safe and easy to use when users understand them. But, by the same token, they can be easily distorted by the uninformed. Your challenge is to become informed.

We ended with a quick summary of your professional responsibilities, emphasizing that your concern first and foremost should be for the well-being of your students. Under all circumstances, we must demand accurate assessment of the local curricula. Each of us should strive to be an activist with a voice of reason in this arena. Only then will we be able to use this form of assessment productively.

In Chapter 10, we established certain conditions that must be satisfied to achieve effective communication: mutual understanding of the targets tested, accurate scores, and an interpersonal communication environment amenable to productive sharing. When using standardized tests as the means of gathering information and communicating about learning, we maximize the chances of success if all of the following are true:

1. Both message sender and receiver understand the nature of the achievement targets reflected in the exercises of the test; they know and understand what was and what was not tested.
2. The tests are developed by professionals who have the technical credentials to create tests that provide dependable information; tests developed in the absence of this expertise are likely to be of inferior quality.
3. The interpersonal communication environment is open to good communication:

   - Everyone involved knows what the scores can and cannot be used for, and uses them accordingly.
   - Message sender(s) and receiver(s) share a common language; in this case, both know what the scores mean and how to interpret them correctly.
   - Opportunity is created by message senders where they and all receivers are compelled to attend to the test scores being shared.
   - During this time, message senders ask receivers to restate in their own words what the scores mean and what their implications are.

The End of Our Studies of Classroom Assessment

As educators, our job is to teach ourselves out of a job. By this, we mean that we must take our students to a place where they don't need us anymore. Any students who leave school still needing to rely on their teachers to tell them they have done well have not yet learned to hit the target, because they cannot see the quality of their own performance. We must turn our achievement expectations and performance standards over to our students, to make them independent of us. Only then can we assure ourselves that we have helped our students become the lifelong learners they will need to be in the new millennium.

Covington (1992) advises us that, "Indeed, at its best, education should provide students with a sense of empowerment that makes the future 'real' by moving beyond merely offering children plausible alternatives to indicating how their preferred dreams can actually be attained" (p. 3). We submit that you can fulfill this mission only if you rely on student-involved classroom assessment combined with student-involved record keeping and student-involved communication.

This ends our journey together through the realm of classroom assessment. By way of saying farewell, let us leave you with the final entry in our set of assessment quality rubrics—this time centering on principles of assessment FOR learning as articulated in a continuum of quality. As you read them in Figure 14.2 (and at the end of Appendix B) remember, physicians have a creed that says, "Above all, do no harm." Let's adopt an educator's version of that creed: *Above all, do nothing to diminish hope.*

Final Chapter Reflection

1. *What are the three most important new insights to come to you as a result of your study of this chapter?*
2. *Which of your previous questions about assessment can you now answer based on your study of this chapter?*
3. *What new questions have come to mind as a result of your study of this chapter that you hope to have answered as you take charge now of your ongoing professional development in assessment?*

Practice with Chapter 14 Ideas

1. Assume that your careful analysis of commercially available standardized tests reveals that only one half of the items in any subtest covers material specified in your curriculum at the specified grade levels you had planned to test. This means that you will not have taught one half of the material tested during the year you test it. Yet your school board and administration compel you to administer a test anyway. How should you proceed?

   What should you do to maximize the value of this assessment and minimize harm to your students?

2. Pretend you are explaining standardized test scores.

   Part A: How would you explain the following to a parent? Prepare a written set of responses:

   a. Raw scores, percent correct, percentile, and grade equivalent

Still Needs Work	Well on Its Way	Ready to Use
There is no awareness of the student's self-assessment role; there is no acknowledgement of the instructional decisions students will be making during learning. No student-friendly version of the achievement target has been developed. No samples of student work have been selected to reveal the path students will follow on their journey to success. There is no plan for or evidence of student involvement in the creation or use of practice assessments to help students progress toward competence. Students play no role in communicating assessment results; that is, in telling the story of their own achievement status or progress over time.	Students are seen as assessment users, but in an incomplete sense; potentially important decisions and roles are overlooked, thus keeping users from taking full advantage of assessment FOR learning opportunities. The student-friendly version of targets developed is incomplete or is not clearly defined in vocabulary student are likely to fully understand. Samples of student work selected are incomplete, thus failing to map a complete path to academic success. The self-assessment role students are to play is superficial or incomplete, thus failing to take full advantage of the opportunity to support learning. Students tell part of the story of their journey to success but because of shallow involvement elsewhere, their story is likely to be incomplete.	The ongoing instructional decisions students must make are clearly understood and are woven into assessment use during learning. A student-friendly definition of achievement expectations has been prepared—perhaps with students playing a role in its development. Samples of student work have been selected to illustrate levels of proficiency, from beginner to fully competent. Students are expected to play a role in the creation and use of practice assessments along their journey to academic success. Students play a prominent ongoing role in communicating with others about their level of achievement during learning.

FIGURE 14.2
Guide for Evaluating Assessments for Student Involvement

Note: This key to quality only becomes relevant when the assessment context makes it advantageous for students to play an assessment role; that is, in assessment FOR learning contexts.

b. When each score should be used

c. The implications of such scores for your instruction

Part B: Now pretend you are explaining them to your students. What would you say about each of the items in Part A? Again, write out your responses.

Part C: Do your responses suggest to you that you understand how to communicate about standardized test scores? Comment on your sense of self-confidence in this arena.

3. With advice from your professor, go online to the webpage of a standardized test publisher and search out a sample score report from one of their tests. With that report in hand, address the following issues:

- Identify as many different kinds of scores reported as you can and discuss their meaning.

- What do you understand from this report? Is there anything you do not understand? If so, how might you secure clearer understanding?

- What are the possible implications for instruction of these results? That is, does it tell you where students performed well? Less well?

- Would this score report be useful to you as a classroom teacher? Why or why not?

4. Mark True or False for each of the following questions.* Explain your reasoning. After you have done so, check your answers against the scoring key and rationale that follows the quiz. Note: You will need to rely on information provided in the chapter text and Appendix C in formulating your answers.

T F 1. Tim is a sixth grader. He obtained a grade equivalent score of 9.2 in reading. This means that Tim scored well above average sixth graders in reading.

T F 2. Tim's grade equivalent score of 9.2 in reading means that Tim could well be put in a class of ninth graders for material in which reading skills were important.

T F 3. Juanita is a sixth grader. She got a percentile score of 70 in reading on a published standardized test. This means that Juanita got 70 percent of the items correct.

T F 4. Susie, a third-grade student, scored at the 30th percentile in arithmetic at the end of the school year. According to school grading policy, scores below 65 percent are regarded as failing. Therefore Susie should be retained for another year in arithmetic instruction so that she will not be handicapped in the future.

T F 5. Mary is a sixth grader who received a stanine score of zero on her standardized test in math. This means that Mary's score is very low compared to other sixth graders.

T F 6. Each stanine range contains 10 percent of students.

T F 7. Mr. Rivera wondered about his student, Elena, whose stanine score in reading comprehension went up from the fourth stanine to the sixth stanine. That big a difference is important.

---

*Adapted from "Interpreting Percentile Scores" by John R. Hills, *Educational Measurement: Issues and Practice*, Summer 1983, p. 24-25.

Answers to Test Score Quiz

1. **True.** A grade equivalent score is the average performance of students on the test at each of several grade levels. A sixth grader who has gotten a grade equivalent of 9.2 has performed like a ninth-grade student on the sixth-grade test. Therefore, he has performed above average for students in his grade.

2. **False.** A grade equivalent of 9.2 means that Tim does as well as ninth graders on sixth-grade work. It does not necessarily mean that he can do ninth-grade work.

3. **False.** Percentile scores indicate the relative standing in a group, not the percent of items that are correct.

4. **False.** Scores at the 30th percentile are really not far below average. The 30th percentile means that the student has scored better than 30 percent of similar students taking the test. Usually no more than a few percent of a class are failed, say 3 or 4 percent, not anywhere near 30 percent. Besides, a nationally standardized test may not accurately sample the arithmetic skills covered in Susie's class.

5. **False.** There is no such thing as a stanine score of zero. There has been a scoring error.

6. **False.** The first and ninth stanine of each have about 4 percent of student scores; the second and eighth about 8 percent; the third and seventh about 12 percent; the fourth and sixth about 16 percent; the fifth about 20 percent. Envision a bell-shaped curve.

7. **True.** When scores differ by two stanines, we tend to think of there being a real difference, not an error of measurement. A difference that large is unlikely to be an accident so it deserves further investigation. Perhaps Elena has benefited from some effective teaching, or she may have become more motivated, or she may have found more time to read, or something in her life that was impeding her progress may have been removed.

Now go to www.myeducationlab.com to take a Pretest to assess your initial comprehension of chapter content, study chapter content with your individualized Study Plan, take a Posttest to assess your understanding of chapter content, practice your teaching skills with Building Teaching Skills exercises, and build a deeper, more applied understanding of chapter content with Homework and Exercises.

APPENDIX A

Detailed Analysis of Assessment Users and Uses

Classroom Assessment

DECISION MAKER	DECISIONS	INFORMATION NEEDED	ASSESSMENT IMPLICATIONS
Student	• What am I supposed to learn?	• Learning targets described in student-friendly language	• Accurate assessments must reflect these learning targets
	• What have I learned already and what do I still need to work on?	• Evidence must allow students to track progress and understand where they are now in relation to expectations at any over time	• Classroom assessments must provide descriptive feedback in student-friendly terms
	• Have I met or am I progressing toward the important standards?	• Status regarding mastery of each standard in student friendly language	• Assessments must provide evidence of standards mastered every few weeks
	• Have I met the state achievement expectations?	• Status regarding state standards in student-friendly language	• Annual state assessments reporting standards mastered
Teacher	• What are my students supposed to learn?	• Must have clear information about assigned achievement standards along the road map to each standard	• All assessments must reflect these targets; it must be clear which target any assessment reflects
	• What have they learned already and what do they still need to learn?	• Continuous evidence revealing of each student's current place in the learning progressions leading up to each standard	• Continuous accurate classroom assessments during the learning describe progress
	• Which students need special services?	• Evidence of how students are doing in relation to grade- or age-level expectations	• Assessments must provide evidence to determine eligibility

	• Have my students met or are they progressing on the important achievement standards?	• status of each student's mastery of each standard	• School or district needs periodic assessments of standards mastered throughout the year
	• Did they meet state achievement expectations?	• Status regarding each student's mastery of each state standard	• Annual state or district tests must reveal each student's mastery of each standard
Parent	• What is my child supposed to learn?	• Learning targets in family-friendly language provided from the beginning of learning	• Assessments must accurately reflect these targets
	• What has my child learned already and what does s/he still need to learn?	• Assessments providing information on current status on each learning target	• Continuous accurate classroom assessments used during the learning need to provide picture of progress
	• Is my child progressing satisfactorily in meeting the teacher's classroom learning expectations?	• Information gained from my child's self-assessment, or from the teacher	• Periodic summative classroom assessments must feed into report card grade or summary of classroom standards met
	• Does my child need the services of a specialized program?	• Student's learning status in relation to grade- or age-level expectations	• Assessment evidence must show status relative to expected achievement levels
	• How is my child progressing on the state achievement expectations?	• Status regarding state standards	• Evidence needed periodically during the year
	• Has my child met the state achievement expectations?	• Status regarding each state standards	• State assessments must provide evidence of mastery of each standard

Interim/Benchmark Assessment

DECISION MAKERS	DECISIONS	INFORMATION NEEDED	ASSESSMENT IMPLICATIONS
Building Principal, Teacher Teams	• What standards are students expected to master by subject across our range of grade levels and classrooms?	• Learning targets in the form of achievement standards organized by subject as they unfold within and across grade levels	• Assessments must accurately reflect these standards

	• Which of these standards are students mastering or progressing appropriately toward? Are there problem areas?	• Information revealing mastery patterns over time within the school year within and across classrooms of this school	• Comparable evidence of student learning status needed periodically during the year
	• Did enough of our students meet standards this year?	• Proportion of students meeting and not meeting each standard	• Annual state or district assessments reveal how student did on each standard
District Curriculum Leaders	• What standards are students to master across all classrooms grades, and schools?	• Standards mastered by grade and subject mapped within and across grade levels across schools	• Assessments must accurately reflect these standards
	• Did enough of our students meet standards this year?	• Proportion of students meeting each standard	• Annual assessments reveal how each student does on each standard

Annual Assessment

DECISION MAKER	DECISIONS	INFORMATION NEEDED	ASSESSMENT IMPLICATIONS
Superintendent	• What standards are to be met?	• Learning targets in the form of achievement standards organized by grade and subject	• Assessments must accurately reflect these standards
	• Which of these standards are students mastering or making appropriate progress toward in what schools?	• Information revealing patterns of achievement within and across schools	• Comparable evidence of student learning status collected periodically during the year
School Boards, Legislator, Departments of Education, Business and Community Leaders	• What standards are students expected to master in our schools?	• Learning targets in the form of achievement standards organized by grade and subject	• Assessments must accurately reflect these standards
	• How many of our students are meeting standards?	• Scores reflecting patterns of achievement within and across schools and districts	• Comparable evidence of student learning status collected periodically
	• Did enough of our students meet standards this year?	• Proportion of students meeting each standard	• Annual assessments show how each student did on each standard

Rubrics for Evaluating Assessment Quality

Key to Quality 1: Purpose

Still Needs Work	Well on Its Way	Ready to Use
No reason for assessment is apparent and none can be inferred from the context; it is not clear why the assessment is being conducted.	Users and uses can be implied but are not made explicit.	Intended users and uses are explicitly stated.
There seem to be too many purposes (users and uses) and the assessment could not possibly serve them all.	There is some question about whether the assessment can fulfill its intended purpose.	It is clear that the assessment will help them.
The specified purpose is inappropriate—the information gathered will not serve the needs of the intended users.	If an assessment FOR learning application, the assessment may be encouraging to learners.	If an assessment FOR learning context, the assessment will provide motivational support for students to strive for excellence.
If an assessment FOR learning context, the assessment will not serve to build student confidence.		

Key 2: Achievement Target

Still Needs Work	Well on Its Way	Ready to Use
The learning targets to be reflected in the assessment are not specified.	The learning targets are stated, but their coverage and quality is uneven.	Clear and explicit learning targets are stated and easy to find. They reflect obviously important achievement standards and reflect the best current thinking of the field.
Or, targets are very broad and vaguely defined.	Some targets are vague, others are clear.	
There is no connection to relevant state or local achievement standards.	Some reflect relevant standards, others do not.	
The targets do not reflect the best current thinking of the academic field.	Some reflect the best thinking of the field, others do not.	

Key 3: Assessment Design

Still Needs Work	Well on Its Way	Ready to Use
The assessment method selected is not capable of reflecting the achievement target to be assessed.	Some targets are correctly reflected in The assessment format(s) used.	Proper assessment methods built of high-quality exercises and scoring procedures sample student achievement properly so as to minimize distortion due to bias.
Exercises or scoring procedures are of poor quality.	The exercises are mixed in quality—some are good and some are not.	
Sampling will not lead to confident conclusions about student achievement.	Some learning targets are adequately sampled, some are not.	
Key sources of bias have not been eliminated and results are likely to be distorted.	Some sources of bias have been eliminated, but others remain and can distort some of the results.	

Key 4: Communication

Still Needs Work	Well on Its Way	Ready to Use
The assessment designer has given no thought to managing information as a foundation for effective communication; the designer has paid little attention to matters of evidence gathering, record keeping, data summary, or reporting, whether in assessment OF or FOR learning contexts.	Information management has been a consideration in planning for effective communication; however, the evidence gathering, record keeping, summary, and reporting requirements of the assessment OF or FOR learning context necessitate fine tuning.	Information management systems are in place for gathering, storing, retrieving, and summarizing information on achievement.
There is little evidence that the assessment designer understands either the proper use of the various communication options to meet the information needs of various assessment users or the essential conditions for effective communication.	The assessment designer has selected appropriate ways of communicating results, but some of the essential conditions still need work to ensure the effective delivery and use of achievement information.	Procedures are in place for delivering assessment results in a timely and understandable manner to all who are to receive and act on it; communication strategies align productively with assessment OF or FOR learning requirements, depending on the context.

Key 5: Student Involvement

(Note: This key to quality only becomes relevant when the assessment context makes it advantageous for students to play an assessment role; that is, in assessment FOR learning contexts.)

Still Needs Work	Well on Its Way	Ready to Use
There is no awareness of the student's self-assessment role; there is no acknowledgement of the instructional decisions students will be making during learning.	Students are seen as assessment users, but in an incomplete sense; potentially important decisions and roles are overlooked, thus keeping users from taking full advantage of assessment FOR learning opportunities.	The ongoing instructional decisions students must make are clearly understood and are woven into assessment use during learning.
No student-friendly version of the achievement target has been developed.	The student-friendly version of targets developed is incomplete or is not clearly defined in vocabulary students are likely to fully understand.	A student-friendly definition of achievement expectations has been prepared—perhaps with students playing a role in its development.
No samples of student work have been selected to reveal the path students will follow on their journey to success.	Samples of student work selected are incomplete, thus failing to map a complete path to academic success.	Samples of student work have been selected to illustrate levels of proficiency, from beginner to fully competent.
There is no plan for or evidence of student involvement in the creation or use of practice assessments to help students progress toward competence.	The self-assessment role students are to play is superficial or incomplete, thus failing to take full advantage of the opportunity to support learning.	Students are expected to play a role in the creation and use of practice assessments along their journey to academic success.
Students play no role in communicating assessment results; that is, in telling the story of their own achievement status or progress over time.	Students tell part of the story of their journey to success but because of shallow involvement elsewhere, their story is likely to be incomplete.	Students play a prominent ongoing role in communicating with others about their level of achievement during learning.

APPENDIX C

Derivation of Common Norm-Referenced Scores

For those interested in greater detail about the derivation and meaning of standardized tests score that compare students to each other for interpretation, here are specific descriptions of the two most common types of scores:

PERCENTILE SCORE OR PERCENTILE RANK

Table C.1 shows you how a student's raw score can be converted to a percentile score. It describes the performance of our norm group on a new test. We will study this table column by column to describe this conversion.

Column one tells us we will be analyzing student performance on a 30-item test. The maximum number correct is 30 and is the score at the top of the column. Possible raw scores range from 0 to 30. If the test is a four-choice multiple-choice test, students can score 7 or 8 with random guessing. Therefore, scores under 7 are assigned a percentile score of 0.

Column two tells us how many students in our 1,500-person norm group (see "Total" at the bottom of the column) actually got each raw score. For instance, 20 students scored 25 on the test, 70 scored 13, and so on.

Column three presents the percentage of students who got each raw score. Look at raw score 20. One hundred and fifty students actually achieved this score, which represents 10 percent of the total of 1,500 examinees in the norm group.

Column four is where it begins to get tricky. This column presents the percentage of students who scored *at or below* each raw score. Start at the bottom of the column. What percent of students attained a raw score of 7 or lower? One-half of one percent. Move up the column. What percent of students attained a raw score of 17 or lower? 38.5 percent—the sum of all the percentages for raw scores 0–17: .5 + .5 + .5 + .5 + 1.5 + 2.5 + 4.5 + 5.5 + 6 + 8 + 8.5 = 38.5. So, a student who attains a raw score of 17 scored equal to or higher than 38.5 percent of those in the norm group.

Now on to percentile scores—see column 5. For each raw score, by definition we need to know *what percentage of those who took the test scored lower than that score.* Look at raw score 26. These students outscored everyone with scores of 25 or lower. We see that 93.5 percent of examinees attained a score of 25 or lower. If we round to whole numbers, then the percentile score for a raw score of 26 is 94. Anyone attaining a raw score of 26 *outscored* 94 percent of those in the norm group; thus, a raw score of 26 converts to a percentile score of 94.

Test publishers calculate each of these conversions and then place them in the computer. From that point on, all students who get a certain raw score have its

TABLE C.1
Understanding Percentile Scores

(1) Raw Score	(2) Number of Students	(3) Percent of Students	(4) Cumulative Percent	(5) Percentile Score
30	10	0.5	99.5	99
29	10	0.5	99.0	99
28	20	1.5	98.5	97
27	20	1.5	97.0	96
26	30	2.0	95.5	94
25	20	1.5	93.5	92
24	40	2.5	92.0	90
23	60	4.0	89.5	86
22	80	5.5	85.5	80
21	120	8.0	80.0	72
20	150	10.0	72.0	62
19	180	12.0	62.0	50
18	170	11.5	50.0	39
17	130	8.5	38.5	30
16	120	8.0	30.0	22
15	90	6.0	22.0	16
14	80	5.5	16.0	11
13	70	4.5	10.5	6
12	40	2.5	6.0	4
11	20	1.5	3.5	2
10	10	0.5	2.0	2
9	10	0.5	1.5	1
8	10	0.5	1.0	1
7 (Chance)	10	0.5	0.5	0
6				
5				
4				
3				
2				
1				
Total	1,500		100	

corresponding percentile score printed on their score report. So, for example a raw score of 29 reflects a level of achievement on this test that is higher than 98 percent of the examinees in the norm group. This will remain true as long as this test is in use.

When test publishers norm a test, they create conversion tables for their national norm group, and typically also offer percentile conversions based on geographic region, gender, race/ethnicity, and local performance only. This means that exactly the same kind of conversion table is generated for students who are like one another in these particular ways.

GRADE EQUIVALENT SCORES

Let's say a test publisher is norming a newly developed 40-item test of fifth- and sixth-grade math. It administers the test to large numbers of students in those two grades at the very beginning of the school year. Each student receives a raw score ranging from 10 to 40. On further analysis of test results, let's say that the average score for fifth graders is 23, while sixth graders score an average of 28 correct. With this information, as represented graphically in Figure C.1, graph A, we can begin to create our conversion table. The first two conversions from raw to grade equivalent scores are those for the average raw scores. Because 23 was the average score for fifth graders, we assign that raw score a grade equivalent of 5.0. Because 28 was the average raw score of sixth graders when we administered our test, it is assigned a grade equivalent of 6.0. That accounts for 2 of the 30 raw score points to be converted. What about the rest?

Under ideal circumstances, the best way to convert the rest would be to administer our new test to students each month, so we could compute averages for them and complete more of our conversion table. Unfortunately, however, real schools will never permit that much test administration. Besides, the cost would be astronomical.

So, as an alternative, we can simply assume that students grow academically at a steady and predictable rate between grade levels. By connecting the two dots (averages) with a straight line that depicts that steady rate of growth, we create a mathematical equation that allows us to convert the scores between 23 and 28 to grade equivalents, as in Figure C.1, graph B. By projecting each raw score point over to the straight line on the graph and then down to the corresponding point on the grade scale, we find the grade equivalent to assign to each raw score.

But what about scores above and below this grade level? How shall we convert these? We have two choices: (1) Administer the new test to students at higher and lower grade levels, compute averages, and complete the table, or (2) rely on our assumption that students grow at a predictable rate and simply extend our line down from 23 and up from 28. Option 2 is depicted in Figure C.1, graph C, where a raw score of 40 converts to a grade equivalent of 8.5.

Once the conversion table is completed and enter into the computer, henceforth, any student who attains a given raw score will be assigned its corresponding grade equivalent. Thus, the grade equivalent score reflects the approximate grade level of students in the norm group who attained that raw score.

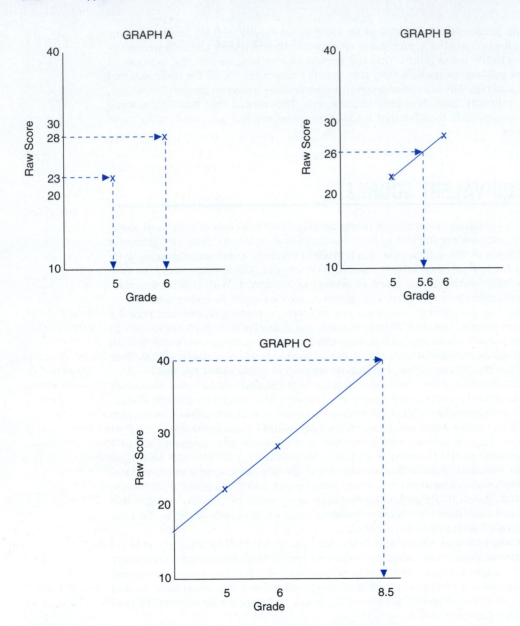

FIGURE C.1
The Derivation of Grade Equivalents

REFERENCES

Anderson, L. W., & Bourke, S. F. (2000). *Assessing affective characteristics in schools,* 2nd ed. Mahwah, NJ: Lawrence Erlbaum & Associates.

Arter, J., & Chappuis, J. (2006). *Creating and recognizing quality rubrics.* Portland OR: Pearson Assessment Training Institute.

Arter, J., & Spandel, V. (1992). Using portfolios of student work in instruction and assessment. *Educational Measurement: Issues and Practice, 11*(1), 36–44.

Austin, T. (1994). *Changing the view: Student-led parent conferences.* Portsmouth, NH: Heinemann.

Bandura, A. (1994). Self-efficacy. In V.S. Ramachaudran (Ed.), *Encyclopedia of human behavior, 4,* 71–81. New York: Academic Press. Reprinted in H. Friedman (Ed.), *Encyclopedia of mental health.* San Diego: Academic Press, 1998.

Bartlett, L. (1987). Academic evaluation and student discipline don't mix: A critical review. *Journal of Law and Education, 16*(2), 155–165.

Black, P., & Wiliam, D. (1998). Assessment and classroom learning. *Educational Assessment: Principles, Policy and Practice, 5*(1), 7–74. (Also summarized in Black & Wiliam, Inside the black box: Raising standards through classroom assessment. *Phi Delta Kappan, 80*(2), 139–148.

Bloom, B. S., Englehard, M. D., Furst, E. J., Hill, W. H., & Krathwohl, D. R. (1956). *Taxonomy of educational objectives, handbook 1: The cognitive domain.* New York: Longman.

Chappuis, J. (2009). *Seven strategies of assessment for learning.* Portland, OR: Pearson Assessment Training Institute.

Covington, M. (1992). *Making the grade: A self-worth perspective on motivation and school reform.* New York: Cambridge.

Davies, A., Cameron, C., Politano, C., & Gregory, K. (1992). *Together is better: Collaborative assessment, evaluation and reporting.* Winnipeg, MB: Peguis.

Gardner, H. (1993). *Frames of mind: The theory of multiple intelligences.* New York: Basic Books.

Hall, C. S., & Lindsay, G. (1970). *Theories of personality,* 2nd ed. New York: John Wiley & Sons.

Hattie, J., & Timperley, H. (2007). The power of feedback. *Review of Educational Research, 77*(1), 81–112.

Johnston. P. J. (2004). *Choice Words.* Portland ME: Stenhouse.

O'Connor, K. (2007). *A repair kit for grading: 15 fixes for broken grades.* Portland, OR: Pearson Assessment Training Institute.

Rowe, M. B. (1978). Specific ways to develop better communication. In R. Sund & A. Carin (Eds.), *Creative questioning and sensitivity: Listening techniques,* 2nd ed. Upper Saddle River, NJ: Merrill/Prentice Hall.

Sadler, R. (1989). Formative assessment and the design of instructional systems. *Instructional Science, 18,* 119–144.

Shepard, L. A. (1997). *Measuring achievement: What does it mean to test for robust understanding?* Princeton, NJ: Educational Testing Service.

Spandel, V., & Culham, R. (1995). *Putting portfolio stories to work.* Portland, OR: Northwest Regional Educational Laboratory.

Sternberg, R. J. (1996). Myths, countermyths and truths about intelligences. *Educational Researcher, 25*(2), 11–16.

Stiggins, R.J., Arter, J.A., Chappuis, J. & Chappuis, S. (2006). *Classroom assessment for student learning—Doing it right—Using it well.* Portland OR: Pearson Assessment Training Institute.

Stiggins, R. J., & Conklin, N. F. (1992). *In teachers' hands: Investigating the practice of classroom assessment.* Albany, NY: SUNY Press.

INDEX